Forearmed

A History of the Intelligence Corps

FOREARMED

A History of the Intelligence Corps

Anthony Clayton

BRASSEY'S (UK)

LONDON · NEW YORK

First English edition 1993

UK editorial offices: Brassey's, 165 Great Dover Street, London SE1 4YA
orders: Marston Book Services, PO Box 87, Oxford OX2 0DT

USA orders: Macmillan Publishing Company, Front and Brown Streets, Riverside, NJ 08075

Distributed in North America to booksellers and wholesalers by the Macmillan Publishing Company, NY 10020

Library of Congress Cataloging-in-Publication Data
available

British Library Cataloguing in Publication Data
A catalogue record for this book is
available from the British Library

ISBN 0 0837701 7

Anthony Clayton has asserted his moral right to
be identified as author of this work.

Photoset in North Wales by
Derek Doyle & Associates, Mold, Clwyd.
Printed in Great Britain by
the Bath Press, Avon

Contents

Foreword By the Colonel Commandant, Intelligence
    Corps.   ix

Acknowledgements   xi

List of Plates   xiii

Prologue: The Role   xv

1. The Forebears of the Intelligence Corps   1
(From Cromwell to Wellington: India; the 1855 Topogra-
phical and Statistical Department, Crimea; Imperial
Experience, and the Field Intelligence Department in
South Africa, 1900–02.)

2. The First Intelligence Corps, 1914.   14
(Creation and Baptism of Fire with the 1914 BEF;
Reconnaissance; Prisoner of War Questioning; Early Air
Photography and Signals Interception.)

3. The Western Front, 1915–18.   26
(Personnel of the Corps; Operational Intelligence and
Prisoner Questioning; Air Photography; Signals Intelli-
gence and Agents; The Evolution of the System 1916–18;
Security.)

4. Other Theatres of Operations and Training, 1914–18.   43
(East Africa, The Dardanelles, Mesopotamia, Egypt and
Palestine; Greece and Macedonia; Italy; South Russia;
Great Britain and Ireland; Recruitment and Training.)

5. The Years of Neglect, 1919–29.   55
(The First British Army of the Rhine; Turkey 1919–22;
Russia 1919–20; Ireland 1919–21.)

Contents

6. The Rebirth of the Corps, 1939–40.   62
(Preparations 1938-39; The Intelligence Corps of the 1939
BEF; Operational Intelligence and Security 1939–40;
Norway and Iceland; The Corps formally established
July–December 1940.)

7. Strategic Intelligence: The Corps Contribution.   80
(The Directorate of Military Intelligence; Bletchley Park
and the Y Service; Prisoners of War; Air Photographic
Interpretation; The Special Operations Executive; The
Political Warfare Executive.)

8. Operational Intelligence: The Corps Contribution.   112
(Signals Intelligence; East Africa; North Africa, Greece
and Crete 1940–41; The Development of the Y Service in
North Africa–Sicily, Italy and Greece 1943–45; Normandy
and North–West Europe.)

9. Security: The Corps Contribution.   152
(Security in Campaign Theatres; Security in Great Britain;
Security in the Colonial Empire and on Shipping Routes.)

10. The War Against Japan: The Corps Contribution.   172
(Hong Kong, Malaya and Burma 1941–42; Strategic Intelligence; Operational Intelligence in Burma; Security in Madagascar, India, and Ceylon; The Ending of Hostilities.)

11. Aftermath.   194
(The occupation of Germany; Denazification; Austria and
Italy; Trieste; Other Liberated Territories—The Far East;
The Run-down of the Intelligence Corps.)

12. Conventional and Semi-Conventional Wars Since 1945.   214
(The Korean War; Suez 1956; Borneo; Belize; the South
Atlantic 1982.)

13. Counter-Insurgency and Military Security Since 1945.   228
(The Middle East—Palestine; The Middle East—Egypt and
Libya; The Middle East—Jordan, the Arabian Peninsula
and Aden; The Middle East—Lebanon; Cyprus; The Far
East—Malaya; The Far East—Hong Kong; Africa—Kenya;
Africa—Cameroons, Mauritius, Zimbabwe.)

14. The Corps Renewed, 1957–90.   250
(Expansion: The Intelligence Corps in BAOR; Strategic
Intelligence; The Corps in the 1990s.)

Contents

Glossary   258

Appendices:

    Appendix A. The Founder Members of the First Intelligence
           Corps, 1914.   261

    Appendix B. Field Security Sections, Second World War.   264

    Appendix C. Wireless Intelligence Sections, Second World
           War.   277

    Appendix D. Awards to Members of the Intelligence Corps,
           1940–91.   281

    Appendix E. The Training of the Intelligence Corps,
           1940–45.   283

    Appendix F. The Intelligence Corps as a Family.   288

Chapter Notes   292

Index   317

Foreword

by

The Colonel Commandant of the Intelligence Corps, General Sir Charles Guthrie, KCB, LVO, OBE

As Colonel Commandant of the Intelligence Corps it is a great privilege for me to write the Foreword to this History. It brings together two separate strands.

First and foremost it is, in the best military tradition, a Regimental History. It traces the antecedents of the Corps, covers in some detail the work of the Corps during the Second World War and, finally, it gives a glimpse of the Corps' activities post-war to the year 1990.

In this context it is appropriate to repeat Sir John Fortescue's words of what a Regimental History should be. He wrote: 'Regimental History is not, if rightly understood, a mere catalogue of dry facts. It is, and should be, the record of past experience alike in failure or success, not only for the maintenance of regimental spirit for that alone is of enormous importance, but for the guidance and instruction of both officers and men against the day when it will be their duty to uphold the honour of their regiment and their country upon the field of action.' I believe the Author has succeeded admirably in this task. No history can be complete but this book gives a marvellous overview of the Corps with many personal vignettes showing resourcefulness, initiative and bravery. The record shows that today's officers and men have much to be proud of and aspire to.

The second strand is that of Intelligence. So much has been written on this subject in the last few years and this book completes part of the jig-saw. Military Intelligence is not the sole preserve of the Intelligence Corps but this book shows that the contribution made by members of the Corps represents a cross-section of almost all military Intelligence work and also shows the very wide variety of Intelligence and Security jobs that have to be done. I should add that, while much of the Corps' work may be secret, the existence of the Corps is not. The Corps is, and always has been, a declared part of the Army's order of battle.

The book also shows the rich variety of people who have at one time or another been members of the Corps, particularly during the Second World War. This for me is the highlight. In later years, members of the Corps became eminent in many fields, ranging from university vice-chancellors and professors, captains of industry and ambassadors, to musicians, geologists, writers, as well as many other occupations. Furthermore, the continuous theme of the contribution made by women to military Intelligence work is notable. The part played by members of the former Auxiliary Territorial Service and the Women's Royal Army Corps who were permanently employed by the Corps was very important. The tradition will be maintained and developed in the years to come as the Corps now includes women members.

The book does have one shortcoming and this is implicit in some of my earlier remarks. Much material has, of necessity, been held back. In particular, the last chapter can do little more than indicate the Corps' and must exclude all reference to recent counter-terrorist operations. The reasons for these limitations are, I believe, self-evident.

It only remains for me to make a few remarks about the Author but, before I do, I, like the Author, would like to acknowledge the invaluable early work done by Colonel Felix Robson.

Dr Tony Clayton joined the staff at the Royal Military Academy Sandhurst as a civilian lecturer in 1965 and two years later became the Intelligence Corps Representative at the Academy and also transferred to the Intelligence Corps as a Territorial Army officer. In 1982 he retired from the Territorial Army having reached the rank of Brevet Lieutenant Colonel in the Corps. It is against this background and that of being a distinguished historian that he has written this book. He has done so through love and loyalty to his Corps and not in any official capacity. In his own words he 'wishes to see the record of our Corps set out.'

I hope that you agree with me that he has achieved his aim and this book is a worthy addition to the history of the British Army.

Author's Acknowledgements

Writing the regimental history of one's own Corps is a very warming experience. The great willingness to help, continually shown by people who have many other calls on their time, strikes a vein of *esprit de corps* that is rich and rewarding. To thank everyone adequately is a most difficult task.

First I should like most sincerely to thank Colonel F G Robson who in his period as Corps Secretary had accumulated so much most valuable historical material as a foundation on which it was possible to extend. No author could have been given a better start to his work.

Colonel Robson's material and my further researches were supported by many serving or very recently retired members of the Corps. These included Brigadiers A K Crawford, M P Ford, B A H Parritt, E P O Springfield and D J Venn; Colonels J H S Burgess, D M Burrill, D Hawker, J J McMullen, H M Sloan, R A S White; Lieutenant Colonels R E Cole-Mackintosh, R Collins, K Dryden, R A Eccles, J Landolt, W Leary, D A O'Connor, R M Richards, R F Pierce, A J Sullivan and A Williams; Majors T Cardwell and R W M Shaw, and the late Warrant Officer 1 (RSM) F R Cloag.

A very large number of the Second World War or immediate post-war years members of the Intelligence Corps gave of their time to send me full accounts of their service or important documents. These included T Allbeury, Sir Robert Andrew, the late L Allen, M Allen, Lord Annan, B Ardill, B Blount, H Boggis Rolfe, V Bonham Carter, S T Charles, K Clifford Cooke, A J Crick, R Dahl, H Eaton, J A F Ennals, Sir Brinsley Ford, Professor N Gash, D Hamblen, J Hillyer-Funke, C I Isolani, B H Kemball-Cook, P M Lee, G D H Linton, W Lough, Nial MacDermot, the late Arther Marshall, M Morgan, E M St G Moss, the late T X H Pantcheff, the late A D Peck, D A Prater, D Peploe, the late Michael Pertwee, T Peters, Mrs E Roberts, the late A Rowan-Robinson, Sir William Ryrie, G A T Shaw, H T Shergold, Mrs M Sherman, H Skillen, J B de Silva, W Stallybrass, K E Sutcliffe, R C Symonds, Mrs D

Taylor, the late J G Charles White and the late A W E Winlaw.

But I am as grateful to the further 70 former members of the Corps, alas too numerous to list, who sent me shorter notes and recollections. Almost all were useful and the footnotes serve to record both the variety and my appreciation.

In addition to these members of the Corps, five others involved in Intelligence but not members of the Corps, Dr H Beckhough, Lord Ezra, J Maclaren and Sir Tom Normanton all gave me especially useful materials. From Valletta, J Agius most kindly produced notes on the Malta Corps members of the Second World War.

The Women's Royal Army Corps kindly gave the Intelligence Corps permission to quote from Colonel Julia Cowper's *A Short History of Queen Mary's Army Auxiliary Corps*; our gratitude to others who have allowed us to quote from family papers is recorded in the footnotes. I have also drawn extensively on two publications of our own, Brigadier B A H Parritt's *The Intelligencers* and Captain H B Eaton's *APIS, Soldiers with Stereo*.

The Corps is most grateful to the Trustees of the Imperial War Museum for permission to use so many of the Museum's photographs; to these have been added several of our own, together with others, for which we are again grateful, from E M St G Moss and Mrs Dorothie Storry. The Intelligence Centre Photographic Section's help was especially useful with wartime snapshots.

Many people have read all or part of this manuscript or some of the material used, or have offered specialist advice and our thanks go out to them. Among these were the late D W King and C A Potts of the Ministry of Defence (Army) Library, and Miss A Ward, J Harding and P Beaven of the Army Historical Branch. My special thanks go also to J O Wright for an early reading of the first sections of the work.

As with many Brassey's authors, I also owe an especial debt of gratitude to Brigadier Bryan Watkins for his most erudite and careful editing of the manuscript.

Lastly, but by no means least, this book owes much to support staff both at Sandhurst and Ashford. In particular, I would like to thank Miss Monica Alexander for her difficult work in converting my manuscript to typescript and to Mrs Miriam Morgan who converted the major part of the typescript to the word processor. The staff of the Intelligence Corps Museum have also been both patient and helpful.

Anthony Clayton
Royal Military Academy Sandhurst
November 1992

List of Plates

1. The bridge at Pontoise, 31 August 1914.
2. An air photograph of German trenches at Loos, 1917.
3. Prisoner of War questioning, Headquarters 1st Army, March 1918.
4. A BEF Intelligence Corps Sergeant questions a civilian, Bethune, May 1918.
5. Prisoner of War questioning, Dardanelles, 1915.
6. Air photographic interpretation, Italian Front, 1917.
7. Lieutenant Colonel Templer with Captain Attfield, France, December 1939.
8. Captain Rowell and Lieutenant MacBride, Medmenham, 1943.
9. Headquarters 50th Division, Western Desert, 1942. The GSO III (Intelligence) at work.
10. Headquarters 50th Division, Western Desert, 1942. Typing an Intelligence Summary whilst under bombardment.
11. Tactical (Y) Signals Interpretation, Western Desert, 1942.
12. Western Desert, 1942. Field Security Section NCOs questioning local Libyans during exchange of gifts.
13. Questioning the Italian General Mannerini, North Africa, 1942.
14. Field Security. Questioning the former Fascist mayor of a Sicilian town, 1943.
15. A booby-trapped German machine-gun, Normandy, July 1944.
16. HM King George VI inspecting 89 (Airborne) Field Security Section, Netheravon, April 1943.
17. Colonel Ewart at the surrender of German forces in North-West Europe, Luneburg, May 1945.
18. Major Storry with his Mobile Section, Burma, 1944.
19. Japanese Kempetai officials being marched to gaol, Singapore, 1945.
20. A National Service NCO of the Corps, Kluang detachment 355 FSS, Malaya, 1945.

21. Searching an Egyptian vessel for hidden arms, Port Said, November 1956.
22. Conducting a body search after a house raid, Aden, 1966.
23. Briefing Royal Marine Special Boat Section personnel, Borneo, 1967.
24. Corporal 'Ali' Barber, Dhofar, 1971.
25. NCOs of the 5th Infantry Brigade Intelligence Cell, Fitzroy Settlement, Falklands, June 1982.

Prologue

The Role

The Intelligence Corps is an Arm within the land forces of the Crown. An Arm is defined as those Corps or Regiments whose role is to be in close combat with the enemy or to weaken his ability to fight—Infantry, Artillery, Engineers, Armour, Army Air Corps and Intelligence Corps.

The Corps is composed of trained officers and men who are concerned with military Intelligence, that is Intelligence that serves the needs not only of the Army but on occasions the other two Services. Without Intelligence a field commander is deprived of an indispensable dimension of command. Essentially, military Intelligence needs are two-fold, providing our field commanders and planning staffs with the Intelligence that they require about an opponent, his armed forces and its equipment, and preventing any adversary from obtaining this type of Intelligence about our Army that we do not want him to have. The terms 1(A) and 1(B) are sometimes used to describe these two sides of the Intelligence coin.[1] The actual work is carried out by a triad. At the top are Intelligence staffs, in the middle are Intelligence officers who collate and assess material provided by the third components, the Intelligence gatherers. The Intelligence Corps have of course never been the only soldiers engaged in any of these duties, but in this century the need for a special Corps for Intelligence work, a reflection of the increasing sophistication of warfare, has become ever greater. And from small beginnings, primarily as Intelligence gatherers, the Corps has now in the 1990s developed its expertise for almost all collation and analysis work, and to the provision of officers for a number of senior Intelligence staff appointments. To meet this role, members of the Corps are and have been first and foremost soldiers, and much, though not all, Corps work is carried out in uniform serving Army commanders in theatres of military operations. But there have been periods, most notably in the Second World War, with port security as one example, when it was convenient for the government to have uniformed military personnel serving as the executive arm of home civilian Intelligence organisations. Also in the Second World War on occasions a number of individuals and small teams engaged in highly specialised covert operations were Intelligence Corps personnel, and such commitments continued in certain of the post-1945 campaigns. But, in the main, after the War the Corps returned to its more purely military Intelligence duties, those increasingly crossing inter-Service boundaries.

Intelligence staff have no executive powers and cannot move a single soldier, they remain purely advisory. In the words of one of the British Army's greatest Intelligence Staff Officers, Brigadier Sir Edgar Williams, the role of the Intelligence Staff '... was to explain what the enemy was doing; not to suggest how to defeat him'.[2] To be effective therefore Intelligence staffs must not only be efficient in collecting, collating and analysing, but also in persuading and presenting. With some commanders in the Second World War success in presentation could only be achieved by packaging Intelligence in such a way that the conclusions to be drawn from it appeared as the product of the commander's own imagination. The rationale of all these duties remains that of conserving life on the battlefield, where Intelligence is a prime weapon of war, and preserving peace in time of international confrontations, through knowledge of an opponent's military capabilities. These are roles vital, professional and honourable.

They are also roles that frequently bring members of the Corps into as great a measure of physical danger, requiring as much plain combat courage, as any of the other Arms of the Army. This work will offer innumerable examples of this courage.

Armies are conservative bodies, conformity is essential for regimental soldiering. Intelligence personnel have on the one hand to conform, but on the other their task must be to question. This duality can prove difficult for other soldiers to accept. Further psychological barriers that have at times impeded Intelligence work include a long standing military belief that any form of covert work is ungentlemanly, together with the view that agents can be unreliable and mercenary. The Corps has, however, been immensely fortunate in being able to overcome these difficulties through the abilities of its members, both Regular soldiers in times of peace and the great body of temporary officers and soldiers that served in the Corps in war and in National Service. Many of these latter have later moved on to high academic distinctions or senior positions in public life.

The view was long maintained that any permanent Corps of Intelligence was undesirable. In consequence an Intelligence Corps as we know it only came into being in 1914, and was to disappear between the two World Wars before reformation, this time more permanently, in 1940. But, prejudice notwithstanding and slowly gaining acceptance as essential in campaigning, there had been for the previous four hundred years organised bodies of men concerned with Intelligence gathering. The Corps may justly view these as its forebears and the first chapter of this history summarises their roles, with one exception under Cromwell, as being very similar to that of the modern Intelligence Corps.

1

The Forebears of the Intelligence Corps

Even before the formation of the British Regular Army, English armies had included among the senior officers a 'Scoutmaster', in command of Intelligence gatherers called 'scouragers' for reconnaissance and field security purposes.[1]

From Cromwell to Wellington

Both Civil War Armies had a Scoutmaster in charge of agents watching enemy movements and handling informers in opponents' camps or areas. The Intelligence so gathered tallies well with present day Intelligence staff requirements, information upon not only movements but also morale, discipline, logistics and equipments being collected. Different from today, however, was the powerful military Security apparatus created by John Thurloe for the Major Generals' régime and continued by Oliver Cromwell as Lord Protector. This exceedingly efficient and well funded system installed agents in streets, markets, homes of known Royalists, and the Court in exile. The distaste it aroused contributed for long to the dislike of Intelligence personnel among other Army officers. The post of Scoutmaster-General declined in standing after the Restoration and its duties were eventually included into the new post of Quarter-Master General created under King James II.

The Duke of Marlborough placed great importance upon Intelligence during his great campaigns in the War of Spanish Succession, 1702–1713. In the field, Marlborough's Quarter-Master General, Cadogan, moving ahead of the army, recruited guides for tactical Intelligence, so ensuring that Marlborough could plan correct movements. At strategic level, Marlborough maintained agents at the French court who on several occasions supplied vital material concerning the composition and plans of the French Army. Unfortunately for the payment of these agents, Marlborough used funds allocated for other purposes. After his replacement as Commander in Chief, political opponents alleged corruption or misappropriation and proceedings were opened. But in the words of one Intelligence historian: 'For the British intelligence officer, Marlborough's fate is a salutary lesson. To obtain good intelligence is not sufficient, the methods used must also be above reproach. Today this rule still applies, and whether it be the use of pressure during an interrogation, or the use of public monies to pay informers, the military Intelligence officer must be ever careful that he never pursues his aim in such a manner, or to such a degree, that he cannot subsequently justify himself in open court-martial.'[2] Members of the Corps, like the rest of the Army, are aware both of their responsibilities and their accountability.

The style in the later eighteenth century wars changed little. In the Seven Years War, 1756–1763, the British Army in Germany, under German Intelligence officers, relied on agents, spies, informers and advance reconnaissance parties to gain Intelligence. In America and Canada, however, occurred the first examples of a tradition to grow massively 200 years later, of co-operation between Britons and Americans (at that time, of course, still under the British Crown) in the field of military Intelligence; a unit named the 'Yankee Rangers' existed for scouting duties. But in planning his brilliant seizure of Quebec, General Wolfe kept most Intelligence in his own hands, personally interrogating deserters, questioning spies and Rangers, reading intercepted letters, conducting his own reconnaissance and including a deception plan—the leading assault boats masqueraded as French provision vessels and a feint attack to distract the enemy was mounted. General Amherst, who took Montreal, also used Rangers and guides for Intelligence work with great skill and success. The experience of the War of American Independence was, however, less successful. André, the intelligence officer of General Clinton, the British Commander in New York, was running a dubiously reliable network of agents and informers, sometimes behind the American lines. On one such mission, in negotiation with an American general prepared to change sides if suitably rewarded, André was captured by the Americans and executed.[3]

Early reverses in the French Revolutionary Wars, in particular the failure of the Duke of York's 1793–5 Flanders expedition, were a consequence of the neglect of Intelligence work. The lesson was first appreciated by the Territorials of the day, mostly Yeomanry and Fencibles, under the threat of invasion. Kent led the way with the formation in 1798 of a Corps of Guides, 3 officers and 60 soldiers (mostly gamekeepers), a unit modelled on Napoleon's *Corps des Guides—Interprètes*. Sussex followed in the next year. Their concern was to be experts in local terrain, roads, supplies and water with, if the enemy landed, a reconnaissance role. The two Corps were disbanded after the 1802 Treaty of Amiens, but Corps for all the south coast countries were formed when the war was resumed. At Army headquarters level, a Depot of Military Knowledge was established in 1803 in the Horse Guards, at the instigation of the Duke of York; it was to gather Intelligence in respect of movements, plans, topography and publications. After Trafalgar, however, the threat of an enemy invasion receded. The Depot fell into decline, its abler officers seeking active service and the whole organisation being tainted with the scandal surrounding the sale of commissions by the Duke of York's mistress. The Guides Corps were either disbanded or became yeomanry, a few lasting to the 1820s.

But the lessons of the Flanders expedition were not lost on those in command in the Peninsula. Operational Intelligence as we know it now developed well. A small informal, locally recruited, Peninsula Corps of Guides were serving with Moore on his advance to Salamanca and retreat to Corunna. In 1809, under Wellington, a Corps of Guides was formally established, 6 officers and 38 soldiers, the numbers increasing in the next years. Its members included French deserters, and some of the officers were Portuguese. Initially their duties were purely as guides, but with proficiency their duties extended to agent-handling, interpreting, tactical questioning, reconnaissance targeted upon French movements, force sizes and commanders some way behind the front, and for a while also certain provost commitments. In addition, a small group of specialist junior officers were at work on local topography, reporting or making maps and sketches of terrain. Others, selected for riding and language ability, were tasked with the observation of enemy movements. Some of these stayed behind in territory occupied by the French. In particular, French units crossing bridges were counted. Others ran a network of agent informers, all duties becoming increasingly specialised, involving deeper penetration or covert means and as such distinct from ordinary cavalry reconnaissance. Captain (later General Sir George) Scovell, who had commanded Moore's Peninsula Corps of Guides, and served Wellington as communications staff officer, was able with remarkable technical skill to decode intercepted French dispatches.

The most remarkable of these officers was Major Colquhoun Grant, appointed by Wellington to command the Guides in March 1814. Grant's career had already been adventurous. Fluent Spanish had enabled him to roam around Spain and report back with great accuracy on French activities and personalities. Captured while on one of his patrols he was taken to France, where he escaped and, pretending to be an American, managed to relay information on French plans and movements back to Wellington from Paris. Grant was officially styled 'Head Intelligence Officer' in the Waterloo campaign, though by this time the Corps of Guides had been—prematurely—disbanded.

India; The 1855 Topographical and Statistical Department; Crimea

After 1815, interest briefly moves to India where Intelligence needs led to the formation of an Indian Corps of Guides in 1846. The intention had been to create a small unit of specialists in terrain knowledge, drawn from any ethnicities and so familiar with most Indian languages and as such also quietly capable of gathering Intelligence. The unit and its redoubtable commander, Lieutenant H. Lumsden, soon developed wider ambitions, evolving into the forerunner of some of the most famous Frontier fighting regiments of the Indian Army, the role for they had been specially designed becoming subsumed. Regimental officers were then inspanned for tours of Intelligence staff duties; this proved successful in a campaign against Persia in 1856, when a Corps of Guides was organised and a small informer network run by General Outram's Intelligence officer, Ballard. The concept was, however, to prove disastrous in the following year. The outbreak of the Mutiny represented a major failure in Intelligence assessment, there being no trained specialist staff to collate the numerous danger signals. But in Europe peace, to last nearly 40 years, had followed the end of the Napoleonic Wars; the Army and defence needs were neglected generally, Intelligence particularly so. War when it came in an obscure corner of the Russian Empire, therefore caught the Army in almost total ignorance, the single redeeming feature at the outset being some idea of the fortifications of Sevastopol itself, thanks to the discovery of secret Russian and Austrian topographical maps in a Belgian back street shop, a discovery made by an undistinguished and prematurely retired Bombay Sappers and Miners major, Thomas Jervis, the first of a line of Royal Engineers officers to be concerned with Intelligence. But of the Crimea, its terrain, Russian garrisons, their organisation, equipment and capabilities nothing was known. As his reward, Jervis became Director of a newly created War Office Topographical and Statistical Department in February 1855. This department, after a very slow start in a converted stables at 9 Adelphi Terrace, Whitehall, can be seen as the forerunner of the Directorate of Military Intelligence, in turn to become the Joint Services Directorate of Intelligence.

The field operations in the Crimea, in addition to lack of preparation in Intelligence and almost every other branch of logistics and staff work, highlighted another besetting weakness of the British Army: officers' squirearchical disdain for Intelligence work as ungentlemanly. The heavy fighting at Inkerman, where the British Army was caught without forewarning, was a typical consequence of the neglect. A civilian, a consular official with knowledge of the Crimea named Cattley, was appointed Head of Intelligence to the Commander in Chief, Lord Raglan. On his own for most of the war, Cattley, who changed his name to Calvert for security reasons, was able to offer a very limited service until his death from cholera in July 1855. He arrived with a measure of information on the terrain and Russian garrisons. Interrogating Polish deserters and dissident Tartars, and using a network of Turkish spies, Calvert was able to collect some material on Russian reinforcements, equipment and morale, material often ignored or not properly used. A Corps of Guides also existed briefly from June 1855. Field Security lay outside Calvert's duties, it was in any case non-existent, with war correspondents providing the world and the Russians with details of all that they might want, and Russian officers disguised in French uniforms wandering unchecked in the British sector. Calvert did however warn that Russian agents in the form of Greeks masquerading as Tartars might be used as spies, a warning proved to be true by the identification of one after Calvert's death.

But the best that can be said of Crimea is that its fearful shortcomings were eventually to lead to reform. Initially, the reverse was the case, a plethora of committees examining all military policy but no motivation for any resolute action following. The Topographical and Statistical Branch united with Ordnance Survey and became totally preoccupied with civilian survey and maps. The Franco–Prussian War, with its glaring lessons of equipment, tactics and speed in mobilisation, acted as a catalyst, with Edward Cardwell, as Secretary of State, as the innovator together with, within the Branch, another Engineers officer, Captain Charles Wilson. Ordnance Survey was detached, the Branch now a Department, split into a Topographical section, tasked with producing British and foreign maps and fortress plans, and a Statistical section to collect other military information; attaches in foreign countries were to assist. A little later, the formal staff procedural links between 'Intelligence' and 'Operations' as we know them now was at last established with the creation of a new Intelligence Branch headed by a Major-General in 1873.[4] Within two years, the Branch had settled down to collect information and compile manuals about certain foreign armies in respect of strength, equipment, tactics, organisation, mobilisation and deployment, together with biographies of their senior officers. The Branch was at the time composed of seven permanent officers and four enthusiastic regimental officers, one or two of whom made 'fishing', 'tourist', 'painting' or 'shooting' trips abroad to areas of especial interest. The young Robert Baden-Powell, for example, went to Germany as a tourist to be an uninvited observer at trials of a new machine-gun, though he found it necessary to pretend to be drunk when challenged by a Prussian soldier. He visited Tunisia to paint pictures of Bizerta, and the Dalmation coast as a butterfly collector, sketches of wings representing fortifications. The Branch became a Division in 1887-88, with the title of Director of Military Intelligence (DMI) for its imaginative chief, Major General H Brackenbury.[5] Notable among the 16 officers of the Division was Captain (later Major General Sir James) Grierson, who, fluent in both German and Russian, visited both armies together with that of Austria-Hungary, developing formidable expertise.[6] The study of foreign press reports and military publications, and liaison with other major government departments and Naval Intelligence was to some extent systematised, though still more haphazardly than by any planned staff requirement. This random approach is illustrated by some of the Division's pre-occupations in the early 1890s—a Russian invasion of India, a French invasion of Britain, an American invasion of Canada, Finland, and a Spanish threat to Gibraltar. At the end of the decade, however, the Divison was tasked with a role as vital then as later, the provision of accurate general and technical intelligence against which arms limitation, mutual force reduction, and international security negotiations, could proceed; a Russian diplomatic initiative in 1898 had led to a conference being convened at the Hague in the following year.

Imperial Experience and the Field Intelligence Department in South Africa 1900-02

In the late nineteenth century for small scale colonial operations, where no permanent Intelligence staff existed, wiser commanders created a small Intelligence Branch often using local civilians with knowledge of languages, terrain and the opponent. In India, an Intelligence Branch was formed in 1878, but its own strength, three officers and three draughtsmen, together with the two very small Bombay and Madras Guides Corps produced no real Intelligence service—the Bengal Corps of Guides had long become élite combat units. In the 1875 Ashanti campaign, Captain (later General Sir Redvers) Buller improvised an Intelligence organisation using informers, interpreters, questioning of captives and bribes to compliant chieftains and threats against others; a small locally recruited Corps of Guides engaged in forward reconnaissance. Immediately before the 1879 Zulu campaign, a civilian border agent had compiled a small but very detailed manual, this was distributed to sub-unit level but at the outset there were no military Intelligence officers. The manual's warnings were negated by two defects in British command which were to last for some time—a prejudice against Intelligence collected by civilians and a measure of racial under-estimation. The result was the early disasters of 1879, notably the decimation of the 24th Foot, (South Wales Borderers), at Isandlhwana. By March 1879, the Commander-in-Chief, Lord Chelmsford, had a rudimentary Intelligence organisation of two locally recruited officers, one with his own privately raised force of local scouts, and more professional scouts from the Natal Volunteer Guides.

The usual mix of deep reconnaissance reports, deserters, agents and a few spies yielded useful Intelligence, though one of the officers was killed. On succeeding Chelmsford, Sir Garnet Wolseley used trained regular officers, with success, for Intelligence work in the hunt for Cetewayo, tracked down after an interrogation of captive Zulus.

The 1882 Egypt expedition benefitted from very full military Intelligence, carefully gathered during a previous shooting and tourist trip by one Major A B Tulloch, who, together with the young Kitchener, both in disguise, also conducted a clandestine railway reconnaissance in 1882. For the actual campaign, an Intelligence organisation was formed, largely from Britons living in Egypt, these included telegraph engineers who intercepted Egyptian government cables. In the field, Tulloch and others operated agents and questioned captives. In the two 1884 campaigns in the Sudan, small Intelligence staffs, two or three regular officers, reconnoitred, controlled agents and questioned captives, among them was Kitchener who, using his command of language and with only a small escort sworn to secrecy, would penetrate deep into the desert disguised as an Arab. Twelve years later, in the 1896–99 campaign, Kitchener, now the Commander-in-Chief, benefitted from the help of an exceptionally efficient Intelligence service created by Colonel R (later Sir Reginald) Wingate whose spies and agents, in the words of Winston Churchill 'disguised as traders, as warriors or as women' provided a complete picture of the movements of the Khalifa and his supporters; raw information was collected by Lebanese interpreters. Immediately before the final battle of Omdurman, in 1898, Kitchener averted a night attack on his own position by sending out local people briefed to warn the Khalifa of a planned British attack at midnight. The Khalifa withdrew his force until the next day by which time British preparations were complete.

One of the emerging British dominions, Canada, had also recognised the need for military Intelligence. In the 1885 campaign in North West Canada against the dissident Louis Riel, a scout unit of 3 officers and 30 men, all from the Dominion Land Survey, was formed, under the title of Intelligence Corps, to assist the militia forces.

The Second Boer War, in which Britain found herself opposed by a well-equipped enemy with mastery of terrain, was the first example of the new Intelligence needs arising from advances in technology and speed in mobilisation and movement. During the war, the largest and most developed combat operational Intelligence organisation in British history to that time, the Field Intelligence Department (FID), was created; its duties, as will be seen, closely resembled the work of the Intelligence Corps of today. At the outbreak of war in October 1899, however, the keynote was one of operational Intelligence failures, a major cause of the British Army's early reverses and casualties. In London the DMI, Major General Sir John Ardagh, lay sick, exhausted by his efforts at the Hague Disarmament conference, with other key officers on tour or posted. The Branch, in particular its over-worked colonial section, was woefully undermanned and also, headed by a two-star officer only, lacked 'clout'. In South Africa the first Commander-in-Chief, Sir George White, had no concept of the importance of Intelligence and was in any case very quickly entrapped in Ladysmith; his successor, Buller, despite his earlier Intelligence experience in the Ashanti war was no better, having no professional Intelligence staff at his headquarters when he met his reverse at Colenso. Paradoxically, the information they needed was available and very full. Ardagh and his Intelligence Division, anticipating war, had from 1896 onwards been collecting information and warning of the probable cost and scale of a conflict they correctly assessed as likely to be with both Boer Republics, the Orange Free State and the South African Republic (Transvaal). They had provided details of Boer arms purchases and foreseen the difficulties of the long frontiers, dissidence among Boers living in Natal and the Cape, and a probable British numerical inferiority at the outbreak of fighting. A handbook produced in June 1899 had given exceedingly accurate reports on the totals of men, rifles, machine-guns, ammunition and artillery likely to be available to the Boers.

But three underlying factors negated the value of this Intelligence. The first was a failure to appreciate the advantage that the Boer armies would have fighting on ground and in conditions totally familiar to them.[7] The second was a political attitude, nothing must be done that could, if learned by the Boers, be seen by them as provocative. The Division's reports, therefore, were not shown to the Cabinet nor discussed with the field commanders. Similar political constraints negated the efforts of 10 Army officers sent out to South Africa primarily for Intelligence work in July 1899. The third factor, in part a consequence of the low standing of the Division, is clearly pinpointed by Parritt. The Division had failed to make the 'clear, sharp distinction between general worry over a deteriorating situation and the crucial moment when positive action is required'.[8] Ardagh incurred much immediate public blame, but when details of his work were revealed public attitudes changed.

On the ground, a Natal political figure and farmer, T K Murray, formed a Natal Corps of Guides of approximately 100, white and black in about equal numbers. In the Cape one of the 10 officers sent out in July, Major Rimington, formed a similar force; this body was known under several names, the more general being 'Rimington's Scouts' but among the names was an 'Intelligence Corps'. On his arrival, Buller appointed Murray as Head of Intelligence but the appointment was too late and Buller was in any case replaced by Lord Roberts after his defeat at Colenso. Roberts arrived with his own Head of Intelligence, Colonel George Henderson, later succeeded by Lieutenant Colonel C V Hume. Henderson's work included a notable deception plan to deceive the Boer commander, Cronje, on the British line of advance, and after the relief of Kimberley a correct assessment of Cronje's next move, an assessment based on the report of an agent in Cronje's forces and on the work of Rimington's Scouts.

The war fell into two phases, the formal war ending with Cronje's surrender and Roberts' entry into Pretoria and the defeat of the remaining Boer field forces a little later, and a protracted two year guerrilla campaign by those Boers who refused to give in. In the first phase the need for the triad was at last recognised, the components being a headquarters Intelligence staff, Intelligence officers at brigade level trained to collate material and to co-ordinate and task the different agencies, and the agencies themselves, these latter possessing specialist skills but not qualified to assess the material they acquired from their variety of sources.[9] Also perceived was the need to link Counter-intelligence work, on which personnel were engaged, with the Intelligence staff. As important for them and his successor, Colonel (later Lieutenant General Sir David) Henderson Hume, saw the need for planning and preparation, including the training of personnel, in peacetime. Colonel George Henderson had laid the foundations with his creation of a 'Local Intelligence Organisation', later the Field Intelligence Department (FID), with, under Colonel David Henderson, interpreters, scouts, guides and 'native scouts', in fixed grades. By 1902, the FID's strength totalled 132 officers, over 2,000 white soldiers, and a large number of black 'native scouts', small units locally raised by individuals, farmers and others providing most of the men. Under a DMI (South Africa), this organisation was structured upon four districts, a number of sub-districts, each with its own Intelligence officer, with others in independent columns. From the top, reporting procedures were standardised and Intelligence concerning Boer strengths, equipments, morale and likely courses of action distributed down to combat units, accompanied by guidance on Intelligence required at headquarters and descriptions of wanted men.

Its greatly expanded size was a consequence of the second, equally testing phase of the war, Boer commando raiding upon the British Army's stretched communications and small outpost detachments scattered over South Africa. For the FID, the testing was complicated by the absence of training among many of the FID personnel and the command's habit of imposing other administrative or logistic duties upon them.

The day-to-day work of the FID reveals the new professionalism. Colonel George Henderson arranged leaks of false operation orders as part of a deception plan. A particularly successful local farmer officer, Woolls-Sampson, carefully recruited black natives who rode into townships and villages collecting information of Boer commando sightings from agents. Other scouts would track commandos on the move, lying out watching them for several days and nights. Deserters, white or black, from Boer forces were questioned. Boer papers and captured documents were translated.[10] The mail of Germans and others working for the Boers was intercepted and read. Parties were sent out to lie up and intercept Boer heliographs. For the first time, reports from balloon reconnaissance, a Royal Engineers responsibility (the balloons usually being tethered to a balloon cart) occasionally provided material, including sketches—and the first air photographs. The observers had an exceedingly uncomfortable time as the balloon revolved in the air or jolted with the movement of the cart. They also found recognition of the movement of men on their feet or even terrain features very difficult; at Magersfontein, balloon reconnaissance was a notable failure. In London, a new Cable Censorship section was added to the DMI's division, its staff contracted from Aden was able to keep well informed on Boer supplies through intercepts, and one operator intercepted and decoded a message from Boer commando generals to the exiled President Kruger. A very small, highly secret, section endeavoured to keep a watch on arms shipments to the Boers from Europe. One Scout, a Minnesota-born American named F R Burnham operating behind Boer lines, sabotaged a Boer railway line. Some of the techniques may appear quaint, such as the Scouts' use of single and tandem bicycles running on the railway lines. A few covert operations took place, notably perhaps that, after the war, of Captain E (later Field Marshal Lord) Ironside who, despite his 6' 4'' height with build to match, disguised himself as a Boer wagon-driver to penetrate dissident Boer groups and German military install-ations in the German colony of South West Africa. Colonel Baden-Powell, besieged in Mafeking, had been kept well informed about his besiegers through agents in the Transvaal. Pigeon communication was used, with mixed results by columns but very riskily by scouts and agents; if found in an agent's kit, the birds proved a give-away, that would prove fatal in a few cases. Courses for FID personnel were arranged, subjects taught being interrogation, field-sketching and report-writing.[11] Lastly, and by no means least important where Intelligence relies upon persuasion, the 'image' of the Intelligence gatherer improved greatly. In the words of Colonel David Henderson 'The spectacle of an Intelligence man entering camp in the early morning on a tired horse tends to raise the Intelligence Corps in the esteem of the army.'[12] Exploits of personal gallantry by members of the Corps served the same useful purpose.

Some of the other difficulties encountered, too, were not for the last time. Most difficult in the war phase was the control of journalists, their press reports being a major source of Boer Intelligence. Another was the question of whether or not to arm scouts, especially black 'native scouts'; if taken unarmed they were defenceless, if taken armed, they were liable to violent Boer maltreatment. In the commando phase it was exceedingly difficult to recognise which Boers were farmers by day but turned—or harboured—commandos at night. Plots to seize armouries, kill co-operative Boers or senior military officers were uncovered. The large area of ground and distances between formations and units presented especial problems for the speedy dissemination of Intelligence.

Interesting detail of some of these activities appears in documents in the Corps Museum. The notebook of an FID officer, Major (later Colonel) H F Coleridge, contains numerous entries such as:

> 7 Dec 1900.
> Native in from Lamoeinfontein last night reports there are about 300 Boers not mounted, 10 wagons, there are 2 tents, Piet Marais is there, they have one English soldier as prisoner. The horsemen are at Witpoort.

Another reads:

> Native Pete left Palmisfontein at 12 noon and saw 19 Boers with General Liebenberg. They went in the direction of Rhaibokfontein.

Despatch riders, some of whom were black, were evidently a useful source of Intelligence, and unexpected indicators, such as compulsory growing of mealies by Blacks, could reveal Boer interests in an area. The Intelligence reports of the Ladysmith garrison reveal the whole wide range of sources now providing pieces of the Intelligence jig-saw puzzle. In addition to cavalry reconnaissance, FID scouts and agents, police, railway officials, missionaries, Boer deserters and civilians weary of the war, and balloons (most useful here for noting convoy movements or camp fire smoke) all contributed. The reports of many native scouts, among them 'Kaffirs John, Joseph and Johannes' and 'Hans Hottentot' were especially valuable.

The FID's activities were not without casualties, which totalled 15 killed and 11 died of disease, 1 missing, 28 wounded and 20 captured by the Boers.

Colonel David Henderson, on the basis of his FID experience later, recommended that all persons, other than Staff Officers permanently engaged on Intelligence duties in a campaign should be formed into an 'Intelligence Corps' for reasons of co-ordination and *esprit de Corps*. He went on to portray the ideal Intelligence officer in terms that need no amendment today:

> The successful Intelligence officer must be cool, courageous, and adroit, patient and imperturbable, discreet and trustworthy. He must understand the handling of troops and have a knowledge of the art of war. He must be able to win the confidence of his General, and to inspire confidence in his subordinates. He must have resolution to continue unceasingly his search for information, even in the most disheartening circumstances and after repeated failures. He must have endurance to submit silently to criticism, much of which may be based on ignorance or jealousy. And he must be able to deal with men, to approach his source of information with tact and skill, whether such source be a patriotic gentleman or an abandoned traitor.[13]

In all, military Intelligence had come of age. The FID was already being referred to colloquially as the 'Intelligence Corps'. Colonel David Henderson's manual *Field Intelligence, Its Principles and Practices* evolved into the War Office *Regulations for Intelligence Duties in the Field* of August 1904 and pointed the way onwards. No future war could be fought without a body of professional military Intelligence personnel as an Intelligence Corps.

2

The First Intelligence Corps, 1914

The British Empire declared war on Germany and Austria-Hungary on 4 August 1914. An *ad hoc* Intelligence Corps for the British Expeditionary Force destined for France began mobilising at Southampton on 5 August.

Creation and Baptism of Fire with the 1914 BEF

Much had happened in the twelve years between the ending of the Boer War and August 1914 to enable this speedy reaction. In South Africa, the FID had been disbanded, but the locally-raised forces that suppressed the 1906 Natal Zulu Rising had included an 'Intelligence Corps'. Most important, the study of the lessons of the Boer War had led to a succession of reforms in the War Office. The Military Intelligence Division had been briefly amalgamated with the Mobilisation staff in 1901—a significant linkage. Greater attention to foreign armies' studies was begun, but no need for any particular training of Intelligence staff officers was yet accepted.

The Indian Army had created a field Intelligence unit at Peshawar in 1904; this unit was referred to as the nucleus 'Intelligence Corps'. It served the Intelligence Branch of the Quartermaster-General's Department, officers who served a tour with the Corps moving later to the Branch for a second Intelligence tour. The organisation worked well in the 1908 frontier expeditions.[1] The only campaign waged by the British Army in the years between 1902 and 1914 was in Somaliland, against Muhammed Abdile Hassan, 'The Mad Mullah'. Intelligence was gathered by a staff of three officers, 350 *illaloes* or scouts who operated in groups of 50, and 150 interpreters. Intelligence was regarded as all-important.[2]

At home, more progress was achieved from 1904 onwards with the implementation some of the major recommendations of the most important of the post Boer War committees on Army reform, one chaired by Lord Esher but much influenced by one of its members, Admiral Sir John Fisher, the volcanic creator of the Dreadnought battleship. The antiquated post of Commander-in-Chief of the Army was abolished, and a General Staff created. Within that staff, Intelligence lost its linkage with Mobilisation and was placed under the Director of Military Operations, a Directorate comprising four sections, MO1 Strategical Section, MO2 Foreign Intelligence, MO3 Administration and Special Duties (including agents), and MO4 Topographical Section.[3] MO2 and MO3 officers continued the pre-1900 practice of continental tours to glean Intelligence, sometimes paying agents for material. In 1907 a new MO5 was created for the Special Duties (protective security, censorship of posts and telegraphs and ciphers), in turn leading in 1909 to a Special Intelligence Bureau under Captain V (later Major General Sir Vernon) Kell. This, the earliest form of MI5, the Security Service, despite its title and the serving officer at its head, employed only two Army officers and quickly became a Service whose staff were almost entirely civilian, police and a few retired officers.[4] An MO6 was also created for medical Intelligence. As early as 1905, the first studies of a German onslaught on France through Belgium were made; Anglo-French staff talks followed in 1905–06. The next step, under the far-seeing Director from 1919, Major General H (later Field Marshal Sir Henry) Wilson, was study increasingly focussed upon the German Army and road and rail communications in North France and Belgium. Further staff talks, as in 1905–06 including some exchange of Intelligence information, also took place.[5] In 1912, the War Office published a *Staff Manual—War (Provisional)*. This manual covered all aspects of field Intelligence work, it also specifically laid down that 'All persons (except secret service agents) permanently engaged in Intelligence duties will be formed into a special Intelligence Corps for the time being, under the Brigadier General in charge of the Intelligence Section at General Headquarters'.[6] Equally useful was a *Handbook of the German Army* first produced in 1912 and amended in January 1914. The information for this was in part derived from photographs of a secret German staff manual which had provided detail down to field ciphers.[7]

Lord Esher's committee also made specific recommendations in respect of field Intelligence personnel. One of these called for the peacetime training of Intelligence staff officers, with particular reference to what they were to collect and how the material should be collected, collated and presented. This recommendation was acted upon, Eastern Command beginning a series of 'Intelligence and Reconnaissance Courses' in 1908.[8] Staff Rides often included Intelligence problems. The Committee's second major proposal was that the nucleus of a corps of Intelligence gatherers, capable of expansion on mobilisation, should be raised in peacetime. This proposal was reinforced by the reference in the *Staff Manual—War (Provisional)* to the need for an Intelligence Corps of Scout officers, Guides, Interpreters and Intelligence Police for any European expeditionary force.[9] But the recommendation was acted upon only half-heartedly, to the extent that a list of suitable men was collected in 1913 by the Directorate's staff officer in charge of MO5, the exceptionally able Major G M W (later Lieutenant General Sir George) Macdonogh. In addition to existing prejudices, a major brake upon action had been a typically British political and military reluctance to accept a significant continental military commitment for the Army. In the colonies local officials and settlers had sufficed; the creation of a corps tasked for Europe implied a commitment to Europe. This commitment was only finally accepted by the Government in 1911, from which time preparations to despatch a seven division British Expeditionary Force to aid France against a German invasion were at last made, and with increased urgency.

The list furnished most of the first 50 men: 1 major, 4 captains, 7 lieutenants, a quartermaster and 42 'Scout officers', who set sail for France at the end of August 1914.[10] The original establishment had provided for 81, including 25 'Officer Scouts' and 25 'Detectives' from the Metropolitan Police. But not all those called, or those who volunteered, were found suitable, and there were difficulties over terms of service. Those called included academics, businessmen, journalists, writers, artists and others selected for expertise, linguistic (French or German) or other, useful for operations in France. Each had received a telegram (most to their total surprise) inviting them to join a body referred to as the 'Intelligence Corps'. They were graded as Second Lieutenants (Interpreters) or as Agents (First Class) and wore General List badges and buttons. Their Commandant was a Major T D Torrie, an Indian Army officer on leave from a staff posting, who was afraid he might miss the war if he returned to India. Their adjutant was Captain J (later Colonel Sir John) Dunnington-Jefferson, Royal Fusiliers, also on leave from India who advanced his claim on the basis of a knowledge of French. The Corps was organised into a Headquarters Wing; a Dismounted Section; a Motor-Cycle Section using Douglas, Premier, Rudge and Triumph motor cycles with varying degrees of skill; a Mounted Section using Grafton Hunt horses; and a Security Duties Section. The latter, initially 12 men of various grades, was recruited from Metropolitan Police Special Branch officers but was later reinforced by further Metropolitan Police officers together with others from Indian Police forces; their role was lines of communication security.[11] Many had previous military experience. At this stage the Corps' only private soldiers were orderlies. Later, soldiers selected for the Corps were posted and badged, for administrative convenience and perhaps also as a cover, to a special '10th Battalion, Royal Fusiliers, Intelligence (B).' From Southampton the Corps moved to Le Havre by the troopship *Olympia* and, after issue of a rifle and 100 rounds of ammunition in a rain-swept camp, thereafter to the front. Macdonogh himself left MO5 to become Colonel GS (Intelligence) at the General Headquarters (GHQ) of the BEF at Le Cateau, where initially some of the Corps were located, others being sent to lower headquarters.[12]

The Corps had been given a very clear directive on its duties prepared by Major (later General Sir Walter) Kirke of the pre-August 1914 MO5 staff. These were:

(a)   To provide experienced officers with linguistic qualifications mounted on horses or on motor cycles or in cars.

(b)   To supplement the Intelligence staffs of various headquarters which were obviously inadequate both in numbers and in the two essential foreign languages—those of our French allies and German opponents.

(c)   To provide officers for the anticipated expansion of the Secret Service.

(d)   To provide the nucleus of a 'Contre-espionage' organisation with the Army in France in accordance with the Staff Manual 1912.[13]

Unfortunately, the hastily assembled body of volunteers lacked any specific training, apart from a few hurried days at Southampton, for these military roles; there was also frequent misunderstanding of, or even contempt for, their role at headquarters. The result was that in the first months of the war personnel were often misused as ordinary soldiers, and under-valued. The war, too, was still in a mobile phase with endless moves of headquarters. The theme, however, soon develops from one of improvisation and amateurishness to a nascent professionalism, to develop yet further when the race to the sea had ended and the front lines were stabilised. Initial work included distant reconnaissance by car or motor cycle around the German outer flank acquiring information on enveloping movements; arranging for the reporting of German movements by Belgian and French civilians; co-operation with the French police; military liaison work with the French; cipher work; the control of passes and permits; the questioning of prisoners; motor cycle despatch work (knowledge of French proving invaluable); organising civilian working parties; searching for lost units; clearing roads of refugees and prepositioning stores for Army units in retreat; accompanying cavalry patrols and bridge demolition detachments; investigating reports (usually false) of enemy stay-behind snipers; examining tunnels and coal mines that the Germans might use, and, in the final stage of this initial phase of the war, the advance north from the Aisne, the spreading of false information to conceal the Army's real movement plans. While the Westward open flank remained, reports of agents and observers could be passed back with little difficulty. The Corps suffered its first casualties, among them Second Lieutenants A Sang, dying of wounds received on the Marne, J M Smith, J T Seabrook and A H Smith Cumming killed, and Second Lieutenants F H Beavan, T Breen, C A Gladstone and H W Le Grand taken prisoner. Second Lieutenant R Rolleston-West was awarded the DSO, the Intelligence Corps' first award, for his part in the destruction of an undemolished suspension bridge at Pontoise le Noyon on the line of advance of Von Kluck's 1st Army on 31 August. Rolleston-West's brigade commander had considered this further attempt to lay charges to be 'suicidal' but with a volunteer from 59 Company, Royal Engineers, Lieutenant J A C Pennycuick, Rolleston-West finally succeeded in dropping the trackway into the river.

Reconnaissance

The first reinforcement draft for the Corps arrived at St Nazaire on 24 August and moving forward were able to assist in the retreat from Le Cateau in a variety of ways. Major Torrie left the Corps to command a cavalry squadron, his place being briefly taken by Major A P (later Field Marshal Earl) Wavell, who had been serving as a Russian specialist in MO2. Wavell, however, wanted to return to infantry warfare and in December Dunnington-Jefferson was appointed to command the Corps; a second reinforcement draft arrived from Britain, among them Second Lieutenant (later Major General) F E Hotblack. After service as a despatch rider, Hotblack's two first specific Intelligence taskings were both to produce results useful even if negative. The first was to reconnoitre coal-mine tunnels to see if they could be used to enter the enemy rear areas, but the Germans had blocked the entrances on their side; the second was to study a sector of the Belgian coast in the context of a landing from the sea, a project later abandoned. Hotblack later turned his interests to tank warfare, becoming GSO2 Intelligence to the Tank Corps and winning a DSO and bar. Another early entrant to the Corps was an artillery subaltern, Lieutenant J H Marshall-Cornwall (later General Sir James Marshall-Cornwall). Both were fluent in French and German. Temporarily attached to a cavalry unit after a brief period in Movements staff, Marshall-Cornwall's troopers overran an area occupied by totally exhausted Germans. From questioning and examination of requisition notes left in the village, Marshall-Cornwall was able to reconstruct the complete order of battle of the German 2nd Cavalry Corps.[14] Another officer, whose identity has unfortunately not survived, identified the German 9th Cavalry Division entering Nivelles on 21 August, the Official History noting that the officer 'was in Nivelles when the Division entered but escaped by motor'.[15]

Also noteworthy was Second Lieutenant (later Captain) S Payne-Best, Intelligence Corps, despatched to Antwerp to establish a liaison with the Naval Brigade. After reaching Antwerp and vainly attempting to warn retreating Royal Marines of dangers on their route, Payne-Best proceeded to Bruges. There, observing from the Belfry and notifying GHQ by normal telephone, he was able to report the arrival of the Germans. During his final return to the British Army Payne-Best talked his way out of capture by the German cavalry, using his fluent German.

The diary of Major J L Baird (later Viscount Stonehaven), a former diplomat and a forceful Member of Parliament for Rugby, provides a more personal account of some of the activities of the new-born Intelligence Corps.[16] Baird, a linguist, was attached to it from August 1914, and the account carries with it something of the heady excitement of the first weeks of the war.

Aug 11—Left War Office, London, in car with M Howard and De Trafford at 12. Reached Southampton (Rest Camp) 4.45. Some grousing among Intelligence Corps owing to men who thought they had joined as officers being told they must look after their own horses; also no messing arrangements or organization. After being embodied a week, and having bought kit, a French exam was held and 12 'plucked', ie sacked.

Aug 12—After breakfast, it occured to me that it would be well to take Jilling, my steward, as batman. He is dismantling *Gertrude* [yacht]. Approved and Jilling willing. Took him to enslisting officer and tried to arrange to enlist him as Horse Transport driver. Unfortunately, it was too late, as Doctor not available to pass him. Made all arrangements. Railway company played up wonderfully; laid 4 lines through the town to the quay in 48 hours. EO said the arrival of the first lot at Le Havre yesterday seemed unexpected, as no arrangements had been made to receive them, and there was much delay in getting off. The reason was probably that all heads of departments had gone to the front in France. Starting at 8 pm. Men in splendid spirits, cheering and singing 'God Save the King' and patriotic songs. The route across was patrolled by 3 lines of warships, so disposed that if a ship gets through one line in the dark, she cannot reach the third line before daylight. The ships were ten miles apart. A perfect sight! The lights on Southampton at sunset were a beautiful sight. We steamed very slowly.

Aug 13—Picked up a pilot off Havre at 9 am, alongside quay at 11. There was much difficulty in getting a motor lorry off. Started for Rest Camp 7 at 4.—Boy Scout as guide; arrived at 6. Scorching hot day!

Aug 14—Motored into Havre for Orders. Disembarkation HQ in offices of Transatlantique Coy on quay. GHQ expected at 11 pm. Dined with Churchill (Consul General) at Cercle Francois 1er. GHQ arrived 3 hours before expected. I met Colonel Macdonogh and took him to Hotel Continental. Torrie, Lane and I started motoring back to Rest Camp at midnight in rain. Luckily petrol gave out just outside small house and we got shelter for the night there.

On 15 August Baird was posted by Macdonogh, now at GHQ as Chief of Intelligence, to the Adjutant General's Department of GHQ for IA duties; that evening he drove with Kirke to Maubeuge to establish intelligence liaison with the French Army. On 19 August, Captain J A Cuffe, the British liaison officer at the headquarters of the 2nd French Army, arrived from Belgium where he had been establishing an Intelligence reporting network. Baird accompanied him to Mons, spending two days

developing a reporting system in and around Mons which provided useful information in the early stages of the retreat. After the
early October battle of the Aisne his diary continues:

Oct 12—Was ordered to take charge of a Secret Service organi-
zation which had hitherto been run from Dunkirk. Went to St
Omer with Wavell at 12.30 followed by eight Intelligence
Corps motor cyclists.

Oct 13—Started 7 am in three motors with four cyclists to try and
locate Germans N and NW of St Omer. Also had a Rolls-Royce
with *mitrailleuse* manned by three Marines in charge of Lt
Smyth IC. After Cassell went on to Wormhout where Wavell
branched off with *mitrailleuse* car eastward, intending to work
round and locate German patrols in Poperinghe district. I
went on with others to Dunkirk, thence to Furnes, Nieuport,
Bruges and Ecloo where we learned from Belgian gendarmerie that German patrols had reached Ghent this morning.

Oct 20—Kirke came up from Ghent and explained that I am to act
independently (as Intelligence liaison) from IVth Corps
(Rawlinson) and 1st Corps (Haig). Kirke who is anything but
an alarmist is not comfortable about our situation and thinks a
deplorable lack of vigour has been shown and opportunities
missed (to counter-attack).

Oct 22—Battle of Ypres. I went again to Dixmude and saw French
Admiral Ronach holding off German attacks with marvellous
grit in most gallant fashion. To spend days and nights
ceaselessly shelled, losing men heavily, and not knowing
whether help is coming or not requires a vast amount of grit
and courage in all concerned. Luckily these qualities are being
displayed in a superlative degree both by our men and our
Allies right along the whole huge front from Verdun to the
sea. ...

Nov 4—Was ordered to join British Mission attached to Belgian
GHQ which consists of Colonel Tom Bridges and Prince
Alexander of Teck (later Duke of Connaught)

Nov 11—King Albert (of the Belgians) came to lunch with us
together with his ADC. The King is a brave man and has done
more than anyone to save a corner of his country. Recently he
stopped a panic when Furnes was under German shell-fire by
going into the square and walking about.

On April 23rd 1915 Baird went to Buckingham Palace to
receive the DSO from King George V. But by the end of the year
he had been strongly urged, in particular by Sir Henry Wilson, to

return to Parliamentary work and speak for conscription and strengthening the war effort. He felt obliged to respect this and his diary comes to an end.

The variety of backgrounds of members of the Corps contributed to the whole; Second Lieutenant Rolleston-West was an engineer who could repair motor cycles, Second Lieutenant Sang had considerable pre-war business experience of northern France. Others, paradoxically benefitting from the absence of any previous training that routinised procedures and discouraged originality, were often able to use initiative in a variety of situations. It was not surprising that French immediately ordered an expansion of the Corps.

Despite the fact that volunteers from civil life also did not always conform to the 1914 Regular Army concepts of Mess behaviour and dress, observers and colleagues all commented upon the high morale and enthusiasm with which the new Corps entered into the campaign. This is reflected in the London *Gazette* of 14 January 1915, publishing Sir John French's first BEF Honours List: 26 names appear under the heading 'Intelligence Corps'. Work was under conditions of extreme fatigue and often under fire. Members of the Corps were, clearly, prepared to put their hands to anything when required. The Hon. Maurice Baring, pre-war diplomat and journalist, commissioned into the Intelligence Corps in August 1914 despite his age of 40, used his intellectual and linguistic talents as personal assistant and staff officer to the General Commanding the Royal Flying Corps (RFC), firstly General David Henderson of the Boer War Field Intelligence Department, and then General Hugh Trenchard. Baring's personality contributed greatly to the excellent co-operation between the British and French air forces, and was to have important consequences for the development of air photography later in the war. Before his death in September 1914, Second Lieutenant J M Smith, attached to the 9th Lancers, was among some 40 volunteers from the regiment and artillery who saved the six guns of 119 Field Battery, Royal Field Artillery near Mons on 24 August. The guns had been under very heavy German fire with many of their gun crews and horses killed or injured. Their rescue by manhandling was a task for seasoned professionals; Second Lieutenant Smith's service was but three weeks.[17]

The first six months of the war had fulfilled all General Henderson's predictions, and in a number of fields the importance of accurate and timely Intelligence had been highlighted. Some examples of operational Intelligence work undertaken by other agencies may be cited; comparable work in the British Army of today would fall to the Intelligence Corps.

Prisoner of War Questioning

A number of Regular and Territorial Army officers were employed under the General Staff (Intelligence) on liaison reconnaissance and other duties, graded as GSO3 or Staff Lieutenants. Among them was the young Leopold Amery, detaching himself from his political career and serving as an Intelligence staff officer with the 4th Army Corps in the Ostende and later the Ypres areas. Using his knowledge of German, he began tactical questioning of prisoners. On 19 October he questioned prisoners taken by the French; these offered unidentified regimental numbers, from which Amery established the menace of three new German divisions poised to attack the left flank of a British division advancing on Courtrai.[18] Amery describes his questioning:

> I soon developed a technique, based on my knowledge of the German character, which I found worked unfailingly with the naturally obedient German private—officers rarely gave away anything. This was to treat them exactly as they would be treated by one of their own officers on recruitment, beginning systematically with their ages, Christian names; religion, occupation, residence, etc, of their parents; date and place of mobilisation, and so on. By the time I got on to the information I really wanted I had nearly always got them well into a routine, regarding it all as a necessary formality, whereas any other kind of opening easily awakened suspicion and stubborn evasion.[19]

Early Air Photography and Signals Interception

More important was the development of air reconnaissance and the beginning of air photography.[20] Four squadrons of General Henderson's RFC were flying air reconnaissance flights in the first weeks of the war, Sir John French later asserting that these had helped him 'avert danger and disaster' at Mons.[21] The Official History repeatedly notes the value of their reconnaissance reports; perhaps their greatest day was 4 September when the bivouacs of all the corps of General von Kluck's First Army across the Marne, clearly indicating his line of advance, were all identified. Wireless sets were first fitted into aircraft in September 1914. The first air photographs of German artillery positions on the Aisne, were taken on 15 September 1914. The RFC then formed its first experimental air photography section early in 1915; at this stage the camera had to be held in the photographer's grasp.[22] A small team led by Lieutenant J T C Moore-Brabazon (later Lord Brabazon of Tara) designed a new camera mounting for air photography.

A thorough knowledge of the German Order of Battle, too, enabled the Intelligence Staff to make correct assessments. Early in the war, a German paper noted that *Minenwerfer*, trench mortar companies, had been attached to certain corps. During the First Battle of Ypres agents in Bruges reported a sighting of one of these, from which the Intelligence Staff correctly assessed the arrival in the area of the German XVth Corps from the Aisne.[23] Identification of certain German Reserve units again resulted in the denial of surprise to several German Corps newly arrived in the Ypres area. By March 1915, largely thanks to the work of Captain (later Brigadier-General) E Cox, the first edition of a booklet setting out the German forces in the field was issued.

Also significant was the development of wireless interception in the field, a development largely limited in these months to direction finding.[24] Interception of German signals was begun in the first months of the war, but in a random, insufficiently co-ordinated way. German messages at this stage of the war were generally *en clair*. During the Marne battle, the temporary loss of contact by General von der Marwitz's 2nd Cavalry Corps with von Richthofen's 1st Cavalry Corps was clearly recognised from plaintive messages. Wagon-mounted transmitters designed for cavalry use provided the vehicle. From October 1914, wireless 'compass stations' arrived in France. These were designed to give the bearing of an enemy station. Any two stations obtaining a bearing were able to provide a cross-reference 'fix' of position.[25] More sophisticated work could only follow later, cryptanalysis—breaking codes—having been neglected by Britain in the pre-1914 years. One early success was the interception of a German signal concerning a visit by the Kaiser to Courtrai on 1 November: an artillery fire and RFC bombing programme was arranged on his anticipated route.[26]

But the significance of good Intelligence collation and assessment as an instrument of war, more important than ever before, was already established; new techniques widened the possibilities. The German threat to the British Army that led to the First Battle of Ypres had been clearly identified by Intelligence supplied through the traditional tactical questioning of prisoners, together with agents' reports and the new agencies of air reconnaissance and signals intercepts.[27] Commenting on a GHQ Intelligence Summary concerning German dispositions in the Ypres Salient early in November 1914, the Official History notes its 'amazing accuracy'.[28] Also, the First battle of Ypres provided a good example of a skilled Intelligence Staff seeing through an enemy attempt at disinformation. Rumours were circulated in Amsterdam that the Germans were reinforcing their forces at Ypres. Macdonogh recognized the rumours for what they were—an attempt to conceal the withdrawal of German formations, from Flanders to Poland.[29] The opportunity and the technology for the growth of the Corps were at hand.

But one lesson, although perceived, was not acted upon. The early months of the war began the close wartime staff linkage between 'Operations' and 'Intelligence' without which neither can function efficiently; this was satisfactory. But although the Intelligence staffs accepted that they had been surprised by the effectiveness of German artillery and machine-gun fire, the conclusion was not drawn that such surprise could have been averted by systematic studies of possible opponents' weapons systems linked to ground and tactics. In consequence the BEF arrived without the defensive battle planning and equipment that could have saved hundreds of lives—machine-guns, hand grenades, barbed wire and shovels. The same Intelligence failure was to be made in the years prior to the Second World War. Such thorough study, and the dissemination of its results to the units likely to receive an enemy onslaught, is part of the work of a regular peacetime Intelligence Corps.

3

The Western Front, 1915-18

In mid-November 1914, after the end of the First Battle of Ypres, the system of always muddy and often waterlogged trenches ran from the sea to the Swiss border. Warfare lost its mobility as defence, in the form of barbed wire and machine-guns, mastered attack. The exhilaration of August 1914 became replaced by a spirit of grim slog at the Front. But other processes had also to be at work, ingenuity and innovation to try and breach the trench deadlock. These in turn led to a need for better educated officers, and more alert Intelligence. In this climate the Intelligence Corps grew and developed its skills.[1]

The Personnel of the Corps

The BEF expanded from its original format of one Army composed of two Corps each of two Divisions, plus a Cavalry Division. At the end of 1914 a Second Army was formed, a Third Army in July 1915, a Fourth Army in March 1916 and a Fifth (initially the Reserve) Army in July 1916. As the new Armies were formed they received Intelligence Corps sub-units and all personnel permanently employed on Intelligence work were incorporated into the Intelligence Corps. The Corps was controlled operationally by the Head of the Intelligence Branch at GHQ, and in respect of its own administration, pay, promotion, organisation and deployment training and discipline by the Commandant of the Corps. The Corps role remained essentially that of supplying specialist Intelligence personnel to assist the Intelligence Staff Officers of the General Staff, and to relieve them of routine work and detail. But in effect the Corps' role advanced from purely the lowest level in the Intelligence triad, gathering, to include much of the middle level work, collation, interpretation and dissemination. Final responsibility, what material to collect, the usages of material and its presentation to commanders remained with General Staff Officers (Intelligence). By the end of 1917 the organisation was as follows:

Revised Establishment agreed by GHQ France with War Office (DMI), 7 December 1917

INTELLIGENCE CORPS HEADQUARTERS

Officers	2	Cars	10
OR	16	Motor Cycles	15
		Riding Horses	2

Headquarters Company		*5 Army Companies* (One per Army)		*L of C Company* ('Intelligence Police')	
Officers	98				
OR	124	each Company con-		Officers 26 incl 5	
(incl WAAC		sisting of:		Met Police officials.	
Cars	2	*HQ Section*			
Motor Cycles	16			OR 222 incl 9	
GHQ Section		Officers	9	Met Police Sgts.	
War Trade Section		OR	36		
Cav Corps Section		Cars	3	Cars	1
Tanks Section		Motor Cycles	10	Motor Cycles	17
RFC Section		Cycles	8	Cycles	110
Wireless Section					
Special Duties Section					

4 Corps Section
each consisting of:

Officers	5
OR	17
Motor Cycles	7
Cycles	10

Also: For every Cavalry and Infantry Division and Tank brigade

Headquarters:

Int Corps Officers	1
Batman	1
NCO on Motor Cycles	1

Total: 1225, incl. 12 WAAC.

Source: GHQ(1) letter, ref IC7084 dated 7 December 1917, copies held in the Public Record Office and the Intelligence Corps Museum.

At GHQ was kept, in the Headquarters Company, a permanent pool of Corps personnel for the support of formations not permanently attached to an Army, such as the Tank Corps and RFC airfields; this pool could also reinforce others when necessary. The Wireless Section remained concerned with direction finding and wireless Intelligence. The Special Duties Section assisted Secret Service work, much behind enemy lines. The WAAC (Women's Army Auxiliary Corps) members were the forerunners of the former Women's Royal Army Corps personnel attached to the Intelligence Corps; on account of the secret nature of their work they were known as the 'Hushwaacs'. A description of the work of the first six survives:

> It was not long before all six were engrossed in what was perhaps the most fascinating work carried out by the WAAC. All were excellent linguists and their task was to interpret, or try to interpret, the wireless code messages of the German army intercepted by operators at stations near the line. Usually there were three or four codes in use at a time and each had its own room in the office to which intercepted messages in that code went. Every now and then the actual code books would be captured by Allied troops and the Germans would then change it. Feverish activity went on until the new code was 'busted' and had its own room for decoding. The work was exacting, the hours long and inconvenient, on seven days a week. Once a week each operator was off from 4 pm but it was not until May 1918 that a day off a month was introduced. Many of the messages turned out to be routine requests for war material but other supplied vital information about movements of troops. At times the work was very exciting; it was always absorbing and as speed was essential there was no let up. Even on Christmas Day the only thing which marked the occasion was a tiny bunch of flowers on each desk occupied by a WAAC, presented by her male colleagues with a Christmas card written in pseudo-code.[2]

Most Corps Headquarters also possessed an Intelligence Corps Scout Group. The role of these groups, which varied in size, is noted below. Divisional Headquarters included two Intelligence Corps officers, one for Intelligence and one for Security, censorship and publicity. The Intelligence Corps was not represented at Brigade Headquarters.

Dunnington-Jefferson remained Commandant of the Corps until February 1916 when he was succeeded by Captain (temporary Major, later Colonel) A A Fenn. All Intelligence

Corps officers, other than those at GHQ, were provided with a motor cycle for their work.[3] A special pool of cars and motor cycles was maintained for those at GHQ. The Intelligence Police were issued with either a motor or a pedal cycle.

Operational Intelligence and Prisoner Questioning

It is most convenient to learn of the functions of the BEF Intelligence Corps in the years 1915–1918 by subject rather than by chronology. Corps officers were expected to compile expert enemy orders of battle and deduce enemy intentions, information for this rarely came at once. Identifications would arrive in scraps requiring most careful piecing together. When these innumerable scraps had been collected and collated, it was generally possible to pinpoint locations and to foretell the role of each hostile formation, the size of the enemy's reserves and the likely boundaries of any enemy attack. Indicators could be new activities revealed by an air photograph; identifications found upon prisoners showing the arrival of new divisions; the discovery of a new issue gas-mask in February 1918, which helped the Intelligence Branch at GHQ to predict the exact date and hour of the German attack upon the Fifth Army. Big coups were made from time to time, but these were the exception and not the rule. Once a patrol captured a mail bag which contained information regarding work that was in progress in front of Laon. On one particular postcard, later well known as the 'Laon postcard', the correspondent mentioned 'that the result of their works would soon be seen'. This served to give the French early intimation of the German attack against the Chemin des Dames which took place on 27 May 1918. Essential elements of operational Intelligence also included any material that could be found relating to German General staff work, administrative procedure, artillery, ordnance and engineering work. But much of the Intelligence gathering was hum-drum and repetitive.

Prisoners of war remained a main source of Intelligence. Prisoners would be seized by fighting patrols mounted by front line units, often without particular enthusiasm for the task. A questioning immediately after capture, particularly by a disarmingly friendly interrogator, who would offer a cigarette, was found to be especially productive. Captain W L Blenner-hasset, one of the Corps' founding members was notably skilful. A frequent target for questioners was whether the Germans had anticipated a particular British attack. At divisional level, prisoner of war cages were set up near main dressing stations so that wounded prisoners could be examined quickly—and generally briefly—for material of immediate tactical value. At Corps level, a more thorough examination of selected prisoners would be made. Each Army generally possessed only one cage with an interrogator permanently posted to it; two or more would be at work at the Army Casualty Clearing Station (CCS). Ethnic minorities in the German Army, Poles or men from Alsace and Lorraine, were often quite willing to volunteer information, some in 1918 even deserting to do so. Some were even tasked to return across the lines and gather Intelligence. The young Captain Hotblack also noted: 'There were still a good many prejudices within the Germany Army which could be exploited in conversations. Prussians despised all the others: Bavarians didn't think much of Wurtembergers or Saxons ... Other topics of conversation might well be hunger, German prisoners were usually thankful for an early issue of food ...'[4]

Stool pigeons—or 'special examination' in the term of the time—were found to be most effective when used forward, at Corps, CCS or Division, time being saved and the prisoner again less likely to be suspicious. Stool pigeons, some of whom were Intelligence Corps officers in German uniforms, had however to be very carefully briefed with an up to date knowledge of colloquial, sometimes regional dialect, German.[5]

Prisoner's documents, in particular his pay-book, which recorded a company number, were especially useful. If a soldier was, through death or injury, replaced by another he was allotted a sequential number. These related to establishments and could provide valuable material on manpower wastage rates. They were collected by Intelligence Corps members and passed to a special unit of three British ladies, Miss C Bosworth and Miss L Brooking, later replaced by Miss S Bosworth who were employed by GHQ to work in Paris. These ladies, also forerunners of the permanently employed WRAC serving with the modern Intelligence Corps, produced exceedingly accurate overall totals.[6]

Front line units maintained—often at great risk from enemy artillery and sniper fire—observation posts, and sent out reconnaissance patrols. In the observation posts panorama landscape drawings would be made, often by Intelligence Corps officers.[7] From 1917, Brigade headquarters were to form a section of observers, under the Brigade Intelligence Officer. The information gained contributed to the Intelligence jig-saw. Sometimes accompanied by an escorting reconnaissance patrol, sometimes on their own, Intelligence Corps officers would crawl into the no-man's land between the trench systems to try and identity the dialects of German spoken by opposing Germans: these could serve to identify formations.[8] Artillery observation posts watched enemy gun flashes at night, aiming to form a triangle of bearings so as to pinpoint a location. Sound-ranging techniques were learnt from the French. On occasions, Intelligence Corps officers could use a deserted mine to pass under the German trench system, and have a quick look around at the other end.[9]

Air Photography

Air reconnaissance and air photography developed very greatly in the years 1915–1918. Balloon observation continued also, primarily concerned with enemy artillery. Marshall-Cornwall served in an aircraft as an observer and photographer 'leaning out of the cockpit with a hand-held camera at a height of 800 feet being peppered by German machine guns'.[10] Photography fully came into its own at the Battle of Neuve-Chapelle in March 1915 and a tendency for observers to exaggerate was corrected. Photographs could unmask camouflaged positions not spotted by an observer, though later in the war German use of dummy camps and artillery positions could confuse. A further benefit was that air photography taught the Royal Artillery how to conceal their own positions. At First Army Headquarters the GSO1 (Intelligence), Lieutenant Colonel (later Brigadier General) J Charteris controlled an Intelligence staff of two regular and three wartime officers, one a diplomat, one a barrister and one a stockbroker, all for most of their time permanently employed on Photograph Interpretation work. The barrister was Captain C Romer, whose training had included both law and surveying; he devised a rule for measuring map scales on air photographs. A little later air photography came to be a vital indicator of German preparations for the use of gas.

Early in 1915 also, an officer of No 11 Squadron RFC, Lieutenant Bingham produced the first example of stereoscopic aerial photographs using a modified standard Thornton–Pickard camera and a portable viewer purchased in Amiens, so adding, literally, a further dimension to the value of air photography. By the end of 1915, the General Staff were committing ever more men and equipment to this prime source of reliable Intelligence. A School of Photography, Mapping and Reconnaissance was opened at Farnborough in September 1916. During the Battle of the Somme, July to November 1916, the RFC took more than 19,000 air photographs from which 430,000 prints were made.

This huge volume of raw photography to be examined emphasised the need for extra staff so by December 1916 and following a proposal of Major General Trenchard, now commanding the RFC, every RFC Squadron and Wing engaged on amy reconnaissance was given an Intelligence Section, consisting of one Intelligence Corps officer, two draughtsmen and a clerk. On 30 March 1917 their duties were formally defined by Brigadier General Charteris, now Head of Intelligence at GHQ. The definition covered the briefing and debriefing of observers after reconnaissance flights, the examination, annotation and issue of all photographs obtained, with explanatory sketch maps when necessary: and the dissemination of information gained as quickly as possible, especially to Army and Corps headquarters.

The new significant, importance of the Intelligence Corps in this work was marked by the arrival of the freshly trained and appointed photographic interpreters from January 1917. Captain the Hon. Maurice Baring, Intelligence Corps, arranged their reception at RFC units in his capacity as Trenchard's personal staff officer. Among the interpreters was Captain O (later Sir Oswald) Birley, the distinguished portrait painter, who was attached to First Army Headquarters. In April 1917, an additional Intelligence Corps officer was posted to RFC headquarters to collate reports sent in by the various sections; by the end of 1917, the RFC section of the Intelligence Corps in France totalled nine officers and six clerks, distributed around airfields and squadrons. The first photographic interpretation manual appeared in January 1917, the work of Major Moore-Brabazon. A more advanced publication to last a number of years, *Notes on the Interpretation of Aeroplane Photographs*, was produced by the Intelligence Staff at GHQ in February 1918. This work clearly shows the developing expertise. An example of this growing skill was demonstrated in July 1917. A landing on the coast of Belgium had been proposed to strike behind the German right flank. No 2 Squadron flew the coast between Nieuport and Middelkerke every twenty minutes between 11.25 am and 5.36 pm on 2 July, whilst a diversionary reconnaissance was flown over Ostende. From the photography obtained, the interpreters were able to calculate the rise and fall of the tides on the beaches. Although the pictures had been taken from a height of 14,000 feet, the slope of the beach was measured to within six inches. The photography was of such quality that interpreters were able to distinguish the black crosses on the wings of German seaplanes outside their hangars at Ostende— this in photographs taken from 17,000 feet. The planned landings never took place, but the photographic interpreters' reports were later ground-checked and their calculations were found to be extremely accurate.

In 1917, the photo-interpretation staff were mostly concerned with examining photographs of German defensive systems before the major Third Ypres offensive. Despite German fighter interception of reconnaissance aircraft, there was also a great increase in reconnaissance and aerial photographic activity immediately before the last German offensive early in 1918. In one week, in March 1918, 10,440 photographs were examined. After the offensive had opened, and throughout the last months of the war, the totals increased further. On one day, 12 April 1918, 3,358 photographs were taken. By September 1918, 5,287,000 prints had been issued, the figure rising to almost six million at the Armistice.

Signals Intelligence and Agents

Communications Intelligence was a third main source. The small-scale interception work began in the early days of the war, using equipments no longer required by the cavalry, continued, the intercepts being collated by the Intelligence Corps. In the trenches themselves, the Germans set out a network of copper wires and metallic rods capable of picking up the faint current transmitted by the British telephonic system's ground return. Amplified by a very sensitive amplifying tube, this enabled the Germans to intercept communications through the ground.[11] The system was only discovered when, early in 1916, the French captured one of the devices in a raid near Arras. The machine was copied and developed for the British Army, where it was known as the 'Amplifier' or 'I Toc'.

Improved devices in the last two years of the war facilitated a steady increase in the distance away from a telephone line that a telephone conversation could be monitored. The early devices were limited but with the use of wireless receivers fitted with repeater coils, and low resistance telephone receivers planted in the ground, monitoring up to 3,000 yards became possible. Two examples of the actual operation of this in practice may be given. Corporal V Shirley, of German origin and fluent in German, was serving with Royal Engineers (Intelligence). He worked in a four man team led by a Corporal, with two linesmen and himself, at the time a private, as an interpreter in the VI Army Corps area. Their quarters were either in cellars of old farms, in barns or in the trenches.[12] Their unit was independent, working to VI Corps

Intelligence Corps. Such Intelligence gathered could be vital, plans for an ambitious German mining project were listened to—and frustrated—in 1916 on one sector of the front.[12]

The wireless intercept system was developed in the conditions of static warfare. In the rear areas the line of wireless 'compass' stations was extended, enabling all German formation signal stations to be picked up. Changes of radio station often indicated relief of formations, changes in procedures or locations might indicate new activity. These could quickly be identified, so providing the Intelligence for the production of clear enemy Orders of Battle, notes on locations and on some occasions artillery Intelligence, if an enemy headquarters was within range. The Corps' role here was limited to collation, the technical work being that of the Royal Engineers signallers. Increasing numbers of German signals were decoded and translated, others served to provide unit and formation identifications. From early 1917, each Corps had an interception unit, many had two.

Another field in which the Corps was concerned with collation was information from agents behind the German lines, brought in by pigeon after the seaward open flank was closed. The original 1914 use of pigeons on the Western Front had been for intelligence purposes, Captain A Waley of the Intelligence Corps organising the Carrier Pigeon Service. So valuable did pigeons become, however, that they became increasingly seen as a secure signals service and they were used on ever larger scales for the transmission of situation reports and other operational messages from front line units to headquarters. They, and Waley, were accordingly transferred from the Corps. They remained important for Corps personnel, however, in one field, the relaying back of messages from agents in German-occupied France and Belgium. Beginning in March 1917, small balloons were released to blow across the trenches in suitable wind conditions. The ballons lifted a small wicker cage to which was attached a parachute and in which was a pigeon and a fuse, timed in relation to the strength of the wind and the distance desired. The fuse released the cage, in the cage was a questionnaire, up to eight pages in some cases, on German installations, strengths, morale and movements to be completed by any Frenchman or Belgian minded to do so. The completed questionnaire was to be placed in an aluminium capsule attacked to the bird's leg or fixed by wire to its tail.

Pigeon releases, into a wind generally western, took place early in the night, answers were often arriving at breakfast time. Informants naturally took care to conceal their identities as any discovered by the Germans were dealt with severely, on occasions being shot.[13] An unsuccessful variant method was the enclosure in the aluminium capsule of a deflated balloon, together with chemicals for inflation and instructions that the return balloon should only be inflated and released when the wind flew towards France. Much useful information was gained by 'pigeon post'.[14] As time passed, however, care had to be taken in cases where cages and birds had fallen into the hands of Germans who attempted disinformation.[15] But similarly, German use of pigeons behind British lines was, when discovered, used by Corps officers for disinformation to our advantage.

A very special group of Intelligence Corps officers were engaged in work foreshadowing the Second World Wars. Special Operations Executive. These men were parachuted by night into German held territory, they wore French peasant clothing or on occasions the uniform of a German regiment in the area. They were tasked to collect urgently needed Intelligence and pass it to agents, or French or Belgians known to be active resisters with pigeon or other communication facility. The officers themselves would then return by a carefully pre-arranged route, or make their way to the Swiss or Dutch borders.[16]

Information was also collated by members of the Corps from agents in occupied France and Belgium specifically tasked for train-watching, a pastime not unknown to the present-day Intelligence Corps. Some of the 6,000 or so of these agents were controlled by agencies in which were serving officers of the Corps, notably among others Payne-Best, Philip, Macewen, Storrs and Woolrych; others were involved in the collation of information received. Train-watching yielded a great amount of valuable information, often information that air reconnaissance could not provide. But train-watching operated under immense difficulties. At the top the several organisations including two military ones, one in London and one at Folkestone (the port linked to the Kent–Holland ferry service), were in rivalry, a rivalry that led to waste of effort, risk, frustration and bitterness never satisfactorily resolved, demarcation of areas proving impracticable. The second in command of the London organisation was Payne-Best, who began his duties with the questioning of Belgian refugees arriving from Holland at Tilbury; he achieved some successes, material then being cabled on to GHQ.[17] But on being sent to Holland to supervise Intelligence collection his excellent work was handicapped by unreliable agents and the inter-organisational rivalries. The Folkestone organisation provided a measure of training. This was facilitated by the rigidity of German staff work—so many wagons and carriages of a particular type denoted one formation or unit—between 40 and 52 trains an hour meant a divisional move, cavalry trains included horse boxes, infantry unit trains had cookers on platforms at the rear. In theory one agent could report a move, another an arrival. The agents themselves were often recruited from Belgian and French refugees, which at least facilitated preliminary training and briefing. In the case of the Belgians, *aumoniers*, or chaplains, would make an initial selection. The agents then returned via Holland, attempting to dodge or talk their way through German border patrols. Some set up their own networks, Belgian housewives proving especially useful as watchers.

At the outset, reports were conveyed (or flown by pigeon) to, and agents tasked by, the British military attaché at The Hague. But the Germans quickly countered this by building high voltage electric fence systems along the Belgian–Dutch border, well patrolled by sentries. *Passeurs*, many ex-smugglers, climbed the fence in insulated clothing with the aid of a climbing frame. They secreted concealed messages, written in Indian ink on tissue paper four inches square enclosed in a rubber capsule (often a condom), upon their bodies. Others threw beetroots with the messages concealed within across the wire fence. Other smuggled reports into Holland by barge.[18] But the Intelligence still had to be transported back to Britain from Holland. Numerous agents were caught by the Germans, especially on the fences and also especially after the interception of ferry steamers by German warships began in 1916. Many agents were tortured and executed. The information that did arrive was not limited to troop movements but contained items the significance of which was not always realised, for example, the commandeering of cotton fabric assessed to be for bandages but in fact for gas masks.[19]

In 1917 Captain the Hon. G Bruce, (later Lord Balfour of Burleigh), Intelligence Corps, using a Luxembourg officer and a Luxembourg citizen married to the Luxembourg Railway doctor, arranged for the opening of a train-watching system of agents in the Grand Duchy, also occupied by the Germans. The information gained by agents – from all walks of Belgian and Luxembourg life—was ingeniously encoded and published in a Luxembourg newspaper which was on sale in Switzerland, a delay usually of some four to five days; key members of the newspaper's staff were among the agents. Other methods of passing information back by and large failed. In 1917 the RFC refused to fly agents in by night any more, the cost in pilots having proved too great. Parachuting had to be limited to certain conditions of moon and weather, conditions to which the Germans soon became alert. Ballooning agents was tried with some real success. But when safely landed, the agents' real problems began. Pigeons, apart from their inconvenience for a man on the move, were a fatal give away even when doped to ensure quiet. The air-drop supply of fresh pigeons was exceedingly risky. A light wireless set proved a technical failure. In all the circumstances, the large measure of success obtained was a remarkable achievement. The Germans reacted by setting up an office in Aachen to provide false train reports to any agents that they had identified or captured and turned.

The Evolution of the System 1916–18

A useful tactical level development in 1918, when warfare once more became more mobile, was the provision, noted earlier, of Scout Groups with most Army Corps. The strength of a Corps Scout Group depended upon circumstances, but was usually 2 officers and from 30 to 40 non-commissioned officers and men. These included some 15 scouts and observers, 10 signallers, 5 runners, 2 batmen, a cook, a wagon driver and a chauffeur. Of the officers, at least one had to speak German; it was also the practice to include a few linguists in the rank and file. The primary task of Corps Scout Groups, both in open and in positional warfare, was to observe approaches and areas not allotted to divisions, watching enemy hostile communications and distant movements along the whole front, and also the flanks of the corps. In open warfare the scout groups were best divided into sections, usually from two to four strong. Each section was further sub-divided into two parties, one for collecting information, the other for passing it back; the former consisted of scout observers and the latter of the signallers, runners or cyclists. To our own Intelligence gathering was added material supplied by the French and, in 1918, American military Intelligence.[20]

The end product of all these sources and agencies was remarkably accurate Intelligence concerning the German Order of Battle. From early 1916 onwards this was all set out in an *Index to the German Forces in the Field*. Compiled by Major Marshall-Cornwall and known as 'The Brown Book', the index was revised at intervals. Most of the arrangements of the German offensive of March 1918 were identified by a mix of train-spotting reports—the movements of divisions to the West from Russia and Romania and the movement of other divisions from the flanks to the centre of a line; aerial photography of new emplacements; the analysis of billeting areas; observation of abnormal numbers of artillery units training near Liege; reports of special assault training and other additional information from prisoner interrogation.

Other less important but useful roles included sub-sections at Army level, concerned with economic intelligence ('War Trade'), the provision of officers to assist the training of Dominion forces, and a measure of duties concerned with the briefing of visitors, publicity and propaganda.[21] Evidently some of his Intelligence directorate's propaganda work was successful; after the end of the war General Ludendorff admitted that it had a serious effect on morale on the German Army and nation. John Buchan, later Lord Tweedsmuir, was commissioned as a lieutenant in the Intelligence Corps in 1915 to assist with the communiqués for, and later for an official account of, the Battle of the Somme. He remained in France until February 1917 by which time he had become 'Lieutenant Colonel and Agent 1st Class' but had acquired a stomach ulcer, necessitating a return to the United Kingdom.

Deception plans and misleading information were used by GHQ Intelligence on occasions – false reports being given to the Press or drafted into carefully prepared political speeches.[22]

Security

Trench warfare, too, contained an I(B), Counter Intelligence, dimension; in the terminology of the time, this was called *contre-espionage*.

The Security Duties Section had not been used for its proposed role in the early months of the war due to the mobile nature of the campaign and the unfamiliarity of the Metropolitan Policemen with an army in a major war. Further, there was neither any prepared Army Security procedure system nor any agreement with the French on security arrangements.[23] The section members, referred to as the Intelligence Police, were largely reduced to messenger, guard and VIP escort duties. Nevertheless their importance was real. An example may be cited. In mid-September 1914 a French farmer, evidently one of a number, was found telephoning movements of British troops direct to the Germans. He was found to have been given 50,000 francs by the Germans.[24]

When the front became stabilised, discussions with the French and Belgians opened. The first meeting, at Boulogne on 4

January 1915, was not encouraging: 'The meeting was pandemonium, there were two agendas (English and French) and we came to no conclusions after four hours of chatter', Baird wrote in his diary.[25] But the next day saw accord on interim arrangements for control at ports. Under these, any Briton entering France would require a pass, only issued after enquiries. British detectives would assist French detectives in the coastal areas, and voluntary workers would require authorisation by the Red Cross or St John Ambulance. Baird wrote further:

> This will create a desperate storm in the dovecote of numerous ladies and gentlemen who think that by putting a Red Cross Armband on they are entitled to roam freely in the Allied lines, but it is the only way to get rid of these undesirables. Our Home Office representatives were shocked by these provisions, which they thought would interfere with Englishmen desiring to travel on ordinary legitimate business in France. ...[26]

The BEF sector was divided into four areas from North to South, each approximating to an Army area. These areas were in turn divided into a Forward Zone, to which entry was controlled by a line of examining posts, a Middle Zone where the bulk of the troops were billetted, and a Rear Area, line of communication. Armies were responsible for the Forward and Middle Zones, referred to collectively as the Controlled Army Area. In detail, for example, the Second Army, responsible for Area B, was sub-divided into 21 Intelligence Police Stations, each comprising 8 to 10 communes covering 50 square miles and each under a sergeant and 1 other NCO.

The Intelligence Police built up a considerable local knowledge, strangers entering a station area being quickly reported to them by French civilian *indicateurs* or informers. Particular attention was paid to the following; travel documents of people wishing to enter the area, these documents being checked against a list of suspects; reports of 'security incidents' such as flashing lights (almost invariably accidental); drinking houses and brothels, the movement of prostitutes being closely controlled; the issue of permits to local inhabitants with genuine cause to visit their homes; and the collection of topographical information from refugees from areas now occupied by the enemy, with particular reference to likely areas of advance. Other commitments included watch on foreigners, unfamiliar men in French or Belgian uniforms in our areas, civilians repatriated by the Germans, guests in hotels and inns, commercial travellers and traders, bargemen, miners, photographers, pigeon movements and lofts. Expert knowledge of the different British and French military and civilian documentation and pass systems was necessary. In the last year of the war, evidence accumulated that some German deserters were in fact double agents, tasked to desert and be recruited into a labour unit from which they were meant to desert again and report: uniforms to facilitate line crossing were found concealed in barns. One unpleasant task that fell to Corps members was the investigation into violent disturbances at the Etaples transit camp in September 1917, and the subsequent rounding-up of deserters. Political agitation was suspected though war-weariness and camp maladministration were the real cause. Sergeant E T Woodhall was among those engaged in the investigation under Captain F D H Joy. Woodhall did, in fact, recapture Percy Toplis, the 'Monocled Mutineer', but Toplis subsequently escaped. Woodhall had earlier achieved a notable success at Le Havre, in which port Prussian Guards prisoners from a nearby British-run camp were at work but also succeeding in escaping. Woodhall learnt the technique of crane driving and with a false identity went to work in the docks. From the cab of a crane he observed a Belgian labourer passing papers to a German officer; enquiries revealed an escape scheme.[27]

The static line system had perforce to adapt to the events of 1918. During the great German offensive in March 1918 Intelligence Police Stations carried on until under enemy shell fire, their tasks now having to include aiding and finding transport for civilians wishing to evacuate their homes, ensuring all communal documents and stamps were removed from offices, pigeons destroyed, and civilian telephones disconnected. After their own withdrawal, new posts had to be opened. With the resumed Allied advance in September, the Intelligence Police static area system ended, the personnel being grouped in teams of 10–12 controlled by Corps Headquarters, an I(B) officer being attached to every two Corps Headquarters. On entry into an area, the first task was to search for concealed telephone lines, mines and booby traps, pigeons and documents. Their task was, where possible, to identify and detail French and Belgian civilians who had worked for the Germans, though the majority of these had, in fact, withdrawn with them. There remained a large number of others about whom doubts existed and whose presence, therefore, in an Army area was undesirable. These had to be rounded up and evacuated. In the Second Army area some 300 were so removed. In addition, the increasing number of enemy deserters had, if possible, to be questioned, and abandoned headquarters' documents and equipment examined. The Corps work in these fields continued with the entry into Germany.

Bodyguards were provided for important visitors such as King George V or the Prince of Wales. One example was Private Louis Seigne, a British national of French parents who served as bodyguard to the King on a Western Front tour in 1918. Seigne was awarded the Meritorious Service Medal for his work. Good security is the result of good training. In two fields, thorough security training bore fruit. The first of these was training in resistance to interrogation, special training teams being at work by 1918. German sources record the extreme difficulty that they experienced obtaining any information from British, Australian and Canadian captives. Soldiers were instructed to provide number, rank and name only, in line with the 1899 Hague Convention. The second concerned German trench 'listening in' sets. Listening teams were established to monitor the communications of our own forward units. These revealed a poor level of security, but the follow-up action made the listening teams very unwelcome and unpopular guests in the trenches. Eventually German listening-in to telephones in the trenches was negated by the introduction of the Fullerphone, though the Intelligence Police retained the commitment of searching any trenches to see if any concealed listening device had been left behind. Germans also listened in to British wireless communications, on one occasion a request for maps sent *en clair* providing them with evidence of a proposed attack.[28]

The massive campaigns and casualties on the Western Front have been the subject of much on-going post-1918 controversy, in which both the BEF Commander, Haig and his Chiefs of Staff (Intelligence) notably Brigadier General John Charteris who replaced the excellent Macdonogh early in 1916, have been represented as over-optimistic and out of touch with reality. At this stage in its development, however, the *ad hoc* Intelligence Corps of the time was only at work at the two lower levels of the Intelligence triad, collection and collation. The final analysis of Intelligence and its presentation to the Army commander, the upper level, was not then an Intelligence Corps responsibility. For this reason, this work does not therefore propose to enter the controversy, apart from noting that many Corps officers had grave worries over the matter.[29] At the lower levels, at which Corps members were operating, the story is one of growing professionalism and, in consequence, growing acceptance of their lower level Intelligence dissemination by the Army as a whole. At first, the green-tabbed officer of the Intelligence Corps aroused suspicion by his curiosity and questions, but as relevant expertise came to be displayed, and correct Intelligence Summaries created conditions for local successes, suspicion was replaced by regard.

4

Other Theatres of Operations and Training, 1914-18

The BEF's *ad hoc* Intelligence Corps proved so successful that, as the war expanded, other Intelligence Corps, Branches or Departments were formed in most theatres. These theatre Intelligence units varied in size and organisation according to local needs. Like the BEF Intelligence Corps, on the one hand, the members of the various Corps were not formalised into a discrete, cap-badge-wearing Corps, but on the other, they were proud of being an Intelligence Corps, seeing themselves as special units with special, professional roles. The procedure was given official authority by an instruction issued by Macdonogh, on his appointment to be DMI in 1916, commending the formation of an Intelligence Corps in areas where one did not already exist.

East Africa

One campaign to last the whole four years of the war was in German East Africa, in modern terms mainland Tanzania, at the time a German colony. Here served, in a local Intelligence Department, two operational Intelligence officers of marked genius, Major PJ Pretorius, a South African, and Major (later Colonel) R Meinertzhagen, a regular officer of the Royal Fusiliers. Meinertzhagen was the creator of the Department, being greatly helped by the Liwali, (senior Arab dignitary) of Mombasa. Together they arranged for several hundred informants in German East Africa to provide reports, and also to organise an anti-espionage system to counter German indigenous informers, several being caught and executed. The Department also recruited local big game hunters as Agents. They ranked as Warrant Officers. These, some 20 in number acquainted with knowledge of Swahili and of local conditions and accompanied by 3,000 picked Africans as scouts, would depart for days, sometimes weeks, into German territory to gather Intelligence. On some occasions, they were supported by air reconnaissance and small reconnaissance groups of the King's African Rifles. Pretorius, a pre-war big game hunter, played a large part in tracking down the concealment of the German cruiser *Königsberg* in the Rufiji River. Pretorius was landed by the Navy during moonless nights to patrol the river for two or three days and was then collected again, until the ship was found. Meinertzhagen tracked down the *Königsberg's* battle ensign for himself as a prize, but his significance in East Africa lies in some of his methods. In a pre-development African colony, cut off by the war from the metropole, many essential necessities of life were lacking. Meinertzhagen ordered his African agents to collect used toilet paper, it frequently produced yester-day's messages, notes on coding, routine or administrative orders, so containing useful information.

Two of his other practices included the surrounding of water holes in German areas with dead animal carcasses together with notices in German saying 'poisoned', and sending letters, enclosing German money, to known German agents, thanking them for their services to the British cause, a ploy which resulted in the execution of their own supporters by the Germans. Long-range patrolling and raiding by Intelligence Department agents in charge of small parties of scouts continued throughout the campaign.[1]

The Dardanelles, Mesopotamia, Egypt and Palestine

A small Intelligence Department was created for the Gallipoli landings, its staff consisted of a GSO1 (Intelligence), two officers each for 1(A) and 1(B), and a cypher officer. A few British businessmen who had been working in Constantinople before the war were given Royal Marines commissions to act as interpreters/interrogators for the Department. Two other notable officers were Captain G Lloyd (later Lord Lloyd of Dolobran), a Member of Parliament, who had already become involved in Intelligence work in Egypt, and the author C (later Sir Compton) Mackenzie. Lloyd's biographer records Lloyd's own description of an Intelligence Department officer in the front line.

> We started out from Lemnos, on the 25th I think it was. I was told to land with the Australians at Kaba Tepe ... to represent GHQ and keep them informed of all that I was doing. The job was going and I offered to do it and I am glad that I did. ... at 3 am we were

five miles off the land and we put the men from the *Prince of Wales* into small boats over the side, a picket-boat towing the boats from each of the four ships. Then we steamed up closer to the land which we could faintly see ahead of us—all absolute silence and dark, very very thrilling—not a sound from the beach. I was to land about ten minutes after the covering force, and before any of the main body, who were in transports behind. Then rifle fire sounded and we knew the boats had reached land; it went on for a few moments and ceased. We got into the boats and went ashore, where we found the first wounded and dead. We heard that our fellows had stormed the Turks at bayonet point and rushed up the steep hills from the beach and disappeared. Immediately the transports began to come up and landing began, but the Turks had got the range of the beach pretty accurately, and every boat landed under heavy fire. I worked at the beach all day. By 8 am we had 8000 men landed but many casualties. We then heard that the covering force was at the top of the hill holding the ridge against heavy attacks by the Turks and under cruel fire—they had no time to entrench. All that day and night were very anxious ... we managed to hold on till morning after which as more men landed things improved. But for three days the battle never let up at all, the din incessant—no words can describe.

Lloyd remained engaged in this work, described by his biographer as 'days of paper work [at GHQ] in comparative silence, interspersed with an equal number of days at General Birdwood's Anzac Headquarters, or collecting first hand experience and information in the trenches' until September 1915.[2]

A paper proposing an Intelligence Staff establishment for the 1915 Salonika force noted its members might include some 19 who remained from the Gallipoli Intelligence Corps. The Official History notes tactical questioning of Turkish prisoners at W Beach, establishing the presence of four Turkish divisions on the peninsula.[3] Other main sources of operational Intelligence information were signals sent from the British Embassy in Athens, where the Embassy was running a network of not very reliable informers, and military attachés in Balkan countries not yet at war.

Mackenzie was concerned with 1(B) work, the difficulties of which were worse than in France, with repeated rumours of flashing lights and spy mania. The culture gap in relation to local Greeks suspected of acting for the Germans was however greater than anything in Western Europe. It was also, of course, a consequence of the absence of any pre-war trained Intelligence Corps. Of one family that had been the subject of prolonged investigation Mackenzie wrote after interrogating the head:

> And gradually as I went over and over again the suspicious circumstances, questioning him each time more closely and finding each time that these circumstances were susceptible of an alternative and innocent explanation, I began to decide in my own mind that the behaviour of the Vassilaki family had been entirely prompted by a low kind of commercial cunning, and that the more sinister motive attributed to their activities had no basis in fact.[4]

Much security effort was, also, directed to the wrong area. The Turks gained most of their intelligence from Egypt, where British and Imperial troop movements were easy to watch and report. One success that Mackenzie achieved, however, was on a July 1915 trip to Mytilene, tasked to spread a rumour that a seaborne assault on Smyrna was in preparation, in order to distract attention from the real assault, Suvla Bay.[5]

The entry of the Ottoman Empire into the war on the side of Germany in November 1914 had created new Intelligence needs in Egypt. By December, an Intelligence Department, though not an Intelligence Corps had been formed under a Regular artillery officer Brigadier G (later Sir Gilbert) Clayton. Its staff included Lloyd and another Member of Parliament, Aubrey Herbert, concerned with political matters, and two archaeologists, L (later Sir Leonard) Woolley and T E Lawrence, concerned with propaganda and material on the Turkish Army respectively. When the Turks moved against the Suez Canal early in 1914, Lloyd was in the front line Intelligence gathering.[6]

After the end of the Dardanelles Campaign, the British Cabinet returned to the possibility of an Arab uprising in the Arab provinces of the Ottoman Empire, and an Arab Bureau, headed by Commander D G Hogarth, RNVR, another noted archaeologist, was formed to study and encourage Arab uprisings. And it was this Bureau, a primarily political organisation, that was to sponsor the adventures of Lawrence rather than the later-created Intelligence Corps (Egypt).

But other officers of the original Intelligence Department were also at work in the area. After a brief visit to Russia in 1916, Lloyd was sent to Mesopotamia (now Iraq) on work that was primarily economic, and then to the Hejaz (now Saudi-Arabia) to report and advise upon the military and political situation, with particular reference to the advisability of the use of non-Moslem troops in the Mecca and Medina areas. Lloyd, accepting that there would be some risk for them in the event of a Turkish recapture of the Holy City, recommended against it—in the event, sound advice. He returned to the Hejaz to serve as an Intelligence Officer accompanying Lawrence in deep penetration raids.

Earlier, however, 1915 had seen a serious Intelligence failure in the war against Turkey. All Turkish reinforcements both for Mesopotamia and for Palestine had to use a railway that passed near the sea at Alexandretta, and was watched. Reports of a Turkish reinforcement for Mesopotamia were sent to France and to India, but not to the Mesopotamian force commander, a major cause of General Townshend's rash advance on Kut el Amara.

For the Mesopotamia campaign an 'Intelligence Branch' was established. Its main sources of information were prisoners, deserters and captured documents—in particular diaries recording timings of Turkish troop movements; travellers, and paid agents. Useful Intelligence was also supplied from Cairo and, until 1917, by the Russians. By the end of the campaign, signals interception was also providing Intelligence on Turkish withdrawal routes. The whole of the branch was, however, complicated by the unreliability of Arab and Jewish agents, and the total lack of any pre-war preparations. Further, the Turkish practice of renumbering and amalgamating units and of increasing or decreasing them substantially above normal establishments, together with the very different fighting qualities of Turkish and Arab soldiers, made intelligence work exceedingly difficult.[7]

For his 1917–18 campaign, the commander, General Sir Edmund (later Field Marshal Lord) Allenby, was able to benefit from a newly-formed military Intelligence Corps (Egypt). The Cairo Intelligence Department had opposed this idea, but their opposition was overruled. On formation in August 1916, the Corps comprised a Commandant graded as a GSO3, four Staff Captains (1st Class Agents); eight Staff Lieutenants (four 2nd and four 3rd Class Agents) and three Special Service officers. A year later, the Corps had increased to over 30 officers and three clerks, with a facility to engage further Lieutenants (4th Class Agents). By the end of 1917, the total had reached 57 officers, to peak at 86 in September 1918, by which time a small new Economic Intelligence Section had been added. Several of the 3rd and 4th Class Agents were locally engaged Egyptians, Palestinians, Sudanese or local Jews. Among the latter was Lieutenant A Aaronson, a product of one of the earliest *kibbutzim* settlements, who on several occasions penetrated the Turkish lines, sometimes by sea. Aaronson was awarded the DSO, a singular honour for one who was, technically, the national of an enemy country; but the Turks exacted severe reprisals against his family.

The Corps applied Western Front Intelligence activity to the campaign: air reconnaissance; air photography; tactical questioning of prisoners, with later agent handling, and signals intelligence (for unit and formation identification), together with security duties. Intercepts of signals proved especially useful in the third Battle of Gaza, when Allenby deduced the German plan for strengthening the coastal flank would entail a weakening of the centre. At work were some of the ablest operational Intelligence officers of the war, including Lloyd, Commandant from mid-1917, and Meinertzhagen, the latter being the originator of one of the classic deception plans of all time before the Second Battle of Gaza: the placing of documents and maps marked to mislead in a haversack which Meinertzhagen deliberately allowed to fall into Turkish hands. Another successful deception plan was the provision to the press of false reports of severe malaria amongst the cavalry in the Jordan Valley, to conceal the move of the cavalry to a new area. Success resulted from careful observance of the first principle of deception, that deception should always aim to strengthen an opponent's preconceptions. Meinertzhagen also used his East African method of a letter of thanks to a well-known Arab controller of agents, which compromised him with his Turkish masters. Another asset for the Corps was a body of irregulars, the Guides and Interpreters Corps (Egypt), of detachments varying in size according to need, but with a cadre of two Intelligence Corps officers and two NCOs. One curious by-product of the mixture of political and military Intelligence activity in the area, a consequence of the considerable British financial support for the 1916 Hejaz Revolt, was an outbreak of gold-smuggling from the Hejaz back into Egypt. A solicitor serving in a London Territorial regiment, Captain K G Groves, was transferred from France to the Corps in the rank of 1st Class Agent and, wearing green staff tabs for work in controlling the smuggling, he took part in two major trails.

Greece and Macedonia

A separate Intelligence Corps was formed for the Macedonian front in later 1917 engaging, as at Gallipoli, pre-war British residents of Greece and the Ottoman Empire. From 1915 onwards, the major problem was the ferocious inter-Allied, inter-Command (Gallipoli and Macedonia), inter-Departmental and inter-Service rivalries and frictions, and the absence of any personnel who could combine local and linguistic knowledge with military and military intelligence training. Compton Mackenzie's writings reflect the frustration. From June 1915, he was working as an 1(B) staff officer in the British Embassy in Athens, funded by GHQ Gallipoli.[8] With the assistance of Captain E Knoblock, Intelligence Corps, Mackenzie ran a system of agents. One was a bell-porter at the German Legation, which had been active in disseminating propaganda and was a main target of Intelligence interest until Greece formally entered the war in mid 1917, and the Legation was closed. Mackenzie later wrote that through this agent he was able to keep the German espionage system in Greece under effective surveillance.[9]

Counter-intelligence was important in this area both before and after Greece's formal entry into the war. Mackenzie secured documentary evidence of espionage by German and Turkish attachés. After Greece joined the Allies, security work developed. All 22 men, described as Macedonian but with names mostly suggesting Turkish origin, faced capital charges of spying before British military courts in 1917–18. Three were acquitted, the remainder convicted, eight being executed. For operational Intelligence, the British Army headquarters at Salonika included an Intelligence Corps of 30 officers.[10]

Italy

In late 1917, after the defeat of the Italian Army by that of Austria–Hungary at the battle of Caporetto, five British Army divisions grouped into two Army Corps of the Second Army were sent to northern Italy. An Intelligence Corps Company, that of the Second Army, was despatched from France to supply Intelligence support. In June 1918, this Company totalled 19 officers and 90 soldiers, some at Corps others at the Divisions' headquarters. Among those serving were Lieutenants L (later Sir Louis) Gluckstein and J (later Sir Julian) Huxley. In addition, there were a further 10 officers and 12 soldiers employed on censorship. All were directed by a General Staff (Intelligence) of 12 officers and 22 soldiers.[11] The principal sources of Intelligence appear to have been wireless Intelligence, trench Intelligence of the Western Front pattern, and close liaison with the Italian Army.

There were some differences in Intelligence Corps operations between the Western and Italian fronts. The prisoners of war, from the multi-ethnic Austro–Hungarian army, provided an increasing flow of information. The Austrians and Hungarians, as the ascendant races in the Habsburg Empire, were the least cooperative. The Czechs and Slovaks became so keen that they deliberately acquired useful Intelligence before capture. The Poles were generally similar, but less observant, while the southern Slavs were so apathetic and disinterested in the war that they generally had little to offer. The Romanians were 'fanciful and imaginative' but 'so romantic and voluble in speech' that their material was overloaded with useless detail.

The arrangements for interrogation were similar to those in France, though use had often to be made of interpreters: sometimes these would be volunteer prisoners. Special difficulty arose from the frequent Austro–Hungarian changes in unit composition and their deliberate practice of keeping soldiers uninformed of plans, in view of their unreliability. Deserter numbers steadily increased, especially prior to an Austrian offensive, a useful indicator. Italian refugees also contributed material. The Austrians were more careless than the Germans over their documents, which often revealed very over-optimistic plans.

The other main sources, air reconnaissance, ground observation and reconnaissance patrols, operated generally as in France. The Intelligence Corps sections attached to the Royal Air Force lived on the airfields, and comprised an officer, who briefed and interpreted, clerks and orderlies. The trench listening devices were used to effect in the mountain areas. Wireless interception could only begin in mid-1918, when the Austrians began using wireless equipment; it then became useful. Some messages were decoded and translated by a section of 2 officers and around 20 men, including German and Magyar speakers. But most messages served almost as well by indicating locations and volume of traffic. Enemy aircraft fitted with wireless were tracked.

A number of prisoners volunteered to act as agents, but arrangements were barely completed by the end of the fighting, at which time a very few had been dropped by parachute. They then moved to other pre-arranged dropping sites to collect pigeons. Security, ('Intelligence Police') work differed from the Western Front in that the Intelligence Police's concern was limited to British troops, the Italian Carabinieri gendarmerie concerning itself with Italian civilians. As in France, spy-mania was constant but with few real suspects. Other miscellaneous Intelligence duties included topography and maps, supervision of war correspondents, and the provision of a News Sheet for the troops;

translation and censorship. This latter was conducted by means of sample surveys of the work of the regimental censoring at unit level, some minor material on civilian military relationships emerging. A close liaison with the Italian Army, providing for a full exchange of Intelligence, was maintained.

South Russia

In late 1917 and early 1918, a small Intelligence Branch was established to support a British force tasked to occupy the Azerbaijan and western Caspian areas, to deny their resources to the Germans. As time passed, the force had additional commitments in stemming a Turkish advance on Teheran and later briefly containing Bolshevik operations in the Caspian areas. The Branch comprised two Staff Officers and nine 'Special Service' officers. Its work was handicapped by language difficulties and the fact that some of the Intelligence gained was not well used. But useful contributions in the fields of photo-interpretation, prisoner questioning, security and censorship were made.[12]

Great Britain and Ireland

For the United Kingdom itself, an Intelligence Corps was formed after the German naval bombardments of Scarborough and Hartlepool in late 1914. In December 1916, the Corps comprised a Staff Captain, 15 Staff Lieutenants and 2 Pigeon Service officers. By August 1918, the establishment of this Corps had risen to 19 Staff Lieutenants, Intelligence Corps, and 3 officers for the Pigeon Service. The BEF system of service within the Corps of members of police forces was also repeated in the United Kingdom, largely for personal bodyguards. Kitchener's personal security detective, MacLaughlin, who was drowned with his master aboard HMS *Hampshire* in June 1916, was one of these.

In Ireland, early in the war, the senior officer of the Royal Irish Constabulary's Special Crimes Branch, I Price, was made head of a new Special Intelligence Branch of the Army's Irish Command, and given the rank of major. A system of district military Intelligence officers was established, but these officers were not specialists, and the results achieved were limited, not recognising the military potential of the Sinn Fein movement.[13]

Recruitment and Training

In the War Office, Intelligence was removed from Operations and restored to independence as a Directorate by General Sir William Robertson, after he became Chief of the Imperial General Staff at the end of 1915. Macdonogh became an outstandingly successful DMI, with a staff that, at the Armistice and for all sections, totalled over 5,000, including eleven GSO1s, 24 GSO2, 33 GSO3s, 70 attached officers and 274 civilians of officer status. Among its sections were two known as MI1(b) and MI1(e), concerned with Signals Intelligence. MI1(b) became staffed by some 80 German speakers, mainly academics, and concentrated on German communications with stations beyond Western Europe. In MI1(e) one of the notable officers was Lieutenant R (later Sir Ronald) Nesbitt-Hawes, who wore the green tabs and cap-band of the Intelligence Corps superimposed upon his Royal Engineers uniform. The sections' main tasks were the breaking of German codes; detecting and observing the movement of German ships and airships by direction finding (DF)—crossing bearings of signals intercepted from two listening posts, and where possible translating messages. Six DF stations existed in Britain, as did one intercept station. Other intercept stations existed overseas.[14] The skills of 'traffic analysis' and cryptoanalysis were developed, the latter under an academic historian serving in the UK Intelligence Corps, Major M Kay.

All the DF stations were linked to the War Office Telegraph Room, itself linked to tables in the Plotting Centre. Plotting staff relayed the latest Intelligence to the Admiralty and GHQ Home Forces in Horse Guards. The tables contained maps of Great Britain with a hole for cord and protractor at the site of each DF Station. From DF reports, the slow movement of Zeppelins could easily be tracked and foreseen. Prior clues to German Zeppelin intentions were often available both from our own weather forecasts and the intensity of German weather report signalling.

The title 'Intelligence Corps' appeared for the first time on a list of distribution of duties in the office of the DMI in April 1915. Staff lists for the various headquarters in the field were issued by the War Office from the first winter of the war; these showed an Intelligence Corps where one existed. But the Corps as such never figures in the Army Lists until the 1919 Graduation List, where some but not all, officers were shown. In the war years, Intelligence Corps officers appeared under their respective regimental or General Service headings but noted as serving on the staff.

Until 1916, the BEF Intelligence Corps, being still only a theatre unit under the control of GHQ, wore no distinctive dress. Regular and pre-war Territorial officers continued to wear their own regimental uniforms and the wartime volunteers General List badges. In 1916, the Corps officers began to wear green tabs and a green hat band with their previous regimental or General List badges; green remains the Corps' colour to this day.[15] Francis Dodd's painting 'Interrogation', now in the Imperial War Museum, illustrates this distinctive dress. The picture showns an Intelligence Corps officer in green tabs and a cap with green band questioning a German prisoner. Standing next to him is a General Staff Officer (Intelligence) with red tabs and red hat band, superior in authority but almost certainly weaker in German. NCOs on Intelligence Policy duty often wore a brassard with the letters IC or a bracelet noting the soldier's name, number and '10th RF INTceB', with the number of the Army to which the soldier was attached. Throughout the war, soldier entrants to the Corps, including the Intelligence Police, destined for service in France, Britain or, later, Italy, continued to be badged to the 10th Royal Fusiliers (Intelligence B). Most joined at Hounslow barracks. Some soldiers were recruits from other units in France. One such was Private M H Cousins, a pre-war employee of the Standard Bank of South Africa, accepted as he was a French speaker. Cousins joined from the Honourable Artillery Company and insisted on retaining his HAC badge. Another was Inspector J W Camp of the Hull City Police. Camp served as a Sergeant in Port Control first at Le Havre, under Captain J H Priestley, Intelligence Corps, in peacetime Professor of Botany at Leeds University, and later at Calais under Lieutenant the Hon. M Baring, Intelligence Corps.[16] BEF Honours and Awards, published in the *London Gazette*, listed the Intelligence Corps as a separate entity in respect of officers; soldiers were of course, in theory, Royal Fusiliers. First World War medals noted regiments but not battalions, the case of the Royal Fusiliers is complicated additionally by the fact that a front-line 10th Battalion existed as well as the 10th (Intelligence). Mr D Buxton has entered into meticulous research, based on soldiers' ranks, acting ranks, numbers and the likelihood that medals such as the Military Medal would be more likely to be awarded to a front-line unit, while the Meritorious Service Medal was a more likely decoration for the Intelligence Police. Buxton estimates the 10th Intelligence Battalion was awarded one Military Cross, one Distinguished Conduct Medal, 7 Military Medals and 36 Meritorious Service Medals, with 31 Mentions in Despatches. The MC was awarded to

Lieutenant J T Curry in February 1915. The DCM and one of the MMs were awarded for immediate post-war operations in North Russia. The remaining MMs and MSMs were all for service in France or Belgium, except one MSM in Italy.[17]

Training of Intelligence Corps personnel had first begun in the brief tenure of Wavell as Commandant of the Corps, with a special course run in France. Officers joining the Corps in Britain received only very rudimentary training. In the case of Second Lieutenant (later Lieutenant Colonel) S H C Woolrych and his batch, including seven other young officers, this training amounted to attachment to a Territorial Army Cyclists Battalion at Putney.[18] Later an Intelligence Corps school was opened in London, near Wellington Barracks which supplied an apparently indispensable drill element of the 10-week course. The subjects included all the aspects of Intelligence work practised on the different fronts. In 1918, the School, now at Harrow, included US Army officers among its students.[19]

By the end of the war the various theatre Intelligence Corps totalled approximately 3,000 men. The contribution made by these men, who by November 1918 had acquired considerable expertise in the whole field of Intelligence duties in addition to the linguistic or other specialist qualifications that had brought them to the Corps, confirmed the lesson of 1899–1902, that no modern war can be fought by an army without its body of trained specialists in military Intelligence.

5

The Years of Neglect, 1919-29

The whole period between the Armistice of 11 November 1918 and the outbreak of the Second World War makes discouraging reading. In the search for economies military Intelligence soon became an easy target. There was a public—and a military—reaction against any major European commitment, and in the Army's imperial security roles the various territories' police services were used to supply Intelligence when required. There seemed no particular requirement for standing professional military Intelligence Corps and, after a brief period of use in supervising the various Armistice terms, the wartime Corps were all run down. Intelligence was seen, once again, as ungentlemanly. There was no Intelligence School and the subject was not even taught at the Staff College. The reawakened appreciation of the need, when it appeared in the 1930s, was met very inadequately.

The First British Army of the Rhine

The Allied entry into Germany however did provide the Corps with final commitments. Major Marshall-Cornwall had in fact been at work earlier assisting the Director of Military Intelligence with the drafting of the Armistice terms.[1] The British delegation to the international Armistice Commission that assembled at Spa in Belgium included at least one Intelligence Corps officer, Captain E A Baring-Gould MC, and an Intelligence Section concerned with codes and ciphers, documents, censorship and air photograph interpretation. Intelligence Corps personnel were employed in the special 'Evacuation Liaison Groups' formed by Army Corps headquarters to keep GHQ informed about German withdrawal, stores, transport, minefields and booby traps.

Intelligence officers were tasked to detect enemy agents, watch for anti-Allied propaganda, and look out for German soldiers unwilling to return home, other matters relating to morale, reports of atrocities and any breaches of the Armistice terms. The British Second Army, the formation selected for the occupation of the British Zone, the Cologne area, included a Security Organisation with its Headquarters staff. At the outset, in December 1918, the organisation totalled 44 officers and 209 soldiers all carefully selected. It was composed of a Signals Security Section, concerned both with our own signals security and the interception of German military messages, a Contre-Espionage Section, concerned with German propaganda, sabotage and espionage, and a Censorship (Postal and Press) Section.[2] Also at work were Intelligence Corps officers with the food relief missions despatched into Germany to alleviate the near-starvation conditions of the civil populace. These provided 'accurate information about the progress of demobilisation, as well as about the distribution, strength and morale of the dissolving German Army'.[3]

From the start, the Germans attempted to thwart the provisions of the Armistice in respect of the surrender or destruction of military equipment. Further there were strident German propaganda offensives against the Allies, some from the Right seeking to create dissension between the Allies, others from the Left attempting to subvert the occupying troops with the Communist doctrine of 'soldiers' Councils'. But despite these challenges, reductions in the Intelligence staffs soon began. By January 1920, the ratification of the Treaty of Versailles, the organisation had been scaled down to 32 officers and 134 soldiers equipped with 11 motor cars, 33 motor bicycles, and 40 pedal bicycles, all tasked for operational Intelligence, secret service and propaganda and censorship.[4]

After Versailles the rundown accelerated. By May 1920 the Intelligence Corps had disappeared from the duties allotted to sections of the Directorate of Military Intelligence, and in 1922 the Directorate itself was once again combined with Operations. The separate post of Commandant of the Corps was abolished, and what was left of the Corps was run by the GSO1 Intelligence with the Assistant Commandant of the Corps acting as his Adjutant.

By December 1921, the organisation had been further reduced to 10 officers and 62 soldiers. For no very clear reason, the counter-intelligence commitment and staff were made responsible to London in 1922, leaving operational Intelligence and censorship only to the Cologne GHQ. This unsatisfactory division lasted until 1927.[5]

The personnel were distributed around the main centres of population; in the British Zone at Solingen, for example, 2 officers and 10 Intelligence Police were posted. Sources of information were British Consuls, customs and permit authorities; Army Chaplains; NAAFI canteen staff; YMCA and Salvation Army staff who picked up gossip; the Military Police; Railway Traffic Superintendents and Transport Officers; hotel managers and porters, with, on occasions, local German police; and French 2eme Bureau personnel.

In addition, some members of the organisation were serving with British military units in border areas of the former German Empire in which plebiscites were being held to determine the frontiers with the newly recreated state of Poland. Early in 1922, Polish nationalists murdered Sergeant Storer of the Intelligence Police near Katowice in Silesia.[6]

Further reductions followed the move of the headquarters of BAR, the (first) British Army of the Rhine, from Cologne to Wiesbaden in 1924. The few surviving Intelligence Corps personnel—still referred to as such—were used increasingly for civil affairs, and the term Security, politically acceptable, adopted. From 1927, the organisation was known as the Civil Affairs and Security Branch. Up to 1929, this G (CA and S) Branch was headed by a GSO2 Intelligence who acted also as Commandant Intelligence Corps.[7] It comprised a Civil Affairs Section which also looked after the Field Security Policy (FSP) (the new name for the former Intelligence Police) detachments, a Clerks and Cipher Section, and a Security Section. This latter was headed by Captain K W D (later Major General Sir Kenneth) Strong, and included five Field Security Police for investigations, press registry and translations. Their particular concerns were the reduced-size German Army's Intelligence Department (Abwehr); German espionage; the monitoring of German politics, meetings and demonstrations, especially if meetings appeared subversive; German Communism and industrial organisations; the control of *Reichswehr* (the Weimar Republic's Army) officers visiting the occupied Rhineland; the supervision of German newspapers, films, theatre and wireless; a watch on marriages between soldiers and German women; liaison with the French and Belgian military occupation commands; the security of GHQ; and investigation of works contractors and local labour.[8] From the mid-1920s, the numerous German societies that were trying to conduct clandestine military training under a variety of guises—art, literary, music, naturalist, aviation, disaster relief, sports and games of all types, religious groups and ex-service men—were watched.[9] By the end of the decade, attention was focussing upon the emerging National Socialist (Nazi) party. The movements of Goering on his visits to the Rhineland were watched as his oratory invariably led to disorder. On one occasion, Strong arrested another frequent visitor, Goebbels.[10] But anxiety, although expressed in London, led to no nation-wide firm action.

As they had done in war, the FSP personnel engaged in this work wore Royal Fusiliers uniform, though most of their work was carried out in plain clothes. They received extra-duty pay of 3/- per day and a civilian clothing allowance. FSP personnel were allotted numbers; these, and not the soldier's name, were attached to reports, the Intelligence staff only retaining an index. Cover addresses were used for postal correspondence. No member of the FSP ever used his home for correspondence, and a special room was set apart for interviewing the agents hired by the FSP.[11] Agents were never taken to or allowed to telephone offices. Corporate social life revolved around the Corps cricket team, disciplinary problems never arose, and the Army Commander, Sir William Thwaites, ensured that the Corps enjoyed the social cachet necessary for its work.

Day-to-day work included the security training of Army units, surveillance of German civilian movements, telephone and telegraph exchanges in an Army exercise area, checks on German police lists of new arrivals in particular areas, and a watch on soldiers' fraternising with the civilian population. Particular attention was paid, largely unnecessarily, to any reports of British Communist and German anarchist or Communist linkages seeking to subvert Army units.[12]

After the August 1929 Hague Conference, the three Occupying Powers began withdrawal from the Rhineland, the last British troops leaving Wiesbaden in December. In this final phase, GHQ classified documents had to be processed and weeded; the majority were destroyed but some were retained and taken back under guard to the UK with the assistance of a Security Service officer. The departure from Wiesbaden on 12 December 1929 of a rear party comprising the GSO2(Int), Captain Strong, and one FSP NCO can be seen as the conclusion of the work of the most important of the First World War Intelligence Corps.

Turkey 1919–22

The collapse of the Ottoman Empire led to a similar requirement for the supervision of armistice terms. Officers of the Macedonian and Palestinian campaign Intelligence Corps were tasked with inspecting Turkish demobilisation and disarmament arrangements; later, others were sent to the Caucasus to oversee the departure of German and Turkish troops. Officers engaged in these duties became known as control officers, but were shown in a January Army List of 1922 as an Intelligence Corps, a branch of the GHQ staff. More seriously, the resurgence of Turkish nationalism under Kemal Ataturk and the despatch of considerable British military and naval forces to Istanbul and western Anatolia, had created an Intelligence requirement. Marshall-Cornwall was then serving in the area with the Royal Artillery, and was extracted to become Special Intelligence Officer to the Commander-in-Chief, General Sir Charles Harington, in 1921. Marshall-Cornwall was tasked with the surveillance of all Turkish military activity. He ran a small network of agents. Of his work he later wrote 'In fact one of Mustafa Kemal's senior officers has been in my pay for months and we were fully informed about the Nationalist order of battle'.[13]

Russia 1919–20

Some of the other immediate post-World War I military commitments facing Britain also required Intelligence support from personnel who had served in the various theatre Intelligence Corps. A small number of the Intelligence Police were sent to the two expeditionary forces serving in North Russia, at Murmansk and at Archangel. One member serving in Murmansk was awarded the DCM for bravery, another received the MM. The citation for the DCM awarded to Sergeant C Smith ran as follows:

> On 11th June 1919, he, finding a company of local troops wavering, went forward alone, under heavy fire, and by his fine example encouraged them to advance. He led them forward two miles and during the advance attacked and overcame enemy posts single-handed. His splendid courage and example saved a critical situation. On several occasions he has obtained valuable information.

At the Far-Eastern end of Russia, at least one World War I Intelligence Corps officer, Captain, acting Brigadier, Bernard Hughes, DSO OBE MC was serving at Vladivostock with the Allied Mission to White Russian forces.

Ireland 1919–21

With one exception, in all the imperial policing and counter-insurgency operations of the years 1919–29, the provision of Intelligence was seen as the task of the police force or if there was one, the civil Intelligence service of the territory concerned. This limited approach, essentially one of security information to secure convictions in court and restore law and order was generally adequate to contain protest movements not inspired by any militant ideology nor supported by any major foreign power. But its inadequacy, and the limitations imposed on an Army engaged in major counter-insurgency if that Army is not provided with an effective specifically military Intelligence system tasked to study 'contact intelligence'—insurgent organisation, tactics and supplies—was fully shown up in the 1919–21 Irish campaign. Here, demoralised under the strains of the campaign, the Royal Irish Constabulary, and the Dublin Metropolitan Police could not meet the Intelligence requirement. There was no military Intelligence system at the outset, and uncertainty over government policy prevented an effective one ever being established.

Even as late as the end of the summer of 1920, the Intelligence Staff still only comprised two staff officers, a records officer and four more officers serving in outstations. The formation of any larger and more credible military Intelligence staff had not been allowed. But this small nucleus was able to control a network of agents who refused to work under the police; some useful material was thereby gained from this source. This nucleus could also use from late 1919, division and brigade Intelligence staffs, but these were posted so frequently that their value was very limited. In 1920 battalion Intelligence officers were sanctioned. Some of these were very effective, but the work of many was amateurish and impeded by other unit duties.[14] But IRA Intelligence opened what is best described as an Intelligence war, aiming at the elimination of the British Intelligence Officers, 13 of them being killed and 6 injured on the first 'Bloody Sunday', 21 November 1920.[15] The system that then emerged, a military partnership with the disintegrating police forces, was a failure.[16] One perspective on this failure was offered by the Army

Commander in Chief, General Sir Nevil Macready, who wrote: 'It would have been better to have relied on a purely military organisation ...', a view echoing the earlier GHQ regret over the absence of an Intelligence branch that studied Sinn Fein.[17] Nor were there any specialist trained personnel capable of vetting the Irish labour employed by the Army, some of whom were IRA Intelligence gatherers. The campaign was the Army's least successful counter-insurgency campaign in the first 40 years of this century, the absence of a professional Intelligence Corps being an important contributory reason.

In Britain itself one other commitment of First World War theatre Intelligence Corps and the present day regular Intelligence Corps, that of the security of the Army against sabotage, espionage and subversion, was made over to the civilian Security Service, MI5, assisted by a War Department Constabulary. Also in Britain, the Army correctly and steadfastly refused to allow itself to become actively involved in the gathering of Intelligence concerning domestic, political or industrial unrest. But in another of the series of retrograde steps, the excellent signals Intelligence systems established in the First World War was also reduced, especially in purely military work. Some work continued in Britain but in civilian hands. Military listening stations in the Middle East were closed down in the early post-war years, with the only Army sections remaining at Aldershot, Sarafand (Palestine), Cherat in India, Malta and Aden.[18]

The only consolation to be drawn from these years was that at least a small number of military personnel were retaining and practising two major skills. Signals Intelligence skills were maintained, albeit reduced, by the Code and Cypher School, and the Royal Air Force's Army Co-operation squadrons continued and developed photo-interpretation work, particularly in the Indian North West Frontier and the Middle East and later, in 1935, flying over Sicily and Italian Africa. Courses in interpretation continued to be run for Army officers, and a new manual, *The Interpretation of Air Photographs*, was produced in March 1939.[19]

6

The Rebirth of the Corps, 1939-40

With very little Intelligence expertise to help it, the British Army embarked for a second major continental European War in September 1939. In the words of the Official History '... there is no sign that the War Office circulated any study of the possibility that the German Army would use armoured Blitzkrieg methods, though evidence to this effect was certainly coming in'.[1] One reason for this was the absence, until 1940, of a permanently established Intelligence Corps. This absence, an important contributory cause to the Army's early reverses, requires some brief analysis.[2] These reasons are useful for both students of the past and for defence planners of the present.

Preparations 1938–39

Perceptions of financial stringency, the '10 year rule' a 'rolling' policy assumption that there had to be no major war for 10 years, an illusion that the spirit of the Locarno Treaty of 1925 was ushering in a new era of international goodwill, a consequential horror of a Continental military commitment, and a failure to appreciate the need for specialist operational study of effects of new technology upon battlefields, especially the probable area of North West Europe supposedly covered by Locarno, were all to blame. Also important was the fact that the War Office was supposed to have responsibility for both strategic Intelligence and the supervision of the Army's own Intelligence personnel; this dualism led to neglect of the second, and an 'it will be all right on the night' belief that this role could be left to theatre commands when these were established. All this can clearly be perceived at work in a brief study of the post-1916 fate of Macdonogh's magnificent Directorate of Military Intelligence, the directorate that would have to sponsor any re-formation of the Intelligence Corps.

By 1 January 1921, the post of Deputy Director had been scaled down from Brigadier General to Colonel, MI5 had become almost exclusively involved with counter-espionage; MI6 was finally removed from a, by now, largely fictional War Office control later in 1921, and MI7 (press censorship), MI8 (cable censorship) and MI9 (postal censorship) had all been abolished as separate branches.

In the next two years, the Directorate of Military Operations and Intelligence were once again combined. Notwithstanding the aggression of Japan and the emerging Nazi threat in Berlin, contractions continued steadily until the mid 1930s. In 1936, three years after Hitler became leader of Germany, the Deputy Director responsible for all branches of military Intelligence had a staff of only some 57 officers and 80 civilians.[3] Intelligence had become a military backwater. By February 1939, a measure of wisdom had belatedly returned, the staff by this time totalling 189, of which 69 were officers. But the small numbers available for actual operational Intelligence precluded both any complete preparations for a trained Intelligence Corps to be available at the outbreak of war, or even the availability of a sound, up to date, tactical handbook on the German Army. Only in September 1939 did the Directorate of Military Intelligence again become independent of Operations.

These constraints, then, largely limited preparation for operational Intelligence and field Security work to paper planning for units similar to those of the 1914–18 war, recruited from professional and academic sources and operating in conditions of static warfare. In 1931, an Establishment Table was drawn up by the War Office for a 175 strong Intelligence Corps to accompany a future British Expeditionary Force.

This establishment was revised and re-issued in 1936, the revision centring around the extension of the work of the Corps to include Security. This new establishment in detail provided for a Corps HQ and Headquarters Section at GHQ; a Section each for the headquarters of Army Corps, Cavalry and Infantry Divisions; a Lines of Communication Section for two ports, and Intelligence Liaison Sections for each RAF Bomber Wing and Army Co-operation Squadron, together with cipher personnel at all brigade headquarters. The GHQ, Corps, Division and Lines of Communication Sections all included Intelligence Officers,

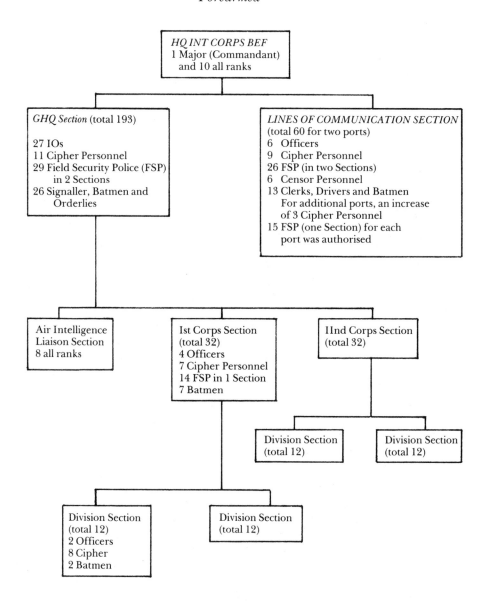

NOTES:
1. It was intended that two Cipher Personnel would be attached to the twelve Brigade Headquarters by their Divisional Commanders.
2. Provision had also been made for a further section of 12 All Ranks to be posted to a Cavalry, Mobile or Armoured Division if one had been included in the BEF.
3. The general pattern of an FS Section was one of an officer, a sergeant major, two or three sergeants, four corporals and five or six lance-corporals.

Cipher Officers and, as a basic counter-intelligence sub-unit, an FSP officer with an FSP Section.[4] This body was to mobilise at Aldershot and proceed to France between 4 and 13 days later.

After further thought and changes another establishment was prepared in late 1938 and it was in this configuration that the BEF's Intelligence Corps was formed on mobilisation in 1939. Essentially the structure was one of a small Corps Headquarters; a large Section to serve GHQ; specialist Sections; and detached Sections for Army Corps and Divisions. In detail, the Corps comprised (see table opposite):

The Intelligence Corps of the 1939 BEF

The personnel actually assembled for this *ad hoc* Corps were a varied mix. Some were Regular Officers and Soldiers from other Corps and Regiments, others from Reserve units, or lists prepared prior to mobilisation. Some had military and Intelligence experience, but others had little of either.

The roles envisaged were those of the 1914–18 Corps, Intelligence and Security; for the latter, the 1920s term Field Security Police were retained. Mobilisation took place at Blenheim Barracks, Aldershot, with the assistance of the 1st Battalion, Argyll and Sutherland Highlanders. The Corps Commandant was Major the Hon B M O S Foljambe with Captain (later Lieutenant Colonel) A Sullivan as Adjutant; both were former Regular Officers who had been selected and briefed for this task several months previously by Lieutenant Colonel G W R (later Field Marshal Sir Gerald) Templer, at the time serving in the Operations and Intelligence Directorate. Less No 15 FSP Section and a small number of other personnel who reached France from 4 September onwards, the whole Corps paraded on 11 September 1939 as a complete unit, a unique occasion.

The selection of the possible officer members of the proposed Intelligence Corps before the outbreak of the conflict was both belated and hurried, virtually no interest being shown until the mid-1930s when the mobilisation appointments in the War Book began to fill with names. But no plans were made for the training of I(A) or I(B) officers until after Munich in late 1938, following the arrival of Templer in the Directorate. A somewhat out-of-date card-index system was used to produce a list of suitable retired officers for training; after interview by Templer, those selected were invited to attend special evening courses, at their own expense. A few others, all over 31 to avoid any clash with the conscription arrangements, also volunteered.

The first of these courses in General Intelligence duties was held on nine evenings in March–April 1939, at the Royal United Services Institution (RUSI); it was attended by some 180 students. The course consisted of a series of 18 lectures, including Intelligence in the Field; Air Intelligence; Defence Security; Demonstration of an Intelligence Office and an introduction to the German Army. During this course Templer himself took the part of a German PW in an interrogation scene.

As the war clouds darkened more up-to-date lists of potential Intelligence officers were prepared in 1938–39; among those concerned with talent spotting was Professor J M Wordie, at Cambridge.

A further 150 candidates for Intelligence appointments attended a second General Intelligence course at the RUSI in July–August 1939. A week-end Security Course was run in May 1939 for 35 civilians, specially selected, and brief attachments were arranged for other personnel earmarked for Intelligence duties. A very few, and very carefully selected, potential officer recruits for Signals Intelligence work were also listed and interviewed. But, in sum, little more that the mere provision of names for slots had really been achieved.

Rather more thought had been given to the recruitment and training of the FSP. In 1936, the War Office had envisaged Port Security as the main requirement. In 1937, a former Intelligence Corps officer, recently retired, Captain (later Lieutenant Colonel) F C Davis MC, a fluent German speaker, had been appointed to train Port and Field Security personnel, Major K Strong being instrumental in this arrangement.[5] In the summer of 1937, it was decided that two week security courses, each for some 12 students, were to be arranged. The students were soldiers and NCOs nearing the end of their service, who could be recalled when required.

The Royal Fusilier fiction was now finally abandoned, and the Corps of Military Police instead provided both the 'cover' and much of the administrative back-up.[6] The courses were held at the CMP Depot at Mytchett, the course building carrying a signboard 'Security Section Corps of Military Police'.[7] The students wore the CMP cap badge with the words 'Corps of Military Police' filed off, together with a new brass shoulder title, FSP. Students were examined at the end of the course; all notes had to be destroyed. Two sections of FSP participated in the important July 1939 Army manoeuvres in East Anglia, and on mobilisation, Davis (now a Major) was joined by two veteran Intelligence Corps officers from World War I, Captains S C Woolrych and L Wallerstein.

The organisation and the CMP linkage began to create

problems on mobilisation as the FSP had a UK sponsor while the rest of the Corps in France did not; GHQ's authority over them was limited to operational work, administration still being controlled from Britain. In France the FSP continued to wear their distinctive shoulder badges, also light green cap covers rather than the red of the CMP.

Recruitment and Training

Before recounting the work of the Intelligence Corps in France before and during the German *Blitzkreig*, it is convenient to look at the recruitment and training of the growing numbers required both for the Corps in France and for certain specific military Intelligence duties in Britain. This remained centred on the CMP Depot at Mytchett, the staff comprised Major Davis, three captains, three sergeants, two corporals and five ATS members, these latter being some of the 1939 version of the present day Corps' permanently employed WRAC and successors to the 'Hushwaacs' of 1916–1918.[8] The early days were ones of great effort to launch the new organisation. Accommodation was poor, the staff were greatly overworked, and much had to be improvised. The recalled reservists, being trained, could be assembled into FSP sections and sent across to Blenheim Barracks for despatch to France immediately, but men that followed required increasing amounts of training. Some of the first arrivals were potential or emergency reserve officers selected before the outbreak of war, others were volunteers with TA or OTC experience. A few, in the words of Sullivan 'were Great War veterans who though gazetted as Second Lieutenants, insisted on wearing the insignia of their former ranks, causing some confusion; the majority were simple honest-to-God civilians, members of the Officers Emergency Reserve, who were keen chaps and competent linguists, but totally lacking in knowledge of the Army and all things military. They could not march, salute or tell the difference between a platoon and a division.'[9]

As the need was foreseen for increasing numbers of FSP to accompany further divisions to France, the unusual step of advertising by the BBC and in the national press for linguist volunteers was taken. This quickly brought a further inrush of some 500 volunteers to Mytchett. These included retired colonial police officials, laywers, schoolmasters, university professors, farmers, publishers, artists, bank officials, journalists and businessmen with even less experience of the Army that the Officers Emergency Reserve members. To quote Malcolm

Muggeridge, who was one of them, 'the Red Caps looked with ill-concealed distaste and disdain at we Field Security men, mostly schoolmasters, journalists, encyclopedia salesmen, unfrocked clergymen, and other displaced *New Statesman* readers. Under their outraged eyes, in the course of a few months, I moved successively from unpaid lance corporal to corporal to sergeant to sergeant major, becoming finally a fully-fledged war-substantive captain'.[10]

Training for these new recruits included basic military training and a two-week field security course, which included interrogation techniques, morale and propaganda, the German Army, and motor cycle instruction. A few of the pre-war FSP NCOs were retained as instructors, some of the ablest of the new arrivals also proved valuable assistance to the training staff—particularly young volunteers awaiting officers' training including not only Muggeridge but also C Skilbeck, D Bloodworth, R M Brooker and B Commins, two being future Lieutenant Colonels. In all, Mytchett can be seen as the first Corps Depot of the Intelligence Corps.

Operational Intelligence and Security 1939–40

In France itself the Corps operated under the BEF's GSO1 (Intelligence), Templer, whose GHQ I(B) staff were located initially at Aresnes-le-Comte receiving reports from division and corps sections via their respective GSO2 I(B) officers. A separate Lines of Communication Headquarters existed in Le Mans, to which the L of C Sections reported. One major impediment, the consequence of the absence of any proper Intelligence training for staff officers, was confusion over the role of the Corps: the term Field Security Police led to much misuse of specialist Intelligence personnel.[11] Three further especial problems existed in addition to the usual routine duties. The first was Communist opposition to the war, strong in France's industrial north and producing intense propaganda activity. The second was the particular problem presented, immediately north of the BEF area, by the frontier with Belgium—at that time still neutral. The French tolerated illicit trafficking despite British objection. To counter this traffic, additional FSP personnel were allocated, some working in Paris and others under Captain Arthur Marshall at Lille. The third problem lay in the French use of a large Italian labour force for fortification construction in the area, a problem requiring Italian speakers. Early in 1940, the problem of a group of well-connected British civilians in Paris opposed to the war also attracted attention and in April 1940 an FSS was stationed in Paris, where it operated in plain clothes.[12] Among its areas of interest were Communist anti-war organisations which were infiltrated. The need for continuing routine work was high-lighted by the tracing of eight French women found to be enquiring after British Army unit addresses in late November 1939, a time when the offensive originally planned by the Germans would have been in progress.

During the 1939–40 winter months, the Intelligence Corps underwent both a sifting process, a number of those on the pre-war lists proving either unsuitable or unfit, and a very considerable expansion to match the build-up of the BEF. By the spring of 1940, the Corps was distributed in over 50 locations from Calais to Marseilles, with an estimated total of 800 officers and men, of whom the very large majority were NCOs.[13]

Of this total the most important element was the Field Security Sections of which the first 18 were, by May 1940, deployed as follows:

No 1. 2nd Division, I Corps	7. I Corps HQ	13. LoC, St Nazaire
2. GHQ, BEF	8. II Corps HQ	14. LoC, Le Havre
3. 1st Division, II Corps	9. LoC, Dieppe	15. LoC, Le Mans
4. 3rd Division, II Corps	10. LoC, Cherbourg	16. LoC, Marseilles
5. 5th (later 4th) Division	11. LoC, Brest	17. LoC, 5th Division
6. GHQ, BEF	12. LoC, Nantes	18. LoC, Boulogne

A further 12 also served with the BEF, and 2 more were en route but turned back in June 1940. This greatly increased command responsibility led to changes in command. In January Major Foljambe departed, Sullivan briefly succeeding him with an assistant for the Lines of Communication Sections. In April the post of Commandant of the Corps was combined with that of the senior Intelligence staff officer, now styled Director of Military Intelligence of the BEF, Major General Mason-Macfarlane. Sullivan became Assistant Commandant for the forward area and retained responsibility for promotions. Four Intelligence Officers and 36 Liaison Officers (Intelligence) were at work in the GHQ Intelligence Section.

The sources and agencies for operational Intelligence for the BEF in the pre-*blitzkrieg* months differed somewhat from those of World War I in that the most significant material—sometimes heeded sometimes not—came from elsewhere: a Czech agent in the Abwehr, dissident Germans such as the Deputy Chief of the Abwehr, Colonel Oster, and the produce of Bletchley Park, where work on German cipher signals was beginning on the Enigma cipher machine, help provided by the Poles. Arrangements similar to the later Special Liaison Units (SLUs), the high security Intelligence sections that passed on Bletchley Park Intelligence to field commanders were set up in France at Army and RAF Headquarters respectively.[14] But with one exception, noted later, Bletchley Park did not really get into its stride until after the fall of France. One break, to produce mixed results, was the forced landing of a German aircraft in Belgium in January 1940, one of two officers on board carrying instructions to units of No 2 Air Fleet about the plans existing at the time for a German offensive through Belgium. GHQ assessed, wrongly, the documents to be a plant; the Germans in alarm altered their plans. Much useful order of battle material was however gained.

The traditional sources were not productive. Although prisoners were taken and German units identified by infantry patrols, the BEF held only a small sector of the actual front, and that not the one where the German attack was to fall. The RAF was facing technical difficulties which impeded air photography before the opening of the German offensive.[15] In the improved spring weather conditions, the camera-equipped Spitfires were able to gather some useful Intelligence immediately prior to, and during, the German offensive. Major T B L Churchill, the author of the 1938 manual, and three other officers had been appointed to a special air photograph interpretation section, GSIA(V) at GHQ. Their role over the winter months was largely that of training regimental officers, but they also received some material from French military Intelligence for study; unfortunately none of this was long range cover.

On mobilisation, No 1 Wireless Regiment at Aldershot had been re-designated No 2 Company GHQ Signals, and attached to GHQ BEF for signals Intelligence work. At the outset, intercepts were passed to Section 1(a) (iv) of the BEF's DMI staff, one Staff officer, four Intelligence Officers and some clerks.

The Intelligence Officers were all straight from civilian life and were experts in German and Germany, but their signals and general military experience were those of the First World War. Some expansion had been effected by May 1940, three Special Wireless Sections, 101, 102 and 103 being in the field. No tactical (and exceedingly little strategic) signals Intelligence, however, indicated the Ardennes as the area for the main weight of the German offensive. Further, on 1 May, the Germans made changes to the Enigma machine for which Bletchley Park was, in any case, not yet ready. The French Army, which ought to have been a prime source, remained convinced the Ardennes were impassable for armour.

Train movements were once again an important source of Intelligence, though who was actually collecting the material and how it was being relayed back to Britain is far from clear. But among the sources appear to have been friendly neutrals and Italians—and some dissident Germans. One may surmise that the channels used included the military attachés in Belgium and Holland. At the request of GHQ BEF, the German usage of Belgian roads in August 1914 was carefully reviewed, and a watch kept for road widening in Germany.

The measure of success was that overall, by one means or another, on 9 May 1940 GHQ BEF had 'almost an exact estimate of the numbers and positions of the German divisions and air forces facing us in the West, and we knew from this that an attack could not be long delayed'.[16] But the measure of the failure was that neither the time nor direction were predicted and the Allies were caught totally by surprise.

Arthur Marshall, commanding his FS Section at Lille provides some account of FS work in the first months of 1940. The duties included lecturing military units on the importance of security; the questioning of people suspected of espionage, sabotage and subversion; the investigation of reports of flashing lights—almost invariably groundless; and reporting on the morale of the civilian population. Much work required close co-operation with the French authorities.[17] A further account is provided by Captain Sir Basil Bartlett, who adds the interception of an occasional German carrier pigeon, snap pass control checks on trains and trams, the investigation of a report of a secret trial mobilisation by Belgium and the investigation of a farmer apparently ploughing his fields in the shape of arrows pointing at airfields and petrol dumps, to the list.[18] At GHQ Templer also initiated certain deception measures to confuse the Germans in respect of British troop movements.

Only inadequate material survives of the work of the BEF's Intelligence Corps in May–June 1940. Except for the Air Liaison personnel, most of the Corps—Intelligence Officers, Cipher Personnel and FSP Sections all moved into Belgium. The speed and overwhelming nature of the Germans onslaught made Intelligence work of all types increasingly difficult. Another contributory difficulty was the practice of the BEF Commander, Lord Gort (to his cost, no great believer in Intelligence), of operating from an Advanced Headquarters often on the move. The Corps organisation for the collation and dissemination of Intelligence, centred upon Arras, was generally unable to pass material up to, or receive material down from, the Advanced

Headquarters in time to be of use. Partly in frustration, the DMI took to the field at the head of a battle group.

But wherever possible some Intelligence work continued. In the Field Security Sections, the German speakers were engaged in the questioning of prisoners, and the French speakers in reconnaissance and liaison. Perhaps the most important Intelligence success was that of the translation of documents belonging to Lieutenant General Kinzel, the German Commander-in-Chief's Liaison Officer with Army Group B. First to see the documents was one of the Intelligence Officers of 3 Division, Captain Osman, in civilian life a German teacher at Oundle School.[19] One of these contained a full Order of Battle of the German Army with commanders and staffs down to divisional level as at 1 May 1940, the other—even more important—was the German Sixth Army's orders for an attack begun on the day of the capture of the documents, 25 May 1940. These orders revealed the direction towards Ypres and Wytschaete of the German two Corps size attack; crucial Intelligence later corroborated by an *Ultra* intercept. Gort's measure, the move of two British divisions to close the gap opening between the British and the Belgians, prevented an encirclement, cut off from the sea, of the BEF.[20]

Among accounts that survive are those of Lieutenant (later Major) R C Symonds, Lieutenant (later Major) A F Bosworth, and Lieutenant T (later Sir Tom) Normanton. Symonds was a Divisional Intelligence Officer I(A) with 44 (Home Counties) Division. Unusually, as I(A) officers were not normally tasked with I(B) work, his first task on entering Belgium was to secure the arrest by the Belgian authorities of two German sympathisers in Ypres. In the event, one had fled. He later interrogated some of the few prisoners taken when the Division was holding their Escaut line. Symond's first prisoner immediately revealed his unit (and thereby his formation), others later were too confident in the Army's victory to assist. Interrogators used the two DMI handbooks on the German Army, a Brown Book showing their composition and history of all known German divisions, with notes on their commanders, and a Yellow Book which was in effect an index to the Brown Book, enabling a unit identification to be assessed fully.[21]

Lieutenant Bosworth was attached to GHQ and then later to I Corps for prisoner questioning. He also records questioning captives on the Escaut Line:

> ... mostly Bavarians and from Baden. Their morale was pretty low,

partly due to the fact that they had had no food for three days, but chiefly due to the stiff opposition they had encountered. They were all active soldiers, and every one of them was only too willing to talk, not that they knew very much but most of them kept diaries, just the same as they did in the last war from which we could check their movements.[22]

Lieutenant Normanton was an SLU Intelligence Officer at BEF main headquarters at Arras. In the final stages of the campaign he was seriously wounded (and his driver killed) in a German air attack. But, in possession of important Intelligence, he directed a French motorist at gun point to take him to a cafe from where he reported by telephone to London, firstly to the Military Assistant to the Chief of the Imperial General Staff. He then found himself speaking directly to Field Marshal Ironside.[23] At this stage of the campaign the SLU channel of communication was often the only channel functioning between London and the BEF.

The BEF cipher personnel were, quite simply, overwhelmed. The German Army had made little use of its field signalling network and their low and medium grade codes prior to May 1940, preferring to use landline. In the turmoil of the *Blitzkrieg* personnel had no time to master field signals, in particular the Wehrmacht's signal proforma systems, when these began to arrive, or even to return their intercepts back to Britain. The Luftwaffe's signals were easier to interpret.[24] They often gave safety lines behind which aircraft were not to bomb or machine-gun. On one occasion these indicated speeds and lines of advance. A parachute attack on the bridge at Maastricht was monitored. Other successes included intercepts from aircraft that led to the deduction that the Germans were about to thrust for Peronne and, linked with reconnaissance aircraft, some further reports on train movements. But Signals Intelligence (Sigint) remained useful only in the early days before conditions became too disorganized. The small air photograph interpretation staff, GSIA(V) now commanded by Major W Venour, similarly found themselves increasingly unable to operate after the first few days in which they were able to contribute Intelligence—often of Dutch and Belgian movements about which GHQ had not been informed.[25] Of his own doing Sullivan recorded:

> When it was decided that the General Staff Branch of Rear HQ should move up closer to the fighting line, I was given the job of reconnoitring and allocating office accommodation and billets at the new location. Things moved so fast that I carried out this task

in three different towns, and it was at the last of these, Hazebrouck, that the Intelligence Corps went into action as a fighting unit and received an Operation Order all to itself.'

Sullivan was tasked to hold part of the perimeter defence of the town which lay on the German line of advance to the Channel but before long it was ordered to withdraw to Dunkirk from where, after some bombing, he and the men under his immediate command were evacuated by destroyer.

Captain Sir Basil Bartlett again provides some impressions of FSP work for this period. FSP Sections were tasked to enter Belgium with forward units. Their principal concern were Flemish militants, *'les Flamingants'*, a number of whom were reported to have been recruited by the Germans for Intelligence gathering from September 1939 onwards. Bartlett gives the example of a leading Nazi sympathiser in Courtrai, arrested by the Belgians but whose papers, incriminating a number of people, were left to his Section to follow up. The Germans had also infiltrated agents among the numerous Jewish refugees.[26] Other major concerns were the prevention of rumours and also on occasions of sabotage.[27] But overall, as with I(A) work, the picture presented is one of a system unable to meet the strain.

In the last dramatic days of the campaign, the Dunkirk evacuation, operational Intelligence for the BEF was effectively that based in Britain where the Y tactical signals organisation 'jammed the communications of the German dive bombers with decisive effect, and supplied from GAF intercepts the Intelligence which helped the naval authorities at Dover to control the shipping off the beaches'.[28] Most of the members of the BEF's Intelligence Corps was evacuated via Dunkirk, the various FSP Sections' French-speaking NCOs having performed useful service in reconnoitring withdrawal routes for their formations and units. 21 FSP Section, serving with 51 Highland Division, fought on the Somme and, most of the Section was obliged to surrender with the Division at St Valéry-en-Caux on 21 June.

During the campaign, two other Intelligence operations in which officers who were to join the formal Intelligence Corps on its formation, were taking place. The first of these was censorship, in which a small number of personnel were engaged, and the second propaganda. Lieutenant Viscount Strathallan (later the Rt. Hon. the Earl of Perth) recalls being '... sent to Paris to liaise with French Intelligence on Propaganda to Germany ... I recall drafting and printing leaflets during the phoney war which were in due time dropped by planes over Germany'.[29]

Overall, in the campaign, three NCOs, Sergeant J P Kingscote, MM and Lance Corporals V V Williams and A A Calthorpe-Newman were killed in action. No list of wounded survives; 1 Warrant Officer and 11 NCOs were captured by the Germans. One of the NCOs captured was Lance-Corporal J A R Coulthard, an Oxford lecturer and post-graduate Fellow. Coulthard was taken to a camp in German-occupied Poland, from which in 1942 he and a companion escaped. They proceeded by train to Berlin, Magdeburg and Munich, touring and dining in some style. Unfortunately, however, their documents were recognised as faked at the Swiss frontier. Coulthard escaped again in 1943, but was picked up at Gdynia, where he was hoping to board a Swedish ship. Tragically, he died of exhaustion on a forced march on 24 March 1945.

Lieutenant W I Brinkworth was awarded the MBE for his services. Other awards included the DCM to Sergeants A B Corbett and S Naish, who had formed a human bridge on a bomb-damaged mole at Dunkirk to assist walking wounded. The MM was awarded to Sergeants D M E McGillycuddy, J F Kingscote and E Jouault together with Lance Corporals D M Crane and W B McGee. Sergeant Jouault and Lance Corporal Crane both escaped from capture by the enemy, returning with useful Intelligence. Corporal McGee's award was for a hazardous journey bringing reports from a Belgian headquarters through enemy held territory on a damaged motor-bicycle. Corporal Coulthard was mentioned in despatches.

Norway and Iceland

The France and Flanders campaign had, of course, been preceded by operations in northern Europe following the German invasion of Denmark and Norway in early April 1940.[30] An immediate British military reaction had been the occupation of the strategically important Faroes Islands on 13 April 1940. The occupying force included a 'Field Security Unit Faroes' under Captain O Larsen. The unit's NCOs, capable between them of speaking in 14 languages, began the routine security work of port and military installations, access control and censorship.

Norway itself was, however, to provide the emerging Intelligence Corps, and indeed the whole British Army, with its first experience of *Blitzkrieg*. A number of FS Sections were landed in support of the various British forces, a further three were earmarked but not used. 26 and 27 FSP Sections were located with the GOC of the North-Western Force at Harstad; 35

and 36 FSP served briefly with the Central Norway force that landed at Andalsnes, and a further section served with the Anglo-French force at Namsos. The Harstad and Andalsnes Sections contained a number of Scandinavian language speakers, that for the Namsos force included a number of French speakers.[31] Finally, 39 Section was landed at Bodo on 12 May.

39 Section was the most successful in operational terms, carrying out Intelligence and Security duties inland as far as the Swedish border until evacuation through Harstad on 11 June. In the course of these duties Lance Corporal Le Grand was seriously injured in a German air raid. Elsewhere, British Army Staff inexperience of the contribution Intelligence Corps personnel could make, and also the ferocity of the German attacks, combined to make Intelligence work impossible.[32] The NCOs of the Andalsnes Sections were used for security screening duties covering the British Troops retreating from Dombas to Andalsnes; at Namsos the Section's French language capability was useful. The late Michael Pertwee, who served at Namsos, recalled the campaign as a succession of air attacks in which virtually the entire town, of wooden houses and without air defence, was burnt down. The Section was employed on other non-specialist duties; for his services in one of these, Pertwee was later Mentioned in Despatches.

One wider consequence of the Norwegian campaign was a realisation of the Army's weakness in topographical information, a realisation to lead a little later to the formation of the Inter-Service Topographical Department, ISTD, in which a number of Intelligence Corps personnel were to serve. ISTD was tasked to collect—sometimes from pre-war holiday makers' seaside photographs—and collate topographical information for commanders and staff planners. The forces sent to Norway would also have benefited from Signals Intelligence personnel; none were sent.

On 10 May 1940 a British force occupied Iceland to forestall any seizure by Germany; early reinforcements of the force included 40 FSP Section, which established itself in the former German Consulate. The Section despatched NCOs to different areas, two such, for example, being H T Roberts and C F Heron sent to Sigulfjordur and Akureyri to detain German nationals. The Section also took on the supervision of an improvised coast-watcher organisation that had been established immediately after the occupation. When the garrison was raised to a divisional command in July, No 60 Field Security Section (Lieutenant E A Gook) was posted to Iceland, No 38 FSS arriving in the following month and a fourth Section, No 74 a year later. WOII McRoberts and Sergeant McNaghten were both commissioned as Port Control Officer and Base Censor respectively. The commitment lasted to January 1943 when the United States Army took over.

A number of FS Sections formed in the first months of the war were stationed in Britain; these were initially referred to as the Home Ports and Home Airfields FSP Sections, but the title was later expanded to that of Travel Control Security. As mentioned earlier, preliminary planning for these Sections had begun in 1937, when Security Control Officers were appointed by MI5 for British sea and air ports. These SCOs had generally either experience as officers in the First World War or commercial or shipping experience. Each officer was required to recruit his own section to establishments of 1 officer and 13 NCOs for ports and 1 officer or a warrant officer and 4 NCOs for airfields; later an assistant SCO for the larger ports was authorised with a second section in some cases. The personnel selected tended to be from the same fields of commerce as the SCO; a few had attended the pre-war Mytchett FSP courses.[33]

Their duties on mobilisation on 4 September 1939 were the safeguarding of ports and airfields against enemy agents or couriers; the collection of any material of Intelligence interest from travellers and seamen; and the security of military personnel and equipment on the move. The different port sections were responsible not only for the port itself but also adjoining coastal areas, so forming a complete chain. Inland, coverage was provided by Sections for each of the Home and Military Commands. Surviving records are incomplete, but it would appear that by the end of 1939 37 Sections (numbered 101–133, 135–137 and 139) had been formed for Home Ports, some 11 (numbered 200–211) for Home Airfields and 6 (numbered 301–306) for the Home Commands.

Other Intelligence personnel, mostly officers, were concerned with censorship though, at the end of 1939, a special committee recommended the transfer of this subject away from the war Office. It eventually became a Ministry of Information responsibility.

The Corps Formally Established, July–December 1940

The Army's rapidly expanding Intelligence needs had made it clear, even by the turn of the years 1939–1940, that the training and administration requirements could not be met by *ad hoc* groupings of officers and soldiers from different arms;

emergency General List commissions, or even by a theatre Intelligence Corps such as that of the BEF. A formal Intelligence Corps with its own administration and Depot, its own badges and insignia to foster esprit de corps and discipline, was essential. In the War Office Major W F Jeffries, a Staff Officer in the MI Directorate, argued the case successfully with the DDMI, Brigadier K J Martin, and the DMI, Major General F Beaumont-Nesbitt.

Preparations followed. In early May 1940, the FS Wing moved away from Mytchett to form an FS Training Centre and Depot at Sheerness. The move soon became complicated by the arrival of personnel from France, the urgent need for additional FS Sections for the control of French refugees; and a further move to King Alfred's College Winchester, which was styled the 'Other Ranks Wing, Intelligence Corps'. On 19 July 1940 Army Order 112 formally authorised the British Army's Intelligence Corps, a little later almost all the personnel of the FSP Sections were transferred to the Corps, the term 'Police' being finally discarded. A search for an officers centre or depot was begun. The Secretary of State for War vetoed a proposal to take over the Royal Holloway College at Egham, on the grounds that the education of women could not be intefered with. The quest then moved to Oxford, where offices for the Commandant in Pembroke College and a much wider use of Oriel College as a headquarters and officers training centre were secured by a MI Directorate Staff Officer, Captain J (later Lieutenant Colonel Sir John) Russell, a former Oxford Union President. The first Adjutant of the Officers Wing was Captain (later Major) the Earl of Northesk. In December 1940, Major Jeffries, promoted to Colonel, was appointed the first Commandant of the Corps.[34]

Following the establishment of the Corps, a very large number of officers and soldiers engaged in Intelligence work were either transferred into the Corps or commissioned into it. But some specifically asked not to be so transferred, either on grounds of sentiment in favour of a former regiment, a remaining anti-Intelligence prejudice; a belief that the Corps would not be able to offer promotion beyond the rank of captain, or as some saw it, for reasons of professional military Intelligence itself, the transfers and gatherings of Corps personnel representing a breach of security.[35] Also, and very much more important, the Corps never became responsible for policy in respect of any branch of Intelligence in the way, for example, that the Artillery could voice policy on guns. The Corps was still viewed as a wartime necessity for which there would be no need in times of peace, and career-minded soldiers looked elsewhere.

The story of the work of the Corps, both during and immediately after the Second World War becomes, then, one of contributions made by members of the Corps, as individuals, small groups or FS Sections, to almost every type of military Intelligence work, the term military Intelligence having, for obvious reasons, a very much wider ambit in time of war than after its ending.

Members of the Corps would be the first to want their contributions placed in this wider context of the work of the entire Intelligence community. But the Corps' contributions were varied, distinctive and substantial as will be seen for the examples given in the chapters that follow. The contributions also mark another major advance in the role of the Corps in the Intelligence cycle, the contributions now being as much involved with collating, analysing and presenting as with collection. The measure of this can be seen in the 1944 and 1945 *Army Lists*, with the very large number of Emergency Commissioned Intelligence Corps officers holding acting ranks of Lieutenant Colonel or Major. The chapters that follow will set out contributions made by Corps personnel in the fields of Strategic Intelligence, of Operational Intelligence and of Security, with two further chapters concerned specifically with the Pacific War and the occupation of Germany. Intelligence Corps training in the Second World War is set out in Appendix E.

Hitherto in this work officers mentioned by name have been engaged in duties later undertaken by the Intelligence Corps upon its formation. In the chapters that follow, officers and soldiers mentioned by name are all members of the badged Corps unless this is noted to the contrary.

7

Strategic Intelligence: The Corps Contribution

Strategic Intelligence, the Intelligence component of grand strategy, was of vital importance in the Second World War. The amount of material that could be available was much greater than in the First World War. Military reverses and weakness were a major incentive for the development of Intelligence work, an important contribution to damage limitation. Intelligence soon became an area of conflict in which the Allies, notably Great Britain, generally secured the mastery. Of the main sources and agencies by far the most important was Signals Intelligence, but also exceedingly useful were air photo interpretation, Special Operations, prisoner of war questioning and certain other organisations such as the Political Warfare Executive. In overlap several of the same sources and agencies also at the same time contributed to both the rather different operational Intelligence needs of field commanders fighting campaigns, and to Intelligence staffs concerned with Security; in their turn the Security staffs also on occasions contributed to Strategic Intelligence. Another overlap was the requirement for almost identical skills in a very special mix, the military expertise of the professional soldier with wider knowledge, often academic, of talented amateurs. For success, it was not sufficient to compile Orders of Battle, note movements or even simply to set out decisions thought to have been reached by enemy commanders in purely professional terms. Skill lay in an understanding, often highly intellectual, of the factors likely to be conditioning an opponent's mind at a time of his decision-making, the ability to recognise that two or three apparently totally unrelated facts together formed an indicator, and the patience that could on occasions require long night hours, perhaps for several weeks, in front of a signal receiver that was apparently dead, or days in confrontation with a prisoner who was unwilling to talk.

A final, domestic Intelligence Corps overlap, was that in all fields of Intelligence, Strategic Intelligence, Operational Intelligence and Security were a number of Intelligence Corps personnel at work in plain clothes for other agencies either for a particular posting or for most of the war. Of these personnel little further can be said beyond recording that their Intelligence input could be of great value. During the war, for example, some Intelligence Corps Officers seconded to the Security Service, and some Security Service officers were provided with military rank and badged as Intelligence Corps officers. The best known example of the former category was Major J C (later Professor Sir John) Masterman, who after service in the Directorate of Military Intelligence was engaged in the control of double agents working with the XX Committee.[1] Other officers served the Security Service with language expertise, major concerns being refugees from Axis-occupied Europe and the Germans and Italians resident in Britain and in Ireland.[2]

One from the second category was Lieutenant Colonel Lord Rothschild, who brought his experience of biological research to work as varied as sabotage and anti-sabotage devices, and the precautionary analysis of cigars sent to the Prime Minister from all over the world.[3] He was awarded the George Medal for rendering safe a bomb concealed in a box of Spanish onions; food store warehouses were seen as useful sabotage targets by the Germans.

Before turning to the separate sources and agencies, it is most important to stress that all worked in linkage with each other—a signals intercept would be set alongside a prisoner interrogation report or air photographs and patterns would emerge. Reports from refugees or other sources would be used to task an SOE officer—or a double agent.

The Directorate of Military Intelligence

In the more strictly military field, the Directorate of Military Intelligence was expanded very greatly from September 1939 onwards. At the outbreak of war, there existed MI 1 (Administration, Personnel, Training, Language needs, Liaison, Security, Censorship and Y Signals Intelligence; MI 2 (Middle East, India, USSR, Northern and Eastern Europe, North and South America); MI 3 (Western Europe); MI 4 (Maps); a very small

THE DIRECTORATE OF MILITARY INTELLIGENCE

1. 1939–1940

Director

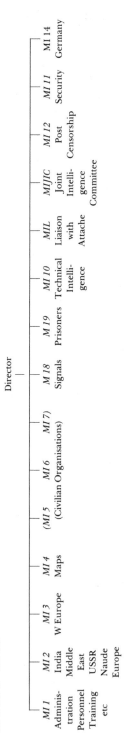

MI 1	MI 2	MI 3	MI 4	(MI 5	MI 6	MI 7)	M 18	M 19	MI 10	MIL	MIJIC	MI 12	MI 11	MI 14
Adminis-tration Personnel Training etc	India Middle East USSR Naude Europe	W Europe	Maps	(Civilian Organisations)			Signals	Prisoners	Technical Intelli-gence	Liaison with Attache	Joint Intelli-gence Committee	Post Censorship	Security	Security Germany

2. 1942-45

Director

MI 1	MI 2	MI 3	MI 4	(MI 5	MI 6)	MI 8	MI 9	MI 10	MI 11	MI 12	MILL	MI 4	MIJIS	MIL(R)	MI 19	MI 15	MI 17	MI 16
Adminis-tration Person-nel Training	India Middle East	W Europe	Maps	Civilian Organisations		Signals	British Prisoners	Tech. Intelli-gence	Liaison with Attaches	Post Censor-ship	Security Germany	Security Germany	Axis Planning Staff	Liaison with USSR	Enemy Prisoners	Anti-aircraft Intelli-gence	Co-ord-ination	Scien-tific Intelli-gence

(MI 16 was an immediate post war creation)

MI R (Special Forces) with also, as largely civilian organisations MI 5, MI 6 and MI 7 (Press and Propaganda). Very shortly afterwards were formed MI 8 (Y Signals Intelligence); MI 9 (Prisoners); MI 10 (Technical Intelligence); and MI L (Liaison with Attachés, British and Foreign) and an MI Joint Intelligence Committee. In April 1940, MI 4 was transferred to Operations, but a new MI 12 was formed for Post and Telegraph Censorship liaison following transfer of this commitment to the Ministry of Information. The liaison staffs, of which some were military and included Intelligence Corps members, were concerned with censorship of the mail of special forces, mail between Britain and Ireland, and the mail of certain allied forces, and also with the base censorship organisation. In the following month, MI 14 and MI 11 opened, the former to take all German Intelligence from MI 3 and the latter for work in connection with purely military security. A little later, MI R ceased to exist, following the formation of SOE, and MI 7 was transferred to the Ministry of Information.

The following year, 1941, saw the formation of a MI (JIS) (an 'Axis Planning Staff') and an MI L(R) for liaison with the Russians, this later became a 'Russian Liaison Group'. MI 9 was split, the section retaining work in respect of British prisoners in enemy hands but a new MI 19 was formed for work in connection with all enemy prisoners. In 1942, MI 15 was formed to be responsible for Air Photographic Intelligence, but this was later transferred to the Air Ministry. In 1943 a new MI 15 was formed of joint artillery, RAF and United States officers for anti-aircraft Intelligence. The system had become so complex that in August 1942 an MI (Co-ordinating) Section was created, but this was later merged with MI JIC to form MI 17. The other changes in 1943 were fewer, with a reformation of an MI 15 for air defence Intelligence and some small reorganisation within MI 8. This configuration lasted with only minor changes to the end of the war.[4] Each of these sections had, of course, numerous sub-sections; other related organisations included the 1940–45 Inter-Services Security Board, the 1942–45 Intelligence Section (Operations) concerned with operational planning, the Inter-Services Topographical Department, and the immediate post-war MI 16 for the study of scientific and technical Intelligence.[5] In April 1942 the Directorate became linked to the Cabinet Office through a small co-ordinating cell, the Intelligence Section (Operations) which itself worked to the policy of the Joint Intelligence Committee.

A few examples of the work undertaken by many members of the Corps in the different sections are instructive.

MI 1 was the sponsor branch for the Intelligence Corps. Within it, on occasions, Intelligence Corps officers served, notably Lieutenant Colonel J G S Barrow in 1942–43. One of its sub-sections MI 5, concerned with Corps recruitment, was located in Oxford. Amongst the officers who served in it was Captain (later Lieutenant Colonel) J Cobban. In MI 3, from 1942–45, was serving Captain (later Professor) L Schapiro. This branch included a number of Auxiliary Territorial Service (ATS) girls, the Second World War forebear of the WRAC. Among these, from early 1943, was Lieutenant Margaret Sherman.[6] Her first duties were the compilation of information in respect of accommodation that might be available for Allied troops in Italy, hotels, schools, hospitals, together with water and energy supplies. She worked from a Baedeker's guide, south to north. She was then moved to study of the Yugoslav scene, tasked to compile a partisan Order of Battle with brief biographies of partisan field commanders, her sources being SOE, liaison officer reports and signals intercepts. The work of MI 8 is considered later.

MI 9 (Prisoners) had its headquarters at Wilton Park, Beaconsfield. Its work was concerned initially with facilitating the escape of British prisoners in Germany, and the morale of these prisoners. It soon developed into the means of communication, in code, with prisoners in their camps. Lieutenant Colonel L Winterbottom and Captain B (later Sir Brinsley) Ford served with this organisation. The initial material was intended to guide prisoners to escape with equipment concealed in parcels including such items as compasses in fountain pens, advice on safe houses in Germany (a brothel reserved for non-Germans was one of the best), and asking them to look out for useful Intelligence material. The code procedures, devised by Colonel Winterbottom, were based on an English-German dictionary; a small number of staff officers and RAF officers liable for capture were given special secret briefings. The airmen's wives were brought into the picture, devising suitable domestic detail for the code correspondence. Although some 1,000 words of military Intelligence per month reached the War Office in his way, the system was never discovered by the Germans; its main successes were an additional indicator concerning the V2 Peenemunde rocket site and certain specifications of the German Mark VI Tiger tank. The long delays in correspondence were a difficulty. On one occasion, Ford went in a motor gunboat to German occupied Brittany to make arrangements with MI 9's local agent, a French Canadian.[7] A small specialist staff was established to assist prisoners escaping in Italy and the Balkans, over 3,000 being rescued. For the final

North West Europe campaign a special inter-Allied 'Intelligence School' was established to brief units on escape and to plan for the rescue of escaping prisoners. A number of escapees were assisted in this way after Arnhem. The work of MI 9 staff could be hazardous Captain F A AD Baker, for example, entered enemy territory in France and Holland on several occasions to assist escapees, in so doing also acquiring useful tactical intelligence. He was awarded an MC for his work. Later, Wilton Park, Beaconsfield housed British prisoners who had escaped or been liberated and were being debriefed, itself a skilled process.

Intelligence Corps personnel at work in MI 11 included at different times Lieutenant Colonels J G S Barrow, A Collard, K H Vignoles and E P Wallis-Jones (later Justice), and Captains R (later Sir Rupert) Speir, and P M Lee before their transfers to MI 5 and SOE respectively. The principal commitment, Security in the Army, involved the formation, allocation and co-ordination of the work of Field Security Sections of the Corps, and work with other agencies and individuals. Another commitment, at times requiring tact, was Security within the War Office. Captain Lee was concerned with the clearance of books and articles written by Services personnel. He records that the guidelines were commonsense, caution and an assumption of the presence of watchful German agents.[8]

MI 12's Base Censorship organisation controlled Base Censor Sections, one for each 20,000 troops; Special Mails Sections in Operational areas, one for each 60,000 troops; Prisoner of War Censor Sections; and Telegraph Censor Sections. The principles governing censorship were to prevent transmission of military or political information of value to the enemy, but in addition picture postcards, all codes and ciphers in private correspondence, and letters to 'pen pals' were forbidden.

MI 14 was the most interesting and important of the sections. In 1940 it was headed by Lieutenant Colonel K Strong, later its deputy commander was Lieutenant Colonel W B P Aspinall, of the Corps. At its peak strength MI 14 totalled 58 officers working 8 specialist subsections. Several Intelligence Corps officers have described work in this section. Captain N (later Lord) Annan was from 1940 to 1942 concerned with German transportation, trying to assess the number of units on their way to the Balkans or North Africa. The main source here was a network of agents employed in the Hungarian and Romanian railway systems. They provided material on the volume of traffic, with also divisional emblems. Later *Ultra* supplied details of movements to North Africa.[9] Major J L Mowat and Captain K D Sutcliffe were staff officers in the co-ordination sub-section, Captain the Hon R W H P Lyon-Dalbert Acton was a specialist in German officer personality profiles.

Major W I Combs's duties were initially study of German Logistics, supply and transportation, developing specifically into studies of these subjects in respect of North Africa, Italy and Northern France in preparation for operations.[10] Captain, later Lieutenant Colonel C R Tangye specialised initially in Order of Battle compilation before moving on to operations preparation. Captain V Bonham-Carter and Major (later Dr) J Mark were engaged in the same work in 1942–43 and 1944–45 respectively. Captain (later Professor) N Gash's schedule was the study of the SS, Waffen SS, and ancillary non-Germanic units. (Some, but not all, German police and SS units ciphers were broken by Bletchley Park). Accurate assessment of SS was of particular importance in the closing stages of the war.[11]

MI 14's sources were reports from signals intercepts, German newspapers and periodicals, SIS reports, prisoner of war interrogation reports and captured documents, orders, Army Lists, etc.[12] A generally complete picture of all battlefronts from the enemy's point of view, with dispositions and strengths was maintained, and a daily map and briefing sent to the Cabinet Office. The main difficulties were fluctuations caused by the destruction of German divisions, their re-formation and re-deployment, and the creation of new divisions of very varying sizes (some being only two regiments) and quality. Co-operation with the US Army in this work of which initially they had no knowledge was close, 'agreed combined estimates' being produced from early 1943, and an Anglo-American Military Intelligence Research Section, for German army study being established.

Towards the end of the war, Lieutenant Sherman in MI 14 also began the preparation of a massive card index of German school and university teachers; these were divided into black, grey and white according to their association with the Nazi Party.[13] The material was later made over to the occupation authorities. Another women member of the section to achieve fame was Captain 'Pooh' Malcolm, ATS, whose knowledge of the German ORBAT was so extensive that she was sent to advise the Pentagon.[14]

MI 14 issued—and up-dated—two major publications, the 'Yellow Book' *Order of Battle of the German Army*, which listed all identified units; and the 'Brown Book', *The German Forces in the Field*, which provided formation composition and commanders' personalities. Other manuals covered tactics, administration and supply, insignia and badges and periodic updating notes.

When MI 17 was established in 1943, its first chief was Lieutenant Colonel J S Latrobe-Bateman who had served with MI Co-Ord; its last Second World War chief was another Corps officer, Lieutenant Colonel Sir Gyles Isham. Lieutenant Sherman was moved to MI 19 in the last months of the war for work, with other ATS Intelligence officers, in translating German documents. Officers with language or other special qualifications also served with the Military Intelligence Liaison staff, working with Allied and neutral military attaches. This staff was headed from 1940 to 1945 by Lieutenant Colonel J C D Carlisle DSO MC, who transferred into the Corps on its formation, and also included Majors A D Powell, V Bonham-Carter and A Dru. The internal political problems of certain Allies required careful handling if the contribution of those countries was to be maximised.[15] When the Special Russian Liaison Group was created, Captain (later Professor) C Hill was liaison officer with Russian engineers, inspecting British tanks before their shipment to the Soviet Union. Other small groups to which Intelligence Corps personnel contributed expertise were the military Intelligence Research Station concerned with handling and exploiting captured documents; the Inter Services Topographical Department, in which Captain (later Professor) J W House served as head of the Army contingent in the European Section; and MI JIS, tasked to place themselves in the minds of the German Command and anticipate Axis moves and counter-moves to Allied operations. This section was headed by Lieutenant Colonel A A W L (later Professor Sir Laurence) Kirwan from 1943 to 1945. Captain Annan also served in it in 1943–44. Some individuals also merit especial mention. Major A H Birse was the Prime Minister's personal Russian interpreter at the Moscow, Teheran, Yalta and Potsdam conferences; he had earlier served (with the Corps) in the British Military Mission in Moscow where Major F Reade-Jahn had also served. Captain N Stanley-Cary was personal security officer to the King of Greece. Captain W (later Sir William) Barker was liaison officer with the Czechoslovak forces in Britain. Sir Peter Norton-Griffiths was specially employed as Assistant Military Attaché in Madrid before service as SHAEF. Captain P S Montgomery served as ADC to Lord Wavell when he was Viceroy of India. In July 1945, the *Army List* recorded as serving in the Directorate of Military Intelligence, 5 Grade 1, 26 Grade 2 and 27 Grade 3 General Staff officers all members of the Corps, together with a further 28 Corps officers serving as 'Intelligence Officers' and 16 ATS officers. At the very top, one of the two Army officers in the small Intelligence group of the War Cabinet that advised the Prime Minister and Chiefs of Staff was Major Annan.

Bletchley Park and the Y Service

The most productive source of Strategic Intelligence in the Second World War was Signals interception. The Germans, on account of both the immense areas of ground occupied by their forces and their fast-moving style of warfare, had made massive pre-war advances in signals technology, and were heavily dependent on the use of wireless. In broad terms, the interception of German signals fell into two categories, the Bletchley Park deciphering service commonly known as *Ultra*, and the Y Services, more often limited to *en clair* messages, or the analysis of the volume of traffic and locations of stations. The former was controlled by the Secret Intelligence Service (SIS) and the latter mostly by MI 8; Intelligence Corps personnel made important contributions to both.

Bletchley Park was a country house in Buckinghamshire. At its height, the establishment possessed a staff of nearly 6000. It existed, primarily as already noted, as a result of the pre-war acquisition of the German Enigma enciphering machine.[16] This machine, or developments of it, was used in all important German signals traffic. As time progressed, periodic German additions to its complexities required a constant intellectual battle involving mathematicians and linguists, and the development of electro-mechanical devices (known as *Bombes*) for the rapid scanning of the tens of thousands of possible combinations of keys on the sending Enigma machines. To the end of the war, the Germans remained unaware of our abilities to read so much of their traffic. That they should remain so was a major security commitment at Bletchley and at all organisations using Bletchley material. There could never be any indication of the method by which the material was acquired and messages not fully deciphered would carry some legend such as 'Source saw a torn fragment of a message'. The source and material were referred to as *Ultra*.

The 'mechanics' of the system provided for interception, at Chatham and elsewhere, the movement of the message to Bletchley by teleprinter and despatch rider, processing in a Registration Room itself monitored by an Intercept Control Room, deciphering in the Machine Room, with further testing if necessary in the Sheet Stacking Room, and, again if necessary, decoding in a Decoding Room. The message then being clear, it was sent for translation, analysis and interpretation. The system worked round the clock.[17] For a while decrypting, but not of Enigma, also took place in Cairo.

These mechanics do not however bring out the importance of Intelligence back-up to derive the most from an intercepted signal. A signal ordering the move of a Panzer division became infinitely more valuable if placed in the context of other known moves. A massive index system had to be maintained and up-dated continuously. Research staff needed, in the words of our officer, 'a rigorously academic understanding of grammatical niceties and precise shades of meaning and a knack of divining the correct expansion of novel German abbreviations with a trained mechanic's repertory of technical terms'.

From Bletchley, Intelligence was passed to the MI Directorate and to appropriate theatre commands where an officer and a small staff of NCOs were formed into Special Liaison Units (SLU), mostly of RAF officers but on occasions including some Intelligence Corps, to handle—and secure—the material.[18] By July 1944, between 40 and 50 naval, military and air command headquarters were receivers. From 1942 onwards, American officers were progressively inducted into the skills and secrets.

The major and spectacular successes of *Ultra* are now well known. They included important contributions towards victory in the Battle of Britain, vital technical information in respect of German night bombing, strategic information concerning German plans for an invasion of Britain and the later attacks in the Balkans and on Russia. *Ultra* provided British planners with much of the most reliable information on the varying fortunes of the German Army in Russia. This information, in turn and when combined with intercepts of German naval and air signals dealing with movement preparations and logistics in Western Europe, greatly helped the planning by British and Allied commanders in the North African, Italian and North-West Europe campaigns. In 1944, *Ultra* decrypts also added to knowledge of the German V1 and V2 weapons. The value of *Ultra* material in the day to day conduct of operations, in particular in North West Europe is noted in the next chapter, but some idea of the scale of the work may be useful here. At its height, in the weeks after the Normandy landings, each 10 days some 4,800 German signals—military, naval, air, police, railway and diplomatic—were being intercepted; some 2,500 military and air signals were processed for the staffs of the Supreme Commander of the Allied Expeditionary Force.

Some 300–400 members of the Army worked at Bletchley, of

these about 40 per cent were Intelligence Corps. Among the Corps personnel were at one time or another Lieutenant Colonels R Wingate, H L Petavel and R P Tester, Majors D Morley, H F Jolowicz (later Professor), T B L Webster (later Professor), L B Firnberg, C D Black-Hawkins, J H Whitehead, J Manisty, D W Babbage and R F Bennett, (both later Presidents of Magdalene College Cambridge), Captains R I S Bax, J McIlwraith, C J Goodman, F T Prince, A H Diverres (later Professor), N L Webster, I McL Campbell (later Professor), D Jones (later D Craig, Operatic producer), H M Evans, K H E Bowen, L J Wesson, J G Monroe, P M G Eden, J McI Lonsdale and J H Wallace-Hadrill (later Professor). Among the NCOs were Warrant Officers A (later Lord) Briggs, Corporal H Fletcher and Corporal (later the Reverend Professor) F S Lindars.[19] This list is far from complete and it should be noted that rank very often bore little relation to actual responsibility.[20]

The logging, clerical and recording work fell in part to ATS members, a number of these—as elsewhere—wore the Intelligence Corps badge on their tunics. The life, for men and women, was not by any means a soft billet, 26 to 28 slept in barrack huts and military discipline was applied.[21]

A number of organisations were involved in Y work. At the start of the war MI 5's Radio Security Service, established to intercept signals from German agents in Britain, found itself with little work to do and able to identify German military and other stations and log the volume of traffic. These were then analysed by traffic analysts, among them at this stage, Captain H Trevor-Roper (later Lord Dacre). As the war progressed, massive expertise was developed, new codes and call-signs discerned in advance of use, and personality files on operators built up both by the RSS and units entirely military.

The essence of Y work was the interception of enemy signals, noting the volume and direction of traffic, direction finding to locate the sender, measuring the number of priority messages, log reading and recording of Enigma messages, and the cryptanalysis of 'low grade' (ie low in the degree of enemy security) signals some of which could nevertheless be exceedingly difficult to decipher, decode or even intercept. Without the Y service, *Ultra* could not have functioned. Much of the material collected in the UK was Luftwaffe, as the German Army generally used landline. Luftwaffe standards of security remained poor, some messages even being sent *en clair*.[22]

No 1 Special Wireless Group, of Royal Signals and attached Intelligence Corps personnel, was formed in the summer of 1940, with headquarters in Harpenden. Detachments were sent to a number of carefully chosen sites mostly in East Yorkshire, East Anglia or the South coast, one for example was on Beachy Head. As more trained personnel, Royal Signals and Intelligence Corps, became available, Wireless Intercept Sections were posted to Army Corps, and later Armoured Divisions, headquarters in Britain. They operated in large box body vehicles fitted out to take the racks of receivers; these vehicles, known as 'Gin Palaces', were linked to the main headquarters complex by landline or despatch rider. Work was divided into three shifts per day. In 1943, it was extended to include the monitoring of German radar emissions.

A NCO in a detachment commanded by Lieutenant A D Peck devised a process that came to be known as the Predictor, involving systematic study of the idiosyncracies of selected Luftwaffe encoders. The detachment constructed a cardboard ring on which code groups could be rotated against clear. Once two or three clear groups had been 'guessed' against two or three code groups it was possible to read off the whole of the rest of the day's traffic by rotating the ring.[23]

Personnel at work in this field included a number of NCOs who later achieved distinction in a variety of professions, and once again, ATS. All, Signals, Intelligence and ATS worked as closely knit teams. Training for Intelligence Corps personnel took place at Harpenden, for later integration with the intercept personnel.

Y work at theatre level is considered in the next chapters.

One less well-known facet of MI 8's work was that of working out, describing and mapping the telecommunication systems of enemy or enemy occupied countries so that these could be either destroyed or, later used. The main sources for these were pre-war telephone directories and agents reports.[24]

Prisoners of War

Prisoners of War continued to be another important source of Strategic Intelligence. In Britain, the agencies were controlled by a Deputy Director of Military Intelligence at Wilton Park, Beaconsfield responsible for both MI 9 and MI 19.[25] From 1940-41, three Combined Services Detailed Interrogation Centres, CSDIC, existed, one at Latimer, one, initially for Italians, at Beaconsfield and one at Cockfosters, this latter for more senior German officers. Material gained here could cover Luftwaffe organisation and losses, or technical matters such as weapon capacities, Luftwaffe beam transmissions, German radar and identification equipments, logistic arrangements, or political subjects, including the effect of RAF bombing. There was also a Prisoner of War Interrogation Section—Home (PWIS-H)—structure comprising a London District Cage at 6/7 Kensington Palace Gardens, mobile teams, and six Command Cages for the main Army Command areas. The mobile teams worked with the Command Cages for tasks such as the interrogation of prisoners taken on commando raids. Cages and camps were fitted with concealed listening devices; prisoners' conversations could yield useful material, one example being some of the first Intelligence concerning the Luftwaffe's *Knickebein, X-Gerät* and *Y Gerät* radio pulse guidance systems for bombers, and a little later, the success of British electronic counter-measures in re-radiating German beacon signals, so confusing German aircraft. In March 1943, two generals, von Thoma and Crüwell, were left to chat in a specially prepared room; von Thoma let slip some very useful comments on German V2 rocket development. In 1943, the number of German prisoners taken in North Africa, approximately 250,000, necessitated the use of two other camps at Castle Douglas and Comrie by *ad hoc* sorting teams. These were looking in particular for prisoners in possession of information of value to those planning the Normandy landings or information concerning the development of flying bombs and rockets. Further arrangements had to be made for and after the Normandy landings in 1944. The plans proposed that prisoners should reach Britain in two streams, a British stream via Southampton to Kempton Park and an American stream through Weymouth to Devizes: the prisoners would then be sorted and some selected for interrogation before despatch to camps. In the event, a second British sorting camp had to be opened at Devizes; in this latter camp, the US Army interrogators were trained when time allowed. The CSDICs and the London District Cage remained, but the other Command Cages were closed down. Beaconsfield was increasingly made over for the interrogation of senior officer prisoners, for example the German General von Thoma and the Italian Marshal Messe, together with their staffs.

A considerable number of Intelligence Corps officers were at work in prisoner interrogation. Most notable was Lieutenant Colonel A P Scotland OBE, who had served as an interrogator in France and Belgium in the First World War BEF Intelligence Corps.[26] Of especial interest, he described in the book he wrote after the war an interrogation of Rudolf Hess, a German secret service officer, and a mine specialist naval officer rescued from the battleship *Bismarck*, together with interrogators ending a strike led by Nazi militant prisoners of war in one camp. His own specialist knowledge also enabled him to contribute to the organisation of raiding parties and the training of units in prisoner handling. Others at work included Lieutenant Colonel H J Baxter, Majors T X H Pantcheff, A F A I Terry, L G Struthers; Captains C J G Raven, W Allen, C H Stokes, W A Morgan, J Dill-Smith, G R Coate, G Sinclair, H K Kettler, A V Magnus, A C Bennett, G Paton, A E Wernly, and Lieutenant W Kieser.[27] Some officers had particular specialisations, Captain Wernly, for example, being concerned with economic warfare. There were also NCO interrogators, among them Sergeant (later Professor) A Nove. ATS personnel included Junior Commander the Hon Mrs Agar, C Townshend and D Rockingham Gill. Working to them were a number of ATS NCOs and privates engaged in the translation and typing of interrogation reports and maintenance of records. German prisoners conversations were recorded and then transcribed on to large documents in both the original German and English translation. These, prepared night and day, were sealed and sent on to Whitehall. One ATS clerk, Private Stainier, recalls 'We proudly wore our Intelligence Corps badges'.[28]

Successful interrogators had first to have a complete command of German (or Italian) training in interrogation and an up-to-date briefing on the aims of the interrogation. As important, also, were the abilities to 'think German'. Prisoners were most likely to help, after an initial attempt to resist shock, within the first 10 days of capture. Listening devices were often valuable, enabling conversations between selected prisoners, from the same or similar units, to be overheard. Conversations would either be recorded on 12 inch discs, or listened to—no easy matter during an air raid. Sometimes co-operative prisoners would serve as stool pigeons; German dissident refugees were also used for this purpose. It was noticeable that the Germans depended greatly on group support and found any form of segregation destabilising, as they also found alternation of harsh and friendly questioning.

Major Pantcheff also recall some interesting Prisoner of War Interrogation Section (Home) (PWIS-H) detail. U-boat crews were usually highly motivated and secure but their cooks were often a weak link. One, an undeclared socialist, admitted his captain had taunted the drowning crew of a torpedoed ship, which in turn enabled the interrogators to pressure the captain. A shot-down Luftwaffe NCO under interrogation gave a description of a German night fighter radar device that had been causing serious RAF bombers losses. As a result of a mendacious allegation by one German prisoner that he had been shackled, a number of Allied prisoners in Germany were chained; the prisoner was persuaded to admit his falsehood to representatives of the Protecting Power, Switzerland. Officer prisoners brought from North Africa attempted to conceal their rank, but gave themselves away by bowing to a Camp Commandant rather than saluting. Some prisoners were taken out to dinner and a cinema or theatre in London as part of a process of convincing them that the Allies were winning and they themselves might gain long-term benefit from co-operation. Other work included the uncovering of German abuse of hospital ship privileges.[29] Very frequently interrogations revealed clues on both German morale and manpower issues.

Non-Germans once again proved very useful sources. A Polish soldier drafted into the German Army had, prior to capture, worked on bunker construction in the area of the planned American landings in Normandy; he was able to supplement the air photographs with precise details of thickness of concrete and depth of soil cover.[30] Polish officers worked in a number of camps and later, in view of the number of Soviet citizens (usually non-Russians compelled to work as auxiliaries for the Germans), a Soviet liaison officer appeared. There were frictions—between the Poles, the Soviet officer and the Soviet prisoners, many suicidal in their despair. As in the First World War, Alsatian men drafted into the German Army proved valuable on occasions—a group who had refused to participate in the mass killing of the inhabitants of the French village of Oradour sur Glane in June 1944, and had later deserted, were able both to give details of the massacre and to identify at Kempton Park the senior survivor of the killers. Another group of prisoners generally willing to talk were concentration camp inmates of German nationality released to join the Wehrmacht. These were posted to a special formation, 999 Infantry Division, and given especially dangerous tasks to perform. They were only given weapons when very far forward. They provided not only military information but also material on the concentration camps.

Less spectacular but almost as important was the security of the prisoners. American interrogators got wind of a mass escape project, almost certainly involving attempts to kill the British guards, at Devizes in December 1944. A British team headed by Major Pantcheff was sent to investigate and found that some German prisoners had already made nocturnal escapes to reconnoitre nearby air and tank installations so as to purloin weapons. They then planned to fight their way to the East Coast in the hope of rescue by small ships or other German forces. The Prime Minister's staff believed such a mass escape could be timed to coincide with some last desperate military gamble—in the event the Ardennes offensive.[31] Pantcheff's team soon discovered what was afoot and, dramatically, the plot leaders were all arrested—the effect on the mass of prisoners being stunning. It would appear that German troops were instructed to plan escape wherever possible. Aboard the troopship *Derbyshire* in the Mediterranean in 1943 were a number of German prisoners and a small detachment of British troops, the latter including a handful of German speaking Intelligence Corps personnel. These picked up a German plan to seize the ship and arrangements were made to foil it.[32] A few other Intelligence Corps officers served briefly in camps for Italian prisoners, their tasks were mostly simple interpreting with from 1943 onwards 'talent spotting', finding those of anti-fascist views prepared to serve the Allied cause.

The mail of prisoners also offered valuable material from time to time and a number of officers and NCOs of the Corps were at work studying such mail, both in Britain and in Canada.

The Intelligence Corps found itself becoming, in the words of one officer, 'The receptacle and guardian of the cumulative experience of interrogation', a role it still maintains today.[33]

Air Photographic Interpretation

Another field of Strategic Intelligence, and as useful and important as any of the others, was air reconnaissance and photographs. As with all previous fields, the Intelligence Corps provided a large percentage of the specialist personnel, but so did other Services and units. Archaeologists were a preferred source for recruits.

A Royal Air Force Photographic Interpretation Unit had opened at Wembley in 1939 but of it the GOC Home Forces, General Sir Alan Brooke observed in August 1940: 'The RAF interpreters are not trained in Army requirements nor in the recognition of objects of military importance and the need for an adequate skilled Army Interpretation Unit at Wembley has become apparent. I consider an Army Section should now be formed'.

In the next month an Army Photographic Interpretation Section (APIS) of 22 officers was accordingly formed for Wembley. The first Corps officer to join was Lieutenant N L Falcon, in civil life a geologist; another early member from the infantry was Lieutenant E Espenhahn who later transferred to the Corps.

At the end of the year, the RAF PIU became tri-service as the Central Interpretation Unit, CIU, and moved early in 1941 to Medmenham.[34] The Intelligence Corps representation increased with the arrivals of Lieutenants M Blundell, N C A Simon, J Booth and J Upcher and then Major R Rowell, Captains W G Duncalf and P W Murray-Thriepland.[35] Lieutenant G Farmer and some NCO interpreters arrived later. As the war progressed, rapid developments in aircraft range and camera technology greatly increased the capabilities of air photography. Specialisation began, an F Section of CIU specialising in railways; individuals also specialised, Lieutenant Farmer developing expertise on minor defences such as wire and minefields and Lieutenant Simon in artillery and harbour defences. Overall, German artillery and anti-aircraft artillery were the special commitments of the Army personnel.

The other main taskings for the Army personnel in 1940–41 were German preparations for the invasion of Britain ('barge counting'), German airfields and German defences on the French Channel coast, initially in preparation for our Commando raids.[36] In March 1942, R Section was formed to provide the air photographic support for Combined Operations Headquarters, the first commitment being that of the construction of a model, from air photographs, of St Nazaire in preparation for the raid. R Section contributed to the planning of the other raids into France—Dieppe, Bruneval, Le Touquet and Boulogne. Of this work Captain Simons recalls:

> In the course of building up these records, both George Farmer and I had observed an emplacement being constructed in the clifftop grounds of an attractive villa at Bruneval. Although I first recorded it as an artillery emplacement, this interpretation was later discarded, and the alternative of a machine gun emplacement became equally unlikely on further observation. The matter was resolved by a now famous low oblique print which enabled Squadron Leader Claud Wavell at Medmenham and Dr R V Jones at the Air Ministry to identify it as radar (or RDF as it was then called). The resulting commando raid to capture the equipment afforded the first opportunity for direct co-operation between a small team from APIS and the combat troops involved.

Another specialist task was a study of the anti-aircraft defences of the Mohne Dam made by Captain Espenhahn in preparation for the RAF attack, and the selection of landing strips for the landing of light aircraft carrying SOE personnel or others on similar secret missions. Great expertise in the recognition of German bomb decoy sites—some of them vast to represent factories or whole cities—and camouflage was built up.

More important for the future was the search, begun as early as April 1943, for evidence of German V weapons, flying bombs or rockets; other Intelligence linked the development of this weaponry with Peenemunde, in northern Germany, and numerous works in the Pas de Calais.[37] For this search, a special section was formed under Captain Simon, assisted by Captain Espenhahn, then in a section dealing with Germany. Good weather in November permitted a full photographic coverage, and a detailed report was prepared by a special mixed Army and RAF section, named *Bodyline*, commanded by Captain Simon.[38] The report was laid before Sir Stafford Cripps, who had been tasked by Churchill to assess the likelihood of secret weapons and who was assisted by the DMI and Mr Duncan Sandys as assessors. All were agreed on the nature of the threat. By the end of the year, 120 V1 flying bomb launching sites had been pinpointed and were being bombed by the RAF.[39] In early 1944 the *Bodyline* team, now headed by Major R Rowell, discovered the second, better concealed, generation of launching sites. Lieutenant G MacBride recalls that these were usually sited at the edges of woods, the ramp under cover but the bomb flying out into open country. They were difficult to spot unless, as frequently happened, one misfired, leaving a large shallow crater as a useful clue.

Even more important was the additional PI work provided by CIU to supplement the Theatre Intelligence Staff APIS personnel preparing for the Normandy landings. A team of 30 Intelligence Corps PIs, headed by Major Falcon and Captain Simon, were deployed. This work was developed after the landing, a new section being formed for it. Some of its tasks included the location of artificial fords or other forms of underwater bridge being used by the Germans for withdrawal when bridges had been destroyed. Lieutenants Mottram and Tenton sought out German stores and dumps and examined the effect of bomb damage on accommodation areas. Medmenham was also tasked for the PI work prior to the Arnhem landings; these clearly indicated the hazardous nature of the enterprise, and Arnhem remains a classic case of the consequences of a commander ignoring Intelligence advice.[40]

The final major commitment of CIU was the continuing search for V weapon installations, now focussing on the V2 rockets. On this search Lieutenant MacBride comments:

> Most of the reports from agents in continental Europe which came our way and indicated that the debut of a new V-weapon was imminent, spoke of launching ramps or tubes, sometimes on the surface, sometimes buried deep beneath thick concrete carapaces. The unexplained site near Calais (Marquise-Mimoyeques) did of course have this last feature and this lent substance to the reports. In fact the Calais site, which I later examined, was quite irrelevant to V-2; known to the Germans as the *Hochdruckpumpe* [High pressure pump] or *Tausendfusil* [Thousand guns] it was designed to shower London with artillery shells on a continuous, night and day basis, every few minutes, for months on end. So we were going mad looking at photographs from all over Europe for non-existent launching tubes or ramps. No-one on our side could, at this stage conceive of a rocket which could stand upright on its tail-fins and slowly rise up without aid from any launching structure.[41]

Captain Espenhahn headed a small team co-ordinating reports from all sources in London, keeping the War Cabinet informed. Certain selected prisoners were closely questioned and a few more clues picked up. Information from Resistance groups in Occupied Europe added some detail, though this was often confusing. Bletchley Park intercepted signals warning German missions abroad to prepare a propaganda campaign about new destructive weaponry. As the team's investigations continued, a new factor was discovered. Lieutenant MacBride describes the developments:

> Our attention was being focussed more and more intensively on the new underground factories in the South Harz area (Niedersachswerfen near Nordhausen) which were manufacturing V-1s and V-2s; also Junkers jet engines and a new ground-to-air rocket, *Wasserfall*. We targeted the site for the first RAF raid; this failed to penetrate the 180 odd feet of anhydrite which protected the factory but wrecked the entrances and exits. During the widespread searches which preceded identification of the Niedersachswerfen complex of underground factories both the army team and the aircraft section had spotted an enormous number of underground sites all over continental Europe. Some were of course simply storage depots; but very many of them were factories, (the provision of sewage disposal facilities was a great help in distinguishing the two categories). It was realised that the Germans were putting a great deal of their war industry underground, not merely V-weapon manufacture, but optics, electronics, conventional aircraft, and many other things. The

Germans were even crazy enough to put a small oil refinery underground in Austria. Two thirds of the total energy used in the plant was needed for fans to keep temperature down to 45°C—almost beyond endurance. We found detailed plans for putting a thermal power station underground in the Harz. It was becoming an obsession with them.[42]

Eventually, in October 1944, a special section, B6, headed by MacBride was formed to develop the specialist photo-interpretation expertise needed for this work. The complexity of the work increased as the Germans resorted to deceptions— decoys, dummies and carefully planned camouflage, fighter aircraft would, for example, be dispersed in an artificial housing estate. Expertise in the use of aerial photographs taken at night was also developed.

CIU itself was undergoing changes at this time, becoming Allied, ACIU, with the arrival of a large number of US interpreters. Its total strength reached 700 of which the British Army contingent numbered 61 officers and 33 soldiers all under the command of Lieutenant Colonel Falcon. Eight of the officers and some of the soldiers were ATS. To assist in all these tasks undertaken by the interpreters of the ACIU, a close liaison was also maintained between Medmenham and the various Combined Services Detailed Interrogation Centres. Any information or clues obtained from prisoners of war would be followed up by aerial reconnaissance to verify, or negate, any items of value.

The Special Operations Executive

The last, and most adventurous if not the richest, source of Strategic Intelligence was the Special Operations Executive (SOE) in which a number of Intelligence Corps officers and NCOs served. In addition to these, the Corps also provided a facility which allowed SOE, who needed their recruits for administrative and operational reasons to have Army Commissions, to have personnel commissioned into the Corps. The exploits that follow therefore belong jointly to the histories of SOE and the Corps. A full record cannot be given as material is not available and certain award citations have not been made public, but the number of gallantry awards made to personnel badged to the Corps serving with SOE is a measure of the Corps's contribution.[43] SOE was formed—from the previous DMI research cell and a special section, Section D, of the SIS, specialising in irregular warfare and clandestine action, in July 1940. Its task was described in dramatic terms by Prime Minister Churchill as that of 'setting Europe ablaze'. More prosaically, SOE was basically concerned with organising supply for and co-ordination of resistance movements in readiness for their uprising at the time of an Allied invasion, although many disruptive operations were also undertaken whenever the risk of reprisals seemed acceptable. The challenge to occupying German forces were to be mounted by local resistance groups armed and supplied either by British air drops or by submarine or caique. Leaders of these groups were to be trained first in Britain before return to their own country by submarine, parachute or under cover of a coastal forces raid. In some cases British liaison officers, sabotage experts and signallers were also landed. A number of the liaison officers were Intelligence Corps, selected for linguistic abilities. Controlled from headquarters in Baker Street, SOE later established a local headquarters in Cairo and in 1942 one in India as well.

This work can only concern itself with the roles of the individual members of the Corps serving with SOE. Lieutenant Colonel M J Buckmaster was in charge of SOE's Section F operations in France and the Low Countries. Under him from December 1941 to February 1943 Major (later Lieutenant Colonel) C C Blizard was in charge of the Dutch section.[44] Also in Section F was Lieutenant Colonel P M Churchill, who co-ordinated SOE operations in the South of France, landing four times either by submarine or parachute drop. His chief commitments were the organisation of escape lines for Allied personnel seeking to escape from France, and the co-ordination of various espionage and sabotage operations. He was tasked to ascertain the best method of introducing agents into France. He personally tried a variety, motor boat to Brittany, felucca from Gibraltar, on foot across the Pyrenees and landing on a secret airstrip.[45] After various adventures, including romance, he was captured in April 1943 by occupation forces, suffering severely in a number of camps. Another notable Corps member of Section F working in a different style was Major (later Professor) H Rée, who operated under the alias of Henri Rechman, a travelling watchmaker. Rée's main success was the application of carrot and goad—'You bring your factory to a halt or the RAF will destroy it' to the management of a Peugeot factory near Montbeliard, manufacturing tank turrets for the Germans. Roger Peugeot demanded proof of Rée's status; this was provided by a personal message chosen by Peugeot and broadcast by the BBC a few days later. Rée and his resistance fighters then made a number of sabotage attacks co-ordinated with the management. The factory produced little for the rest of the occupation.[46] Rée was obliged, a little later and after a fist fight with a border guard, to escape over the Swiss border, seriously wounded. He returned later to continue the work of directing and leading sabotage groups. In the words of the citation of his OBE: 'his prestige and authority was enormous'. Engaged in similar work in occupied Lorraine was Major D M Pearson, who operated under disguise. He was able to persuade the Germans to use him an interpreter with their forced labourers, and in this role visited numerous Luftwaffe bases. Among his achievements, following such visits, were the arranging of an air strike which destroyed a number of new German jet aircraft, and the careful briefing of advancing US Army units on the enemy's defensive arrangements for the city of Nancy.

Other members of the Corps were at work in Occupied France, though not under Section F direction. These included firstly Major W R Probert and Major A Macdonald who were despatched into Southern France from SOE's Algeria headquarters. The general nature of their role was that of training and arming French resistance members together with reporting on suitable dropping zones. As Allied Forces approached the resistance fighting became more open. Major Probert won his DSO leading an attack on the German garrison of Foix, in south-west France, and after some street fighting securing their surrender. A third was Captain G Marchant, a member of one of the Anglo-American French liaison teams parachuted into France to work with resistance groups in support of the Normandy landings, an operation known as *Jedburgh*. He was awarded a well-deserved MC for an eight hour covering operation near Paris which enabled some 200 French ill-trained resistance members to withdraw in face of a very professional German infantry and artillery attack. The services of others can be only briefly touched upon. They included Captain P L LeChene, who survived Gestapo interrogation and two years in Mauthausen concentration camp. Captain E A G Bisset, who had previously served in the Dieppe raid, was parachuted into south-central France in July 1944, but was killed while fighting with the French Resistance harassing Germans; he was posthumously awarded a French Croix de Guerre. Captain J Macalister served as a French agent and was captured and killed in Buchenwald concentration camp, as was Captain D Hubble. Major P Dehn and Captain A W Fielding served in Occupied France in 1944, the latter being arrested but later enabled to escape with the help of another SOE agent. Captain N G Whytlaw, created several Intelligence organisations in Occupied France in the winter of 1943–44, making liaison trips to France in a motor torpedo-boat. On nine of these trips he landed despite heavy enemy defences and patrolling; on one occasion he narrowly avoided capture.

For their services to SOE in France, the DSO was awarded to Colonel Churchill, Major Probert and Major Rée, with the MC to Major Marchant and Captain Whytlaw.

In SOE's Italian operations an organisation known as No 1 Special Force was formed. Its Security section under Major P M Lee worked for a while under a cover title of 300 FSS. The force operated from a base near Bari in southern Italy, aiming to co-ordinate all anti-Fascist partisan activity in German occupied north and central Italy, especially after the fall of the Mussolini régime; the Corps personnel played an important role in the negotiations leading to the Italian armistice.[47] The Force's first tasks carried out in late 1943 were to ascertain which Italian partisan groups were really combative (against the Germans rather than internal political opponents), and to train Italian specialists, such as wireless operators and saboteurs. The first eight months of 1944 tended to reflect the switch in the emphasis away from Italy to France, with only limited scale operations being possible. By the autumn and winter, however, partisan activity had increased with German road and rail movement severely harassed. The pace was increased early in 1945 with large scale 'drops' of former Italian soldiers retrained as partisans.

With them were dropped key British personnel, including several Intelligence Corps members. Among them was Captain J P Amoore, parachuted into Piedmont in Northern Italy with a British mission working with Italian partisans. On the capture of the mission's leader, Amoore became second in command of the mission, rendering exceedingly valuable service in arranging for the parachute supply drops for the partisans, co-ordinating their actions with the advancing Allied forces and Intelligence gathering. Also parachuted into Piedmont in late 1944 was Major A Macdonald, who organised an effective partisan group, but one which attracted increasing German harassment and pursuit. In the course of this, Major Macdonald was captured. By posing as a model prisoner he reduced German watch upon him and succeeded in escaping to Switzerland.

Other members of the Corps operating with No 1 Special Force included Majors A M Baird, J Henderson, G Morton, J P T Linklater, C N Macintosh, Captain J Stott and Warrant Officer L Norris. Major Morton was parachuted into the Aosta area in early April 1945, tasked with co-ordinating Italian partisan action to support a final Allied land offensive. This he conducted successfully, the German garrison of Aosta surrendering and Fascist Italian Engineers subverted to the extent that they neither blocked roads nor destroyed industrial plant. Major Macintosh played a key role in the final capture of Florence.[48] At a time when British and Indian leading elements were facing a massive Axis counter-attack Macintosh and Norris crossed the Arno and contacted the Italian partisan leaders in the city. These had placed their own agents in the German SS Commander's office in the Palazzo Vecchio. Major Macintoch was able to pass back, by concealed line, details of the German defence arrangements, including passwords, and arrange for the partisans to guide the advancing Indian Army brigade into the city. Norris was, unfortunately, wounded by a sniper. Major Henderson was awarded an MC for his work in directing sabotage and guerrilla activities in the Ancona area of Italy. The services of the others can no longer be traced.

Working upon Intelligence supplied by SOE and 15 Army Group was a parallel programme entitled *Italia Combatte* which broadcast to Italian partisans in North Italy. This was run by Major I Greenlees, with two other Corps officers, Major C I Isolani and Captain J Vernon, among the staff. A partisan order of battle was kept and daily instructions, some in code, sent out. Partisan leaders were also brought in for discussions. Major Greenlees had earlier been commissioned to drive along into Bari to take over the radio station at a time when the city was still patrolled by the Germans.

Of great importance to the work of SOE in Italy was the Security side. On arrival in Italy, Lee made over routine station and personnel Security to Major A Baird with most of the FSS members, now including two Maltese NCOs of the Corps. He himself ran an operational Security system questioning returning agents and looking out for penetration and double agents, so arranging Intelligence that if an agent were arrested by the enemy, all who had been in contact with him in his work would be notified within 48 hours. He also devised means of recognising reports from agents arrested and operating under duress. His small staff gained formidable expertise in recognising Fascists and determining who were likely to be reliable agents.[49]

After the capture of Rome and the move of the headquarters of No 1 Special Force, an additional Field Security Section, 301 FSS, was provided. Not the least of No 1 Special Force's achievements was first training and then developing a partnership with American Special Forces at work in the same field.

Of the SOE contribution to the Italian campaign the SOE commander later wrote 'Without the partisan victories there could not have been an Allied victory in Italy so fast, so complete and with such light casualties'.[50] Awards to Intelligence Corps personnel serving with SOE in Italy included the DSO to Majors Macintosh and Morton, the MC to Major Henderson and Captain Amoore, and the MM to Warrant Officer Norris.

To work in Hungary, Captain J G Coates was dropped by parachute, but was almost immediately arrested, to suffer torture from his Hungarian and German captors and interrogations from his Soviet liberators. He kept the secret of his mission secure despite the torture, and organised the escape firstly of two other British officers and then himself, passing through the front to the Soviet lines amid great danger. He was later awarded the DSO. Major R Truszkowski, (later Truscoe), who had previous served as a liaison officer with Polish forces, worked in various SOE offices concerned with Poland in London, Moscow, the Middle East and Italy.

In the variety of complex tasks in Greece the SOE's Intelligence members included an Oxford scholar, Colonel the Hon. C M Woodhouse, and Major N G L Hammond, a Cambridge classics tutor.[51] In late 1942, Woodhouse was appointed second-in-command of a party ordered to contact a Greek Resistance Group and to destroy an important mountain railway bridge used by trains carrying supplies destined for the Afrika Korps to small Greek ports. Tall and fair, he had, wherever possible, to conceal his hair while in Greece. The task was executed in conditions of extreme cold; local difficulties unfortunately delayed its execution until after the battle of Alamein, which it was designed to assist. The mission was then ordered to remain in Greece for what was in effect a new role. Two Greek Resistance Groups, one of moderate Republicans (EDES) and one of Communists (ELAS) had co-operated in the destruction of the bridge, thereafter their relations became strained, ELAS units beginning to attack those of EDES early in 1943. The complexities of the situation were replicated on the one hand by other local resistance groups, and on the other by friction between the long term political aims of the Foreign Office and the military aims of SOE. Throughout 1943, Woodhouse's linguistic and intellectual abilities played a vital role in limiting the strife and securing brief spells of co-operation. His missions most successful sabotage of German transport was the destruction of a big railway viaduct in June 1943. This and the work of the Greek groups was valuable not only in itself but also in fostering German concern about an Allied invasion, with consequential reinforcement of their garrisons[52]. At the personal level Woodhouse had to face constant danger and strain, at the political level the growing strength of ELAS.[53]

As military prospects increased—a secret airstrip was actually built in Thessaly—Woodhouse, by the end of the year in charge of the mission, found the ELAS challenge ever stronger. Their strength was fortified by Italian weaponry acquired after the Italian armistice and being used increasingly against EDES and other non-Communist groups. At times officers of the Allied mission were treated by the Communists more as hostages than military leaders and advisers. The work of the mission had become so politicised that Hammond explained his preference for living in a different village to the one occupied by the forces to whom he was attached by saying that it was 'well worth three hours march not to be continually on the doorstep of political intrigues'.[54]

In 1944, the Germans began to withdraw from Greece. The mission directed ambush and sabotage harrassment of the withdrawal, but by now the Greek population, starved, war weary and with villages burnt by the Germans, were chiefly concerned that they should go. A non-communist government was set up in liberated Athens, but this was met, in December 1944 by a large-scale Communist uprising which needed British forces to suppress. In post-war assessments of the work of his mission, Woodhouse considered that its military successes were overall disappointing, but that if there had been no Allied mission in Greece from 1942 onwards, the Communists would have taken an unchallengeable control of Greece when the Germans withdrew.[55] And not the least of Woodhouse's achievements, to be of especial importance in 1944–45, was his work in convincing American officers on the spot of the realities of the Greek scene; these were very different from fashionable thinking of the time in Washington.

Hammond's equally adventurous work was mainly in Thessaly.[56] He found the ELAS guerilla movement passing under such firm Communist control and propaganda that he eventually asked to be withdrawn. Other Intelligence Corps officers to be dropped into Occupied Greece included Majors A W G Winlaw, A Andrews, I S Nevill, P R Musson, L F Sheppard and Captain G J Tsoucas. The operations were rigorous not only from the military and political conditions but also those of climate, terrain and disease, in particular malaria.[57]

Woodhouse had earlier served in the 1941 Crete campaign and had been returned there by caique for five months at the end of

1941 to assist in the extrication, under German and Italian noses, of British and Commonwealth Servicemen still in hiding or in the hills. In occupied Crete were also at various times Major T J Dunbabin, an Australian-born Oxford archaeologist, Major P Leigh–Fermor, Captain R G Turrall, Captain R H Stockbridge, Captains I Scott-Kilvert and A W (Xan) Fielding and Lieutenant S Verney.[68] Dunbabin was SOE's senior officer in Crete, spending some two years there, generally disguised in a long black shepherd's cloak and hood. His duties were concerned with the organisation of resistance groups and the collection of military and air Intelligence. Leigh Fermor, who combined the talents of a writer, scholar and adventurer, was generally engaged in similar work while also disguised as a shepherd. He achieved a special distinction by leading a party which kidnapped the German garrison commander, General Kreipe. Kreipe was seized in his car and pinned down. Leigh Fermor placed Kreipe's cap on his own head, and masquerading as the general, negotiated the car's way for over 100 miles and through a number of German control posts, down to a beach and a waiting submarine. Fielding also signalled Axis aircraft movements at Maleme airfield so enabling the RAF to intercept aircraft taking supplies to north Africa. He built up an effective local guerilla network, negotiating a working arrangement between the Communist and anti-Communist Groups. Verney was despatched to Crete to try to work for a mutiny in the German forces. Based in Khania he made contacts with Poles and Austrians serving in the Wehrmacht but his chief success was in persuading a whole battalion of Italians to desert into the mountains and arranging their subsequent removal by British warship.[59] Finally, concerned with the planning of Greek operations from Cairo was Captain F Noel-Baker.

In connection with operations in Greece and Crete Colonel Woodhouse and Majors Dunbabin, Hammond and Fielding were awarded the DSO and Captain Stockbridge an MC.

In Italian-occupied Albania, the Corps was most notably represented by Major P N Kemp, who in 1942 and 1943 had participated in several small-scale cross-Channel commando raids. Kemp was sent on liaison with the Albanian partisans for seven months in 1943. He was twice surrounded by the occupying Axis forces, once shooting his way out and once escaping disguised as a woman. Kemp even spent four days in Tirana in plain clothes, bluffing German patrols. He was awarded the DSO for his actions. Another Corps officer, Major S P M Leake, was killed in Albania during a German air attack on a partisan camp.

Kemp went on to participate in an SOE mission in German

occupied Poland, a mission which could not achieve its objectives due to a breakdown in communications. The British personnel, including Kemp and Major P Solly-Flood, linked up with the advancing Soviet Army, only to be placed under arrest by the Soviets. From Cairo, Major P Howarth directed SOE operations, involving Polish agents in Eastern Europe. In the course of this work, Major Howarth discovered a half-formed plot among certain Polish officers to assassinate General Sikorski, the head of the Polish government in London.[60]

British military personnel had been attempting to assist effective resistance in Yugoslavia from 1941 onwards. Initially, resistance had seemed most effective under the Royalist General Mihailovic. It soon became clear however that Mihailovic was husbanding his forces with an eye to the post-war scene, and the communist partisans led by Tito were very much more effective. In 1942–43, when it seemed that Mihailovic's followers were active, British missions parachuted into Yugoslavia to assist him included Major Solley-Flood and Captain J Stott. But, as in Greece, members of these missions soon found themselves caught in the cross fire, sometimes literally, and British military support was transferred to Tito's partisans.

Among those sent to assist the latter were Major S V McNeff and Captain J A F Ennals. The latter was sent by motor launch to the islands off the Yugoslav coast in late 1943, first to establish contacts with the partisans—achieved only after they were finally convinced that he was not a German in disguise—and then to locate a small Axis cruiser. This ship, the *Niobe*, was found, Brindisi alerted and the cruiser sunk. In 1944, Ennals was parachuted into North-East Yugoslavia to work with the Xth Corps of Tito's partisan Liberation Army.[61]

Other Intelligence Corps officers served with SOE in the Western Mediterranean area based on Gibraltar; these included Majors Musson, and Kemp and Captain Macintosh. Their duties included assistance to personnel escaping from occupied Europe, the gathering of Intelligence concerning Axis plans and projects in the Maghreb, and certain special preparations for the Allied landings in North Africa.

Not all personnel working with SOE were officers. Lance Corporal G Cini was awarded a DCM for bravery as a wireless operator working under very dangerous conditions in two missions in enemy occupied territory.

In addition to the operational work of SOE, Intelligence Corps personnel were tasked with a Security role at the various SOE Special Training Schools, over 20 at their greatest extent. Their training role, with the agents, with whom they participated in all training was to develop the agents' senses of Security; this involved observing drinking habits, their handling of money, behaviour with women (extending to practical testing), or any other facet of personal behaviour that might give an agent away.[62] In addition the FSS NCOs had usual Security responsibilities in areas such as premises and staff—one infantry captain, for example, was found to be passing copies of the SOE War Diary to the Soviet Embassy, for which he was court-martialled.[63] For this work special linguistic, character and temperament qualities were required and the Corps personnel were carefully selected.[64] An SOE document later commented:

> The importance attached to the judicious selection of agents was at all times self-evident. Mistakes were inevitable, but anything which reduced the margin of error was an important contribution to the ultimate success of SOE in the field. The reports of FSP on trainees were of great assistance from this point of view and this represents the most important service rendered to SOE by FSP.

Initially three FSS Sections, 63, 64 and 65 were engaged in this work, being joined later by 2 and 84, in total 77 NCOs at maximum strength, in Britain. In addition 12 NCOs were despatched to SOE headquarters in North Africa with 7 more in Cairo; in Algeria, the NCOs were concerned with possible contacts that might be made by Axis submarine raiding parties. One member of 84 Section was posted to the Dieppe Raid force. By 1944, Nos 64 and 65 had been re-deployed in preparation for the Normandy landings, and 84 FSS had taken over all other personnel in Britain. The Corps' contribution to SOE work in the Pacific War is considered later.

Intelligence Corps personnel also made important contributions to the training of future resistance leaders for work under SOE direction. Major S H C Woolrych, returning to Intelligence work, was chief instructor at the SOE training school at Beaulieu, eventually becoming a Lieutenant Colonel and Commandant. Other Intelligence Corps instructors and administrators included Majors P Follis, J Lonsdale, P E Dehn, N Mott and E Hardy Amies, with also Captain R Angelo. Another officer who offered very distinctive expertise was Major (later Colonel) B Blount, who provided specialist knowledge in the organic chemical and biological fields, in particular poisoning and corpse disposal. He also advised on parachute jumping into water, an experience uncommon at the time. His expertise was needed in the Middle

East and in 1943 he was dropped into Greece for two months training and liaison work.[65]

Another Intelligence Corps expert was Sergeant A M Baird whose field was that of 'railway sabotage without explosives'. As noted earlier, Baird was later commissioned and served with SOE in North Africa and Italy. SOE operations and training, it is a pleasure to record, was also the first of many occasions when Intelligence Corps personnel have been greatly assisted by members of the Women's First Aid Nursing Yeomanry, (FANY), numbers of whom possessed special language qualifications useful for SOE's communications. Several FANY members developed the greatest expertise in recognising 'morse hand-writing', the individual personal styles of German signals personnel.

The Political Warfare Executive

Complementary to SOE was another organisation, the Political Warfare Executive (PWE). Its major work, subversive propaganda targeted upon German soldiers and U-Boat sailors, was viewed askance by some as 'below the belt'. The tone of the propaganda was sometimes scabrous, highly spiced accounts of the lives of senior German officers and the behaviour of wives and girl friends of absent servicemen. Many of PWE's leaflets and broadcasts were fashioned to appear as though they came from inside enemy or enemy held territory.

One Intelligence Corps officers, Major R Dahl, became involved with this work in the Mediterranean theatre where PWE sought to undermine German morale and boost that of the civilian population in Greece and Yugoslavia by broadcasts and carefully slanted political leaflets, the latter dropped, after some arm-twisting, by the RAF.

He was then moved to London for further PWE work of which he wrote:

> It was a fascinating but often frustrating organisation to work for. Civilians strongly outnumbered Service personnel. The work of the Department, focussing on many European countries, demanded the employment and co-operation of many eminent foreigners—some of them rum characters—but most of them were of distinguished intellect with whom it was a pleasure to work. My work with PID at Bush House, London at first brought me into contact with some who were active there in many small conference gatherings ... like Dilys Powell (then Austrian Section), Heinz

Koeppler a high-powered German propagandist, Richard
Crossman and Hugh Greene, who was then Head of the BBC
German Service. On about six occasions I was called upon to
broadcast from Bush House in German in the *England diese Woche*
programme, from brilliant scripts composed by Professor Lindlay
Frazer. He was a great authority on recent German history. I
remember one broadcast in particular, a talk in which, as a
captured German U-Boat commander I was voicing the opinion
that for Germany the war was virtually over and lost ... 'we've had
it!'.[66]

Also at work in political warfare was Lieutenant T B LeCren,
broadcasting to Germany, and Major I Greenlees broadcasting to
Italy. For a while, in late 1943, these roadcasts were represented
as being made in Italy, while in fact they were sent out from
Woburn Abbey. Occasionally an operational Intelligence staff
officer would also broadcast; in June 1943 Colonel Prater
broadcast from Cairo to Germany and Austria speaking from his
own personal first hand knowledge of the effects of RAF attacks
on German industry and communications, and refuting Goebbels'
propaganda claims of the advantages of shorter internal lines of
communication. The 8th Army Intelligence Staffs under Colonel
Prater drafted propaganda leaflets for dropping over the
German lines in Italy.

In Cairo from 1943 to 1945, Colonel R F StG Lethbridge was
head of GHQ's Psychological Warfare Branch. At least one
Intelligence Corps officer, Major Probert, served for a while with
PWE, being concerned with propaganda in Madagascar. There
were also PWE officers engaged in immediate operational
intelligence work. An example is noted in the next chapter.
Finally, PWE, to be effective, required an immense amount of
Intelligence briefing but in return acquired much useful material,
particularly on Axis personalities, later used in war guilt and
denazification proceedings.

* * *

In December 1945, a conference to consider the future of Army
PI was attended by some of the most experienced officers
concerned with photographic interpretation during the war. The
PI representation was headed by Lieutenant Colonel Falcon. As a
result of experience gained during the war, the conference
considered the qualities required in a good PI: 'It is probable that
qualities count more than qualifications. Of the qualities, visual

memory, speed of decision, patience and attraction to detail head the list. The best interpreters have a research-type of mind and realisation of the significance of events'. The same could be extended to all in every field concerned with Strategic Intelligence.

8

Operational Intelligence: The Corps Contribution

Any boundary between Strategic and Operational Intelligence must be unclear. Inevitably there was considerable interface between the two at theatre level. Signals Intelligence, SOE agents and UK based air photography could, for example, all report on the day to day logistics of Rommel's Afrika Korps or von Rundstedt's armies after the Normandy landing. A second overlap was with Security, personnel whose primary task was Security on our side of the front line could often acquire information about events on the other side. A third common area was the use of the same qualities and skills, questioning, analysing, comparing and the relating together of seemingly unconnected happenings. The differences lay in the use and the speed required to process Intelligence to fight a running campaign day to day, and in the more dangerous field conditions for Intelligence personnel. For the contributors badged to the Intelligence Corps there was a further difference also; the Corps contribution in theatres was not only that of individual specialists but also that of specific Intelligence Corps sub-units, in particular Field Security Sections (FSS). These, despite their title, quite often contributed as much to I(A) Intelligence, as to I(B), Security.

Signals Intelligence

Before entering into a succession of campaigns, some words first about *Ultra* and secondly about Y Signals Intelligence are necessary. In a paper produced after the war, Sir Edgar Williams highlighted certain features of *Ultra* from an operational command perspective.[1] *Ultra*'s information could often engulf other sources, letting a lazy intelligence officer neglect other local and perhaps quicker sources; the German sender was not always himself correct in what he was saying and its use was especially limited in fast moving warfare. In a static or in a planning phase, such as Alam Halfa or the planning of the Normandy landings, *Ultra* possessed immense corroboratory value enabling an officer to select the right information from overt sources. This was to be of special value when used parallel with the reports of agents. The actual handling of the material also presented problems. The material was so rich that it required handling by trained, experienced personnel if it was to be placed correctly in the context of other sources and agencies. It was necessary at Army level, on occasions tactfully to persuade lower formations that Army knew a little more than it could say—not always easy, for example when a Corps was heavily embattled. Verbal appreciation proved the most acceptable method of achieving this, certain items being attributed to a prisoner. The Security of material was a major priority and there were occasions when Intelligence acquired from *Ultra* could not be put to use as the Germans would have deduced that their signals were being read. But ensuring Security (by dire threat if necessary) could lead to a reduced attention to the Security of Y material. And finally, as the war progressed and moved nearer Bletchley, dialogue with the *Ultra* readers proved very valuable—explaining that a half-broken message delivered quickly in a key theatre could be much more useful than a full broken one relayed later. Both *Ultra* and Y work made important contributions to assessing the success or otherwise of deception plans.

To Sir Edgar Williams' specific observations on *Ultra* might be added one more general comment. The end of the war in sight, commands—and Intelligence staffs—became over confident. Sources and agencies provided correct Intelligence but vital clues, such as the *Ultra* intercepts pointing towards some coming big operation just before the Ardennes offensive, were overlooked. (In fairness it should be noted neither of the other two important agencies, the Y Service and air photography had provided any clues at all). On these occasions the skill of entering an opponent commander's mind as he moved towards decision-making was neglected. In this atmosphere danger signals were either not seen and not assessed or, as in the case of Arnhem, if assessed correctly could not be presented effectively to commanders. The two setbacks of the final North West Europe campaign, Arnhem and the Ardennes, were the consequences.

The Corps contribution to operational Y work was constrained at the outset by decisions to send a high percentage of personnel, linguists and non-linguists, in 1939–40 to India—some were even taught German there.[2]

After the fall of France, General Headquarters Home Forces, located at St Paul's School Hammersmith, took on the role of an operational command headquarters in face of the German invasion threat. Matters such as whether the daily pattern of enemy bombing offered clues to further enemy plans, reports of damaged rail and road communications that affected GHQ's ability to move our reserves, and reports (often rumours) of parachutists and objects dropped from the air became the concern of staffs and Intelligence officers, as much as 'barge counting' and the location of Stuka dive-bomber squadrons by *Ultra* or Y Service. These concerns lasted until the end of 1941.

An early overseas example of the interaction between operational Intelligence and Security was that of 522 FSS which was embarked for the unsuccessful September 1940 project of seizing Dakar, in French West Africa. Two members of this section were tasked to seize the French Governor-General. In the event the Force never landed and the section was moved on to Freetown. Here useful Intelligence concerning French naval forces was acquired by two German speaking members of the section who disguised themselves as neutral seamen. The section remained at Freetown for some months at work on local security and the borders with Vichy French territories, and was then moved to Gibraltar.

East Africa

The Italian East African campaign owed much to signals Intelligence. Interception in Britain, in Cairo and in Nairobi provided the field commanders with complete and up-to-date Intelligence on Italian operations, movements and plans; no Italian code or cipher remained secure. For the British and imperial forces, an East African Intelligence Centre was set up. It controlled a small theatre Intelligence Corps of the First World War style comprising some four or five Sections formed in Kenya and eventually totalling 86 officers and 146 soldiers. Forward Intelligence teams conducted interrogations and studied captured documents which yielded Intelligence on minefields and confirmed what was already known of the Italian Order of Battle. The speed of the advance tended to overtake the process. Somalis and Ethiopian irregulars were used—and paid in specially minted Maria Theresa dollars. One Intelligence priority was the location of any Germans in the area.[3] Two FSS, 255 and 269, served with the forces entering Ethiopa from the Sudan, the latter with forward units. Also entering Ethiopa at the same time was *Gideon* Force, one of Captain Orde Wingate's first experiments in deep penetration and disruptive warfare, later to become famous in Burma where Wingate, by now a Major General, conceived and commanded the Chindit operations. Before very strong Italian positions near Debra Marcos, the Force decided to attack rather than fall back on its own supply lines. With *Gideon* Force were at least three Intelligence Corps officers on loan to the Sudan Defence Force. One, despite an age of 47, was Lieutenant R G Turrall who won an MC for cool leadership—with a shell splinter wound in the skull. A second was Lieutenant K F Sheppard who was awarded a DSO for his work in leading and organising Ethiopian guerillas behind the Italian lines. He was able to direct the activities of over 5,000 insurgents with the help of only two British NCOs. After the campaign was over, the various FSS took on security commitments. These included the pursuit or tracking down of Italian soldiers, stay-behind parties and deserters. An unusual but useful contribution to the campaign was the psychological operations work of Major G L Steer, who had been a *Times* correspondent in East Africa before the war. Major Steer produced news sheets which were passed into Italian territory by traders or dropped by aircraft. These served to bolster the morale of Ethiopian partisans and encourage desertions from Italian or Italian colonial forces. Particularly successful were leaflets carrying photographs of the vast concentrations of Italian prisoners taken after Wavell's defeat of Graziani in the Western Desert.

North Africa, Greece and Crete, 1940–41

The North African Desert campaigning began, effectively, with General Wavell's December 1940 offensive. This opened with the recapture of the Sidi Barrani border areas lost to the Italians in September, and swept on to occupy all Cyrenaica (Eastern Libya). At least two FS sections accompanied General O'Connor's Western Desert Force, under Lieutenants R P Peel and A W Sansom, the latter being replaced by Warrant Officer F Whitty.[4] The former, with XIII Corps, was chiefly at work in captured Italian headquarters collecting documents and strength returns, but on one occasion Lieutenant Peel and Sergeant Jacobs, accompanied by only two New Zealand soldiers, persuaded an Italian company in a dug in position to surrender.[5] This section was among the first units into Derna and Benghazi, and later was part of the garrison of Tobruk during the 1941 siege. Lieutenant H E Stewart, an Italian speaking officer attached to 9 Australian Division, was captured in April 1941, and transported to Italy. He escaped from a prison camp hospital, and with the help of false documents made earlier, managed to cross the frontier into Switzerland. He was awarded an MC for his exploits.

A particular feature of Wavell's Desert campaign was the Long Range Desert Group (LRDG) concept—small deep reconnaissance patrols operating on the desert flank of the Western Desert Force, in both reconnaissance and harassment roles. The Corps from time to time contributed personnel to the LRDGs. A number of the patrols from August 1940 onwards were led by Captain (later Lieutenant Colonel) P A Clayton, one of the four original officers who founded the LRDG.[6] Among other tasks was the harassment of the Italian garrison at Kufra oasis, and the setting up of a 7000 gallon petrol supply cache in the middle of the Libyan desert. In an even deeper operation into the Fezzan, involving two patrols, the capital of the Fezzan, Murzuk, was occupied and, accompanied by Free French from Chad, Clayton advanced again on Kufra. His patrol was, however, attacked from the air and then by a ground force; in the ensuing action, Clayton was injured and captured. In captivity, Clayton forged documents for escapers and, after the Italian armistice in September 1943, he walked out of his camp to wander, either in groups with other escapees or on his own, around German occupied Italy. A diary records his travels and contacts—some with Allied agents. He was eventually betrayed and recaptured. He was awarded a DSO for his LRDG work. Other awards to LRDG members of the Corps included first an MBE and then an OBE to Captain W B Kennedy Shaw, who was the LRDG's Intelligence Officer from July 1940 to February 1943; Sergeant E S Davies was mentioned in despatches.

Also active in Axis held territory was Captain, later Lieutenant Colonel, J E Haselden whose pre-war civilian employment in Egypt and knowledge of French, Italian and Arabic gave him immense local expertise of great Intelligence value. His first major exploit was in October 1941 when he led a party of Arabs in an important ten-day intelligence gathering reconnaissance. The party was landed by boat from a submarine, though Haselden swam ashore first to see that the coast was clear. In the next month Haselden conducted a 100 mile deep 10-day reconnaissance in enemy territory, after having been dropped off, dressed in Arab clothing over his battledress, by the LRDG. The reconnaissance assisted the subsequent raid on Rommel's headquarters at Sidi Rafa; on his return, Haselden disrupted important Axis communications. For the first of these exploits, Haselden was awarded an MC, with a bar for the second. He was, unfortunately a casualty on his next mission, leading the land group of the commando raid on Tobruk in September 1942. The commando comprised 80 soldiers masquerading as prisoners of war, with sub-machine-guns concealed under greatcoats. They approached in this disguise from the desert in three vehicles driven by Palestinian Jews in German uniforms; these transported them to the outskirts of the town where disguise was dropped. The group, joined by men landed from the sea, destroyed the wireless station and certain fort guns, but, by mischance, they were identified by the Germans before they could attack their main target, supply ships. Almost all were killed or captured, including Haselden.[7]

A component of the success of both campaigns against the Italians which was to increase greatly in importance, was Signals Intelligence, expanding from the pre-war experience. An 'Intelligence School' was opened at Heliopolis; this covered the East African campaign obtaining valuable results from Italian traffic.[8] In Cyrenaica, one mobile Y detachment reading Italian W/T links operated with the Western Desert Force under the direction of the General Staff Signals Intelligence and, ultimately MI 8. But at this early stage in the desert war commanders still viewed the, unfortunately intermittent, signals Intelligence with reservation, and full benefit was not always drawn from the material available which, in any case, tended to be more informative on order of battle than deployments and locations.

Trained photo-interpreters were not available from the Middle East in 1940 and there was an acute shortage of Italian speakers for prisoner interrogation. The task was immense, some 130,000 prisoners but with information liable to date. The need led to the recruitment of over 70 Italian-speaking Maltese into the Corps, a large number of whom were commissioned. The majority of these were Maltese inhabitants, some 10 appear from their names to have been British resident in the islands. They were mostly civil servants, teachers, clerks and police officials. Many continued to serve the Intelligence Corps in theatres far from their homes, and it is a pleasure to record the gratitude of the Corps to them.[9]

The success of Wavell's campaign could not be followed up on account of the Axis threat to the Balkans and the need to deploy troops in Greece. Three weeks after the Italian invasion of Albania, in October 1940, a British Military Mission, including an FSS under Captain G Household, arrived in Athens. When

British and Commonwealth troops arrived, four FSS were included.[10] As in France in 1940, the speed of the German advance precluded almost all battlefield Intelligence work other than the depressing tasks of reconnoitring withdrawal routes and securing airfields. No air photo-interpreters were available, a very serious weakness. Of wider use, as a continuous contribution to the actual tactical situation on the ground, were *Ultra* intercept decrypts sent out from Britain, and Y Signals Intelligence, No 101 Special Wireless Section being at work in Greece in March 1941.[11] It was able to read traffic from German reconnaissance aircraft, their reports on Italian naval movements being of special value and contributing to the victory at Matapan. *Ultra* intercepts later warned of the German airborne landing preparations for Crete. The Y service provided a steady stream of information on German troop, naval and merchant shipping movements, the German occupation of off-shore islands and, later, German landings. But these could only be used in part. The Crete operations provide the major example of a Commander-in-Chief ordering a battlefield commander, in this case General Freyberg, not to use *Ultra* Intelligence as use of it might reveal the source. In the evacuation, one FSS section was returned direct to Egypt from Greece, and the other three were withdrawn to Crete, only to undergo the same experience again.[12] Corps personnel participated in the fighting, Lieutenant H M Trethowan, as a liaison officer with the civilian authorities, accompanying General Freyberg in the preparation and briefing of a Maori battalion tasked to recapture Maleme airfield. The FSS always had to be the last to be evacuated, as they were responsible for certain civilians who had to be screened prior to embarkation. Two officers, Lieutenants A Shama and E F Kinsey, were captured and Warrant Officer B Merritt was wounded in these operations.

More successful was the brief campaign in June–July 1941 against the Vichy French régime in Syria and Lebanon which was being used by the Axis powers to sustain anti-British eruptions in Iraq—of which *Ultra* had provided useful advance warning. Preparations, in which Intelligence corps personnel were involved, included the clandestine training of Jewish youths selected by the Jewish Agency to masquerade as Arabs and seize a bridge ahead of the invading Allied forces, the planting of agents in Syria from a secret caique base in Cyprus, and the training of a group of Dodecanese Island Greeks in the application of limpet charges to ships' hulls.[13] Photo-interpretation support was to have been made available, but the small team arrived too late. After the campaign was over, one British FSS and two Australian sections, all under Captain Household, handled the Intelligence aspects of the withdrawal of 25,000 French troops and 7,000 civilians from Beirut to France or French North Africa.

In the meantime, however, the arrival of Rommel's Afrika Korps and the subtraction of British and Commonwealth forces for Greece had led to reverses in Libya. Although signals Intelligence had reported the arrival of the German troops, their resources and the expertise available at the time were not adequate enough to warn of the speed at which the Germans were able to deploy for combat. The Army of the Nile was pushed back to the Egyptian border and Tobruk was invested. General Wavell was replaced by General Auchinleck, who was soon able to benefit from improved Intelligence assets.

For the first time, the Intelligence Corps badge began to be seen on battlefields. A number of Captains were posted to Army, Corps and Division Headquarters as Intelligence staff officers. The first was probably Lieutenant (later Brigadier) D A Prater, serving with XIII Corps from September 1941. In addition to the routine work of piecing together Intelligence from captured prisoners, documents and air photographs, Lieutenant Prater's duties included briefing of units on the 'going' conditions, generally by map overprints indicating passability. With XXX Corps were Captain R Dahl and Lieutenant A (later Sir Anthony) Part. Captain M E Allen served with XII Corps in North Africa and onwards into Sicily and Italy. He describes the routine daily round as being concerned with tactical questioning of prisoners, compilation of lists of unit identifications from German Army field post box numbers, and collection of enemy personnel, weapon and ammunition strengths; more interesting work included participation in the planning for the invasions of Sicily and Italy.[14] Headquarters officers did not however remain deskbound, in a forward reconnaissance in early 1942 Captain Prater was severely wounded. Each Corps and Division, too, could now be given its own FSS.[15]

An Army Air Photographic Interpretation Unit (AAPIU) had opened in Cairo in April 1941 with a limited number of trained personnel among whom were members of the Corps. Detachments from AAPIU were posted to Syria and Iraq, but most important was the Western Desert Section, tasked to locate and plot enemy positions for the autumn 1941 British offensive. Mobility was gained by the development of a mobile PI office to fit in the back of a three ton lorry and air photographs were made available down to battalion level. One Divisional Commander remarked 'You are the eyes of my division'. Perhaps the first

Corps recruit to photo-interpretation in the desert was Lieutenant A MacIntosh.

The Development of the Y Service in North Africa

Another major asset was a developing Y Service. German medium frequency traffic—the reconnaissance elements of armoured forces, or combat units in communication with headquarters or workshops—began to be read together with both German and Italian low grade traffic. Returned from Greece, 101 Section was attached to XIII Corps, with forward detachments experimentally with 7 Armoured Division—an arrangement in the end found too difficult in view of constant movement. Major J M Makower was awarded the MC and Sergeant W T Swain the MM for their interception work under exceedingly difficult conditions in this period.[16] The next step was the formation of a Y Section at Headquarters 8th Army (as the Army of the Nile was now called). This, for the first time in the Middle East, provided for interception at Army level, with Intelligence Corps membership for translation, collation and assessment.

Auchinleck's November 1941 offensive secured a brief success, only to turn to disaster, leading to the loss of all Cyrenaica with Tobruk as well, and the retreat to El Alamein in the summer of 1942. One very full and interesting account of these reverses as seen by a Corps officer exists, written by Captain E H S G Moss serving in an Intelligence staff appointment at the Advanced HQ of 50 Division in the 8th Army.[17] He recorded that at the opening of the Gazala battles, early in June 1942, the enemy strengths and equipments were known well, but the speed of their movements surprised our Army. Useful intelligence for the battle came from prisoners of war and captured documents, but the analysis and briefings had on occasions to be done under shell fire with German tanks visible less than half a mile from the Advanced HQ. A German general, Crüwell, was captured, he revealed nothing but his notebook contained 'several interesting scribblings'. The collapse of the Gazala defensive system (brigade-size boxes supported by armour) on 13–14 June necessitated a withdrawal to the frontier, then to Mersah Matruh and then on to the Alamein position, all over a two weeks period during which time the division was harassed by German armour and aircraft. The Division's G3 Intelligence was wounded and Captain Moss found himself entirely responsible for the Division's Intelligence work. Certain other Corps activities were, however, not successful. The personal bravery of Lieutenant C (later Sir Con) O'Neill 'crawling close to the enemy lines in the Western Desert so as to disseminate propaganda through a loud hailer' was an unsuccessful exercise in psychological operations.[18]

Auchinleck was then replaced as Commander in Chief by General Alexander, with General Montgomery in command of the 8th Army. The latter found himself supported by a well-developed and exceedingly efficient Intelligence system, to which the Intelligence Corps was now beginning to make further operational Intelligence staff contributions, though most Corps personnel were still in specialist roles. The Field Security Sections were now well experienced in their desert battlefield tasks.[19] In the open desert, much work was done on a detachment basis, assisting in the preparation of an Intelligence picture and assessment, route finding, liaison work and identifying and escorting prisoners. But the three main assets were properly developed air photo reconnaissance and interpretation, *Ultra* and Y signals Intelligence.

In the field of photo-interpretation, on-going developments now included 'first phase interpretation' immediately after the landing of aircraft, and the provision of photo-interpreters at divisional headquarters where they prepared maps and overlays showing enemy defences and the terrain. Intelligence was therefore available in time to be of use. Photo-interpretation work was facilitated by cloudless sky and the absence of ground cover, which enabled even small positions such as slit trenches and machine-gun posts to be clearly visible. Two constraints, however, were the fact that only 20-inch lenses were available and that low flying was almost impossible on account of the nature of the terrain; these made the location of enemy armour difficult.

Spectacular progress on the basis of lessons learnt had also been made in the field of Y Signals Intelligence, in particular traffic analysis, with closer observations of enemy signals behaviour, procedures and techniques. Enigma messages were also collected for onward transmission to Bletchley. After experiments, the Y cell at Army Headquarters was established under an Intelligence Corps major with a second officer and clerks in support. All were tasked to produce a Signals Intelligence assessment. A little later the major was restyled GSO2 GSI(S), 8th Army.[20]

The 8th Army's November 1941 offensive and subsequent reverses had had a profound effect on Y work. In spite of inadequate vehicle and equipment resources, GSI(S) Middle East had provided staffs with as much assistance as they could and had built the skeleton of an organisation which, with slight modifications, was later adopted in all theatres. During 1941, also, the cryptanalytic problems became progressively less Italian-oriented, and more expert personnel had to be obtained to deal with German traffic. A wireless Network Reconstruction (WNR) staff was brought out from Britain by No. 2 Special Wireless Group, but it was barely adquate for all the tasks. There were also certain procedural shortcomings in the handling of material at Army level.

The first personnel of No. 2 Special Wireless Group arrived in Egypt from Britain in May 1941 and became increasingly able, after a period of training, to cover German Air Force high level networks. In 1942 the Group's sections, six in all, were complete, each with a largely Intelligence Corps Intelligence Section. But again, all the newcomers needed time-consuming training.[21] There were already a number of fixed DF stations in the Middle East; a mobile Direction Finding unit was needed in the desert. One was duly created for 8th Army's Tactical Headquarters, usually operating in three detachments. Wireless controlled DF was also incorporated in certain sections. An internal Signals Intelligence wireless network serving base, Army and Corps sections, and equipment and personnel for the network was also set up, despite the overstretch upon personnel and resources. Suitable ciphers were devised and approved, and personnel were trained as book-cipher clerks. The latter were drawn from two sources: Intelligence Corps NCOs who had failed to reach the standard required for field work, and less fit Royal Signals personnel.

This favourable situation, of six SWS sections together with a mobile DF section, was suddenly offset by the loss of 105 Section, which was with HQ X Corps, cut off at Mersa Matruh on 29 June 1942. Most of the Signals personnel fell into enemy hands, but the Intelligence Section succeeded in filtering back through and round the enemy position without loss or casualty. On the way it even succeeded in blowing up some enemy ammunition stocks with rifle fire.[22]

Terrain affected both tactics and Y work. The vast, barren area had only one coastal road; this gave one main axis of advance/supply line, with a seaward flank and an exposed desert flank. There were few possible defensive positions, no local resources and few amenities of civilisation. The lack of defensive lines meant that fighting ranged up and down the desert in a series of advances and retreats of hundreds of miles at a time. All units were mobile and tactics were often more akin to naval warfare than land campaigning.

Rommel's communication activities were constrained by

distance and a lack of telephone facilities, which meant that wireless was at all times essential for strategic communications. In battle, it made the only possible tactical link, for single or multiple orders. German Lines of Communication, and the complete dependence of forward troops on rear supply points and workshops, resulted in 'Q' and maintenance networks which produced valuable logistics Intelligence, also indirectly indicating their commander's capabilities and intentions. Both sides were forced to maintain constant mobile reconnaissance forces in front and on their flanks, these had to use wireless to report positions and observations. This type of traffic was the first to be heard, and at all times the most consistently listened to and broken. Further, whenever the need arose for co-ordination of German artillery on a large scale, a wireless network with a simple code was set up, which was of considerable interest to Y.

All added together would produce continuous and most valuable Intelligence on Afrika Korps intentions. The Intelligence was, generally, speedily handled on the command networks.

Some idea of the degree of Y success may be gained from the results obtained before and during the Battle of Gazala (May–June 1942) and the period of retreat that followed. Prior to the battle, both *Ultra* and Y had produced plenty of evidence, notably the location of 21 Panzer Division, and that the enemy was preparing to resume his offensive against Eastern Cyrenaica. Y work was able to maintain a continuous flow of Intelligence once the attack was launched. On three occasions, Rommel's operation orders were intercepted at a relatively low level and read sufficiently early for counter-measures to be taken. In the July battles, when Rommel attempted his first attack on the Alam Halfa positions and Auchinleck attempted to push him back—both operations unsuccessful—Y Intelligence was of incalculable value. Air attacks on our troops were also frequently broken up as a direct result of timely warnings.

Much information was produced on the main groupings, moves and locations of enemy formations and units. For example, 5 Tank Regt Workshops (21 Panzer Division) gave daily repair states, including the arrival of new tanks for inspection; 8 Tank Regiment (15 Panzer Division) gave tank states at intervals, enabling a complete and detailed picture of the tank strengths to be built up. Strength returns of other arms, both of personnel and weapons, were also intercepted, and it must be added that, during the more confused phases of a battle, useful information on the position of our own troops was provided by the German reconnaissance units.

In respect of our troops their own signals as intercepted by Y produced much information concerning whereabouts and activities, often greatly needed. This information, known as the 'J' Service, reached Corps Commanders earlier through Y than through normal signals channels. In this type of warfare, speedy information on our troops was of vital importance and, as a direct result of Y activity, the 'J' Service was set up to fulfil this function in a more methodical way.

All this heavy activity placed a severe strain on officers and NCOs alike, and one of the principal lessons learned during this campaign was the need for a larger GI(S) staff.

In sum, it can perhaps be claimed that the period late 1941 to mid 1942 marked a turning point in the history of operational Intelligence. The old sources, prisoners, desert reconnaissance, even air photographs were now increasingly outclassed in value by signals Intelligence. In North Africa, the developing Y Service now complemented Bletchley Park, whose material began to arrive in the Middle East in quantity in 1941. Indeed, the 8th Army staff came to feel that they had failed if they were not in possession of Intelligence before the *Ultra* material arrived. *Ultra*'s value at theatre level in North Africa lay more in static situations than fast moving ones, or in intercepts concerning tank strengths, fuel supplies, ammunition, movements of commanders and morale. In this way it provided an in-depth corroboration to the front line Y service. However there were exceptions. *Ultra*, for example, indicated to Auchinleck that Rommel was not going to halt his advance at the Egyptian–Libyan border, and then later to Montgomery that Rommel planned a final drive on Alexandria by means of a Southern flank sweep in the late August full moon. Rommel's defeat could therefore be well prepared.[23]

Few accounts exist of Wireless Intelligence Section work survive. What now follows is based upon notes from one participant filled in and corroborated in discussions and correspondence with others.

Reported GHQ ME No 5 Int school ... ... before the arrival of Monty. Stationed at Heliopolis under Col Jacobs, with a set of ex-academics. We spent many weary months working day *and* night on German tactical codes.

'Alex' on a visit to us before Alamein said we were worth a 'division' to him, which made it all seem worth while. Monty merely grunted his acknowledgement saying 'good work, good work'.

The daily work was the decyphering and decoding of messages

brought in regularly by messengers from outposts 'in the blue' with forward units, busily at work day and night intercepting Morse messages from major German units:

> We also took turns to go into the desert areas where our units were stationed and collect these code messages and check the operators. Of course we received messages from major German units of all kinds from Rommel down. The longer the better to enable us, by trial of all kinds of experiments between the codes of letters of alphabet and numbers to break into their different codes, frequently changed.
>
> The codes themselves were often 'double-boxes' first changing letters of the alphabet and sometimes changing those code letters into numbers. The more complicated, the greater the indication of the size and strength of the German units.
>
> So ours were the longer term tactical codes, rather than the short-term codes used between units 'in the field' of all three arms.
>
> We worked in pairs or singly, at long tables plain and bare, to all for 'spread' of different messages in the hope of finding clues between them. Fortunately the Germans were always so methodical [as they found at Bletchley Park] that the messages contained helpful clues.
>
> Often, however, we were reduced to hours of trial and error—like adding up totals of most often recurring letters (that is why we needed longest possible messages from our operators) and trying them out eventually as l, or a, n, r etc. Moving from one box to another, trial and error seemed often a patiently slow grind. But when one got a real 'result' and broke an important code—pandemonium sometimes broke out of the dead silence of the night, with a war-dance of triumph on the tables. May sound childish but often nerves were stretched taut after hours of concentration (with breaks between, of course, when the pressure grew too great).
>
> We were a mixed bag, mostly academics, specialists in German or maths, only a few of us in proper uniform, but all engaged wholeheartedly in the important task. As 1942 wore on, we were able, more and more, to inform HQ of the tactical positions of Afrika Korps tank and armoured corps units and strengths in different areas as well as advance plans for movement of armies, battalions, corps etc, to different strategic positions, planned ahead for certain dates. Also admin, orgn and strengths, especially problems of communication and strength and above all, fuel.
>
> So we were able to supply enemy Order of Battle details badly needed at HQ. Thus we did play a significant part in the planning

of the Alamein operation and the speedier movement of our troops of the 8th Army through the Desert Campaign until the joining up with our 1st and the American Armies. Of course our whole operation had to be maintained under strict secrecy. So we were surrounded by barbed wire and well guarded. The capture of Rommel's own complete signal unit together with its staff and leader in the desert (by an 8th Army forward attack unit), with its signals gear and code books intact also helped speed up Int operations, revealing valuable information on enemy formations and overstretched supplies.[24]

Also important was the breaking, following capture, of the German Enigma keys of their Army to Corps (Chaffinch) and Corps to Division (Phoenix) ciphers.[25] Another vital ingredient of success was the location, by the Y Service, of Rommel's Intelligence Unit at Tel el Eisa, a successful raid by an Australian battalion killed the unit's commander and captured valuable records. These revealed lapses in British Signals security which were put right and more valuable still, the documents exposed one of the main sources of German Intelligence, their interception of the daily situation report sent to Washington by the American Military Attaché in Cairo. These daily reports, very detailed, were being sent in American Black Code, known to the Germans. Later, on two occasions in the pursuit of Rommel across Libya, signals Intelligence laid and monitored the success of deception plans; one such prepared by Captain Prater, now serving at GHQ, centred upon a falsely marked map left in an abandoned vehicle at Alam Halfa, a Second World War use of the 'haversack ruse' so successfully employed by Allenby at Gaza in 1917.

From Alamein onwards, for the first time in the theatre, the Y organisation was therefore a unified whole. Formation HQs were served by their sections, which, in close co-operation with other sections, pooled all results by W/T link, despatch rider or telephone. Copies of captured documents of interest to Sigint were made by GSI(S) at Army and passed on to sections with as little delay as possible. In respect of Alamein itself, the major Intelligence achievement was perhaps identifying the movements of Rommel's best division, 21 Panzer Division, at the height of the battle; this provided a clue to German counter attack plans. Later, vital intelligence included early notification of the German preparations to withdraw, the parlous German tank and fuel states and the redeployment to Tunisia of reinforcements originally destined for Rommel. The main difficulties faced by the Intelligence agencies were—initially—location of minefields and uncertainty over which of several defensive lines prepared by Rommel was to be the main one.

Throughout this period, however, enemy security was being tightened. Although, on the whole, Y kept pace with the new security measures, its work was made very much more complex and difficult, and also more time-consuming. Y Sections had, somehow or other, to keep within intercept range of the withdrawing enemy, who in no way let fall his high standards of wireless security. Pooling of information became ever more important, with continuity of coverage an acute problem. The risk could not be taken of missing important messages when sections went off the air for moves. Certain measures had to be adopted to meet these difficulties. First was the rationalisation of cover, so that all sets in the Army area were used to the greatest advantage. This was not always easy as formation staffs tended to regard sections as their exclusive property. During the move of a section, cover had to be taken over by other sections, and moves of sections had always to be made in two echelons. It was also necessary to maintain double cover of groups heard at low signal strength, together, if necessary, with the piecing together of fragments heard by different sections.

In the later stages, the problem of assisting the 1st Army, together with the co-ordination of the 8th and 1st Armies' operations, led to the establishment of GSI(S) 18 Army Group and the provision of expanded intercept resources in North Africa similar to those serving GHQ, Middle East. But trained staff were few and the shortage was further aggravated by the necessity of providing in the rear a large party to work on the medium-grade material produced by operational links. Later, more trained personnel were sent out from Britain and drawn in from elsewhere—a code research party to break particularly difficult or obscure codes was supplied by 5 Intelligence School.

Initially, the provision of satisfactory vehicles, particularly for use as 'I' offices, had been a serious need. One section had been using tents—an embarrassment in mobile warfare and sand-storms—and later, unadapted 3-ton trucks, which also necessitated the packing and unpacking of all documents during moves. The arrival of locally built 1-ton intercept and 'I' vehicles brought about a great saving in time and increased mobility, in addition to vastly improved work conditions. A mobile Y Section could move forward from Army Headquarters when necessary and in the final stages of the advance to Tripoli, 101 Section and the Mobile Section were employed together, performing a leap frogging act in a series of rapid moves. Extreme mobility and the utmost efficiency in erecting and dismantling were thus attained.

Intelligence Corps officers were now also providing operational Intelligence expertise at Army level. One of the most notable was Major A Crick, or whom Brigadier Williams later wrote 'He later served on my staff in 8 Army in 1942 when his personal contribution to unravelling the secrets of the enemy's defensive layout at El Alamein did most, on the Intelligence side, to enable an economy of effort and casualties which was most remarkable'. Wider recognition by formation commanders of the importance of Intelligence was evident from the inclusion of the Intelligence Staff's box-body vehicle as one of four in a formation Commander's immediate command complex—the others being Operations, Air Support and the Commander's personal vehicle. The Intelligence staff of XXX Corps comprised a GSO2, two GSO3s and one or two (each) German and Italian speaking Intelligence Officers depending on availability. Later, as more officers became available, a Corps headquarters might have up to six more Intelligence Officers, each tasked with specific subjects. A Division headquarters would have a staff of a GSO3 and one Intelligence officer together with two NCOs. Intelligence was passed by field telephone, in Intelligence Summaries (ISUMS) sent out in high grade cypher and full Intelligence Summaries (INTSUMS) distributed in written form by courier. The two latter were generally produced daily by Army, Corps and Divisional headquarters. The Intelligence Corps officers engaged in Intelligence staff work at this time included Captains T A Dick, J O'Brien, J W M Willett, W M Nolan, M Marriott and, as we have already seen, D A Prater.

Another Corps commitment was security in rear areas, which at times interfaced with operational intelligence. At work forward from Alexandria, 271 FSS was concerned with stay-behind German and Italian personnel in areas occupied by the 8th Army. On occasions these personnel would even be disguised as priests. The stay-behind parties were principally tasked to gain Intelligence, but they would also engage in sabotage, often by igniting hay bales. Newly-occupied towns had to be searched for hiding places in roof tops or elsewhere, and personalities, noted on the Good (White) List or Bad (Black) List, found. At times of withdrawal, the Section was used to spread disinformation by rumour which the arriving Axis units would pick up. Some Intelligence was also acquired from the local population, a system of informers being operated, but it was often found that the local populace, having little interest in the war, was prone to sell information to all comers.

An account of the work of one FSS Section, 278 FSS which arrived immediately prior to the Battle of Alamein, is also typical of the Corps' sub-units. The account notes their operational work, often under fire or air attack in the following weeks and months as including route finding, liaison and courier work, assistance in compiling enemy orders of battle, Security for conferences called by General Montgomery, questioning prisoners at an improvised camp during the actual battle, house searches and the collection of captured documents at Derna (the section being the first unit to enter the town), the building of an improvised prison in Benghazi, the rounding up of suspects at various points in Tripolitania, assistance to the Free French column of General Leclerc de Hauteclocque in the last lap of his epic trans-Saharan march from Chad, further conference Security and prisoner questioning work in Tunisia, and Security for King George VI during his visit to North Africa. At Alamein, 37 FSS earned the thanks of the Commander of 1 Armoured Division following the find by Sergeant A Potter of a minefield map in a burnt-out German tank, greatly assisting the Division's advance. Captain E L Peters, serving with an FSS of 44 Division, was tasked to escort the captured German General von Ravenstein in a destroyer to Alexandria. Von Ravenstein had earlier tried to escape recognition by claiming to be a sergeant, but had been exposed by Captain Prater. The destroyer was sunk while on the way but Peters safely delivered his prisoner. FSS Sections working forward with the 8th Army would operate from Humber Snipe or Canadian Ford pick-up vehicles, and would live in rough dug-outs or hurriedly built sangers in the desert.

Most of the work done by Intelligence Corps personnel in French North Africa following the Allied landings of November 1942 were second stage post-occupation security, and as such are dealt with in the next chapter. One very early arrival, however, contributing to the success of the actual first stage occupation, was a party of 85 FSS which landed with United States assault forces at Cape Malifou, Algeria. After a short exchange of fire, they seized documents and wireless equipment belonging to the German Armistice Commission staff, a success followed three days later by the arrest of two German agents. Also landing over the beaches were other Corps NCOs serving with Y Service Wireless Intelligence Sections.

Throughout the period, the field organisation was backed up by 5 Intelligence School, working on German and Italian codes and ciphers, and 7 Intelligence School, directing all high-grade cover, both at Heliopolis. These, a little later, combined to form the Special Intelligence Company and including increasing numbers of US Army personnel for training. Further back-up was supplied by Special Wireless Sections in Cairo, Malta and Gibraltar monitoring long range Axis army communications and, in the case of Gibraltar also, some Vichy French traffic as well.[26] Intelligence Corps personnel served with all these Sections.

Members of the Corps also continued to contribute to prisoner of war questioning. A Combined Services Detailed Interrogation Centre (CSDIC), Middle East Forces, was set up at Maadi, near Cairo, tasked primarily to secure detail against which other Intelligence could be assessed. From 1941, CSDIC officers were sent forward, on occasions to help with tactical questioning and from 1942 there were, in addition, mobile CSDICs of some 11 officers and 160 soldiers (including guards) for each Army headquarters, the equipment included microphones designed for use in tents. A number of the officers were Intelligence Corps, they were mostly German speakers but also some Italian linguists. Their work could be exciting; Major F. Cornish recalls interrogating from a slit trench a German major in an adjoining slit trench during a dive-bombing raid. Some Corps officer acted as 'stool pigeons'.

The first priority was the identification of units—and sub-units down to Company level. A frequent and invariably successful method when a number of German prisoners were available was to hold a parade, at which an officer would call out 'All members of—a particular battalion already known—step forward'. After this was repeated two or three times for different units, the remaining prisoners volunteered their units with no difficulty. Others, with a little encouragement, would boast about the achievements of particular units and commanders. Lieutenant Colonel H T Shergold, who joined the Cairo CSDIC as a lieutenant (after no training of any sort whatever) and rose eventually to command it after its move to Italy, personally paraded and identified to Company level many thousands of prisoners after the fall of Tunis, the aim being to establish which units had, in whole or in part, escaped back to Europe.

The usual procedure in North Africa was to site interrogators on the supply lines, supply vehicles returning empty being used to bring the prisoners back. One exception was the Wadi Akarit battle, where interrogators were deployed in the 25 pounder artillery lines intercepting prisoners as they came through. In the desert communication was a problem at times. Colonel Shergold recalls that, on one occasion, an interrogation report had to be despatched 100 miles by truck.[27] More detailed interrogation often focussing on technical intelligence could only take place in rear areas, or in Britain. Documents, other than pay books and personal papers and notes, too were generally taken to Corps or rear areas for study. Of special value was a rich collection of German Army order of battle material found in a captured divisional headquarters near Tunis. Knowledge of German signs and abbreviations was essential for captured operations orders. One less complex success was from a group photograph captured in Tunisia in which, in the background, was a Mark VI Tiger tank—the first intimation of this machine's existence. In the Tunisian stage of the campaign, the more static nature of the battle meant that prisoners knew their surroundings and terrain better than they had done in the desert, and were able to describe them better.

Intelligence Corps air photo-interpretation personnel had earlier been contributing to the planning prior to the Anglo–American landings in French North Africa. A special section of CIU was formed under Captain R Rowell for some of the photo-interpretation work, and Intelligence passed to the ISTD, which collected additional material from pre-war family holiday and professional visitors. A planning staff was set up in Norfolk House, St James' Square; among the staff was one of the Corps's first Staff College graduates, Major A Rowan-Robinson, together with Major C T Tinling.

When operations opened, photo-interpreters were attached to formation headquarters in the 8th Army down to Division level and to the joint air forces headquarters, 12 officers and 26 soldiers at Army level and 2 officers and 4 soldiers at Corps or Division. With IX Corps of the 1st Army was Captain A Gilbert who recalls:

> At IX Corps Headquarters one was a staff officer and carried out many normal duty office duties, in addition one was expected to interpret photos with flashlight batteries and our own home-made devices for illumination. The main problem was to put over or sell the idea of photos to the Commander and, once this was achieved one could start really to damage the enemy ... We found a mountain gun on the Djebel Bon Kournin and had it destroyed. After that, if one saw a target on photos one had only to stroll across to the GSO2 Air and twenty minutes later had the pleasure of seeing two squadrons of Mitchell bombers going over to attack.

Another aspect of this close co-operation was air photo interpretation of the poorly mapped or unmapped desert country. This, for example, enabled the 8th Army first to have a clear Intelligence picture of a hurriedly prepared German defence line in the Marsa Brega/El Agheila area, and then in March 1943 to turn the flank of the German Mareth position. In this latter operation, air photography also facilitated heavy air to ground strikes on the retreating Germans. Numerous other examples of such co-operation occurred, and a local version of Medmenham, a joint Anglo–American North African Central Interpretation Unit (NACIU), was established near Algiers. But poor weather and lack of aircraft often imposed limitations on the 1st Army Front.

Ultra's most important contribution to the campaign was the steady provision of information concerning German rein-forcement arrangements for Tunisia, Intelligence not always acted upon in the early stages, and advance warning to the 8th Army of the heavy German attack at Medenine in March 1943. Other tactical Intelligence was also regularly supplied. Y Signals work, however, did not immediately enjoy the same success with the 1st Army as with the 8th Army.[28] Northern Tunisia was hilly, impeding interception. There had been no Special Wireless Group until early 1942 and no Intelligence School for research and retention. However, the difficulty was resolved in May 1943 by the transfer of personnel, in particular Italian speakers, from Heliopolis to Constantine, but by then the campaign was over. The personnel and their formation staff, trained in and brought out from Britain with the 1st Army, lacked the accumulated experience of the 8th Army Intelligence staffs. The Axis forces were also operating in areas where landline was used more than wireless. Only towards the end of February 1943 did Y work begin to re-assert superiority over other sources and agencies. An outstanding Y achievement was that of March 1943 when a Wireless Intelligence Section attached to the American General Patton's headquarters intercepted a German message deferring an attack for half an hour. The 30 minutes was used to deploy tanks hull-down and the attack was repulsed. Other important successes followed, notably one leading to the destruction of German tank attacks near Medjez el Bab one month later.

Tunisia also provides an example of agent handling by Corps officers. Tunisians—often former French colonial *Tirailleurs*—were tasked to move between the lines, ostensibly selling eggs or vegetables but in fact reporting on enemy concentrations and movements. In semi-political work, Major D Macfarlane served on the staff of the Anglo–American Psychological Warfare Branch in charge of combat propaganda. Here the actual execution in respect of the British Army fell to Captain O'Neil, leaflets being distributed among Axis troops by infantry patrols, aircraft drops and artillery—a special shell for the 25 pounder field gun was produced for the purpose. Evidence of a measure of success comes from the weakened resistance of a few units exposed to heavy propaganda 'fire' and the clear fear that the Germans had of propaganda.

In the hard fighting facing the 8th Army on its entry into Tunisia one of the Corps's ablest operational Intelligence officers, Lieutenant Colonel (later Colonel) J O Ewart, played an important part both at GHQ and with the 8th Army. Ewart had graduated with First Class Honours in Classics at Edinburgh University in 1939, and joined the Army in 1940. Of him in a citation for the award of an OBE endorsed by General Montgomery, Major General F de Guingand, Montgomery's Chief of Staff, wrote:

> This officer has on several occasions rendered the 8th Army particularly valuable service. He is an officer of outstanding ability in the Intelligence world ... He was attached to 8th Army for some weeks during the battles of Medenine, Mareth and the Gabes Gap, and I cannot speak too highly of his work.

Also involved in operational Intelligence in the Tunisian campaign was Major Rowan-Robinson who, after a period with the 8th Army Intelligence Staff to gain field experience, returned to his post at IX Corps headquarters where each evening he would brief the Corps Commander, General Horrocks, on the enemy situation. At a lower level, a corporal of 35 FSS accepted the surrender of remnants of the Afrika Korps 21 Panzer Division headed by Colonel Pfeiffer at 1930 on 11 May 1943. Captain A Lyle-Smith was captured by the Germans in February 1943. He escaped twice from imprisonment in Tunisia; later in September 1943 he—in an Italian uniform provided by an anti-Fascist camp guard—participated in a successful mass break-out from a camp in Italy. He was awarded an MC for his exploits.

Sicily, Italy and Greece 1943–45

The second half of 1943 saw the invasion and occupation of Sicily and the start of the Italian campaign. The period opened with a tragedy for the Corps, the loss of the officer commanding 89 (Para) FSS, Captain J Dunbar, when the glider in which he was travelling as part of the airborne assault on Sicily, crashed into the sea. Intelligence Corps officers contributed to the planning of that assault, Captain Prater with XXX Corps and Captain J B da Silva with the 1 Airborne Division. The latter made a personal reconnaissance in an RAF Beaufighter and later landed in Sicily with his Divisional Commander.[29]

A few further examples may be cited, one being the work of 412 FSS under the command of Captain K A F Hornby attached to XIII Corps. The section was among the first units ashore at Reggio on the Italian mainland on 3 September 1943 and remained in close support of forward units right up to the occupation of Trieste. It participated in a number of major operations including the crossing of the Sangro in January 1944 and the forcing of the Gothic Line in the severe winter of 1944–45. 91 FSS and 312 FSS landed at Salerno with the United States 5th Army together with 276 FSS with the British forces; 276 FSS was among the first units to enter Salerno town while the fighting was still intense on the beaches, with few guns and tanks ashore. Questioning refugees, the section learnt of German preparations for an armoured counter attack from the direction of the Cara di Terreni. The information was passed to the Navy, whose guns aborted the German plan.[30] 3 FSS was working with the British 1st Division at the Anzio landing. Among the first units to enter Rome was 314 FSS. 89 (Para) FSS was among the first units to land at Taranto, where they seized the German counsul.

Y Signals Intelligence found the move from North Africa warfare to mainland Europe difficult, and some time was to pass before its primacy as an agency was re-asserted. The main difficulty was the greatly tightened Axis wireless security measures. One consequence of these was that there existed only a few indicators—mainly *Ultra* and air photographs—that suggested that an Axis withdrawal from Sicily was being planned. These were insufficient to carry weight in operations planning and the Axis withdrawal was not as harassed as, undoubtedly, it could have been had Intelligence advice been accepted. Fortune changed however with the exploitation of German Very High Frequency, VHF, transmissions from October 1943 onwards. This new and valuable source of information provided some 60 per cent of Y Intelligence in the campaign, although still most usefully supplemented by Direction Finding and Medium Frequency low and medium grade traffic.

The Y Service was controlled from Allied Forces Headquarters by an Anglo–American staff, with further staffs at the Army Group and two Army headquarters. The Special Wireless Group headquarters was sited at Bitovito from the end of 1943. Intelligence Corps Wireless Intelligence Sections continued to support the Signals units.[31] With the capture of Corsica one Section, No 101, was posted to Cap Corse, but in July 1944 it was moved to Siena. Later it joined No 2 Group at Castelfidardo, near Ancona.

Intelligence gained was chiefly that of groupings, regroupings and intentions. Some enemy formations and units were heard regularly for months, notably 278 Division and the 103 Reconnaissance Battalion of the 1st Parachute Division. At times, Y knew more of the enemy's locations than its own command, in particular in the Cassino battles. Enemy security measures imposed a check in the winter of 1944–45, but ascendancy returned in the early spring. Direction finding in Italy was notably successful, some intercept sections being able to recognise which aerials German signallers were using, a shorter aerial indicating preparations to move. A particularly important contribution was made by the Special Intelligence Company with its specialist research facilities. Towards the end of the campaign, intercepts of instructions to German submarines in the Adriatic from their base at Pola were being made and some telephone conversations behind the German lines were being monitored.

To some extent, Bletchley Park filled gaps by playing an increasing battlefield operational role. As in the North African campaign, *Ultra* messages afforded the Allied generals a very full picture of German strengths and order of battle, reinforcement capabilities and logistic difficulties. In Sicily and Italy, *Ultra* intercepts, now sent direct to all Army Commanders, increasingly provided Intelligence on front line tactical operations and plans. Among the most noteworthy were Hitler's decision in October 1943 to hold a line south of Rome rather than withdraw and, a little later, his next decision, to abandon plans for a large counter-offensive against the Allies; the advance provision of full details of Kesselring's counter-attack on the Anzio bridgehead, which enabled this counterattack to be contained; details of Kesselring's withdrawal plans after the Battle of Cassino, and Hitler's decision to hold lines across north-central Italy, firstly Pisa to Rimini and then later modified, after the fall of Florence, to the 'Gothic Line'.

Before the invasion of Sicily, the 1st Army photo-interpreters had been reorganised. The 1st Army Photo Interpretation Centre (1 APIC), under Captain C J F Ashby, was formed in March 1943 and began an extensive and vitally important study of Sicily and the Italian mainland. A detachment of British photo-interpreters under Major F R Fugelsang and including Lieutenant R M Richards and two or three other Corps officers was sent from

NACIU to the American 5th Army to form an Allied and joint PI unit, 5 APIC. This received most of its aerial photography from the 3rd Reconnaissance Group of the United States Air Force.[32] The Western Desert Section of AAPIU left Tripoli early in July to take up temporary residence in the Phoenicia Hotel, Malta. The island was still an important target for German bombers. During raids on Malta, the photo-interpreters suffered casualties but continued to 'churn out information on Sicily and Italy all the time we could get sorties'.[33] For the Calabrian landings, a model of the beachhead area, 1:1000 metres, was constructed from air photographs for the final briefings—and then destroyed as a security measure. Location of enemy artillery was the major tactical priority. Divisional reports of the time all record the value of the air photographic Intelligence.

The photo-interpreters of the 8th Army crossed to mainland Italy on 16 September 1943, landing at Reggio with their own vehicles with which they had now been issued. The AAPIU drove to Foggia where it occupied the town hall and began to operate. The 5th Army landed at Salerno and the interpreter of both armies were fully employed in keeping the Allied forces informed of the enemy's activities. One description of the general PI organisation in Italy survives:

> The divisional section consisted of two officer PIs, two draughtsmen-clerks and two driver-batmen. Transport consisted of a three-ton office truck and a jeep. At corps headquarters there was a similar section. The 8th Army Headquarters Section consisted of two divisional sections and its purpose was forward planning. The 8th Army Section lived with 285 Wing RAF and carried out interpretation of all photography flown on the army front. The composition of this unit fluctuated from time to time, but basically consisted of a headquarters commanded by a major with an interpretation unit of eight PIs and four draughtsmen-clerks. Transport consisted of a jeep, two PI offices accommodating four PIs each, a map library truck and a headquarters office. In practice, the section was often complemented by the addition of a surplus divisional section, and sometimes robbed to provide reinforcements for divisional sections. One division left its section behind in North Africa during the invasion of Sicily, and there were other divisions which, on arrival in Italy, had no experience in air photography and more or less rejected their PI sections for some time. There was a tendency sometimes in the opposite direction, when the PI was regarded as a miracle worker and expected to find things which did not exist or others which

would never be visible, or worse still, both![34]

In 1944, the photo-interpretation system was again reorganised to provide for a Mediterranean Allied Interpretation Unit (MAIU) West, under Major Ashby at work in Italy, and an MAIU (East) which remained in Egypt; as more personnel became available PIs were posted to Corps and Divisions, including for example Captain A Gilbert to the 1st Free French Division. Captain Gilbert's team built a large model of the Cassino battlefield for the French commander.

Under static conditions and reasonable weather, each divisional front would be covered daily, but the processing was slow and pictures usually arrived the following day, dropped in a sandbag by a Spitfire. Divisional staff would then cross check these with prisoner and patrol reports. If there was numerous new data, marked maps or mosaics would be prepared. After the photographs had been examined, follow-up action might include preparation of going traces for beasts (large numbers of mules were employed in Italy) or tanks, listing of artillery targets or possible observation posts, and the assembling of material for patrol briefing or prisoner questioning. At times of success, special attention was paid to enemy preparations for withdrawal, likely withdrawal routes, and new defence lines.

The Salerno and Anzio landings were preceded by briefings from models and air photographs; over-printed maps based on air photographs were made available to units. Sometimes mosaics would be prepared for a major assault. Divisional photo-interpreters concentrated on the forward areas immediately to their fronts, Army level staff worked on the rear areas. Prisoners and patrols were used to corroborate findings. In the static phases of the campaign photographs of the whole front, scaled to approximately 1:12,000 were taken, to depth of 10,000 yards behind the enemy's forward positions.[35] The Italian vegetation and broken nature of the terrain made photo-interpretation work much more difficult than in Libya.

Intelligence Corps officers at formation headquarters continued to provide operational intelligence expertise as in North Africa. The senior was Major Prater, who became GSO1 Intelligence, 8th Army as a Lieutenant Colonel in January 1944. Among his staff were Majors J W M Willett and A Colquhoun and Captains R Kinghorn and K Gottlieb. The GSO2 Intelligence at V Corps was Major F J Stoop. The work varied somewhat from North Africa in that much useful intelligence was gained from civilians and partisans. These had however to be questioned as they passed through into the Allied area. On one occasion Captain M E Allen identified an Axis agent because he was wearing his Italian hat the wrong way round.[36] Lieutenant E H M Clutterbuck, who had been involved in the planning of both the Sicily and Anzio landings, was 'Mentioned in Dispatches' for his service at Anzio.

Captain Colquhoun, a fluent Italian speaker, operated with particular style. Landing at Salerno, he telephoned a pre-war friend in Naples—at the time still in German hands—and together they commandeered an Italian naval motor boat with which he set off for Sorrento, liberating it with Italian partisans. Later, Captain Colquhoun acquired an Italian Savoia bomber, complete with crew, which he used for work with partisans in Tuscany.

Captain da Silva, serving with the 1st Airborne Division, also participated in the seizure of Taranto of which he wrote '... the Germans could spare only their lightly armed 1st Parchute Division to oppose us in the south. As neither side had sufficient troops to establish a line, we had to resort to mobile tactics ... The SAS, Phantom and Popski's Private Army were sent over from Cairo and put under command'. In the course of these fast moving operations the Divisional Tactical Headquarters came under fire, the GOC being killed. Captain da Silva and another staff officer carried his body away to an ambulance jeep. Other 89 (Para) FSS personnel commandeered a car and drove through territory still enemy-held to snatch the German consul at Bari.

A second CSDIC MEF was established after the Allied landings in North Africa, and quickly became joint Anglo-American. The British component was however detached after the Allied landings in Italy and was used for the interrogation of prisoners in the Italian campaign from a base in Naples.[37] It was the main unit for this purpose, though later the American Army created its own tactical questioning units. The 8th Army CSDIC officers continued to work forward for tactical questioning. In Italy the communication of reports proved much easier, field telephone systems being generally available and, when not forward, interrogators being supplied with a radio.

The scope of work required from the CSDIC expanded. An early tasking was the identification of any prisoners who had served with German units in the coastal areas of North-West Europe, particularly France, as part of the preparations for the Normandy landings. Any thought to have especially useful knowledge were flown to Britain. After the Italian armistice, CSDIC officers were sent forward to Italian formation headquarters. Poles conscripted into the German Army were identified and recruited for the Polish Corps, and dissident Indians who had collaborated with the Germans were questioned. Towards the end of the campaign, a special camp for Austrian prisoners with a knowledge of Austrian administration and law was opened, and British personnel earmarked for the military administration of Austra sent to the camp for study purposes. After the fall of Rome, the interrogation of Axis spies and agents, and their Abwehr or SS case officers became a priority. At the end of the campaign, a camp for captured German generals or their SS equivalents was opened. At one point, it contained 102 officers, and also Himmler's wife and daughter.[38] Among the CSDIC interrogators was Major H A Freeth, the distinguished water-colour painter.

Captain C I Isolani made an especial contribution to the Italian campaigns in a form of agent handling.[39] After preliminary study at Combined Operations headquarters, concentrating upon Axis orders of battle and beach defence in Sicily, Captain Isolani with a group of other officers including Lieutenant G Whitehead, R Pine-Coffin, J P S Amoore and J P Birch were attached to the 1st Canadian Division, landing with the first units ashore both on Sicily and at Reggio di Calabria. Initially, their main duties were reconnaissance and prisoner questioning. After the mainland landings and Italian surrender however, Captain Isolani was approached by an Italian Army Captain, F Gay, who volunteered himself and seven other Italian parachute soldiers of the Folgore Division as ready to fight the Germans. With the support of another Intelligence Corps officer serving with 8th Army Intelligence staff, Captain Sir Ian McLeod, Captain Isolani was permitted to use, develop and expand Captain Gay's nucleus, which eventually became 'F Recce Squadron', carrying their former Folgore insignia on their vehicles. CSDIC officers were also deployed to help and over 120 Italians came to serve with the unit. They were tasked, in twos and threes, to cross into enemy held territory in civilian clothes and were given precise intelligence gathering tasks and crossing points for their return journies. They were of particular use north of the river Sangro where the line became stabilised; they also suffered a number of casualties—those captured by Axis forces being tortured. Their political value was as great as their military contribution, and recognised in a message of appreciation from General Harding at the end of the war.

The work of Intelligence Corps personnel serving with SOE in the Italian theatre has already been recorded. A few other members of the Corps were committed to special duties, one for example was Lieutenant P Wood whose pre-invasion task involved being flown at low level over Sicily to communicate (in Italian) with agents. He was unfortuntaely killed while engaged in this work. Lieutenant E O'Donnell kept the proposed Allied landing beaches under observation—from the Messina light-house across the Sicilian narrows. There was also a small tactical Political Warfare input into the Tunisian, Sicilian and Italian campaigns, referred to as 'combat propaganda'; the work consisted of disseminating news of Allied successes, controlling existing newspapers and where necessary starting new ones. Lieutenant Colonel D Macfarlane was in command of a small unit tasked to secure and operate local media—radio and newspaper and leaflets. Also at work with Political Warfare in Italy were Major (later Lieutenant Colonel) C V A de V. Beauclerk (later the Duke of St Albans) and Captain D J P Weaver. A photograph survives of Captain Beauclerk smoking a pipe while supervising the typesetting for the *Salerno Times* during a heavy enemy bombardment.[40] Other Intelligence Corps officers were posted to the Allied Military Government of Italy; these included Major Sir Philip Magnus and Captain A E Howell.

The casualties suffered by the Intelligence Corps in the mainland Italian campaign totalled 13 killed, including one NCO who died during the great ammunition ship explosion at Bari.

Before moving to the final campaign in North West Europe, the Intelligence Corp's contribution to Balkan operations in 1943–44 merits mention. After the surrender of Italy in September 1943, it seemed feasible to occupy the Dodecanese islands of Cos, Leros and Samos. A force, 234 Brigade Group, including small detachments from 291 FSS under Captain W J B Gibbon and 470 FSS under Captain M P J C Wood, was assembled but heavy German air attacks necessitated withdrawal, in the course of which Captain Wood was killed. Sergeant C A Thwaites was awarded the MM for his conduct in this operation, in particular the destruction of secret documents while under heavy fire and bombardment. He escaped from Cos in a very small boat, using his steel helmet as a paddle.

The other Greek commitment was conceived, over optimistically, as Security; in the event it proved to be operational Intelligence. In October 1944, British troops returned to Greece.[41] Axis forces being in the process of withdrawal, little formal opposition was met. A major military commitment—for which Colonel Woodhouse had provided warning—arose, however, as a consequence of Greek political faction fighting. On

5 December 1944, the Communist faction, EAM at political level and ELAS at the military, increased their level of insurgency activity to that of open revolt; they were enabled to do this with captured Axis mortars and light artillery. A civil war, bitter, bloody but brief, ensued, in the course of which the British troops in Greece, initially about a division in strength and partly British partly Indian Army, had to be reinforced to over two divisions supported by tanks, artillery and RAF air to ground strike aircraft. On the planning staff for the British landing was Lieutenant Colonel A (later Sir Anthony) Rouse, and posted in from SOE to co-ordinate the arrival of British troops was Lieutenant Colonel L F Sheppard. At its worst stage, the British forces were confined to a tight defensive perimeter in the centre of Athens, cut off from the port of Pireaus. Reinforcements arrived, some—including Intelligence Corps NCOs—by parachute, at the turn of 1944-45. These quickly enabled British forces to secure domination over the ELAS by February 1945.

Four FS Sections were involved in Greece from October 1944. These were 290 FSS (Captain W B Rigg) and 268 FSS (Captain R L Innes) at Salonika, 20 FSS (Captain P W Purves) in Western Athens and 24 FSS (Captain J Fritche) in eastern Athens and Piraeus. The latter two made a number of arrests in the period prior to 5 December 1944, mostly Axis agents, Greeks, Italians, others and one German paymaster. Evidence of direct Soviet involvement with the ELAS uprising was discovered by 268 FSS.

As the situation worsened further, Intelligence support was provided by 94 FSS in the Corinth and Peloponnese areas, 5, 31, 89 and 278 FSS used variously, and a No. 1 Mobile Detachment CSDIC at work in the Athens area. This latter unit, some 80 strong, was involved in heavy fighting near Tatoi airfield, a number of its personnel being seized and held, temporarily, by ELAS. Tragically, Colonel Sheppard died after his car had been blown up by a mine in these operations.

After February 1945, the commitment returned to one primarily of Security, the exception being work more of an operational intelligence nature on Greece's northern border, carried out by 268 FSS (Captain Leitch) with detachments at Alexandroupolis, Florina, Kavalla and the Rupel Pass.

Normandy and North West Europe

Planning for an eventual invasion of North West Europe had begun as early as 1942. Members of the Intelligence Corps were involved in this from the start in a number of fields; some of the work overlapped with Intelligence gathering for raids such as that at Dieppe, St Nazaire and elsewhere in France, the Channel Islands and Normandy. Intelligence Corps personnel participated in some of these raids. Major A I Terry was captured during the St Nazaire raid, after having collected valuable intelligence for the Force Commander. Major P N Kemp served in the raid on Casquets when an entire signal station unit was captured, and in a raid on Point de Plouzes in Brittany. Before their move to the Mediterranean the Corps's first parachute sub-unit, 89 (Para) FSS had provided four men under Captain Dunbar for the Bruneval Raid, the British Army's first parachute operation. The object of the raid was to acquire German target tracking radar equipment used for the guidance of aircraft in intercepting RAF bombers.[42]

For the Normandy landings, a planning staff was established initially at Norfolk House, St James's Square. The Intelligence work lay under the direction of Brigadier K Strong, in his capacity as Brigadier GS (Intelligence) Home Forces, with Lieutenant Colonel J L Austin, an Oxford philosophy tutor immediately in command. The initial 1942 British planning staff was developed after the January 1943 Casablanca Conference, an enlarged Anglo–American staff under Lieutenant General Morgan, a British Army general, known as Chief of Staff to the Supreme Allied Commander (COSSAC) being established in April 1943. COSSAC possessed an Intelligence Branch, but this was a servicing agency only. By November 1943, this Intelligence Branch had become the Intelligence Division of Supreme Allied Headquarters, Allied Expeditionary Force (SHAEF), with activities extended to the collection of its own Intelligence. It had moved to the top floor of Peter Robinson's building in Oxford Street, in a large L-shaped hall. The chatter of waitresses working in the restaurant next door could be clearly heard, though curtains were pulled over the maps when people not vetted entered the hall.[43] A final move took the Intelligence staff to Bushey Park.

The preliminary work was divided by subjects—operational Intelligence, topography, enemy coastal defences, enemy forces, enemy civil administration, engineer Intelligence, APIS, and a Special Study Group concerned with plans of towns. Corps officers appeared in most of these subject sections. Prime sources of Intelligence were air photography, military documents captured in Italy, plans of fortifications stolen by conscripted labourers and decrypts of signals and reports sent by the Japanese attachés in Berlin. Captain W Stallybrass, for example, was first

PLATE 1. The bridge at Pontoise destroyed by Second Lieutenant Rolleston-West, 31 August 1914. (*Contemporary photograph*)

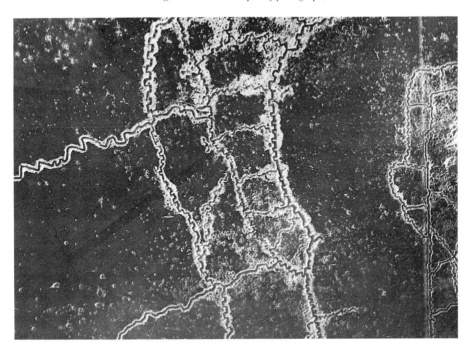

PLATE 2. Air Photographic Interpretation: an air photograph of German trenches at Loos, 1917. (*IWM*)

PLATE 3. Prisoner of War Questioning: BEF Intelligence Corps officers questioning German deserters at 1st Army Headquarters, Ranchicourt, March 1918. (*IWM*)

PLATE 4. Security: A BEF Intelligence Corps Sergeant questioning a civilian in a deserted street during a German bombardment, Bethune, May 1918. (*IWM*)

PLATE 5. Prisoner of War Questioning: Intelligence Corps officers attached to the 42nd East Lancashire Division questioning Turkish prisoners, Third Battle of Krithia, Dardanelles, 1915. (*IWM*)

PLATE 6. Air Photographic Interpretation: An Intelligence Corps Officer at work, Italian front, 1917. (*IWM*)

PLATE 7. The General Staff Officer I, (Intelligence) of the 1939 BEF, Lieutenant Colonel Templer, with Captain Attfield of the IB Staff, France, December 1939. (*IWM*)

PLATE 8. Captain Rowell and Lieutenant MacBride, of the *Bodyline* special photo-interpretation team (German flying bombs) at work, Medmenham, 1943. (*Intelligence Corps*)

PLATE 9. Captain Moss at work as GSO III (Intelligence) 50 Division Headquarters, Western Desert, 1942. (*E H St G Moss*)

PLATE 10. The typing of an Intelligence Summary whilst under bombardment. (*E H St G Moss*)

PLATE 11. Captain Makower and Sergeant Swain in tactical (Y) Signals Interception work, Western Desert, 1942. (*Painting by T Cuneo, Intelligence Corps*)

PLATE 12. Intelligence Corps Field Security Section NCOs questioning local Libyans during exchange of gifts, Western Desert, 1942. (*IWM*)

PLATE 13. An Intelligence Corps officer and NCO questioning the Italian General Mannerini, North Africa, 1942 (IWM)

PLATE 14. Field Security. Captain Bickerton-Edwards questioning the former Fascist mayor of a Sicilian town, 1943. (*IWM*)

PLATE 15. An Intelligence Corps NCO photographing a booby-trapped German machine-gun Normandy, July 1944. (*IWM*)

PLATE 16. HM King George VI inspecting 89 (Airborne) Field Security Section, under the command of Captain Dunbar, Netheravon, April 1943. (*IWM*)

PLATE 17. The surrender of German forces in North-West Europe, Luneburg, May 1945; Colonel Ewart accompanying Field Marshal Montgomery. (*IWM*)

PLATE 18. Major Storry with his Mobile Section, Burma, 1944. (*Mrs D Storry*)

PLATE 19. Japanese Kempetai officials being marched to gaol by Captain Isaac, Singapore, 1945. (*IWM*)

PLATE 20. Lance Corporal Daws, a National Service member of the Corps serving with the Kluang detachment of 355 FSS, Malaya 1945. He is accompanied by Gau Meng, the detachment's interpreter. Kluang was an area considered 'at risk' and personnel of the detachment had the use of armoured cars. (*Intelligence Corps*)

PLATE 21. Staff Sergeant Everson of 1 FSS supervising the search of an Egyptian vessel for hidden arms, Port Said, November 1956. (*Intelligence Corps*)

PLATE 22. An Intelligence Corps NCO conducting a body search after a house raid, Aden, 1966. (*IWM*)

PLATE 23. Staff Sergeant Jackson, Intelligence Corps, attached to the Commando Brigade briefing Royal Marine Special Boat Section personnel, Borneo, 1967. (*Intelligence Corps*)

PLATE 24. Corporal 'Ali' Barber, Dhofar, 1971. (*Intelligence Corps*)

PLATE 25. Lance Corporal Lovett and Sergeant Massey, Intelligence Cell 5 Infantry Brigade, Fitzroy Settlement, Falklands, June 1982. (*Intelligence Corps*)

tasked to produce a handbook on Normandy, then to study the Normany beachhead obstacles and defences, and then finally to produce maps and town plans. Others worked on coast defence guns, orders of battle and railway movements. Among other Corps officers at work were Captains T G S Combe, the Hon (later Sir Kenneth) Younger and Niall MacDermot, the latter specialising in security intelligence for the operation, initially under an American colonel. Captain MacDermot was later moved to 21 Army Group with responsibility, as a Lieutenant Colonel, for the direction of all Field Security work in the combat zone following the landings. Later, after the landings, new special staffs were established for counter-intelligence work when the Allied Armies entered Germany, their main purposes being the liquidation of German Intelligence organisations, censorship in occupied Germany, the targeting for technical Intelligence gathering in Germany, and the acquisition, in Germany, of Intelligence to be used in the war against Japan. Intelligence Corps officers served on these staffs.

Almost as important as the Intelligence gathering work was the careful preparations that had to be made in respect of Security—both in the context of enemy efforts to learn of our plans and for security in rear areas after the landings.

The overall strategic contribution of Bletchley Park has already been outlined. SLUs were established at Supreme Headquarters and 21 Army Group Headquarters in January 1944. Perhaps *Ultra*'s major contribution to the success of the Normandy landings was the monitoring of German acceptance of the Allied deception plan, *Fortitude*—a project involving double cross agents, false signals traffic, handbooks destined not to be used, rumours and decoy movements, all indicating that there would be a major Allied landing in the Pas de Calais. A special staff section for this project working under the direction of the London Controlling Section was established, this included Majors C Harmer and J D Wallace-Hadrill. Perhaps more than the staff realised at the time, the deficiencies of German Intelligence, inter-organisational rivalries, and Hitler's personal beliefs and prejudices, assisted them. Their success was considerable and lasted well into July 1944, a number of German formations and units being located in the Pas de Calais and so not available for the Normandy fighting.[44] Bletchley Park was able to confirm that these formations, in particular the entire 15th Army and other units, were still in place on D Day. This information was of value not only to the deception planners but also the operational staffs who could then assess how long those formations that could be redeployed (and not all could), would actually require for commitment to the battle. *Ultra*'s other main contribution was the provision to Allied Headquarters of a virtually complete German Order of Battle, with in particular, very full information on the location of armoured units and formations and also much detail in respect of German manpower and equipment shortages. The most valuable decrypts were of course those of messages from Berlin and the German field commanders in the west, but Japanese Embassy messages from Berlin and Vichy were also exceedingly useful on several occasions. A late *Ultra* report of German dispositions on the Cotentin Peninsula facilitated a useful change in the plans for American parachute landings. *Ultra*'s relative weakness, however, lay with the coastal garrison divisions who used landlines.[45]

Y work also suffered, until the actual landings and for a while afterwards from the German use of landline and tightened signals security. These latter, however, had a major spin-off benefit for the Allies in that the Germans' experience of the efficiency of Y work in North Africa and Italy left them with such a healthy respect that they frequently felt unable to use wireless communication at all. The organisation in 1944 was built around a number of personnel with experience in the Mediterranean and one unit recalled from that theatre.[46] Sections attached to 21 Army Group were dispersed around Southern England in sites chosen to cover German WT links in coastal France and Belgium. These units had earlier been monitoring German traffic, mostly aircraft, but with the build up of German divisions in France were able to expand their work. In London was No 1 Special Intelligence Company which briefed Y Section personnel and carried out some long term research.[47] 13 out of the 16 officers of this Company were Intelligence Corps. It remains here to note that 2 members of 118 WIS, Lieutenant A Macdonald and Corporal F T Fowler, were awarded the George Medal for bravery in rescuing the crew of an American bomber that crashed carrying a full bomb load at Parham airfield near Saxmundham in April 1944, and that for the first weeks of the campaign a party of 5 officers, of which 3 were Intelligence Corps, were attached to Signals Intelligence, US 1st Army.

In May 1942, a new theatre APIS (GHQ) was formed to work at Norfolk House. Two of its first tasks were air photograph advice for the Dieppe raid for which models and air photograph packs were produced in quantities, and help in the planning for the landings in French North Africa. As more trained photo-interpreters became available, the system expanded, PI sections being attached to Corps and Divisional headquarters and later a new 2nd Army APIS was established in a building near Victoria Station.[48] Following the summer 1943 decision that the landings would be in Normandy, work became increasingly concentrated upon that area. To assist this, the R Section, formerly at work at Combined Operations, was closed down and its staff transferred to APIS (GHQ), the title of which was changed to APIS (TIS) (Theatre Intelligence Staff), all under the Chief of Staff of the Supreme Allied Commander. APIS (TIS) comprised a Major, 30 other officer PIs and 18 draughtsmen, British, Canadian, American and from all three services. Early in 1944, Captain Espenhahn of APIS (CIU) was appointed to command a new 21 Army Group IU, formed to control the APIS of the British 2nd and Canadian 1st Armies, their Corps and Divisions, a total of 25 PI Sections with 65 PIs. Among these latter were some Intelligence Corps veterans from Italy. The parent unit, APIS (CIU) was also tasked with some of this theatre level work. New techniques of value included the use of low level oblique photography and moving cameras.

Every small piece of information available about the German defences, strong points, gun positions and beach and underwater obstacles was collected and up-dated, dropping zones for parachute troops and landing sites for gliders were selected and German troop movements recorded.[49] Models of the beaches and landing areas were prepared. The detail can be judged from the 6 Airborne Division's summary of Intelligence—64 pages and 5 annotated maps. Captain Simon, Second in Command to Major Falcon at APIS (CIU), recalls:

> Although the planning interpretation was being carried out by the new interpretation units formed for SHAEF and 21 Army Group, we at Medmenham were engaged in collation of their efforts and liaison duties, as well as special assignments. One of the latter, which fell to my lot in May 1944, was a detailed interpretation of the defences of an artillery emplacement North of Caen which covered the approaches to the landing beaches. I had the opportunity of some visits from the commander of the Parachute Battalion which was to capture and neutralise the guns on D-Day and together we were able to build up a very detailed picture of what he would have to tackle.

Overall, the size of the effort can be summed up in APIS (TIS) total of photographic prints, 1,093,500. The PI contribution to the success of the landings was massive. There was continuous provision of printed overlays recording German defences for maps, issued down to unit and sub-unit level. A very important source of Intelligence, and one unfamiliar to staffs with experience limited to North Africa was the reports provided by the French and Belgian resistance. On occasions, purloined copies of whole divisional and other railway movement orders would arrive. Other sources also contributing to the overall Intelligence picture were special beach obstacle reconnaissance parties (transported by midget or coastal submarine), and the Soviet Union, occasionally prepared to confirm formation movements.

The Intelligence picture available, then, on D-Day was a full one, though not complete in every detail. One gap, to prove serious, was an inprecision over scrappy Intelligence that one of the best German divisions, 21 Panzer, was covering Caen—a deployment that prevented a quick British capture of the city.

The contributions made to D-Day planning by members of the Intelligence Corps engaged in SOE work and in prisoner of war interrogation have already been mentioned. It remains only to add that at the same time as the final arrangements for the Normandy landings were being made, other preparations were in hand for landings by forces, largely French and American, in the south of France. Some 14 photo-interpreters from MAIU (West) were attached to the American Command, among them still serving with the French forces was Captain A Gilbert. On one occasion after the landings his skill as a PI enabled the French to cut off one German line of retreat. Captain D Hamblen was sent to Corsica to ensure Security in preparation for the landings. The other very small scale Intelligence Corps 'represented' in this operation included two NCOs, Sergeant Granville and Corporal Noritshy, who took part in the airborne landings, and Captain J W Barber, serving with the joint Anglo–US–French No. 4 Special Force Unit (SOE). This arrived at Saint Tropez in August 1944 and moved north east with the US 7th Army. Captain Barber describes 4 SFU's work as playing 'some small part in helping to stabilise the often chaotic conditions prevailing after liberation, what with old scores being settled and the like'.[50]

The Intelligence Corps' contribution to the final north west Europe campaign in the field took the same forms as north Africa and Italy. Some Intelligence Corps officers served as 'in line' Intelligence staff officers at Army, Corps and Division headquarters. Others served in specialist agencies—photo-interpretation, prisoners and documents, Y Signals Intelligence. Others commanded Field Security sections of NCOs and soldiers of the Corps; their work is set out in the next chaper.

After the Allied landings, the two main sources of operational Intelligence for the campaign continued to be air photography and signals Intelligence, in particular Bletchley Park, the Y Service only coming into its own in late July. These sources were supplemented by prisoners of war, captured documents and the reports of agents, resistance movement members, refugees and ordinary civilians. In a campaign so near home, Bletchley Park greatly extended its role, begun in Italy, as a main provider of actual battlefield tactical intelligence. The achievement was remarkable. On a number of occasions, German signals indicating a move or an attack were deciphered and passed back to field formation headquarters directly concerned in five or six hours—frequently in time for precautions to be prepared. Major German theatre-level defensive plans could take five to six days, but the material was still immensely valuable. But, except for a few periods of technical difficulties, a steady daily stream of German operational messages—movements of reinforcements, locations of formations and headquarters, proposed air strike targets and minelaying programmes, were sent by Bletchley Park to SHAEF and onwards from July to September 1944. From these patterns, trends and appreciations could be formed.[51] The flow diminished somewhat when the Germans were forced back into their own country, with its own telephone system.

Three major *Ultra* successes in the Normandy fighting of incalculable value to 21 Army Group may be noted—the tracking of the movements of the German divisions retained in the Pas de Calais after the Normandy landings, the locating of the headquarters of the German armoured reinforcement *Panzergruppe West*, enabling it to be destroyed by bombing at a critical stage in the Normandy battle, and, greatest of all, the preparations to meet—and totally to destroy—the German Army offensives towards Avranches in early August. The first major Y success was in early August, a warning of a German counter-attack on the XII Corps bridgehead east of the Orne.

Army and Corps Y Sections were under the control of a Signals Intelligence staff, supported by No 1 Wireless Intelligence Company. From the spring of 1944 all were located in Kensington. They landed in Normandy soon after the initial landings. The first weeks of the break-out phase, late July to September 1944 were the most profitable period for Y as there was a great increase in the volume of low grade material intercepted. On 14 August, for example, it was possible to produce a Y statement showing the location of almost every important German unit enclosed in the Falaise 'pocket', though the combined results of DF and low grade traffic. The winter hold-up, from September to mid-December, saw a marked decline in low grade intelligence and some decrease in Y activity. However, when the Battle of the Ardennes opened, Y was again able to contribute. The attacking German formations observed strict wireless silence until contact had been established, but therefter wireless traffic totals gradually began to rise. Current Intelligence from the salient was provided by several SS Panzer Reconnaissance Battalions, whose running commentaries on the battle included useful locations.

As 21 Army Group entered Germany, it seemed that Y Service work was drawing to a close, and plans were made to move sections to the Far East. This proved premature, the 2nd Army experienced a need for Y VHF expertise, the B type Sections trained and equipped for this work being added to the different Corps Headquarters. After the crossing of the Rhine, however, German signals Security and overall professionalism began to collapse and the final stages of the campaign proved technically very simple. German traffic became very free, much being *en clair*, so providing very full Order of Battle and tactical Intelligence. Of Y Service in this campaign, Major J M M Sherwood, of No. 1 Special Intelligence Company, wrote in his War Diary: 'Few Y problems have one correct school solution; only an organisation which subjects itself to contrast revision and self criticism can hope to compete with the ever changing problems of Signals Intelligence in the Field'.

One final point on Y work needs mention. From Tunisia onwards there had developed interchanges of personnel with the US Army; prior to the Normandy landings, numbers of British Y Signals and Intelligence personnel were attached to US formation headquarters. By 1945, there were more American than British Y staffs in the field but as late as May 1945 British Y Sections were accompanying General Patton's Army into Austria and beyond.

In the initial stages of the invasion there was only limited air photo interpretation activity, but this changed very quickly. The photo-interpreters of 6 Airborne Division landed with their formation, suffering casualties. By 18 June, the advanced party of APIS 2nd Army had landed, and by 7 August the 21 Army Group Photographic Interpretation Unit had established itself in France in control of all photo-interpretation work on the 1st Canadian and 2nd British Armies. The main responsibilities during the Normandy fighting were bomb damage reports on enemy batteries, German troop movements by day and night, especially over the Seine, and preparation of planning maps of German defences on a 1/50,000 scale. The speed of advance through northern France and Belgium outstripped the provision of prints to forward troops and photo-interpretation did not regain its full status until the end of the year, with the work of photo-interpreters during the German December 1944 Ardennes offensive, the Allied crossing of the Rhine, and the subsequent entry into north Germany.

The expanded role of photo-interpretation at Medmenham in support of the Allied invasion has already been noted. In the field, the technique of linking air photographs to prisoner of war questioning was advanced, photographs would be shown to prisoners who were then asked leading questions. Divisional photo-interpreter sections at this time would usually include two photo-interpreters—officers or warrant officers, a draughtsman and a driver for the section's jeep. Equipment remained simple—an Anglepoise lamp, two Type D stereoscopes and two pairs of dividers, a magnifying measurer, mathematical tables, drawing board and essential stationery. The sections worked to the GSO1, though frequently in contact with the Divisional commander. A good section would plan ahead, trying to anticipate their commander's likely plans and needs. Tact and the ability to work as part of a team were needed both in presenting Intelligence to commanders and staffs and, frequently, in arranging for the necessary aircraft flights.[52]

A few other snapshots of operational Intelligence work by Intelligence Corps officers are of interest. Most notable perhaps was again the work of Colonel J O Ewart, usually at Field Marshal Montgomery's forward Tactical Headquarters. The citation for Colonel Ewart's CBE speaks for itself.

> This officer was responsible for the tactical intelligence throughout the German offensive in the Ardennes. His task was to keep the C-in-C apprised of the enemy situation and to give personal guidance to the Armies put under command in a very difficult situation. By regular visits to the battle and close personal touch with the situation in addition to the usual intelligence sources, he was able to produce a volume and accuracy of information which kept the Armies fully informed of the situation and enabled the C-in-C to make such dispositions as he deemed fit in relation to the tricky problems created by the enemy's earlier successes. He was tireless, accurate, often brilliant in his work at this critical juncture, and without his presence both in close touch with the C-in-C and with the battle it would have been impossible to have produced a coherent view at a time when accuracy and calmness were more

than ever demanded. Colonel Ewart made a very substantial personal contribution to the defeat of the enemy's last gamble in the West.

Tragically at the age of only 28, Colonel Ewart was killed in a motor accident in July 1945.

During the preparations for the Rhine crossing, two Intelligence Corps Sergeants, H J Saunders and L M Gilbert, both fluent German speakers, carried out a notable reconnaissance in the Xanten area. Disguised as German soldiers in Wehrmacht uniforms, they spent several days in enemy territory gathering operational Intelligence, in particular enemy artillery positions and movements. Sergeant Saunders, a native anti-Nazi German, was arrested by German field gendarmerie but talked his way out of an interrogation, and recrossed into Allied held territory with, in the words of his citation: 'information of the highest military importance'. Both were awarded the MM for this work.

The questioning of prisoners remained a useful source and a daily commitment for formation interrogators, mostly Intelligence Corps. Certain officers of especial ability such as Captain T Peters at VIII Corps headquarters were tasked for the interrogation of senior officers, it being held that an officer from a large headquarters would have both the necessary knowledge and, in the eyes of the prisoner, the necessary prestige for a useful interrogation.[53] A special Enemy Documents Unit was formed to seize documents on arrival in liberated territory; these tons of documents provided a mass of information on the Axis military and general war effort and a daily summary of military information was sent forward to the Intelligence Staff.[54] Of particular value were documents captured in Normandy that contained information on V2 rockets. The work was later expanded to include nuclear research and concentration camps after the entry into Germany. One Corps officer, Captain T R Galloway, was awarded the MC for his exploits in December 1944. Interrogating three men in plain clothes captured near the River Maas, he identified them as German soldiers on a special mission. Extracting their rendezvous from them, Captain Galloway lured their recovery party across the river and then killed or captured these also. At one point he was standing amid fire from across the river to direct and secure his captives.[55]

One Corps officer, Captain D Royce, was tasked with special assignments, the first to ascertain the psychological reactions of selected prisoners from German units that had suffered particularly heavy bombardment in Normandy, and then in an exercise of verification a comparison of what Intelligence staffs had assessed enemy positions to be in one sector of Normandy, what those positions actually were, and what effect the different Allied modes of strike obtained.[56]

Other Intelligence activities also developed after the Allied armies entered the Reich. The first was not particularly successful due to the speed of advance after the crossing of the Rhine. Attempts were made to infiltrate Poles and anti-Nazi Germans in the guise of displaced persons across into territory still held by the German Army to gather tactical Intelligence. Major A W E Winlaw, serving with 6 Airborne Division was an agent handler in this role.[57] Six Pioneer (now Royal) Corps companies formed the nucleus of T Force, under Major A Stark, Intelligence Corps, tasked to seize particular Intelligence targets, in particular research and experimental establishments and armament factories in occupied Germany. Five small Intelligence Corps Combat Propaganda units, with smaller leaflets sections attached, served in the North West Europe campaign. The units broadcast over amplifiers to German troops encouraging them to surrender. The leaflet units worked with the Royal Artillery. In the south of France Lieutenant Colonel D Macfarlane commanded a small Political Warfare Branch unit tasked to pass propaganda material and occasionally an anti-Fascist Italian over the frontier to the partisans in northern Italy.[58]

In conclusion, German-speaking officers of the Corps, notably Colonel Ewart and Major Crick, were much involved in the formal surrender of the German forces on Lüneburg Heath as guides and interpreters, translating the surrender terms.

9

Security: The Corps Contribution

Intelligence and Security are a close interface; the Intelligence Corps contribution to Security was as great as the Corps' contributions to other fields of Intelligence. In terms of sheer numbers of personnel, the contribution was of course far larger. Over 450 Field Security Sections existed at one time or another in the Second World War.[1] Their duties covered an immense variety of ground level tasks in most quarters of the globe. Almost all of these were humdrum and monotonous for most of the time. Some were interspersed with a flash of drama or excitement. But all were Intelligence and Security tasks that had to be done—if other soldiers were not to pay for the omission with their lives.

The tasks can conveniently be divided into three main themes—Security in overseas campaign theatres, Security in the United Kingdom, and Security in certain British colonies of importance for reasons either strategic or economic. In campaign theatres most of the Corps' work was under military direction but in some Middle East territories the Corps' Field Security Sections acted as the executive of civilian political or Intelligence departments. In Britain the balance was more even, and in the colonies direction was generally civilian. At a theoretical level, Security operated on the 'Six Controls' system. Identity Cards, (documents), Movement Control (passes), Residence, Communications, (mail, telegraph and in cases of suspects telephone), Publications (media of all types) and Special Control (in particular firearms and cameras). Which particular controls were applied to any area depended upon operational and political conditions.

Security in Campaign Theatres

The occupation of Italian East Africa left a small but on-going Security commitment. In Eritrea, for example, 261 FSS was concerned with port surveillance at Massawa and a limited measure of travel control. In Addis Ababa the locally raised East African Intelligence Corps controlled a small network of informers. Captain T Allbeury was appointed Military Liaison Officer to the Emperor of Ethiopia, a post which was in fact a cover for investigation into Italian stay-behind groups and certain commercial dealings with the Japanese in which prior to December 1941, a few members of the Imperial Household were engaged. Captain Allbeury was later moved to Mogadishu, in former Italian Somaliland, tasked to penetrate a number of Italian underground groups left behind by the defeated Fascist regime concealed amongst the Italian settler population.[2]

In the Middle East proper two organisations, the Middle East Intelligence Centre, MEIC, and Security Intelligence Middle East, SIME, had existed from pre-war days. In the military field SIME policy was executed by FSP Sections in a Field Security Wing, but before the entry of Italy into the war the numbers involved were very small. An Intelligence staff officer and 13 soldiers, the late 1939 total, were used to form the nucleus of two FSP Sections. These were reinforced in early 1940 by a draft of 1 Warrant Officer and 14 FSP soldiers from Mytchett, together with a second trained Intelligence Staff Officer. Personnel were also found for an FSS with the Western Desert Force, later to become XIII Corps. Two Corps officers, Lieutenant Colonels G Kirk and K Jones, were at different times Deputy Director of SIME, and Lieutenant Colonel H N Trethowan was a Section Head in 1944–45.

With the entry of Italy into the war it was clear that Security Intelligence would have to expand very greatly. Many Egyptians favoured the Axis cause, Cairo was a cosmopolitan city, tailor-made for espionage and subversion. To create an efficient organisation GHQ Middle East was given a Counter-Intelligence Branch GS I (B), and an experienced Government of India official who had been head of the Delhi Intelligence Bureau, Sir David Petrie, was brought out of retirement. Petrie, aged 60, was commissioned as a Second Lieutenant in the Intelligence Corps and immediately given a temporary rank of Colonel, probably to facilitate apparently routine military movement around the Middle East. He served in Cairo until the end of 1940 when he was recalled to London first to enquire into MI5, and then to become its very successful Director-General (with the local rank of Brigadier).

Following Petrie's appointment the pace accelerated. Field Security Courses were started, the first two Intelligence Corps FSS officers, Lieutenant FID (later Sir Francis) Astley and AW Sansom were commissioned locally and elements of three FSS began to arrive from Britain. Gradually, personnel were formed into sections to provide a network to cover the Middle East. The first priorities were Egypt and the units of Wavell's Army of the Nile, then Palestine, Cyprus and the Sudan. A training process gradually developed into the first FS centre and depot overseas. An experimental establishment for a composite British-Indian FSS was devised and the first Indian troops selected for training; plans were made for the formation and training of New Zealand and Australian FS Sections.[3]

By August 1940, the first Middle East Sections had been designated 251, 252, 253 FSS—the first formed overseas, and authority to form 10 was received, 9 of which were formed by the end of the year. A further 5, 264–268 FSS were formed at the depot at Winchester in 1940, but did not reach Cairo until later in April 1941. In September, the Field Security Wing, Middle East was established with two depot sections. The Wing was housed in the Hotel Semiramis, its role was to administer existing FSS, raise new ones and hold reserves. The Wing graduated to being 'The Intelligence Corps Depot and FSS Training Centre' a little later. By the end of 1940, 160 men, British, Australian, New Zealand and Indian had received FS training. In 1941 the Centre moved to Helwan; a further 23 FSS were raised locally and others arrived from Britain to meet the extending Middle Eastern commitment, ports, towns and vital installations in Palestine, Egypt, Sudan and Eritrea.[4] The Army of the Nile, later 8th Army, formations were also provided with FSS. These had certain security commitments once Libya was finally occupied; a spy ring in Tripoli for example was identified and broken up. The brief 1940–41 appearance of British forces in Greece gave their FSS traditional roles; airfield security and in the words of Captain G Household 'women, waiters, civilian employees, strangers hanging about Piraeus docks for no good reason, or questioning British troops with native Greek inquisitiveness ...'[5] After the campaign was over, FSS personnel were engaged in the screening of refugees.

The nationalist uprising of Rashid Ali in Iraq in April 1941 was swiftly put down but the rising, and the subsequent military occupation of Syria and Lebanon extended the Field Security requirement. A number of German and Italian agents had arrived in Syria and Lebanon after the June 1940 armistice, their aim being to incite Arab revolt against the British in Palestine and Iraq. Two FSS were despatched to Basra in June 1941 for port and frontier duties, together with four Indian Army Composite FSS. The Security requirement was still further stretched by the Anglo-Soviet occupation of Iran in August 1941. For this three further FSS were despatched, initially to Iraq. After the entry into Iran, a reorganisation of FSS followed. Some personnel from the British sections were posted to new Indian Army Composite Sections, the first four being disbanded.[6] The Indian Sections were allocated to lines of communication duties or to Indian Army formations. Of the British Sections, one was stationed at Baghdad, another at Teheran and a third at Ahwaz with detachments along the Basra–Teheran railway.[7] By the end of the year, in Persia (Iran) and Iraq—PAIFORCE—19 FSS were serving in an FS wing under a Deputy Director of Military Intelligence.[8] The two major concerns were, of course, the oil routes and the military supply route to the Soviet Union; liaison with the RAF was close. German agents were active for some time, a number being parachuted into both Iraq and Iran. These, together with Iraqis and Iranians who were assisting them, were all detained. A few Corps officers served on the Intelligence staff. One, Captain F Cornish, recalls that his work ranged from a study of Turkish Military Intelligence to locust control.

The work of two NCOs of 72 FSS, Sergeants Navarra and Wickens on secondment to the Combined Intelligence Centre led to the arrest of Franz Mayr, one of the most important among the numerous German agents in Iran. However, perhaps the most spectacular of events in Iran was the Tehran Conference (EUREKA) held on 28 November 1943 between the Allied War Leaders – Churchill, Stalin and Roosevelt. Five FSS were deployed for this gathering. A number of Iranians suspected of pro-German sympathies and activities were taken in before the Conference.[9] On a lighter note, in 1944 FSS personnel from Baghdad recovered a large quantity of silver purloined from a leading Baghdad hotel by members of the Shah of Iran's entourage: all was recovered on board the Levant Express on the Iran–Iraq border.

In respect of Syria and Lebanon, initially 12, later 9, FSS had to be committed, under a Defence Security Officer with headquarters in Beirut. Two Australian FSS were also at work. An immediate task was to ensure that the ships sent from France to repatriate the defeated Vichy French garrison landed no Axis agents.[10] The baggage of the 35,000 French troops in Syria was searched, the men themselves screened, and the ship's wireless rooms sealed before their evacuation to France. The later FSS roles included general counter-intelligence and Security, political intelligence gathering and surveillance of civilian movement by rail and road across frontiers, especially that with Turkey.

Some more detailed glimpses of the work of the various Levant FSS are interesting. There were periodic German attempts to land agents either by submarine or parachute descent; these were discovered in advance by *Ultra* intercepts and the agents, Greeks and Armenians, caught. Agents captured were 'turned' to provide disinformation, strategic or operational; in this field the differences and jealousies between the German Intelligence Services, the formal military Intelligence *Abwehr* and the SS *Sicherheitsdienst*, were turned to advantage, sometimes with the actual help of *Abwehr* personnel. On other occasions, specially recruited Allied agents (often German Jews) were used to plant disinformation where it was known that it would be collected. Double agents, and specially created fictitious personalities of supposed Axis sympathisers, were used for the same purposes. At work in Damascus, 264 FSS maintained an NCO at the frontier port of Abou Chamat working with the Syrian Sureté and gendarmerie, their major concern was the bi-weekly trans-desert coach service linking the Iraq oilfields to the refinery and port at Haifa. A good working arrangement with the Free French was established. In Damascus, NCOs worked in plain clothes, with an interpreter and four plain clothes Syrian policemen. In early 1942, FSS personnel arrested an entire spy ring of Palestinians, Syrians and Lebanese in Aleppo after one of its members had informed against the ring; later in the year, an Armenian group parachuted into the area was all rounded up. Other agents and informers apprehended in 1942 included a small party of Italian parachute special forces soldiers, and local coastal schooner captains passing on shipping movements to Axis agents operating from Turkey. Of special concern were the nationalist political parties, pro-Axis 'front' organisations (some with apparently innocent names such as 'The Society to Command Virtue' and 'Condemn Vice'), other semi-secret political clubs, and the rising anti-French sentiments. Nationalist leaders were questioned and screened, assessments being based upon whether their activities would impede the war effort. Arabs watched and identified as disseminating pro-Axis propaganda, especially at times of German success in North Africa, were arrested. This work involved meeting—and feasting—with all the varied Levant communities. Road blocks were occasionally operated, together with checks upon hotels, pensions and cabarets. Brothels were watched and girls who persistently asked servicemen about their units investigated.[11] More mundane, but of military importance, was the reconnaissance and identification of the 1943 hashish crop.

At Kuneitra, near the Palestine border, FSS work was frontier liaison with the Palestine Police, a watch on the illegal sale of Arab land to Jews, and the purchase and smuggling of arms into Palestine for use by *Haganah* or other more extreme Jewish groups.

Along the entire, Syria to Egypt, FSS worked with the Royal Navy's Fleet Base Security officers. Train control on the railway lines to Palestine, Transjordan and Turkey was another important role. On the Transjordan and Palestine lines, FSS personnel would board the non-corridor train some distance from the frontier and clamber from compartment to compartment and coach to coach. The main Istanbul–Eastern Turkey and Iraq railway looped briefly through Syria, FSS personnel had to be present on the train while it did so and accomplish a check of passengers within an hour; suspects were removed from the train and despatched to a centre in Palestine. In Palestine itself the priority security commitment was the Iraq–Haifa oil pipeline. FSS personnel were tasked to secure military headquarters against raiding parties, and investigate certain monasteries, cabarets, brothels and political groupings. The Corps was also increasingly involved in Censorship, 23 special Censor sections being at work in the Middle East.

Egypt's capital, Cairo and her ports remained Intelligence jungles to the end. In Alexandria, the Canal Zone and the Egyptian Red Sea ports, every movement of troops by ships, lighter or train was watched by adverse elements, and the troops themselves beguiled by restaurants, cafe and brothel owners, sometimes even being drugged so that their documents could be stolen. Although the mass of the population were friendly, there were Axis sympathisers well placed in all walks of Egyptian life. Another specialist commitment was that of 251 FSS, concerned with the Syrian, French and Greek communities, the latter creating a special difficulty during the 1942 Greek naval mutiny.

Perhaps the most spectacular case occurred in mid-1942 when a German wireless operator and driver were captured in the Libyan desert; under interrogation they revealed their role as a communication link to a pair of German *Abwehr* agents who had been infiltrated into Egypt. One of the agents, Eppler, had a mixed German and Egyptian background and upbringing; the other, Sandstede, was of German colonial stock who had stayed on under the British in Tanganyika. Sandstede was the wireless operator. Eppler was tasked to set up a spy and saboteur network in Egypt to assist Rommel's 1942 offensive. He made contact with several prominent Egyptians, but was unable to communicate with his own masters following the capture of the German wireless operator. Their reserve contact procedure was through a junior employee at a foreign embassy in Cairo. Their contact was observed by an FSS detachment and their arrest by Sergeant C Benjamin and a 259 FSS team followed; other arrests, including some Egyptian officers, followed.

As important as any security work was that on the lines of communication forward from Alexandria, to Mersa Matruh or further, according to the state of the campaign. 271 FSS provided detachments that worked on the railway line, on wheeled transport and in the transit camps. The detachments on the trains in addition to checking documents watched to see what men could identify each other. At least one German wearing British Army uniform was caught in this way. The trains were liable to sabotage by Egyptian civilians, in particular at Debaa, and a system of screening of labour and civilian movement control had to be established.[12]

The Allied landings in French North Africa, amid a very confused political situation, initially involved 11 FSS, later reinforced by a further five. The duties included security investigations following denunciations by Frenchman against Frenchman, *colon* against Arab and vice versa, frontier security on the Spanish Moroccan borders, smoothing where necessary the delicate administrative and political negotiations with the French, in certain areas reaching understanding with local Berber *caids* or investigating those who were known either to be pro-Axis or had been bribed by the Germans, port control at several ports including searching of ships and questioning crew members, and investigations into stay-behind espionage parties recruited from the large resident Italian community in Tunisia.[13] Later, after the Allied entry into France, remained the screening of the mass of French people who wished to return there, and also the screening of Polish soldiers returned from the USSR via Iran.

Also notable was the Corps' contribution to S Force, a task force under the command of Lieutenant Colonel D Macfarlane and composed of men, British and American from several arms, carefully prepared for the occupation of Tunis. Corps personnel involved represented the equivalent of seven Sections, their task was the arrest of certain personalities, the prevention of sabotage, search of premises and seizure of documents and prisoner control. The circumstances of the fall of Tunis—delayed and with a mass of prisoners—created difficulties but lessons were learnt for the future.

Once again a VIP visit—Prime Minister Churchill's convalescence in Morocco—provided a major security commitment in December 1943 and January 1944 for Lieutenant Colonel the Hon H B Eyres-Monsell (later Lord Monsell) and Major (later Lieutenant Colonel) H Boggis-Rolfe of the Corps.

Field Security work developed from the defensive style of the BEF's 1940 campaign as the Allied Armies entered mainland Europe. The speed with which in 1940 the Germans had rounded up French and Belgian citizens and seized wireless stations and documents had been noted, and was now to be emulated. S Force operations, of the type tried in Tunis but with a role extended to seizure of the media and renamed R Force, were a priority role, 412 FSS being employed in this work in both Florence and Padua and 97 FSS so employed in Rome. By the time the headquarters of FS Wing CMF, had moved to the Naples area in 1944, 41 FSS or Port Security Sections were under command, in many cases working closely with American Counter-Intelligence. The total eventually reached 47.

The daily round was very varied. The arrest of Fascists and the location of documents came first, informers were inspanned to assist. One officer, Lieutenant R Kisrani, secured Mussolini's personal documents in April 1945. Others to be caught included British, Maltese and Arab renegades, and certain Zionists. German and Fascist Italian Intelligence services left stay-behind agents equipped with radio. Right up to April 1945, a steady stream of Germans and Fascist Italian agents crossed the lines, were landed from the sea or were dropped by parachute on Intelligence gathering or sabotage missions.[14] A notable success was that of 314 FSS who caught three Axis agents landing from motor boats in the northern Adriatic; prompt interrogation revealed 17 more agents and saboteurs. Some agents were women. Several score were caught by FSS working with anti-Fascist Italian police; in all the vast majority were quite quickly apprehended. A minority were executed, others mostly 'turned around'.[15] Security measures against German infiltrators and Italians wishing to cross the front line to rejoin families in the north had to be taken. Curfews had to be imposed and all local firearms collected and stored. Publications had to be supervised and controlled, Italian labour required by the military vetted. Brothels had to be watched and applications (mostly from prostitutes) to marry British Servicemen investigated. Bandits—in organised and well-armed groups—remained a menace, as did infighting between exiles from Albania and Yugoslavia. A very stringent control had to be exercised over refugees who had formerly been active in the cause of General Mihailovic. Italian soldiers who had demobilised themselves had to be screened where possible. In ports merchant ships' crews lists had to be checked and desertions investigated. Rumours abounded—of German stay-behind parties, agents and delayed action mines. Some were false, some true, some deliberately planted to impede troop movements. Allied logistic units fed the rumour supply, failing to realise that they were often merely the catspaws of local vendettas. Some organisations and individuals attempted illicit political publishing, these were usually Communist. In Sicily Mafia linkages posed special, and usually insoluble, problems. All had to be investigated in an atmosphere of Southern Italian poverty, at times squalor, compounded by the sickness of defeat which served to sour the relative comfort in which most of the FSS personnel lived.[16] An essential ingredient had been the pre-invasion compilation of lists of Fascist supporters.

The Intelligence Corps mounted a special organisation, Headquarters Intelligence Corps (Field) for the Normandy landings. This organisation was formed in May 1943.[17] From an initial staff of 12 officers and 19 soldiers the Headquarters appears to have administered at its greatest extent 83 Field Security Sections together with 25 Field Security Reserve Detachments, (FSRDs), 3 special Counter-Intelligence Units, an Intelligence Laboratory and 36 Censorship Sections.[18] A special Movement Security organisation was created to cover the embarkation period, the personnel including Intelligence Corps officers and sergeants. Passes controlled access to the ports and certain roads, troops who had been briefed had to be segregated from those who had not, and farewell social occasions closely supervised. Some of the commitments were unusual, such as that of Security cover for the construction of the 'Mulberry' prefabricated port and the investigation of wild rumours, one for example alleging the death of General Montgomery. Headquarters Intelligence Corps (Field) arrived at Arromanches on 11 August 1944; it worked from a seminary at Sommervieu, Calvados until September when it moved first to Amiens and then to Brussels. It had been twice hit by V1 flying bombs in London, the second in July causing the death of an NCO; in Brussels a V2 fell outside the main office killing Sergeant Rosinoff of 273 FSS and injuring 24 others.

Security work had been as important in the planning and preparation months as after the landings. First perhaps, was Security among the planners. 'Cover lists (of those in the know) indoctrination of security-mindedness' safety of secret documents, especially anything concerned with *Ultra* secret breaking of the enemy ciphers, signals security, liaison with MI5 ...' were all day to day concerns of Intelligence Corps personnel.[19] Other security measures included full censorship of all mails to Northern Ireland as well as fully maintained censorship on mails to Gibraltar, the Irish Free State and neutral countries, together with certain 'delays' on letters home from Axis prisoners, the banning of export of local newspapers, certain restrictions on overseas telegrams and telephone calls, certain travel restrictions and some measures of movement control applied to the southern coast of England.

Detailed Counter-Intelligence plans were included in the orders for the invasion, prepared under the direction of the GSO1 I(B), Lieutenant Colonel N MacDermot who was followed later by Lieutenant Colonel (later His Honour) S Noakes. These, in addition to the normal protective Security for our own forces, covered the use of the vast mass of material accumulated about German Intelligence agencies, including personalities' dossiers, the rapid seizure of counter-intelligence targets and identifications of black-listed personnel for arrest, and a control network to collate material gained during these operations and interrogations. Some 250,000 Germans were to be arrested to destroy the Nazi state machine, of these some 50,000 were listed as war criminals. A special section of Supreme Headquarters, the Evaluation and Dissemination Section, headed by Major M Furnivall Jones, was responsible for the dissemination to the armies in the field particulars of collaborators and Nazi personalities. As in other matters, the 1942 Dieppe raid had been something of a rehearsal; 84 FSS practised the expanded commitment.

Two examples of lapses in operational security in the UK illustrate the commitment. A lavatory wall in Colchester was found to have the date of the Rhine crossing airborne landing scrawled on a wall. A policeman kindly returned some marked maps of the landing that had been handed in.

In Normandy itself one Section, 19 FSS of 50 Division, landed over the beaches on D Day and 317 FSS of 6 Airborne Division landed by glider, sustaining a number of casualties, including Captain F C Scholes, killed while serving on the Division Intelligence staff. 19 FSS found two parties of stay-behind agents in Bayeux and mounted patrols in the Normandy *bocage* country looking for enemy line-crossers.[20] By 15 July, there were 18 further FSS ashore together with a number of the FSRDs, whose role was to provide additional personnel when necessary. The final total across the Channel amounted to 27 FSS and 25 FSRDs serving with 21 Army Group. The overall arrangement included provision for one or more Corps or Division FSS to be tasked for specific counter intelligence targets in cities and towns and ports, after which they would hand over to a Lines of Communication FSS. Rouen, for example, required a T Force, as the commitment was termed, of six FSS and five FSRDs, but Lille, occupied at a time of manpower shortage, could only be given two FSS and a handful of FSRD personnel. In Germany six FSS were assigned to Hamburg. FSS tasked for a particular city were, if possible, given time to prepare for the commitment. Sections were sometimes split into smaller detachments. Overall control was centralised at 2nd Army level, where work would be in conjunction with reliable French, Belgian and Dutch police and other agencies, among them Bletchley Park whose decrypts led to the identification of several agents. Resistance Groups were also often very valuable in effecting the seizure of German military and political headquarters, wanted Axis collaborators, equipment and documents.

Booby traps in prestige buildings or abandoned German headquarters were a common hazard. German soldiers would emerge from hiding—sometimes these would include groups that had been tasked as stay-behind radio or sabotage groups but had decided to give themselves up. Pigeon breeders and pigeon lofts, as in the First World War, required special attention.

When the pace of advance was rapid, as in the liberation of Belgium, the FSS were faced with vast numbers of refugees and displaced persons, among whom collaborators and others on the 'Automatic Arrest' lists were attempting to hide. Later, in the winter FSS again used the Resistance cells to mop up German stay-behind parties and secure liberated territory against German infiltrators and agents. With the help of Belgian and Dutch Resistance members, 19 FSS and Canadian Army units operated a control line along the River Maas, effecting an almost complete capture of line crossers despatched by German military Intelligence. Immediately before the Ardennes winter offensive, the Germans infiltrated a number of agents behind our lines to report on troops movements, these spoke English with an American accent and special procedures had to be devised.[21] One section, 273 FSS attached to the US Army for this period, was specifically tasked to screen refugees for infiltrators.

According to German records captured in 1945, 105 enemy agents were parachuted or attempted to penetrate into liberated territory in the last winter of the war. Of these 85 were definitely identified as agents, and all the remainder with one exception held on suspicion.[22] Most were very badly trained.

On occasions of hard fighting, FSS served as infantry. One such was at Arnhem, where 89 (Airborne) FSS's Commander, Captain J E (later Sir John) Killick was captured and all its members, with one exception, either killed or taken prisoner. Captain Killick's description of Arnhem merits full quotation:

> In this operation, 89 FS Section had a rather opportunist brief. For reasons of aircraft space, and in order not to put the whole section's eggs in one basket, we travelled to Arnhem in separate penny packets – 1 Sgt and 2 Cpls with each Brigade HQ, and the remainder, including myself, distributed in parachute sticks or glider loads of Div HQ and Div Tps. On the ground, in the initial stages, there was no alternative to 'every man for himself' and an instruction to RV in the town centre as and when possible. In the nature of the operation this of course never became possible. If it had gone according to plan, we would in any event have had no more than the opportunistic task of rounding up known German intelligence and Gestapo HQs and Dutch collaborators on the basis of a very rudimentary and short list of known names and addresses, carried by myself and senior NCOs in home-made metal tubes and typed on combustible paper. Each tube was fitted with a simple 'pull' igniter for destruction. We were to work in collaboration with SAS 'Jedburgh' teams including Dutchmen, who would liaise with and organise the Dutch Resistance. All this under the overall authority of a Dutch naval officer with plenipotentiary powers from the Queen of the Netherlands. If all this had come off, we would presumably only have operated for the few days until the Division had withdrawn and we had been relieved by another Section. As it was, we of course simply assimilated into the fighting on the ground, and did our best to remember our basic infantry training.[23]

Sergeant Chambers is described as standing in the open on the Arnhem bridge directing artillery fire at German targets. 317 Airborne FSS also fought as infantry in the Rhine crossing. Once in Germany, the problem assumed a new form, one example may be given. Near Mönchen-Gladbach, 19 FSS caught two German girls, telephonists who had been hurriedly instructed in radio and left behind with a transmitter. They were given to an American

Intelligence unit which persuaded them to send disinformation supplied by 21 Army Group; the girls concerned were glad to be well fed and housed.[24]

One NCO with a very special commitment was Sergeant N Kirby, responsible for security at Field Marshal Montgomery's Tactical Headquarters. His main concerns were advance security for proposed moves of the headquarters, and the dangers of infiltration of the headquarters by stay-behind parties of soldiers or Axis collaborators when the headquarters was located in a town.[25]

Finally, the Intelligence Corps provided an FSS composed entirely of Russian speaking personnel for the Potsdam Conference.

Security in Great Britain

Security in Britain had three main concerns: a general Security commitment for the country as a whole, a specific commitment for the security of the Army, and a watch on the Irish Free State in case it was to be used by the Germans as an invasion or espionage backdoor to Britain. Six laws formed the basis of civil security:—the Official Secrets Acts, the Aliens Restriction Act, the Treachery Act, the National Registration Act and the 1939 and 1940 Emergency Powers Acts. These latter authorised Defence Regulations which covered a very wide variety of subjects ranging from photography to propaganda and access to particular areas. The Corps' contribution to home security was, as before, individual specialist staff officers and FSS.

The FSS expansion continued throughout 1940. At the turn of the year there were 50 FSS for Home ports and airfields, 63 with military formations and 9 for the major UK Commands. Further sections were formed in 1941 and by 1 August 1943 the total in respect of the UK had risen to 48 FSS and 68 Port Security Sections, together with 2 Censor Sections. The day to day routine work of, for example, 143 FSS centred on Aberdeen included identity card checks upon fishermen in several small ports, crew checks on crews of ships at Aberdeen, and daily control of civilian passengers flying from Dyce Airport to neutral Sweden. 200 FSS at Perth was similarly tasked with the screening of escapers from Scandinavia and a final surveillance of our own departing agents.

In respect of general security, the majority of enemy agents landed or parachuted into Britain were apprehended by FSS personnel. They were either picked up immediately on arrival because their arrival had been expected as a result of signals interceptions and the work of double agents, or because discrepancies in their personal stores or documents were noticed, or taken later with the FSS personnel acting as the executive for other agencies who had gained further information from later screening. A few examples are illustrative. Three out of a group of four Belgian agents in German service were taken by Sergeant R Barker of 143 FSS near Aberdeen (the fourth was later caught in Glasgow). An agent was caught at Gourock by Corporal (later Lieutenant) D H Smith and, after a civilian flight in from Lisbon, another at Poole. Some claimed to be refugees. One such was proudly displayed by the Americans after his landing in Iceland, but Corps personnel were able to show the Americans the beach where his transmitter was buried. German agents were often poorly trained. In 1940, the documents of many had been based on wrong information provided by an SIS double agent group which facilitated their recognition and capture. Most were 'turned' to become double agents working for the Allies. FSS were also tasked to look out for, and on occasions arrest, civilians of extreme political views of either Left or Right Wing. The whole of the UK was covered by a network of FSS that extended as far north as Shetland where two Sections were concerned with the security of and screening of passengers from the 'Shetland Bus' secret transportation to Norway.

Security of prisoner of war or civilian detainee camps was also a Corps concern, particularly when German military prisoners escaped. Over 400 did so between 1939 and 1945, almost all being recaptured, but much work fell upon I(B) staffs and FSS. In the Isle of Man, where civilian security suspects were held, a special unit known as the IOM Special Section was formed.

Port Security involved the checking of all personnel arriving by sea. In major ports the commitment was consideraable. Liverpool, for example, provided:

> ... a massive security problem covering an extensive range of docks, and with great liners (eg. the *Mauretania*) and hospital ships arriving at Princes Landing Stage. Again good relations with Army, Naval and Merchant Marine authorities were essential in making arrangements for security checks on all arrivals. It is perhaps surprising that the team sent on board to do the checking consisted of lance corporals and corporals with a sergeant in charge. The latter had the job of setting up the practical arrangements, dealing with officers of the rank of eg. chief purser, and always open to accusations of causing undue delay. We worked in co-operation with the Immigration Service in dealing with anyone who could not

be given clearance.[26]

The work could become very intensive at a time of the arrival, by one method or another, of large numbers of refugees. Later, the FSS working at airfields had to be increased for similar work.

Another task of Port Security was the boarding of neutral ships – especially those with a Panama or Liberian registration – that were assembling in a British port to sail in a British escorted convoy. Also of particular concern were Irish ships plying between the Free State, Lisbon and Britain.

NCOs armed with a 'Red Book', listing known or suspected seamen in Axis service, would check crew lists and papers.[27] The various Governments in Exile-in-Britain, in particular those of the Netherlands, Belgium, Norway and Greece, contributed the names of people that their own nationals in Britain considered dangerous; if these were found serving on ships they were then arrested. Not all escapees from occupied Europe were patriots – enemy agents attempted to enter Britain in the guise of escapees. One such was exposed when a key on his keyring was found to be false, containing secret writing material. Occasionally documents would be found, one such was the discovery of details of aircraft production lodged between deck boards on a cargo ship. Certain instances of sabotage also had to be investigated. In September 1944 out of the 34 major port and 2 airfield Security Control officers, 27 were Intelligence Corps, together with the Officer Commanding a Mobile FSS, and Security Control officers at the Isle of Man, Rosyth and 3 of the major military Commands.

When a German invasion of Britain appeared probable, Intelligence Corps officers serving in UK Command and formation headquarters had special tasks in addition to the routine handling of Intelligence reports and training. Studies were made of likely German tactics for raids on coastal targets such as British radar installations. Until the formation of the Directorate of Combined Operations, Army Commands made studies of the French Coast opposite them, Corps officers preparing 'beach profiles' for use by British raiding parties.

Much military Security work was purely routine, though with the huge expansion of the Army there was an internal problem presented by soldiers of fascist, communist, Irish Republican, anarchist and pacifist views. Some 7,000 such cases had to be investigated. The routine work involved visiting units to brief all ranks on the need for security; and investigations, following up breaches that had been reported – careless talk in a public house or documents left behind in a train – and attempts to investigate how the German broadcaster Joyce ('Lord Haw Haw') could obtain local news such as, for example, that the clock on a certain town hall was 10 minutes slow. A number of FSS personnel were at work testing the security not only of military headquarters but also of public utilities such as power stations. Some personnel were involved in censorship. A few commitments were more unusual. An Intelligence Corps captain had to sit by the bedside of a 21 Army Group staff officer while he was given an anaesthetic. The officer knew the plans for the Normandy landings. Immediately after an anaesthetic on a previous occasion he had sat up in bed and revealed highly secret plans; a watch was considered necessary. And on one occasion Captain M Pertwee rugby-tackled a charlady leading a section of cleaners into a hall at St Paul's School where the whole plan of the Normandy landings was laid out in maps and models.[28]

In 1940–41 the Irish Free State was seen as one possible route by which the Germans might enter the British Isle. Of this danger Captain V Bonham-Carter wrote 'The possibility of a German invasion of Southern Ireland facilitated friendly relations with representatives of the Irish Army with whom we conducted occasional war games and map maneouvres. Nor was any objection made to our officers (in mufti of course) driving all over the south to survey the roads and possible landing places.[29] Also engaged in this work was Lieutenant A (later Sir Anthony) Rouse.[30] Irish workers in certain key ports, for example Dover, were screened and certain militant Irish Republicans who were attempting – by bribe or persuasion – to suborn Irish soldiers in the British Army, quietly sent on their way home.

Security in the Colonial Empire and on Shipping Routes

The Colonial Empire provided a number of Security commitments which Intelligence Corps individuals and FSS met.[31] Some arose from the strategic position of the territory, others from the territory's position either as a source or as a route staging post for vital raw materials.

Hardest pressed of the strategic colonies was Malta where an FSS, No 69, was slowly built up from mid 1940 around the personality of Sergeant T Hale. Efforts to strengthen the sections were frustrated by the shipping shortage until early 1942 when personnel were brought in by submarine. A peak of 6 officers and 18 soldiers of the Corps were serving in Malta immediately prior to the invasion of Sicily in mid 1943. These included 69 FSS, Censor Staff Malta, 45 Base Field Censor Unit and from April

1943 to June 1944 a Y Service Wireless Intelligence Section.

Gibraltar was a centre for a number of Intelligence activities; some—Western Mediterranean Signals Intelligence, 'exfiltration' of escaped prisoners from Spain and Portugal—have already been noted. Under a Defence Security Officer—some of whom were officers of the Corps—two FS Sections operated from 1941, concentrating on Counter-Intelligence, the dockyard and the civil port. German agents operating on the Iberian peninsula were attempting to close the 'exfiltration' routes, to recruit Intelligence gatherers among the crews of the Spanish fishing boats, and to mount sabotage operations against Gibraltar's defences and warships in the harbour. This covert Intelligence war necessitated the arrival of a third section, largely for airport security, in 1943. Day to day work involved random searches of the Spanish casual labour that worked in the Colony. The different security tasks brought the strength of the Corps on the Rock up to 17 officers and 42 soldiers.[32] A Corps Censor unit not included in these totals also served at Gibraltar.

In 1942 269 FSS was moved from Ethiopia to Aden for port Security duties. The Section checked between 100 and 200 ships each month for the rest of the war.

Work in other colonies of economic or political significance was under the direction of Lord Swinton's Security Executive. This body had the future of aircraft production as a very high priority. For this the Security of certain shipping lanes were seen as crucial, together with the excavation and transportation of bauxite especially from British Guiana onwards via Trinidad. Threats to Security were seen as sabotage of installations and ships, and agents or stay-behind parties in communication with German U-Boats.

In colonial territories the Field Security Sections worked closely in conjunction with the local representative of the Security Service. The precise duties of Corps personnel varied but Port Security Control, a watch on passengers, crew and cargo was perhaps the most common. Checks on passenger and crew lists were imposed. Discrepancies or a careful watch on these would reveal actual and potential Axis agents and stay-behind operators, a number being caught.

An account of the work of Corps personnel in Newfoundland, not at the time part of Canada, may be taken as a useful example.[33] Installations in Newfoundland itself were all secure under local arrangements, but signals intercepts had revealed that the Germans were attempting to recruit agents among the crews of the Spanish and Portuguese fishing fleets that worked off the

Grand Banks. They were especially anxious to recruit radio operators to report on weather and convoy movements. In August–September 1942 a civilian Security Service officer together with Major B Ardill, a Portuguese speaker, and four Warrant Officers of the Corps were despatched to St Johns.[34]

The procedure followed was to bring ships' radio operators ashore for an extended interview, during which their personal particulars would be recorded and a warning on breaches of neutrality given. Radio intercepts pointed to particular ships. One such was the hospital ship of the Portuguese fishing fleet. On 1 November 1942 this ship was on a course that would have brought her on the route of a convoy sailing for the invasion of North Africa. The ship was stopped by the Royal Navy and her wireless operator arrested, he admitted that he had been using the ship's radio for German Intelligence.[35] The Intelligence communication from Newfoundland to London was by transatlantic cable, in code re-encyphered on one-timepads.

The severe weather conditions in Newfoundland made the posting a testing one for the Corps personnel involved. Other postings were in more attractive climes. Many commented on the comfort of these FSS's war, but the work remained always vital and on some occasions dangerous. In the West Indies and Caribbean there were FSS personnel in Bermuda, Bahamas, Jamaica and Grand Cayman, Leeward and Windward Islands, British Honduras (now Belize), Trinidad and Tobago (plus Barbados) and British Guiana (now Guyana). The work interfaced with Port Security in Britain, in particular the main ore unloading port, Cardiff. Corporal (later Lieutenant Colonel) B H Kemball Cook, a Greek speaker, was tasked to vet seamen on Greek ships.[36]

The Bermuda Section was mainly preoccupied with censorship. Captain (later Major) H Montgomery Hyde notes over 900 personnel Services and civilian, being engaged on mail examination and contraband work in Bermuda, a major port of call for mail ships between the USA and Europe. Mail opened secretly and photographed revealed agents and pro-Nazi sympathisers in the USA. One particularly notable letter, marked for a Berlin address recognised by Hyde as an intelligence post-box, listed shipping movements in and out of New York. The sender was later linked to the writer of another letter, full of details of US aircraft supplied to Britain, despatched to an address in Portugal. Together these provided a lead-in to the exposure of networks of German espionage in the USA. A major contraband haul was an almost priceless collection of over 500

French Impressionist paintings and drawings seized by the Germans in Paris with a view to sale for much-needed dollars in America.[37] There were additional mail examination arrangements in Bahamas and Jamaica and also in the Dominion of Canada.

In the Bahamas work centred upon smuggling. The remaining personnel covered the vital area. Bauxite came from up the Essequibo river in British Guiana or the Orinoco in Venezuela to either Trinidad or to Jamaica, and then onwards to Galveston and New Orleans.[38] The sections in the Leeward and Windwards, and in British Honduras, had to maintain a close watch out for signallers, stay-behind personnel and unusual movement of small coastal craft; it was known that there were pro-Axis colonists among the Dutch population of Curaçao. In Trinidad there was an especial requirement to check passengers on ships voyaging between Buenos Aires and Iberian ports; spies were caught on these ships. British Honduras posed the special problems of the land boundary with Guatemala and also certain off-shore islands. In British Guiana a trail past the bauxite quarries was frequented by diamond prospectors; the trail crossed difficult terrain that offered a life line for agents and saboteurs.

In West Africa the overriding Security concern was convoy safety. Freetown in Sierra Leone was an assembly port for convoys, 70–80 ships being in the harbour at such times; bauxite, foodstuffs and other sinews of war also came from West Africa. Three FSS, controlled by a West Africa Intelligence Centre in Accra, were concerned with assistance to U-Boats and other enemy activities against our interests operating from Fernando Po and, until November 1942, French West Africa. Canoes crossing from Nigeria to Fernando Po had to be intercepted and the crews and cargoes examined. A small residual pro-German organisation in the Southern Cameroons was tracked down and, after the beginning of the massive American air transport flights across Africa to India, Kano airport and city became a Field Security commitment.

Convoy movements were again the main Security priority in East Africa, with additionally the export of Northern Rhodesian copper via Beira in Portuguese East Africa. An FSS was also committed to the Seychelles and Mauritius, the latter territory having the additional problem of a francophone community some of whom were pro-Vichy with contacts in Madagascar—controlled by a Vichy administration until 1942. Security work in East Africa linked—as a consequence of how movements from the East African ports – with the SIME working in the Red Sea, Persian

Gulf and India. Much time had to be spent in interviewing dhow *nakhoda* (skippers) for possible convoy-watchers or other agents in the guise of crew, passengers or pilgrims. There were also six Censor Sections at work in East Africa.

Security work was often dull and repetitive but a lapse of attention to detail on just one occasion could negate long periods of solid hard work; the success of security work also is often measurable more by what did not happen than what did. In both preventive and detective roles, Corps personnel were playing key roles.

Of day to day life one officer later wrote. 'We were never too military, and discipline was informal. When we did go through the traditional motions of parades and inspections, we performed them in a spirit of holiday—for the close, mutual trust between the section and its officer made the continual practice of obedience so obviously unnecessary. Daily relations in a crack section between the Field Security Officer and his NCOs much resembled those between a fatherly sales manager and his salesmen. But each section had its own individual character. In some the smartness of the men – when they were in uniform – and the atmosphere of the section office were reasonably regimental; in others the place looked and sounded like a salesman's office in Soho. And these were sometimes the best when it came to the real job of detecting enemy agents'.[39] In the words of Geoffrey Household's post-war autobiography, Field Security Sections 'became the eyes, ears, languages and mobile resource of I(B)1'.[40]

10

The War Against Japan: The Corps Contribution

The war against Japan, December 1941 to September 1945, was qualitatively different from the war in Europe. The war was remote, fought on the edge of empire; it began some time after the war in Europe to which it always remained secondary in importance.[1] In terms of general military operations and specific military Intelligence Britain was even less well-prepared for it than for war in Europe. Main theatre headquarters in India or Ceylon were far removed from the front line, a situation which sometimes failed to create the necessary sense of urgency. There were formidable language and culture barriers and the number of British Intelligence personnel trained to overcome them was never sufficient; it was exceedingly difficult to enter the minds of the, sometimes unknown, Japanese Commanders.[2] One other general feature of the culture barrier was a tendency for ethnic prejudice to skew Intelligence appreciation—at first in gossipy under-estimation of the Japanese and later in over-estimation of their skills and ferocity. Similar prejudice also led at first to undervaluing of Intelligence supplied by other non-Europeans, in particular Chinese, even when this was almost certainly reliable.

This chapter will follow the same pattern as the previous four, a record of the initial disasters and then in turn consideration of the Corps' contributions to Strategic Intelligence, Operational Intelligence, and Security. In the war against Japan a vast amount of strategic Intelligence and some operational Intelligence was of course provided by American and Australian agencies. In India and Burma, most of the day to day operational Intelligence and Security work was carried out by the Indian Army's Intelligence Corps (India), a Corps established in November 1942 with its own

172

cap badge and organisation, and also the Burma Intelligence Corps, an *ad hoc* 'theatre' Intelligence Corps. The Intelligence Corps (India) included a number of men with previous local experience and knowledge gained in business or government, a number of young British and Indian officers commissioned on to the Indian Army General List and seconded to the Intelligence Corps (India), and a few pre-1941 Indian Army Regular officers from a variety of regiments also attached. The British Army's Intelligence Corps contribution lay in five main fields – a few officers who, through pre-war careers, spoke Japanese; officers hurriedly taught Japanese in Britain and employed in signals Intelligence; prisoner questioning and document translation; towards the end of the campaign photo-interpretation specialists; a number of NCOs and officers (some themselves newly commissioned ex-NCOs) serving in FSS; and, as in Europe, a small number of volunteers serving in special operations. British Army Intelligence Corps personnel were technically 'seconded' to the Intelligence Corps (India), rather than 'attached' to it.

Hong Kong, Malaya and Burma 1941–42

There appears to have been only one member of the Intelligence Corps in Hong Kong at the time of the Japanese attack, Lieutenant (later Major) F S Austin, who became a prisoner. In Malaya a 'Headquarters, Intelligence Corps', had been formally established in August 1941 under the command of Major A B Chamier. It comprised two Field Security Sections, together with Cipher, Interpreter and certain other specialist personnel; a third section, 78 FSS, that arrived a little later, was despatched to Java, at that time part of the Netherlands East Indies. After the Japanese attack, a fourth section, 15 FSS, arrived at Singapore in January 1942 to suffer with the fall of the fortress—10 members being taken prisoner with 5 dying in captivity.[3]

Three further FSS had been raised in Singapore from among the various Malayan Volunteer force units, but these were all also taken prisoner with a further 10 dying in various camps. Of the brief campaign itself little need be said. Two or three officers with pre-war experience of Japan, including Lieutenants R J F Kalberer, G R Storry (later Professor), C W Tait and R Brown, the latter three all later Majors, were available for operational Intelligence work. Lieutenant Kalberer became a GS03 Intelligence at Army Headquarters in Singapore. But the lack of preparation, the absence of air photography facilities and the stress of battle and constant withdrawal all made their work virtually impossible.

A few local residents and officials were commissioned into the Corps on the spot. One of these, Lieutenant G A T Shaw, was first employed rounding up Japanese residents of Singapore—all elated, with suitcases full of whisky and pornographic literature—after which he was posted as a liaison officer to an Australian battalion retreating from Johore. With Shaw, Lieutenant G Rawlings and Lieutenant W Clark (a Japanese speaker), were tasked to escort and evacuate the prisoners captured in the campaign, in total 13. These had all been captured unconscious, their requests to be killed on regaining consciousness were ignored. Four were hospital cases but, of the remaining nine, two were fighter pilots. All faced certain death in the event of a Japanese recapture and opted to remain with the British. Evacuation became a matter of honour. Shaw, Rawlings, two other officers and the Japanese boarded a gunboat which, despite damage from air attack, reached an island off Java. From there, amid great difficulties, the party travelled by junk to east Sumatra and by train across Sumatra to Padang. There the Dutch separated the prisoners from their escorting officers and their fate is not known. Lieutenants Clark and Shaw were moved out by sea to Ceylon, but Lieutenant Rawlings was captured by the Japanese who used him as an interpreter at Changi military Prison.

The story merits the telling as it reflects more accurately the attitude of Intelligence Corps officers to Japanese prisoners than post-war journalist allegations of ill-treatment, allegations that have been totally disproved. The escape of 15 FSS had followed a hard decision. The GOC, Lieutenant General A E Percival, had directed that certain highly trained specialist personnel who could not be replaced should leave. The Divisional Commander of the division to which 15 FSS was attached ordered Captain Lemin to take his four expert linguist NCOs out. The main evacuation of the specialist personnel, in some 30 little ships, was intercepted and all were destroyed by the Japanese Navy. Captain Lemin, however, had had difficulty in assembling his party and was able to sail away with a party of artillerymen and signallers in a small steam launch. They left the blazing waterfront during an air attack in which Captain Lemin was wounded. They first reached Sumatra, which they crossed by land, for a rather safer journey to Colombo in a warship.

The adventures of Lieutenants Storry, Tait and Brown were similar. Ordered, because of their Japanese language expertise, to escape, they travelled to an island between Singapore and Sumatra where their rescue ship was sunk by Japanese aircraft.

Later, with some 70 other military personnel, they were lifted from the island to Sumatra in a motor launch, from there they too were taken by the Navy to Colombo. Two other Japanese speaking Corps officers were also ordered out of Singapore, Lieutenants Kalberer (see page 173) and R T Wait, but the former was killed in a Japanese air attack on his boat.

Even more adventurous was the story of 43 Special Military Mission, sent to Java (part of Lord Wavell's command) early in 1942, commanded by Lieutenant Colonel L (later Sir Laurence) van der Post and including Captain R (later Sir Robert) Black.[4] The mission was tasked to set up a stay-behind party to facilitate raids and also an escape route from Malacca to Sumatra. But the speed of the Japanese advance, together with the surrender of the Netherlands East Indies government, made this impossible, particularly as the NEI government's surrender ended the supply of electric power essential for the mission's long range signals to Colombo. The mission's shorter range signals led to tracking by the Japanese, Colonel van der Post being captured in the spring of 1942. For a while the mission marched on, from ridge to ridge, the Japanese on its trail, until in August the Japanese threatened to bayonet all the women in an area which they knew the mission had reached. The local Javanese administrator pressed an appeal and the mission gave themselves up – to the administrator, not the Japanese. They were fortunately able to convince the Japanese that their radio equipment was nothing special and they themselves only a group of survivors from the fighting.[5]

In January 1942, there was but one FSS in Burma, an all Indian Section attached to 17 Indian Division, the garrison of lower Burma. But this section was poorly trained and was being misused. It was split up and other personnel, British and Indian, were detached from different units to form two additional composite sections. One of these struggled to maintain order in Rangoon, no easy task in a teeming Asian city set alight by massive air raids; the other retreated to Maymyo. These four sections, hurriedly recruited and trained, were deployed with two at Maymyo, one at Mandalay and one on the railway system. Their chief concerns were Japanese infiltrators (in British or British Indian uniforms), agents, order, and refugee control. By June 1942, when the front had stabilised on the Assam–Burma border, IV Corps was able to deploy four FSS, formed from the British Army's 25 FSS, the Indian 26 Division's FSS and the remaining members of the Burma sections.[6]

Strategic Intelligence

In the Far East, Captain P L Leefe, the GS03 Intelligence at IV Corps' Headquarters from 1942 was the first Corps officer to serve in operational Intelligence in India. But generally, the Corps was less well-represented, even by the end of the war, in the major Command Intelligence appointments. These not unnaturally tended to be filled by Indian Army officers appointed by a senior Indian Army officer, the Director of Military Intelligence (India). The most senior British Army Intelligence Corps officer was D S Prater who was transferred in 1945 from the 8th Army (see Chapter 8) to Allied Land Forces Headquarters first as a Colonel and then as Brigadier General Staff, Intelligence. Major J (later Sir John) Figgess served in Intelligence Staff appointments. One other officer who served at GHQ first as a GS03 Signals Intelligence and then as a GS02 Intelligence was Major J J Grant.[7] Another was R G Lock, who began his Far East Intelligence Corps service as a Sergeant and finished as a Captain. He had been at work in Sumatra before the war and spoke both Dutch and Malay, so making him an exceedingly valuable member of the theatre branch of the Inter-Service Topography Department (ISTD).[8] His work was of special importance when, at one stage in the war, a landing in Sumatra was being planned and, rather later, in 1945 when ships of the Royal Navy were operating against Sumatran targets.

Two members of the Intelligence Corps at Bletchley Park, Lieutenant F S Lindars and Captains D A F M Russell, were at work in the small section dealing with the Far East.[9] Captain Russell's field was Japanese Military Attachés and Lieutenant Lindars that of the Japanese Military Attaché in Berlin, which work he was able to continue after the fall of Berlin, as the same code was used by Japanese missions in other countries. Special Liaison Units were opened in Delhi, near Calcutta and in Ceylon.

The role of Signals Intelligence in the Japanese war has been much under-estimated. Although it never enjoyed the primacy it attained in North Africa and Italy, its contribution was very important. The Americans maintained a large Pacific intercept network, but Britain and Australia were responsible for others from south China, India, Ceylon to Australia and New Guinea, with yet others in Mauritius and Kenya. Intelligence Corps personnel served not only in India but also in Melbourne, Darwin and New Guinea. The more forward units concentrated upon immediate low grade signals traffic, passing higher material back for decrypt work. At theatre level, the organisation was at first centred on Delhi, where the Wireless Experimental Centre India Command was established at a requisitioned university college in a suburban hill village, Anand Parbat. There interception masts and equipment were set up, and an organisation created that provided for sections dealing with collation and evaluation, deciphering and translation, traffic analysis, and listening.[10] Messages in apparently meaningless random four digit groups would be taken down by FANY personnel, girls from the Women's Auxiliary Corps India (many Indian or Anglo–Indian), and later West African Signals troops, who bore the monotony of this – to them – meaningless occupation with commendable loyalty.[11] Reception was very good, the highest mast of Radio Delhi being used when necessary. The first outstations were at Bangalore in southern India, and at Barrackpore near Calcutta. Later, as more Special Wireless Section personnel became available, a further interception sub-centre was opened in Ceylon and units deployed on the border for Japanese aircraft intercepts. For direction finding and, where possible, some radio interception purposes, the 14th Army maintained four or five stations on the Burma border – one or two of these were RAF.

The Japanese used a wide variety of cipher systems for their various diplomatic, naval and military communications. Some 30 members of the Intelligence Corps served in teams concentrating on particular subjects at the different centres; Lieutenant A Stripp, for example, was put to work on the Air Force system.

Where the messages could be read, and they often were, the resulting Intelligence varied in importance from the strategic to the trivial, but it was at times available in large quantities. This was because their conquests and the extended deployment of their forces obliged the Japanese to rely on radio for communication and though interception, particularly of radio telephony, was liable to be affected by static, it was not uncommon to pick up messages originating over 1000 miles away.[12] Furthermore, at least in the latter part of the war, the Allies had enough resources to intercept nearly all messages.

Sometimes, however, ciphers could not be read, at least not quickly enough to provide operational Intelligence. In such circumstances, it was nevertheless possible to use traffic analysis – the study of behaviour, procedures and techniques – to deduce the movement, location and size of enemy forces, even to the point of providing tactical warning of air raids. Training in *kana*, Japanese morse, had been started in Britain and the Middle East in 1940 and early in 1941.

A serious operational difficulty was that the Japanese would vary the size of formations for a task, particularly from 1943 onwards. Signals from a Divisional Headquarters, for example, did not necessarily mean that the division was at full strength with complete food, transport and ammunition supplies. Unless there was other corroboration, all that they meant was that a divisional headquarters was commanding some force of indeterminate size. A Burma Intelligence cliché ran 'From signals you get an enemy's bad intentions, from prisoners you hear his heart beat'.

Interrogation of Japanese prisoners could never yield anything approaching the same results as work with Germans and Italians. Japanese soldiers were ordered to kill themselves rather than allow themselves to be taken, an order generally obeyed until the Japanese Army started to disintegrate in 1945. This meant that, for most of the war, the only material available was a slow trickle of private soldiers, a total of 6 in the 1941–May 1942 retreat, 30 during the first Arakan offensive.[13] These had had no briefing on what to do when captured. If well questioned, they would reveal or confirm unit or formation identities and volunteer information on supply bases, other units, the Indian National Army and their own unit or regimental personalities. There was generally no attempt to dissimulate, nor any sense of guilt for atrocities. Sometimes a cigarette served to open a Japanese soldier to further questioning, but there could also be a tendency to say what the prisoner thought the interrogator wished to hear. In view of the small numbers, cross-checking was difficult, and the horizons of platoon level soldiers, often disease wracked, dying or begging to be killed, very limited.[14] Officers, when later they were taken, were generally unco-operative.

The language difficulty was so great that personnel were generally trained either as interrogators or document translators, not normally both.[15] Documents, when available, were at first underrated as, in Europe, prisoners were generally more helpful than documents. In Burma documents proved the more useful but also hard to come by until 1944. One earlier example, though, of the value of document intelligence, was the use made of captured papers indicating the arrival of Japanese reinforcements from the Pacific at the time of the big Japanese Tanahashi Force offensive in February 1943. Other documents provided long-term political or economic Intelligence. Sackfuls of documents would be brought in for 'scanning', a preliminary quick selection process (in which newly arrived translators greatly improved their Japanese), and then those appearing to be important passed to the best linguists. Tactical Intelligence was gleaned from documents ranging from marked maps and operations orders to soldiers' pay books, identity tags, savings books and unit or personal diaries, these latter often in Japanese cursive script. The first identification of a battalion of the newly arrived Japanese 49 Division in the Kabaw Valley in February 1945, for example, was from a unit tag on a Japanese corpse. Sometimes, however, Japanese faced with capture would throw away their identity documents, not for security reasons but in the hope of hiding their disgrace in anonymity. The documents' linguistic challenge was often worsened by thin paper and running ink.

A Combined Services Detailed Interrogation Centre was opened in the Red Fort at Delhi, the prisoners being housed in the elephant stables. The CSDIC was staffed initially by former British residents in Japan, reinforced later by Intelligence Corps personnel trained in Britain. The Centre also interrogated prisoners of the Japanese-directed Indian National Army; these were usually questioned by Indian Army officers. Among Corps officers at work at the Red Fort were Majors Storry, J D Healey (later Professor) and J G C White. Others among the talented team who learnt Japanese at the London University crash course were Major P (later Sir Peter) Parker, and Captains S T Charles, K B Gardner, L Levy, J H Watkins and A Davies, the latter four all to become distinguished scholars after the war. Linked with the CSDIC was the South East Asia Translation and Interrogation Centre (SEATIC), a document sorting and translation organisation.

Signals Intelligence and the Centre were major contributors to the compiling of BOOB, the Burma Order of Battle. The BOOB was however not easy to compile as the Japanese would generally name – and change the names of – units and formations after the commander and would vary the strengths according to needs.

Air photo-interpretation for long suffered from the shortage of trained personnel and the low priority given to the theatre. A skeleton service of 4 officers, originally destined for Singapore, opened in Delhi and Calcutta early in 1942. But by February 1943, the total strength for the theatre was still only 11 officers. Army and RAF drafts sent out from Britain later in the year included the first Intelligence Corps photo-interpreter officer for the theatre, Major (later Professor) S Piggott. He was joined in 1944 by Major P W Murray-Thriepland. The structure now consisted of a Central Photographic Interpretation Section (SE Asia) in Delhi for long term work, with a Photo-Interpretation Department at Calcutta (Alipore), for more immediate tasks.

Photo-interpreters were next attached to 12th Army headquarters at Calcutta, to South East Asia Command in Ceylon, and in inadequate numbers to a few formations of the 14th Army. The CPIS (SE Asia) was commanded by Lieutenant Colonel Piggott until 1945, when the structure was again reorganised to provide for an Army Photographic Interpretation Unit at Kandy in Ceylon under Lieutenant Colonel Fugelsang. By mid 1945, some of the most experienced of the original Medmenham officers, including Major Simon and Captain Upcher had arrived.[16] Major Simon commanded the 12th Army PI Unit which, in his own words:

> consisted of the 14th Army interpreters who were with the HQ and were being regrouped as the newly formed 12th Army, together with some PIs who were being brought in from Delhi and other theatres. I arrived in Rangoon in June 1945 and found that there was plenty to do. The unit was sufficiently new that I was able to organise it as I thought fit; but it was also immediately apparent that both the PI and the organisation had to be very different from what I had previously experienced. Fortunately, I had a few PIs experienced in jungle conditions; but I was responsible for the whole Burma theatre, and the most distant divisional PI under my command was some 400 miles away. We managed, however, to arrange regular meetings at Pegu and I got around to most of their HQs to meet the divisional commanders, most of whom showed enormous enthusiasm for what PI was doing for them. I recollect that I found this particularly evident at 4th Corps HQ where the General (Major General F I S Tuker) was a real PI fanatic. ... In addition to the interpretation of the areas of Burma where fighting was continuing, we started immediately after my arrival to assemble material for the next phase which could have involved Malaya and Thailand. Fortunately, this material was never required owing to the Japanese surrender; but in working on it, I was able to co-operate more closely with other sources of Intelligence than had been possible elsewhere. In this I was particularly fortunate to have contact with Force 136 [SOE] which operated behind the Japanese lines. After 'VJ' Day there was a feeling of anti-climax. One job, however, of an unusual nature was dealt with; it came from Civil Affairs (Burma) who wanted to know what percentage of the ricefields were still under cultivation.[17]

Other very valuable air photograph interpretation contributions to the Burma campaign included topographical detail (of special importance in a territory not well mapped), the observation of Japanese use of the railways and of bridge construction and repair, and the selection of suitable sites for the dropping of agents. In the jungle areas, air photography could, of course, only be of very limited assistance.

A small number of Intelligence Corps personnel were also among the SOE groups in the Far East; in this theatre, SOE operated under the cover title of Force 136. There were two Corps officers with Force 136 in Burma, Majors R G Turrall and I S Nevill; from the end of 1944 a trickle of FSS NCOs were also posted to secure SOE bases and for training. In occupied Burma there were two main tasks, both aimed at producing sabotage units. The first, almost from the outset of the Japanese occupation, was arming and supporting Karen and other resistance groups. The second, from 1945 onwards, was assistance given to groups from the Japanese-raised Burma Defence Army which had decided to change sides.

Major Guy Turrall's individual work merits especial mention. Before his service with Force 136 he had served as an Operations Staff Officer with the Chindits, General Wingate's airborne long range penetration groups, and then with 16 Brigade on deep penetration patrol work in North Burma. After a brief spell in command of the Hong Kong Volunteers, he joined Force 136, despite his age of 51. He was parachuted in February 1945 in a 'blind jump' mission in the Pyagawpu area, tasked to harass any Japanese withdrawal southwards and to collect intelligence. In April, leading an attack on a Japanese supply base at Kyaukkyi by a group of Karen levies (from several hundred that he himself had raised), Major Turrall was wounded by grenade splinters. He later operated in an area east of Kyaukkyi, with his levies killing over 500 Japanese and providing Intelligence to enable air and artillery strikes to kill several hundreds more. In August, Major Turrall was operating with guerillas east of the Sittang River where at the time of the Japanese capitulation he tried, gallantly but a little rashly, to secure the surrender of the local enemy units. He was himself beaten up by the Japanese who did not at first believe the news. For his work in the campaign he was awarded the DSO.

Two Corps officers were also involved in special operations in Malaya. One was Major C (later Dato Sir Claude) Fenner, a pre-war police officer in Malaya. In 1943 and 1944, on three occasions while travelling in either a British or a Dutch submarine, Fenner made a rendezvous with members of anti-Japanese insurgent groups operating in Malaya—on one of these occasions Intelligence was passed in the brain cavity of a dried fish. In June 1945 Fenner was permitted to land—by parachute—in Malaya to work with the Malayan Peoples Anti-Japanese Army (MPAJA) resistance movement. Lieutenant Colonel J P Hannah, who from pre-war days spoke Malay, was also concerned with the MPAJA. After a frustrating spell on training duties in India, Colonel Hannah was parachuted into Perak in February 1944 to train and, in operations, command the MPAJA's 5th Regiment, at the time 130 strong. By August 1945 the 5th Regiment could field 800 men, supported by some 15 British officers and six 20 strong Gurkha Support Groups. This and other MPAJA units would have been invaluable had an invasion of Malaya been attempted; in the event Hannah secured the peaceful surrender of the Japanese in Perak.[18]

Also involved with Force 136 and Malaya were a small number of officers, including Major H W Astor, who were assembled in Ceylon to plan for six Intelligence Assault units to go to Malaya and also Hong Kong, Indo-China, Thailand and Indonesia. The plans were overtaken by the Japanese capitulation. Major P Kemp after his eventual release from Poland by the Soviets, found post VE day London dull and returned to SOE work with Force 136, being dropped into Laos, in Indo-China, to try to liaise between French sponsored and American sponsored anti-Japanese resistance movements. This mission was also overtaken by events.

As in Europe, political warfare was also used in the Burma campaign, with only a very small measure of success against the Japanese but with a much greater measure against the dissident Japanese controlled 'Indian National Army' and the Burmese civil population. The first experimental unit, called 'Indian Field Broadcasting Unit' (IFBU) was commanded by Major Steer, and was developed from his experience in East Africa. The unit began work in early 1943; by 1944 there were five IFBUs in the field numbered 1 and 201–204, each broadcasting by means of a recording machine of sufficient power to cover a frontage four miles long and half a mile deep, and also using two-inch mortars to fire leaflet canisters which burst in mid-air. A small number of other Intelligence Corps personnel, including Captain R Pierce, assisted Major Steer in this work. The Burmese were prepared for British re-occupation by the promise of better times. Trade goods and medical supplies were dropped into an area warned 48 hours in advance, and people who came for them questioned for intelligence. Other Burmese were given more conventional military instruction in guerilla warfare. INA members were promised pardon if they surrendered, considerable numbers so doing.

Operational Intelligence in Burma

Any review of operational Intelligence work in Burma must begin with a reminder to the reader of the three chief difficulties in the theatre, mountains, monsoons and malaria, compounded by numerous other tropical and jungle warfare hazards. Corps personnel sweated and suffered along with everyone else. Several died of disease and two, Corporal J E Harris and Lance Corporal H Ellis died during the enforced construction of the Burma–Siam railway by the Japanese. Members of the Corps were serving in a variety of roles, contributing to all the different operational Intelligence processes. Overall it can be said that serious gaps in the provision of Intelligence remained until late 1943 and early 1944, and that the provision never became complete, even in 1945. But by 1943, high grade decrypts and Y Service intercepts were reaching front line formations and units in greater quantity. It would appear, for example, that from high grade Signals Intelligence at the time of major Japanese attacks on Imphal and Kohima in 1944, General Slim was aware that Japanese reinforcements had arrived in Burma, and that he had some, but an incomplete, idea of their locations with a rather better picture of their logistic problems. The absence of Japanese wireless traffic in particular areas, indicating the area being free of Japanese units, on occasions provided useful Intelligence in planning axes of advance. Another source was also proving very valuable; reliable Burmese had been enlisted into the Burma Intelligence Corps, platoons of which were attached to divisions.

At Operational Intelligence level, the first major source of Intelligence were those Indian and Burma nationals, Naga hill men, Karens and Chins, who had no love for the Japanese. As noted earlier, prisoners taken by units were rare, though documents or identity discs taken from prisoners or corpses could be informative.

The difficulties in connection with air photography have already been noted.

In respect of prisoner of war tactical questioning and documents study, trained officers and NCOs, as soon as they became available, were sent to Corps and Division Headquarters in the form either of Mobile Intelligence Sections for the interrogation of Japanese, or Forward Interrogation Units (FIUs) concerned with the Japanese sponsored India National Army and Burmese country matters. The first two Mobile Sections were commanded by Majors Storry and S M Bardens, with later others including Major C Arab. Within them interrogation work would be done by the officers, occasionally assisted for translation work by other British officers but more often by Nisei (descendants of Japanese immigrants into Canada or the USA) and supported by British and Indian signals and administrative personnel. Interrogation—until early 1945, after which time numbers greatly increased—would often take place as prisoners lay half dead or in the actual terminal stages of malaria, beri beri or dysentery. Prisoners would be isolated from other Japanese for the interrogation. Sometimes interrogators went forward to the unit who had made the capture. When prisoners became more numerous, translator officers would be used as interrogators. The one common feature with North Africa or Europe was the need for interrogators and translators to be 'half living in their minds every day in the enemy's camp over the hill, sidling into the domestic picture of the enemy's daily routine'.[19] The interrogators were not interpreters. In the words of Captain S T Charles:

> Direct, uninterrupted interrogation produces runs of thought that flow with the language, that can naturally pursue the value of an incidental phrase in the answer. From the conversational intimacy of a continuous dialogue, the JPW (Japanese Prisoner of War) became a more vulnerable source; furthermore, the assessment of his personal qualities – his truthfulness, his accuracy, often linked to education or the job he did in 'civvy street' was made on much safer ground.[20]

The prisoner himself, sick and confused, would often believe he was the very first prisoner to fall into enemy hands in the whole history of Japan, and had so lost the right to call himself Japanese. To this confusion could be added the effect of benign treatment, some medical attention, and better food than the prisoner had enjoyed for some time, instead of the execution that the prisoner had expected. The Japanese Army gave no resistance to interrogation training or advice at all. In this vulnerability, therefore, the prisoner's foe could suddenly become his friend, and useful questioning could often follow. A little later, further questioning could be pursued, in the prisoner's relaxed state. This questioning was very frequently preceded by a conversation about the prospect of a new post-war life in India or Britain, return to Japan being unthinkable. A final stage in the Japanese prisoner mentality noted by several officers was – perhaps as a reaction to the boredom of camp life – a return to truculence, a contempt for the British soft treatment provided for them.

As the Japanese Army began to disintegrate in mid 1945, prisoners arrived in such numbers that they could not all be sent to Delhi. Captain J G C White was posted to Calcutta to conduct preliminary interrogations, working in the city's gaols or questioning prisoners on the transport ships. Captain White was then posted to a CSDIC (I) team preparing for the invasion of Malaya.

Some examples of members of the Corps at work on the next most valuable source, Y Signals work, can also be given. At Barrackpore, Lieutenant (later Professor) D L Snellgrove, serving with 25 WIS, was initiated into Y work on Japanese Air Force intercepts. Later, in Ceylon and in Delhi, he found himself in the Special Liaison Unit, at work on top secret material for special recipients only.[21] On occasions, sections would be deployed forward for particular purposes. In January 1943, for example, 115 SWS, with its attached 54, (later renumbered 115) WIS which included Captain (later Professor) H M Knox, was sent into the field in the Arakan to monitor the communications of Tanahashi Force, intercepts being passed back to the WEC. The section was later posted to XV Indian Corps Headquarters. As a good example of the immediate practical value of field intercepts, an event in January 1945 may be cited. Following the breaking of a Japanese formation cipher, useful Y material became available to XXXIII Indian Corps. Lieutenant (later Professor) H Lloyd Jones recalls that the reading of one signal led to the successful ambush of a Japanese battalion—and very sincere thanks from the Corps Commander.[22] The Japanese Army's water transport code was one of the first to be broken by Y Signals; useful results followed. By the final 12 months of the Burma campaign, Y personnel were attached to Army, Corps and Division headquarters. 25 WIS had been at Imphal with IV Corps from October 1943, being joined by 5 SWS, the two together relieving 201 SWS. On the Arakan front 6 SWS, with 6 WIS, had joined 115 SWS with 54 WIS, though in the event, 6 SWS was moved to Imphal in December 1944. The increased capability met new opportunities; as the Japanese military capacity crumbled, messages were increasingly sent *en clair*, reducing difficulties to that of language only.

Other examples of operational Intelligence show the classic principles all at work in the very special conditions of the Burma campaigns. Early in 1944, 50 Indian Parachute Brigade captured Japanese documents in the Sangshak area. A Burmese attached to the Brigade, who knew some Japanese, recognised an operation order. This was taken through Japanese-held territory to IV Corps Headquarters where it served to correct a 14th Army and

IV Corps assessment that the assault on Kohima was to be made by only one regiment; it was to involve the full 31 Division, crucial Intelligence. In February and March 1945 Meiktila battles, Lieutenant Charles, an interrogator, and Lieutenant G Kay, working as a translator, were able to identify the elements of three Japanese divisions that had been hurriedly pushed in to try to break the hold of Major General Cowan's 17 Indian Division on the Japanese lines of communication.

One of the most striking successes was to follow in July 1945. On the night of 6/7 July, a Gurkha patrol killed a Japanese officer on the 17th Indian Division front near Penwegon. On his corpse was an original operation order, dated 14 June 1945, for a Japanese 55 Division break-out operation due to be fully prepared by 19 July 1945. It was translated at 17 Division on 7 July by Lieutenant L Levy.[23] Copies of the translation were distributed the same day. The original document was then sent to IV Corps Headquarters where it was re-translated by Lieutenant Holliday, checked and reissued further on 10 July, a copy being sent to SEATIC who published it on 16 July. V Force (hillmen irregulars locally recruited for harassment behind the Japanese lines) reports confirmed the Intelligence and Y Signals Intelligence later confirmed 20 July as the day fixed for the operation. Prisoners and documents captured elsewhere along the IV Corps front suggested analogous projects for the other Japanese division, 54 Division, and their controlling 28th Army Headquarters in the area. The division most concerned, 17 Division, had two weeks warning, and the Corps ten days warning, of the Japanese plan for a mass breakthrough attempt. The result was a battle which eventually produced a total of some 17,000 Japanese casualties (mostly by artillery fire, aircraft bombing, guerilla harassment and drowning while attempting the crossing of the Sittang river) for minimal casualties of some 90 on the British and Indian side.

In North Africa and Europe it is possible to draw an approximate dividing line between Operational Intelligence and Security in operations, with, of course, numerous examples of interface. In Burma the interface was total, Intelligence and Security being one and the same, and the modern term of 'operational security' is appropriate. The pattern in 1943 provided for FSS to be posted to Divisions, with usually one British and one Indian NCO detached to Brigade headquarters. The prime responsibility was the prevention of Japanese infiltration into headquarters areas at night.[24] Such infiltration attempts could be made by parties of between 10 and 180 men, sometimes all in plain clothes. Other FSS duties varied according to the terrain but included control of refugees, the active patrolling of villages in the immediate rear, the questioning of local peoples to ascertain who was collaborating with the Japanese and who might be prepared to collect Intelligence for the British, the prevention of pilfering and the search for any Japanese documents. Intelligence was often relatively easy to come by in respect of the Japanese-sponsored Indian National Army, photographs of INA parades being found from which identities could be made. Sources of Intelligence could be unusual. One old woman:

> an Opium eater, having consumed all that she had and not being able to carry on without it, has decided to brave the battlefield and cross to Imphal to obtain a further supply. She is an extremely intelligent old woman with remarkable powers of observation and memory. She has given locations of defences, HQs, dumps, types of artillery, details of casualties, food supply, L of C routes and also the names of the chief (local) collaborators, six in all. ... Following information from the old Manipuri woman that the Jap was using culverts along the road as store places all were searched. From one, a 75 mm gun in pieces, 55 rounds, spare kit and four pack saddles were recovered.[25]

On occasions, FSS NCOs of the Corps, in disguise as Asians, would lead a small party of trusted locals into Japanese-held territory gathering Intelligence, ascertaining collaborators, and searching buildings that the Japanese had not thought necessary to secure. One NCO was sent on a mission of this type to Akyab island on to which a British landing was planned. He was able to establish that the Japanese had withdrawn, leaving no stay-behind parties. The Japanese had, however, in their occupation aroused tension between the Moslem and Buddhist communities which had erupted into violence about which he was able to warn the landing commanders. On his return he found a letter from his aunt awaiting him. She had written 'I am so pleased to hear you are in the FSS. You deserve a nice office job after being so long in the infantry'.[26]

A few other examples of Operational Intelligence work by FSS can also be given. Captain R W R Ogden's 604 FSS, working with 20 Indian Division, pursued and captured U Nandiya, a much wanted Burmese working as an agent for the Japanese, on 1 February 1945. The capture was the result of several months of research and pursuit in the course of which U Nandiya twice narrowly escaped being caught. Captain Ogden was awarded the MBE for his work. Captain (later Lieutenant Colonel) R J Isaac, commanding 505 FSS, was awarded the MC for his work while the Section was serving with 5 Indian Division; on one occasion he personally accounted for nine Japanese. No 589 FSS under Captain A Watts and 573 FSS both distinguished themselves in the Pegu area while clearing the main axis of advance on Rangoon in May 1945; one NCO of 589 FSS, Sergeant Caldecot, being killed during these operations.

Other officers were engaged in more conventional, if no less arduous, Operational Intelligence duties. Major W Lough, for example, serving with 2 Division, was sent to learn the fate of one of the Division's brigades loaned operationally to another Division. 'I was sent after the incident in which the brigade headquarters was overrun and the brigadier and all but one of his officers killed. Ordered to report on the state and morale of the brigade I felt I was being put on my mettle as a staff officer'.[27]

Operational Intelligence was also greatly assisted by the theatre Burma Intelligence Corps (BIC), a hastily raised First World War style body reminiscent of the East African Intelligence Corps of 1914–18. Its members, guides, scouts and interpreters, were grouped on an *ad hoc* basis after the retreat to India from remnants of the old Burma Armed Forces, military, para-military police or Volunteer units who had somehow or other managed to reach India in 1942. It was thought that had there been such a local Corps in Malaya in 1941–42 much needless confusion and suspicion over 'fifth column' collaborators could have been averted. The officers, nearly all non-Burmese, included government officials, businessmen, forestry officers, oil men, Anglo-Indian traders, even a few hill tribesmen – China, Kachins and Karens. The other ranks consisted partly of Anglo–Burmans (mixed parentage) who rated as British Other Ranks and spoke English, Burmese and Urdu, and partly of former Burma Army men, rated as Indian Other Ranks and speaking only Burmese and Urdu. Some 16 platoons, each of some 40 men, were formed, a platoon serving each combat Corps and Division headquarters. Platoons were subdivided into Sections to work with the infantry brigades. A Depot was established at Mhow in India as part of HQ Burma Auxiliary Forces.

The BIC engaged in a variety of duties. These were mostly not strictly Intelligence, but in the course of them the Corps acquired information of value to both the I (A) and I (B) staffs. They were highly regarded by their Divisions, and won numerous decorations. BIC platoon commanders were constantly arranging food and medical supplies, explaining malaria control regulations, checking black lists and other minor but useful duties. An example of the working relationship between Field Security and the BIC is set out in a letter from Captain Ogden of 604 FSS dated 1 March 1945, to his staff:

> As you know, I want the whole Section to concentrate on obtaining good information from the locals. Work very closely with the BIC. Major Lutter, the OC divisional BIC is anxious, as I am, that the BIC and Brigade FS dets work very closely together. If they get information, give them credit for it in your reports, and head your reports "FSS/BIC Joint Daily Report".

A notable—and unique—feature of operational Intelligence in Burma was the deployment in action of a specific tactical deception unit, D Force. The conditions were ideal, jungle concealed movement, the Army was moving increasingly to offensive operations, and the Japanese, who tended to a rigidity of tactical thinking, lacked any forms of battlefield surveillance equipment. The Force was composed initially of 6 companies, 2 British, four Indian, each of about 50 men, later raised to 8 companies.[28] It was commanded from January 1944 by Major (later Lieutenant Colonel) P E X Turnbull, who had previously been at work with guerillas in the Chin Hills.[29] D Force was equipped with fire cracker devices (of varying efficiency in the damp Burma climate) simulating small arms fire, together with genuine explosives and a number of sub-machine guns. Success, it was soon found, lay in the use of large numbers of effects in a concentrated area.[30] Initially operations were single company, later two or more were committed. Their aim was to be a multiplier, by creating noise to simulate the presence of a much larger force. The missions included flank cover for one of the attacks to relieve a besieged position, and later appearing to threaten the axis of a threatened Japanese counter attack, both in the Arakan in January–March 1944; diversions covering withdrawal from the Kabaw Valley on the central front in April and cover for a pre-monsoon withdrawal in the Arakan in May; and diversions involving mortar and small arms fire and movement of vehicles to provide a three day cover for a brigade redeploying for a flank attack on Ramree island in January 1945.[31] The apogee of D Force was reached after the fall of Ramree when five companies mounted a series of seaborne landing raids which successfully duped the Japanese as to the British axes of advance, leading them to dissipate their forces.

Companies adopted mobile harrying tactics to simulate a reconnaissance in force.

The story of Operational Intelligence cannot however be presented in the same terms of general overall success as in North Africa and Europe. As late as June 1944, for example, Lieutenant General Scoones, commanding IV Corps on the Central front, was complaining sharply that he had received no prior warning of the arrival of a new Japanese formation, 15 Division, near Imphal. Later, in the autumn of 1944 the 14th Army Commander, General Slim, was unsure whether the battle he planned to fight against the main Japanese force in Burma at the time was to be in front of the Irrawaddy or behind it. Even in 1945, Slim was not fully briefed on the Japanese abandonment of Rangoon. The peculiar difficulties of the Burma campaign were as great for Operational Intelligence as for anything else.

Failures in Operational Intelligence were also matched by numerous failures in Operational Security. The Japanese operated several Intelligence gathering networks, some Buddhist monks, numerous Burmese, Japanese civilians in one or other form of disguise, on occasions running networks of informers, together with small detachments of Japanese soldiers selected for their physical resemblance to Burmese. These all frequently achieved successes in shadowing British columns on the move, or walking in and around British occupied villages where time and the conditions of the terrain prevented the creation of any form of wired perimeter.

Security in Madagascar, India and Ceylon

One of the first purely security problems in the Pacific War was in Madagascar, which lay on the interface between the German and Japanese wars. This French colony had remained under a Vichy régime until the entry into the war of Japan. The Japanese began to threaten Vichy with action against the French colonial position in Indochina unless facilities were made available to Axis and Japanese warships in Madagascar. Allied occupation became imperative. In May 1942 Force 121 of five brigades, British and African, landed near Diego Suarez; with the Force landed over the beaches 29 FSS, commanded by Captain L W Annis. The Section went on to serve with the Force in the second stage of the occupation in September 1942. The Section's tasks were the release of known Gaullists held in prison; surveillance of the French authorities and residents, replacing those with an active collaborationist record; the detention of certain men among the crew of a German merchant ship in harbour who were suspected of Intelligence gathering; screening of numerous Italian seamen; and in the first months the operation of a pass and road check system between the northern area occupied by the British and the rest of the island. For his work in the Madagascar operations, Sergeant R Croft-Cooke of 29 FSS was awarded the BEM. Also at work in Madagascar was Captain R E Colby, in charge of pre-occupation propaganda (leaflets inviting the French garrison to surrender) and, after the initial landings, in charge of a hastily established broadcasting service tasked to counter the pro-Vichy propaganda still broadcast from the unoccupied area.[32]

Rear area Security in the Burma campaign was a major problem as certain nationalists in Burma and in India were active in the Japanese cause. Furthermore, on occasions, the Japanese dropped in agents for sabotage work. An early task was the screening of refugees from Burma. The very large number of FSS committed indicates the size of the problem, stretching back as it did to strategic ports and Lines of Communications installations in India. In 1943, there were 25 sections working in Assam alone. This need for rapid expansion had diluted quality:

> The British Other Ranks were of two categories. The early entrant, coming from the old British Intelligence Corps Sections, were of a high mental and social category. These men gave excellent service and nearly all were commissioned and became in their turn FSOs of new Sections. The other category consisted of British Other Ranks in SEAC and India Command. These men naturally were of a lower calibre but after training and weeding out of the unfit at the Depot, the remainder actually posted to Sections gave good service.[33]

The Indian personnel also had to be subjected to a rigid training and assessment process. Relations between Indian and British personnel were excellent, Sections were housed together and British NCOs accepted discipline from Indian NCOs when the latter were the senior. In 1943, it was ruled that all Intelligence staff officers were to be attached (though not rebadged) to the Intelligence Corps (India), a move designed to prevent able Intelligence officers being posted to other duties; this ruling was later extended to British FS NCOs commissioned in the field or after a course at an Indian Officer Cadet Training Unit.

During and after the retreat from Burma, a major Security problem was that of the Indian nationalist uprising of 1942. Part of the nationalist effort was targeted upon military units, calling for subversion and sabotage. Propaganda in lurid terms was directed especially at Indian and Gurkha regiments from a variety of Japanese sponsored organisations.[34] Some FSS, for example 545 Parachute FSS, were composed equally of British and Indian personnel so as to provide appropriate watch on a Division formed of British, Indian and Gurkha units. When the tide turned and the 14th Army was on the advance, FSS priorities extended to the rounding up of Japanese supporters in areas liberated.

A glimpse of the nature of the work of Port Security can be found in the notebook of Sergeant W L Brown, who served at Colombo.[35] The notebook contains the names of some 450 mariners—including some officers and wireless operators—on a Black List. The men came from a variety of countries including Portugal, Spain, Sweden, Norway, Ireland, France, Greece, Estonia, Holland and Belgium. Against them are remarks such as 'Known to have contacts with Axis agents', 'Courier of Uncensored Mail', 'Reported to have made enquiries about troop movements', 'Known Enemy Agent', 'Suspected of having sold information to German agents in Beira', 'German agent, former member of Spanish Blue Division', 'In close touch with German Consul Lourenco Marques', 'Tried to break radio silence at sea and send messages to Sweden' and 'Strongly pro-Petain and anti-Allies'.

In Karachi, Captain Isaac arranged with the head man of Baba Island, where the local fishing community lived, that sailing and fishing permits would only be issued if he was told which fishermen were carrying cameras to photograph shipping in the harbour. This useful arrangement led to a number of arrests.

A few Intelligence Corps personnel were at work at the Special Censor Unit at Tinsukia, north Assam—these included NCOs who had taken an intensive Chinese course. Tinsukia was an outpost of the main Intelligence Corps (India) Censorship organisation based in Calcutta. The concerns of Intelligence Corps personnel at Tinsukia were both English mail from the local tea planting community and some Chinese mail from Chinese rear echelon units in the area.

The Ending of Hostilities

Lieutenant Colonel van der Post gives a remarkable picture of the end of the Japanese war in his *The Night of the New Moon*.[36] When in prison, Colonel van der Post had collected Intelligence about Japanese military activities in Indonesia, and also about the

Indonesian nationalists; the collection was based upon reports slipped into the camp by Chinese—and one Korean—informers. He came to learn of the Japanese plan for a mass execution of the thousands of Allied prisoners in Indonesia, to be carried out when Allied troops landed. He organised, in conditions of great secrecy, an attempt to resist a Japanese mass execution within his camp. The prisoners were divided into six platoons and caches of stones, to be thrown at the Japanese guards, were prepared. It was hoped in this way that a few might escape slaughter and either hasten the advance of Allied troops or at least provide an account of what had happened. The dropping of the atom bomb led the Japanese to abandon their plans for this carnage.

A postscript should be added to the work of the Intelligence Corps during the Japanese war. The campaigns had been marked by hatred on both sides. The post-war world has seen new relationships develop between Britain and Japan. An important part of these new relationships has been both the post-war teaching of Japanese Studies, the study of Japan, her history, philosophy and culture, and the numerous personal contacts made, by members of the war-time Intelligence Corps. The new relationships have benefited both victor and vanquished.

11

Aftermath

The German and, later, Japanese capitulations changed the nature of much of the work of Intelligence Corps personnel, but in the first months of peace the quantity of that work was only slightly reduced. There arose a very large number of residual commitments, some directly concerned with Intelligence and Security for the Army and some in which the Corps acted as a uniformed military executive arm of wider British government policies. Although many wartime experts were demobilised in late 1945 and 1946, the supply of personnel was maintained by the Corps' use of National Service officers and soldiers. This chapter looks at these wide residual commitments that fell to the Corps, but has also to conclude with the much reduced role that the Army of the time saw for the Corps after the end of those commitments.

The Occupation of Germany

In the final stages of the German collapse and immediately after the surrender, small Intelligence Corps detachments received the surrender of German personnel and units on several occasions. Some liberation commitments were distressing. Sergeant Stagnetto of 317 FSS, with a small detachment from the Section, were the first Allied troops to enter the appalling Belsen concentration camp, taking photographs of the conditions in the camp at the moment of its liberation. Later 53 FSS, under Captain K M Stephens, arrived, Sergeant Turgel of that Section interrogating Kramer, Belsen's Commandant.

The arrest and interrogation of suspected War Criminals believed to be in the British Zone of Occupation was an immediate Corps priority. Among the leading Nazis and personalities arrested were Heinrich Himmler, the leader of the SS, taken by 45 FSS. Himmler had disguised himself by removing his moustache, adding an eye patch and giving himself a new identity as a sergeant in the German Army secret field police. At the head of a small party of close associates he attempted to move from Flensburg in north Germany to Bavaria, but he was cut off by British troop movements. Following up information gathered elsewhere, 45 FSS arranged for a number of checkpoints on important routes to be set up. At one of these, at Bremervoerde, Himmler and two associates were detained, the disguise that they unwisely selected being in an automatic arrest category. However their real identity did not become clear for a further two days, when Himmler admitted all. Himmler's suicide precautions—a small quantity of cyanide concealed in the left cheek—unfortunately escaped his medical examiner until too late. A little later, FSS personnel picked up Hitler's Foreign Minister, Joachim von Ribbentrop, in Hamburg. Other much wanted personalities included Rudolf Hoess, the Commandant of Auschwitz and the entire post-Hitler government of Admiral Doenitz, taken by 61 FSS at Flensburg. This latter group included Colonel General Jodl and a number of ministers and senior officials. Lesser fry included the Commandant of Sachsenhausen concentration camp, arrested by 53 FSS, and the Gauleiter of Magdeburg by 9 FSS, the latter official being, paradoxically, part-Jewish.

The Corps' next task in Germany and Austria was threefold. The first and most immediate was the unearthing of numerous members of the Nazi Party and related Nazi organisations who had gone to ground under one name or another, and at the same time to see if there was any likelihood of a final resistance movement emerging. In the event, the former engaged Corps FSS for many months, while the latter threat, apart from very occasional minor sabotage, emerged only once in any significant form. A widespread movement under the cover of a transport organisation in both the British and American zones was watched for a while and then destroyed by a series of arrests on 31 March 1946.[1] The second task was initially to report on civilian morale and later to provide expert personnel for the rebuilding of a German educational, cultural and eventual political life. The third was to contribute, again in the form of special personnel, to the search for German technology of use to Britain. This latter duty often took the form of a race against other Occupying Powers, a race not always friendly, even among close allies.

Supreme Allied Headquarters had set out the basis for immediate denazification and counter-intelligence work in a 1944 directive. The main features of this included an Allied Military Government, non-fraternisation, control of movement, food, identity documents, education, the media, local government and such productive capacity as remained. Regional governments would later assume much more power than under the Nazis. A 21 Army Group Counter-Intelligence Instruction for the British Zone provided greater detail. FSS, whose name was later to change to Counter-Intelligence—CI—Sections, were to be posted to *Regierungsbezirke* or district administrative centres and other towns over 1,000,000. There were also to be Port, Frontier and Anti-Sabotage sections; for this work 85 CI Sections and 20 CI Reserve Detachments were formed from the FSS of 21 Army Group and new drafts. By the latter months of 1945, this organisation had taken shape, with Headquarters Intelligence Corps (Field) administering 83 FSS (with one additional Netherlands Army section), an Army Refugee Interrogation Team, 20 Military Government Interrogation Sections, 16 area security offices and a Counter-Intelligence laboratory, together with 3 Counter-Sabotage detachments and a small number of Port and frontier Security Sections. The Intelligence Corps played a very large part in the manning of all these sections and sub-units, initially controlling and supervising drafts under Intelligence Corps (Field), after that headquarters disbandment and replacement with the Intelligence Division of the Control Commission Germany, by 273 FSS.

Of these sub-units initially two, 23 FSS and 309 FSS were posted to Berlin; they were joined by a third, 50 FSS, late in 1945 when all were placed directly under Berlin Headquarters Intelligence Staff. By March 1946, only 309 FSS remained, but it was reinforced during the 1948-49 Berlin Blockade crisis by 903 FSS, whose main task was the screening of the 12,000 strong civilian labour force at Gatow airfield serving the airlift.

Denazification

Essentially, the immediate FSS work of denazification can be summed up in four words, search, detain, interrogate, document. For this work good German was essential, together with a knowledge of the now defunct Nazi régime. For this latter the Nazi's own 1943 handbook, *Organisationsbuch der NSDAP*, was invaluable.[2] In command of the Field Investigation Unit of the War Crimes Group North West Europe was Lieutenant Colonel R A Nightingale. The basis of questioning was a 12 page Questionnaire *Fragebogen*, covering every aspect of an individual's life: personal particulars, religious beliefs, schools and Nazi party special schools, University and Nazi Party student organisations, employment, military service, Nazi Party social and professional organisations, income, property, travel and persons visited. Thoroughness was all important. Former Nazi sympathisers faced prison, loss of employment and if illegally acquired, home, and, in lesser cases, disenfranchisement.

In the denazification process, an immediate task was the many thousands of German military personnel, all having to be screened before release. Major T Peters recalls, of this work, that priority release was given to agricultural workers for the 1945 harvest and to entertainers to raise German morale. German speakers from a variety of sources—Jewish refugees, Alsatians and others were often co-opted in to assist as interpreters. Another early task was the purging of German industry, particularly heavy engineering, electrical and chemical concerns.

Officers of the Corps were employed in the interrogation of a number of senior officers and Nazi officials; Lieutenant Colonel Scotland, for example, led the interrogation of Marshal Kesselring, in which Captain M F Cornish also participated. Later Captain Cornish was sent to Moscow to assist in the interrogation of the Gauleiter of Breslau.

Another early commitment was the denazification of universities and *Hochschulen*, and supervision of their return to a normal life. Captain F O P Brann was, for example, responsible for Bonn University. Candidates for entry, students, and staff had to be screened, student societies watched and text books monitored – gifts from British and Swiss universities being especially useful. In the academic year 1945–46, the task was enormous—university buildings lacked water, heating, electricity, doors and windows; students wrote lecture notes on the backs of old envelopes, lived in cellars of ruined houses and worked part-time as labourers to qualify for a hot meal.

Related to University work was that of scientific research. In this field Lieutenant Colonel B K Blount was at work in the Research Branch of the Control Commission's Economic Subcomission. He was tasked to end all scientific research work of military potential, but to encourage other work. His duties varied from the prevention of needless dismantling and destruction to the preservation and funding of numerous research institutes.[3]

Local authorities and public services were another important area for denazification—in Hanover an SS *Standartenfuhrer* with a particularly unpleasant reputation was found by 45 FSS working as a council labourer. Major T X H Pantcheff's investigation into

Nazi atrocities in penal camps at Esterwegen and Aschendorfer Moor provide a good example of the Corps' contribution into war crime enquiries. At the former, French and Belgian resistance members had 'disappeared', at the latter some 200 prisoners were killed with Nazi Party connivance in April 1945, the killings being the work of a lance-corporal posing as an officer. Major Pantcheff's team comprised himself, a captain, a warrant officer and two staff sergeants, all Intelligence Corps. Careful investigations were carried out among the former prison guards (now themselves prisoners of war) and former inmates of the camps, now released. Eventually, a British Military Government court imposed six death sentences in respect of the Aschendorfer Moor killings, and a second court imposed two death and several long-term prison sentences in respect of the Esterwegen brutalities.[4]

Three investigations were especially distressing; two concerned the execution in May 1940 of British Army soldiers who were at the time German Army prisoners. These included a group from the Royal Norfolk Regiment killed near Calais, and a much larger group of some 90, mostly Royal Warwickshire Regiment, killed near Dunkirk. Among those who assisted in this investigation was, again, Major Pantcheff. A third investigation, in which Captain Cornish worked with RAF investigators, was into the murder of British prisoners in a German Camp, Stalag Luft III.

Another FSS task, reflecting the changing international scene, was the investigation of Soviet agents pushed into the British Zone after training at a special unit at Torgau in the Soviet Zone. The agents were generally Germans who had been former members of the KPD (the German Communist Party). About one half immediately gave themselves up on arrival, thankful to leave the Soviet Zone; the rest were not too difficult to apprehend.[5]

At a high political level, Lieutenant Colonel N Annan was appointed to the Political Directorate of the British Control Commission, with the task of advising the military government on such matters as denazification and the renewal of German political life.[6] In the latter context, the British Zone area was of key importance. Almost immediately, in October 1945, a crisis arose from the arbitrary dismissal of Dr K Adenauer from his post as *Oberburgermeister* of Cologne by the local British military administrator, a brigadier. Adenauer had committed no offence, but the brigadier, distrusting Adenauer's known political ambitions to lead a restored democratic and Catholic Western Germany, banned him from entry to Cologne and also from any form of political activity. The unwisdom of this action was recognised by Colonel Annan and his Foreign Office superiors. They did, however, experience some difficulty in persuading the military administration that a return to political life was not only inevitable, but if that life was healthy, also desirable. Colonel Annan then proceeded to call on Adenauer and, in a somewhat delicate interview, reassured him that he could pursue political activities towards his goal.

Early in 1946, Colonel Annan called a meeting of German personalities known to want to resume political activity to advise them that this would now be permitted. Of this meeting he later wrote:

> The response was touching, 'This news is better for us than white bread' said one old Social Democrat. Here were men who had come many kilometers in most cases with extreme difficulty as roads and railways were still so terribly damaged, men with sallow faces and with the strained expression that hunger gives ... At that meeting I saw for the first time that spirit of dedication to democracy as a form of government. That spirit sprang from the knowledge both of what dictatorship had been and what dictatorship still was in the Eastern Zone of Germany.

It next fell to Colonel Annan to guide the Social Democratic Party (SDP) back to a proper political path, guidance involving restrictions on certain party leaders of the 1930s who had been prepared to compromise with the Nazis. More serious was heavy Soviet pressure on SPD leaders in Berlin and the Soviet Zone to merge with the KPD. Colonel Annan and his Foreign Office chief were unable to persuade Grotewohl, the Berlin SPD leader, against the fusion. But by research and the exposure of the pre-war record of Ulbricht, the Communist leader, Colonel Annan was able to ensure that a majority of the SPD delegates at a special conference rejected the merger, despite the fact that the conference was held in the Soviet sector of Berlin. The Soviets then went their own way in their own Zone, but another consequence, however, was a greater appreciation by the USA of the wisdom of British policies. Colonel Annan's reporting of the emerging German political scene went through the Foreign Office to the Foreign Secretary, Ernest Bevin, personally.

These reports used the careful observations of the political scene by several Intelligence Corps officers, among them being Major Peters, Major D Royce and Captain M P Thomas. The latter was in fact a native German but totally opposed to Nazism. The pressurising of the SPD leaders represents a good example of such observation. At first the Soviets had been content to allow both the SPD and the KPD to emerge. The clear, large lead of the SPD over the KPD caused them, as we have seen, to change tack and seek an amalgamated party that would carry out Soviet policy. Paper and publicity facilities were given to the KPD and denied to the SPD, anti-fusionist SPD meetings and officials were harassed and, on at least one occasion, beaten up. Meetings to discuss fusion were convened at short notice with only the KPD members warned in advance, and SPD waverers were bribed by food parcels.

Also at work at the political level was Major N Gash, now head of MI 14(d), the only remaining operational unit of MI 14. During the war, this section had been concerned with Nazi party-controlled military forces; now, as a unit, its ambition was extended to the collation and analysis of all information of a military or security nature concerning Occupied Germany and Austria.[7]

Other, very varied tasks, were carried out by members of the Corps in Germany at this time. Major J C Phipps served as Personal Assistant to Lord Justice Lawrence at the Nuremberg War Criminal Trials. Lieutenant Colonel K Garside, who had from late 1944 been collecting captured enemy documents that might be of use for the Control Commission, continued work on documents that were of importance. He was instrumental in helping the 'Enemy Publications Committee' establish a field organisation to locate German learned and scientific books and treatises produced in the Nazi era. Major (later Professor) N R C Cohn was engaged in similar work in Austria, some of his finds being used at the Nuremberg trials. A NCO, J Packman, organised the main Intelligence Bureau registry at the Control Commission headquarters. Lieutenant Colonel J F E Stephenson, was in charge of an MI5 liaison section concerned with collection of evidence against British traitors in Germany. Major W Stallybrass served with the Commission's Enemy Document Unit. Lieutenant Colonel A A Rowan-Robinson and Lieutenant Colonel C T Tinling were in charge of all German interpreters at work for the Commission. Lieutenant Colonel H Boggis-Rolfe served in the Commission's Legal Division and Major C A Cox was tasked with organising a new police force in the British Zone. Other officers served as Regional Intelligence Officers, Lieutenant Colonel B Kemball Cook, for example, so serving in Bremen. In Britain, some Corps officers were at work in the political re-education of German prisoners of war, Wilton Park at Beaconsfield being one centre for their work. Others were at work in different prisoner of war camps questioning former members of the SS in order to identify the most notorious. In the United States, Colonel D A Prater was bringing his massive experience to the German Military Document Centre at Camp Ritchie in Maryland.

One sensitive issue was the different Allies' attempts to secure German wartime scientific and technological inventions. An Anglo American unit, FIAT or Field Information Agency (Technical) was set up near Frankfurt with a joint staff, among the British officers was Major Stallybrass.

Austria and Italy

A similar FSS system to that in Germany was established for Austria. An initial 12 FSS were deployed in the British Zone of Occupation in Austria, under the control of 2 Area Security Offices at Klagenfurt and Graz with, until 1949, additional Frontier Sections and a further 3 FSS in the British sector of Vienna.[8] Factors complicating the immediate post-war situation were the large number (120,000) of prisoners of war, equally large and ever increasing numbers of displaced persons, the consequence of a brief Soviet occupation of (and some reluctance to depart from) areas of the British Zone, and the fact that Vienna was entirely surrounded by Soviet-occupied territory. In the areas entered by Soviet troops unpopular Communists installed by the Red army had to be removed from office. Actual relations with Soviet military personnel, combat units who had fought their way into Austria, were at first very cordial, political officers often being openly ignored. But from 1947–48 these units were replaced by others who had been heavily indoctrinated politically. There was also the sensitive issue as to whether Austria was an occupied or a liberated territory, the Austrians themselves repudiating the 1938 annexation.

As in Germany, the tasks were the tracking down and arrest of Nazi Party members, zone demarcation and line-crossers, attempts by hundreds of Jewish refugees and displaced persons to depart illegally for Palestine, and, from 1946, the questioning of Austrians returning from captivity and forced labour in Soviet camps. Some had even worked in or near Soviet armaments factories. The three sections in Vienna had wider duties. No 310 FSS at Schönbrunn Palace had special security commitments and 291 FSS located near the British Embassy concentrated on protective security. The third, 20 FSS, was enlarged, totalling some 50, and carried out a wide range of Intelligence and

Security duties over most of the British Zone; these duties included counter-espionage, censorship, screening of prisoners of war and refugees, and some signals Intelligence. Much of its work was carried out in plain clothes. In 1948 a Yugoslav spy-ring trying to stir up the small Serbian population in Styria in support of a border claim was unearthed, and broken up. The stream of refugees trying to cross the Hungarian border necessitated special measures. A photograph library and card index system had to be built up, and dubious refugees questioned with the aid of Hungarian interpreters. Information gained ranged from Intelligence concerning Soviet Forces to breaches of human rights. The massive presence of the Soviet Army both in Austria and Hungary added tension, but also some zest.

With Austria's return to political life at the end of the decade FSS duties were extended to surveillance of political parties, especially the Communist Party. Engaged in similar work to that of Colonel Annan in Germany was Colonel W D Gibson, serving as Colonel I(B). The main political level tasks were inter-allied agreement on frontier control, the vetting of candidates for important civilian positions and the arrest of the worst of the Austrian Nazis.[9] Lieutenant D Hamblen was GS01 (Frontier and Travel Control) in the Intelligence Organisation of the British part of the Allied Control Commission, Lieutenant Colonel C Beauclerk was head of the Information Division for the British Zone, and Lieutenant Colonel D Macfarlane head of the Political Warfare Branch.

In 1949, frontier control was handed back to the Austrian government and the Frontier Sections withdrawn. In 1950, all the FSS outside Vienna were withdrawn with only two Province Headquarters, FS Carinthia and FS Styria and a small number of detachments remaining. In 1955 all British units were withdrawn.

An ongoing FSS commitment remained for a year in Italy; in February 1946 there were still 16 FSS at work. Several Intelligence Corps officers served in the 1944-45 Allied Military Government of Italy. Lieutenant Colonel A E Howell, for example, was successively Provincial Commissioner for Potenza and Aosta, and then later head of a political department of Allied Headquarters. Major A Colquhoun was in charge of a section concerned with former Italian partisans, and Major C Isolani served as Head of the Allied Publications Board in North East Italy, controlling printed media.

Trieste

A problem of special difficulty and to remain an Intelligence Corps commitment until 1954 was the port of Trieste. During the last days of the campaign in Italy, 8th Army and Marshal Tito's Yugoslav partisan troops raced each other to occupy the Italian region known as the Venezia Giulia – Italy's easternmost provinces, Trieste, Gorizia and Udine. An agreement between General Morgan (Field Marshal Alexander's Chief of Staff) and Tito in March 1945 had defined Allied and Yugoslav 'zones of interest'. It had been accepted that Trieste city and its surrounding territory would be liberated and occupied by the Allies as they would need the port facilities for their further advance into Austria. But Tito's partisans entered Trieste first, on 1 May 1945, while the forward troops of the 8th Army were held up at a bridge, allegedly prepared for demolition, over the River Isonzo some 20 miles west of the city. The allegation was deliberate disinformation provided by the leader of a small partisan group later to be one of 35 FS Sections' biggest security problems in the nearby town of Monfalcone, noted in 1945-47 for its large pro-Tito Communist faction.

New Zealand troops entered the city of Trieste on 2 May and immediately claimed the right to occupy the surrounding Trieste Province. But for over five weeks the partisans refused to leave those parts of the provinces of Trieste and Udine which they had occupied and from which came allegations of atrocities and reprisals. Partisans also attempted to deport Italians and repopulate the area with Yugoslav nationals, in order to claim an 'ethnic' right to annex the disputed city. Allied troops were not empowered to intervene officially, though in practice many interventions were made, saving life and preventing deportations.

At the end of the five weeks, XIII Corps Headquarters took over military control of the Allied-occupied area of Venezia Giulia, known from then on as Zone 'A', the dividing line being known as the 'Morgan Line', while the Yugoslavs occupied Zone 'B' the hinterland and Istrian Peninsula. With the departure of the New Zealanders, 56 Division garrisoned the province and city of Trieste, with 88 US Infantry Division at Gorizia, and the British 6 Armoured Division in areas of Udine Province. Lost to the Allies was the whole of the Istrian Peninsula and the city of Pola, where a British military presence, including a Field Security detachment, had been maintained for a few months. Lieutenant General Sir John Harding, the Commander of XIII Corps, became Military Governor of Venezia Giulia, and an *ad hoc* civilian police force called the Venezia Giulia Police Force was set up, initially officered by the British, and carrying out all civil police duties except Special Branch work.

It therefore fell to the Trieste FSS to perform Special Branch duties for the Allied Military Government in addition to their normal counter-intelligence functions, including Port and Frontier control and all the wartime civil Security controls. Port control work included searching ships for clandestine arms consignments to Jewish groups in Palestine. In view of the tense political atmosphere in Trieste, the Military Government applied strict regulations regarding public assembly, demonstrations and the printing and publishing of unauthorised newspapers. From the start, searches of vehicles, homes, factories and other hiding places for weapons, explosives and propaganda material were daily features of FS work, in addition to the routine post-war search for and arrest of war criminals, men in arrest categories and black list individuals. Some telephone tapping and agent handling work was also involved.

The most important single counter-intelligence task facing Field Security personnel quicky became that of countering the activities of the Yugoslav Secret Police, whose efforts included 'stay-behind' agents, local sympathisers and agents infiltrated into Zone 'A' in the guise of refugees, businessmen, railway workers and other trades.[10] Thus Refugee Screening and Travel Control Teams made up a considerable part of the counter-intelligence effort, with Intelligence Corps and American Counter Intelligence Corps personnel both being assigned to it. A converse also existed. Non-Communist Yugoslavs living in Trieste would try to slip across the border in a raid, either to kill Yugoslav soldiers or to distribute propaganda. One gang engaged in this war was infiltrated by an agent recruited by 96 FSS, a success resulting in the capture of the entire gang and greatly improved Anglo-Yugoslav relations. Captain R M Richards commanded a joint Anglo-American Screening and Interrogation Centre at Opicina, in the hills above Trieste. This work could at times become quite dramatic—on one occasion involving first the secret smuggling in and then the secret smuggling out of a very senior member of a foreign intelligence organisation together with his wife and child. Other countries were continually active in the Trieste Intelligence field, the Soviet Union massively so under the guise of a trade mission, and also the Italians, anxious to retain the city. The breach between Yugoslavia and Moscow was reflected by a local split in the Communist movement, both wings requiring surveillance. A Central Counter-Intelligence Index was built up by the Intelligence staff of XIII Corps, and Field Security detachments were active in frontier and Port Control duties along the Zone 'A' borders. By 1950, the Index ran to over 100,000 cards, all laboriously maintained by hand. A Postal and Telegraphic Censorship (later known as 'A' Liaison Section) was officered by the Intelligence Corps, while CSDIC (CMF) Forward Detachment provided detailed interrogation services for cases of suspected agents, high-grade refugees and defectors.

The commitment for the Corps in these years, 1945-47, was considerable. In Trieste city, 412 FSS was deployed on general counter-intelligence duties. 414 FSS was occupied on vettings for the Army and Military Government, and 21 Port Security Section was at work in the port. In the province of Trieste, 35 FSS was stationed in Monfalcone. In Gorizia, 12 FSS worked briefly with the Americans and in Udine 419 FSS was engaged in frontier work to the Yugoslav border, with 411 FSS in similar duties to the Austrian border. In addition to these FSS, there was also in Trieste city No 5 Special Counter-Intelligence Unit, the Censorship Group, and the CSDIC Detachment. Four further FSS were not far away, in north-eastern Italy, until their withdrawal in 1946-47. At XIII Corps Headquarters, Major W I Combs was serving as GS02 Intelligence.

In 1948, after the Italian peace Treaty, the G (Intelligence) Staff of a new Headquarters, British Element Trieste Force, (BETFOR) amalgamated with the American Army Intelligence staff at Trieste. As part of this rationalisation, 412 FSS merged with 429 FSS, 21 Port SS and 5 SCIU to make a 'District Security Office' some 60 strong, which after some months changed its name to 'Trieste Security Office'. In November 1954, Trieste was finally evacuated and the Office was closed down. Trieste had provided the largest field grouping of Intelligence Corps soldiers under one command in one area ever assembled to that time. On 26 November 1954, the very last British Army officers to leave the city were the GOC, Major General Winterton, with his Intelligence Corps personal protection party of Major R M Richards and three sergeants.

Other Liberated Territories

In May 1945, 89 FSS was sent to Norway with the liberation forces, its work on arrival being house-searches, port security and dawn raids on German camps to arrest wanted personnel, generally Gestapo or SS staff seeking anonymity in Army or Luftwaffe uniforms.[11] A number of senior personnel wanted for war crimes were so arrested. These included Vidkun Quisling, the arch collaborator. Captain Cornish, together with Sergeant Blake and a team of some 30 Norwegian lieutenants, processed 52,000 German prisoners in 3 months. A number were selected for further detailed interrogation, some of which Captain Cornish's team conducted. In Copenhagen, 319 FSS was engaged in similar work.

Also despatched to Norway were members of a joint Anglo–American Psychological Warfare unit that had been preparing to serve in Force 134, assembled for an invasion of Norway that, in the event, did not take place. Captain D McColl of this unit was initially concerned with liaison and information but was soon transferred to 109 Special Counter-Intelligence Unit for the detailed interrogation and trials of major war criminals of the SS and other Nazi organisations, and certain German personnel concerned with the killing of British servicemen who had been taken prisoner.

In Greece, an Intelligence Corps commitment remained. At Salonika, 268 FSS under Captain Leitch maintained detachments for some months at Alexandroupolis, Florina, Kavalla and the Rupel Pass. A few other members of the Corps also served briefly in Greece on special assignments. For example, Colonel Macfarlane was in command of the Anglo–Greek Information Service (AGIS); Captain S Verney served in Crete and Greece on liaison and interpreting duties. The last Corps unit to remain in Greece was 24 FSS, based in Athens with later a detachment at Salonika; this commitment remained until 1949.

One commitment near home was the investigation of German misbehaviour in the Channel Island of Alderney during their period of occupation. The victims, some 400, were Soviet Union slave labour or other prisoners; their deaths had been caused by overwork, brutality and under-nourishment, with occasional outright murder. Major Pantcheff and an Intelligence Corps Sergeant carried out the investigation, interrogating survivors and their former German guards, but the three SS officers concerned were all reported dead.[12]

The Far East

In the Far East, Intelligence Corps commitments after the Japanese surrender were equally varied, with, in addition, on-going physical danger in certain tasks. The Japanese surrendered on 15 August but, except in the case of Hong Kong, no action could be taken until the formal capitulation ceremony on board an American warship in Tokyo Bay on 2 September. Thereafter, at least 35 British and British-Indian Field Security sections were despatched to the territories liberated from Japanese rule. The priority tasks were recovery of Allied prisoners of war and internees and the tracing of collaborators and war criminals.

Also posted to Singapore were the Mobile Sections of Interrogators and Document Translators. Their earliest task was simple interpreter work, passing orders to the parties of Japanese prisoners at work in the docks. Later, after nominal rolls of prisoners, Japanese and Indian National Army (the latter comprising both men and women) had been prepared, teams were tasked to discover how much the Japanese knew of our earlier plans to invade Malaya—in the event an alarming amount; how accurate had been the SEAC assessment of the number—and equipment of the Japanese in Singapore—at first sight a serious under-estimate; whether the Japanese had arranged 'stay behind' parties—their plans were apparently overtaken by the speed of events, and who had been local collaborators.[13] The Japanese interviewed on the events of the war, mostly staff officers, spoke freely. Other miscellaneous duties included some war crimes investigations, certain work for the local Counter-Intelligence Co-ordination Bureau, a search, unsuccessful, for the Japanese colonel credited with the 1941 invasion plan, and enquiries into the death in an aircraft accident of the Indian National Army leader, S C Bose.

In the case of Malaya and Singapore, 15 FSS that were included in the 7 British and Indian divisions preparing for the proposed assault landings on the peninsula, Operation *Zipper*, were conveniently to hand and set to work immediately.[14] In Singapore, for example, the rounding up and interrogation of many Japanese *Kempetai*, special police, followed searches among the port labour force in which the Japanese had attempted to hide. Captain J Navin, who had learnt Japanese at the Karachi Training Centre, was among the officers investigating war crimes, serving on a team screening Japanese prisoners in Changi gaol, and later as a defending officer in court. After their arrival, the sections were spread around the peninsula and tasks extended to cover the VIP visitors and much more important, wider political Intelligence gathering at a low level, such as the investigation of early Communist subversion of labour on rubber plantation estates and political murders. In May and June 1946, 1 FSS, which had arrived in Johore in January, found clear evidence of the enforced drafting of young men into jungle based bands for guerrilla training.

From September 1945 to November 1946, the bulk of XV Corps, composed of three Indian Army divisions, was serving in the Netherlands East Indies. Their first tasks were the rescue of Allied prisoners, disarming the large Japanese garrisons and searching out the instant arrest categories, *Kempetai*, certain other Japanese, some Koreans and some Chinese (chiefly Formosans). Next came the restoring of law and order in a confused political situation, the Indonesian nationalist movement being violently opposed to the return of a Netherlands colonial government.

Twelve FSS were at work in Indonesia in these months at Batavia (now Jakarta), Bandung, Surabaya and Tanjong Priok in Java, and at Padang, Medan and Palembang on Sumatra.[15] A few Air Photo-interpreters also went to Java, and one or two Corps officers, including Captain J Pike, were serving in operational Intelligence staff appointments.

Work had often to be carried out in combat conditions. On one occasion, in late 1945, a brigade had to fight a seventeen day long battle against the Japanese trained *Tentara Repoeblik Indonesia*, Indonesian Republic Army. In Surabaya, for example, after the ejection of the TRI, its members sought to re-enter by infiltration. Other subversive organisations also attempted the same, notably a local *Hizbullah* (Party of God) party, and both Chinese Communists and nationalists. The methods employed overspilled into crime and 601 FSS took on strength the few Indonesian police officers who had not been murdered. Crime then extended to piracy, needing a security raid on the island of Madoera— which put a stop to it. Co-operation from the resident Dutch community, suspicious of Britain's decolonisation policies in India, was not always forthcoming.

Other tasks that fell to the FSS Sections included broadcasting on Radio Soerabaja, the recovery of hidden weapons, security arrangements for the British High Commissioner, raids on localities in which insurgents were suspected of hiding, and the identification of victims of a particularly unpleasant political massacre by certain extremists. The work was hazardous. One member of 601 FSS later wrote:

> Because of our special role we each had a price on our heads. The general state of affairs may be adjudged by the curfew, the nightly knocking of distant machine-guns and the daily artillery stonk like the slamming of gigantic doors which served to warn the opposition to lie low.[16]

The work could be physically dangerous, one NCO of 611 FSS on one occasion only escaping a murder attempt by jumping into a canal, and other FSS detachments being fired on during raids. The work continued until later in 1946, when the British and Indian troops were withdrawn.

Other sections were sent further afield. A nucleus of FSS personnel accompanied 3 Commando Brigade which arrived at Hong Kong at the end of August 1945. Their initial role was, as elsewhere, the arrest of war criminals and collaborators with, also, the control of refugees from mainland China, some of whom had been domiciled in Hong Kong before December 1941. Over 600,000 refugees were so screened, at a rate of some 2,000 per day. In Thailand, 568 FSS was sent to Bangkok with the headquarters of 7 Indian Division. In Japan itself, 551 FSS was sent to Kure as part of the occupation Force. The roles of both FSS were principally those of war crime investigation and a measure of reporting on political and public opinions. Also in Japan, Lieutenant Colonel J Figgess served with the UK Liaison Mission from 1945 to 1952.

The Burma Field Security Sections, 354, 358, 551 and 592 FSS, were included in the British garrison. Their routine tasks included monitoring political activity, the security of British personnel and headquarters, and some work against large scale banditry (dacoity). The investigation of war crimes in Burma was pursued only to a limited extent, a major difficulty being that many Burmese who collaborated with the Japanese in the early stages of the war changed sides and became useful co-belligerents from 1944 onwards. Some of these were also either in or clearly destined for political office.

One FS commitment in Burma, that of 354 FSS was however different.[17] China had for long maintained a border claim on an area of Burma north of Myitkyina and Chinese Nationalist troops entered this area in 1945. Intelligence was required, and 354 FSS was tasked to gather information on the strength and order of battle of Chinese forces in the Chinese province of Yunnan, across the border. A headquarters was opened at Maymyo and detachments of two men and a Chinese interpreter were posted to Bhamo, Lashio, Mu Se and Myitkitna; these reported in code twice weekly on the Burma Frontier Constabulary network. Chinese Army deserters proved a useful source, but Intelligence was gathered also from friends, local contacts and travellers. The Chinese Nationalists, however, soon became too preoccupied with the Communist challenge to attempt any further reoccupation. Political reports on Karen attitudes to the Aung San government were also prepared. The FSS, together with all British troops, were withdrawn from Burma after independence in January 1948.

Interest in China led to an immediate post-armistice expansion of the 'China Intelligence Wing' in Calcutta. Chinese speakers, including several members of the Corps, notably Lieutenants J Chinnery and M A K Halliday (later Professor) and Captain R J Gilmore, who had been at work elsewhere, being moved in. The two chief fields of Intelligence gathering concerned the political steadiness of the Chinese community in Calcutta, and the collection of information about the changing conditions in China as seen by travellers and others. A few specialists were sent to Hong Kong and one or two, briefly, to Shanghai.

The immediate post surrender tasks of the Japanese interrogators were interpreting at sword-surrender ceremonies and the tracking down of the *Hikari Kikan*, a Japanese stay-behind organisation. Thereafter, Mobile Sections were sent to Java, Bangkok and Saigon, while the Delhi Red Fort CSDIC moved to Kure in Japan, the headquarters of the British Commonwealth Occupation Forces. With the CSDIC went some of the Corps Japanese linguists. In Java, Lieutenant Gardner was wounded in the leg. In Burma, other Mobile Section interrogators, including Lieutenants L Levy and S T Charles were at work locating Japanese units; often they were better informed than the Japanese formation staffs. Once assembled, the next task was interrogating Japanese commanders and staffs and then drafting outline histories of the Japanese formations in the Burma campaign; these outline histories formed the basis of some of the narratives in Lord Mountbatten's despatches. They also interrogated the Burma *Kempei* '... an unpleasant experience. I rarely had the experience of evil almost physically felt as when traversing a courtyard in Rangoon Gaol to reach their cells'.[18] A distinction had to be made between Japanese Prisoners of War, captured before the surrender and Japanese Surrendered Personnel—even in defeat, the Japanese Command refusing to admit the latter were prisoners. The former category had to be returned to Japan very unobtrusively.

In India too some units that had been training for operations against Japan received new local assignments. One such was 595 FSS, the only unit in 2 Indian Airborne Division to be both up to strength and fully parachute trained. The Section was moved to Karachi and committed to internal security duties of especial hazard at the time of the mutiny of the Royal Indian Navy in 1946. A few Intelligence Corps officers also held staff appointments, Captain R Greenwood, for example, was Army Liaison officer with the Police during the 1946 Calcutta riots.

The Run-down of the Intelligence Corps

The wartime growth of the Corps had been remarkable. By July 1943, the Corps strength had reached 2,537 officers and 4,508 soldiers; those serving in specifically Intelligence Corps unit or sub-units created totals of 177 Field and 69 Port Security Sections, 16 detachments serving with Special Wireless Sections and 35 Censor Sections. By the end of August 1945, the Intelligence Corps totalled 3,027 officers and 6,585 soldiers. There were in addition a further 1,400 officers of other units at work in military Intelligence.[20] But despite the widely varied commitments of the immediate post-war years, the future of the Intelligence Corps was once again in doubt. The Director of Military Intelligence from 1940 to 1944, Major General F H C Davidson, was an enthusiastic defender of the Corps and had as early as July 1943 written a formal paper proposing a post-war retention of a permanent Regular Corps. In his paper, General Davidson stressed '... the starvation of intelligence which adversely affected operations in the early days of the war'. In other papers that followed, General Davidson proposed that this permanent Intelligence Corps should possess its own Depot and School, that short service commissions should be given to specialists in particular fields of Intelligence, and that officers of the Intelligence Corps should be eligible for 117 Intelligence appointments, including that of Director of Military Intelligence.

The Commander-in-Chief Home Forces, General Sir Bernard Paget—who in May 1943 had become the Intelligence Corps' first Colonel Commandment—warmly supported these proposals, adding a number affecting Intelligence in the Army as a whole, and one recommending that Intelligence Corps officers should be eligible to go to Staff College in the post-war Army.[21] Many officers in the field had also come to realise the value of the Corps. In respect of signals, interrogation and operational Intelligence, for example, Major General T S (later Lieutenant General Sir Terence) Airey the Chief of Staff (Intelligence) of the Allied Forces in Italy, wrote a perceptive paper in January 1945. In this paper he noted that 'in the whole of this theatre there are only two regular officers employed in operational intelligence', himself and the Brigadier at 15 Army Group. He was very concerned that all the Intelligence staff officers, both at headquarters and the forward formations, the majority of whom were academics, would be demobilised immediately the war was over, leaving an absence of Intelligence expertise in the Army. He recognised that: 'the problem cannot be solved merely by posting regular officers to intelligence appointments, because a certain indispensable knowledge based on study and experience is required'. He recommended the retention of some officers until a permanent cadre of regular officers 'selected and trained in the requirements of modern intelligence' could replace them. In his more general opening paragraphs, Airey observed 'One of the most remarkable features of the war has been the development of military intelligence from a dimly academic pre-war state to a highly organised and practical science which has had a profound influence on the outcome of the major military operations of the last five and a half years'. He feared the consequences of Intelligence being allowed to 'lapse into its pre-war obscurity, a calamity which would deprive the Army of realism in its preparation and training for battle and would almost certainly lead to disasters ... As an analogy there is the case of tank development between 1918 and 1939'.[22]

Other officers however, saw the Intelligence Corps once again in 1918–20 terms, a wartime necessity for which there would be no need in peace. The Adjutant General's Department argued that Intelligence work could not provide an adequate career structure in times of peace, and would in any case be too small in quantity to justify a separate Corps. For some time it seemed that the Corps was destined to follow the path to oblivion of the Reconnaissance and Glider Pilot Regiments. Others saw the future of the Corps as one of short service officers and Territorials, or Territorial Army only. Fortunately the final 1948 decision, although very far from satisfactory, preserved something of the Corps. This limited measure of survival owed much to General Paget, and to Major General Davidson who later became the Corps' second Colonel Commandant. A small nucleus Intelligence Corps was to be allowed, to provide specialist personnel for such tasks as air photo interpretation and counter intelligence sections, with a few linguists for document study and refugee questioning. An earlier decision, in 1946, had authorised periodic training for Intelligence Corps reserve officers in all these skills.[23] Operational formation Intelligence staff officers were, however, not to be Intelligence Corps. In role terms, the Corps was thereby reduced once again to simple collectors of Intelligence. It was not to be allowed to recruit permanent regular officers direct from Sandhurst, officers who transferred into the Corps were not eligible for the Staff College and very unlikely to advance beyond the rank of Major.[24] The prospect drove a number of the Corps' best officers to seek their careers elsewhere.

It was to take nearly 10 lean years before the short-sightedness of the 1948 decisions was realised. In those 10 years, as will be seen in the chapters that follow, the Intelligence Corps was not able to make the full contribution to military operations that it had done in the Second World War. But by the mid-1950s the significance of the strategic posture of Soviet and later the Warsaw Pact's ground forces was clear, and with it a need for expert operational Intelligence as great as in 1938–39. Fortunately the GS01 of the 1939 Directorate of Military Intelligence was now Chief of the Imperial General Staff. General Sir Gerald Templer was to restore to the Intelligence Corps and the Army the regular officers 'selected and trained in the requirements of modern intelligence' called for by General Airey in 1945. This development is examined in the chapters that follow.

12

Conventional and Semi-Conventional Wars Since 1945

In the period 1945 to 1989 the British Army was engaged in five conventional or semi-conventional wars, conflicts in which the Army's adversaries have generally either worn the uniform, or if not uniform-wearing been on the payroll, of another State. As such, these operations although they may draw heavily on counter-insurgency tactics, are distinct from internal insurgency in a British territory, which forms the subject of the next chapter. The list includes the 1950–53 Korea War, the 1956 Suez operation, the 1963–66 conflict with Indonesia known as *Konfrontasi* (Confrontation), the 1982 South Atlantic war, and the commitment, from 1977 and still continuing, to safeguard Belize. The growing contributions made by the Intelligence Corps to these operations reflect both the lean years after 1948 and the post 1950s increased appreciation by the Army of the Corps' work.

The Korean War

The first two conflicts occurred in the period of drastic cut-back. The Korean conflict began on 25 June 1950 when 10 divisions of North Korean troops crossed the 38th Parallel line that divided Communist controlled North Korea from the non-Communist south. Despite initial North Korean successes, United States and South Korean forces managed to prevent their overrunning the whole Peninsula, while a large international military force was progressively assembled under United Nations authority. The force included initially two British and one Australian battalions, followed and replaced later by two British brigades which, with other Commonwealth units were, in July 1951, all formed into the 1st Commonwealth Division. The successes of the United Nations forces who entered North Korea and took the capital, Pyongyang, in turn led to the entry of the Chinese Army into the war in October 1950. Chinese troops drove the United Nations Army back south of the original 38th Parallel line reoccupying Seoul. In the final phase of the war, after the United Nations pushed the Chinese back liberating Seoul again, the war became static along a line well to the north of the 38th Parallel.

The relatively small size of the British contribution limited the British Intelligence effort. Prisoner of war questioning, for example, was not undertaken by British Army personnel. On the Operational Intelligence side, one Intelligence Corps officer, Captain D C Cullinan served as GSO3 (Intelligence) with 29 Brigade.

For photographic interpretation work, 104 Air Photograph Interpretation Section was sent out from Britain in 1951, under the command of officers not members of the Corps, but including within it officers and NCOs who were, notably Lieutenant M F J Harte. When the line was static, their work was very similar to that carried out in the 1943–45 Italian campaign or even the First World War. A daily print scrutiny to a depth of two miles was carried out. Any fresh reinforcement of Chinese forces was identified; sometimes, due to the hilly nature of the terrain, these were alarmingly close to our own positions. Enemy artillery movements and positions were detected, the use of comparative cover, 'give away' tracks and fresh camouflage enabling positions to be recognised even when self-propelled guns were concealed in caves. Brigade and battalion headquarters were provided with material needed for the briefing of patrols.[1]

A Field Security Section, 904 FSS, was sent to Korea in August 1950. On its arrival towards the end of the year, the Section immediately moved to Seoul and Pyongyang, the latter being in United Nations hands at the time. The year 1951 was a difficult one for the Section, for a variety of reasons of which the chief was overstretch. A Canadian Army FSS was given the overall Security responsibility in the Commonwealth area, 904 FSS personnel retaining commitments only in the 29 Brigade operational and Pusan rear base areas. By 1952, the Canadians had reduced their contingent and 904 FSS had extended its commitments to 28 Brigade and the Seoul Forward Maintenance Area. The Section also suffered its first casualty, Sergeant E M Hall, who disappeared while conducting a security investigation; it was believed that he had been killed by North Korean agents.

The Section secured the full confidence of the Division following the arrival of Major (later Lieutenant Colonel) D Devitt in February 1953.[2] A Divisional Counter-Intelligence policy was at last prepared and implemented. The Section was given the additional personnel it needed for its commitments, totalling 2 officers, 2 warrant officers, 8 staff sergeants, 16 sergeants, 4 corporals and a residual Canadian element of 7. The basic security commitments—the two brigades, Seoul and Pusan remained, but were now carried out with much greater expertise, sufficient staff enabling a useful relationship with the civilian population to be worked up on the basis of study and knowledge of local people at village and peasant dwelling level. The day to day work was again traditional, the control of civilian movement, vetting of civilian works labour, the screening of refugees, the security of certain key installations, the search for and arrest of wanted individuals on a 'black list', the investigation of any reports of espionage or subversion, and, using local knowledge, the briefing and guidance of infantry units engaged in security sweeps. One notable success was the arrest by Staff Sergeant R Davies of a Korean who had blown up a British ammunition dump. The Korean wore South Korean Army uniform but was almost certainly a member of one of several groups of North Korean soldiers who had crossed the lines in this disguise for sabotage and VIP assassination purposes.

Major Devitt also had other tasks. He was initially burdened with responsibility for the work of the United Nations Security Guards, a locally recruited force tasked with the prevention of line crossers from North Korea and provision of guards for ordnance parks and depots. More interestingly, Major Devitt and some of his senior NCOs were concerned with agent-handling—Koreans prepared to cross the line on the Division's 10 mile front, either on a short term mission gathering operational Intelligence about enemy positions and strengths, or on longer term political warfare missions of propaganda or sabotage in the area of the enemy opposite our sector. One of the NCOs, Staff Sergeant G Jackson, on occasions accompanied agents himself. Staff Sergeant Jackson was awarded the MM for this hazardous work.

Security work posed particular problems, the difficult terrain and extreme winter cold, a peasant culture quite alien to British Army experience, and local Korean military and civil officials often of very dubious integrity. In the early weeks of the static phase it was thought necessary, as a temporary measure, to clear all civilians back 10 miles from the front line; an American division that failed to do this was heavily shelled. But, conversely, this unpopular action made the recruitment of local agents for security very difficult for some time, until some limited return home of the civil populace was allowed and the FSS had won acceptance. This acceptance was gained first and foremost through personal contacts with heads of families, but also with help in local medical problems, children's activities and with schools. By early 1953, it was no longer necessary to buy information.

One complication, however, was the indisciplined activities of Republic of Korea (South Korea) Army and Military Intelligence in the Commonwealth Division area, at one point orders for the arrest of Republic of Korea Intelligence personnel even having to be issued. Members of 904 FSS had on a number of occasions to intervene forcibly to prevent harassment and abuse of the Korean civilian populace by soldiers and officers of their own Army. In these incidents the Section, as the winners, gained prestige ('face') and became spoken of by Koreans as the 'protectors of the poor'. The Section's reward was useful Intelligence.

In the last static phase, and after the armistice, an important part of 904 FSS work was the prevention of theft of stores, particularly food-stuffs. Here, once again, the friendly relationships established with the local populace often led to a warning of a planned raid or help in the recovery of Army property stolen.

One final commitment was Intelligence Corps representation, by Major J D Gimblett, on a tri-Service and Anglo-American-Canadian study team analysing the experiences of prisoners taken by the Chinese, formulating guidelines for resistance to interrogation training.

Suez 1956

The Korean War lasted three years. The next conventional conflict, the 1956 Anglo–French landings at Suez, lasted less than three days, after which United Nations and Superpower pressures obliged Britain and France to halt an otherwise successful military operation. Its purpose had been to re-assert control of the Suez Canal following the action of the Egyptian President, Nasser, in nationalising the Suez Canal Company. The size of the force assembled for the operation, 45,000 British and 34,000 French men, was massive. The actual landings, by parachute and by assault from the sea, were preceded by five days of air strikes. After the ceasefire, sometimes under sniper fire, British troops remained in dug-in positions, enforcing curfews and patrolling actively until withdrawal in late December.

The Intelligence Corps contribution lay primarily in the field of air photograph interpretation, together with certain other work at command level, and security and interrogation personnel in the field. The Air Photo Interpretation Unit, Middle East, at Episkopi in Cyprus were at work on photographs of the Sinai Desert and, early in November 1956, on the effects of the five days of air strikes. Corps officers at work included Captains L L Lacey-Johnson and R W Pickwood. APIU (ME) had earlier been reinforced by a hurriedly formed I Air Photo Interpretation Section which included two Intelligence Corps NCOs, Staff Sergeants G A Clarke and P B Watterson.[3] This Section, together with Captain C K Mole of 3 Division APIS, participated in the landings in Egypt.

On the actual scene, Intelligence Corps personnel took part in the assault, providing part of the support for 3 Commando Brigade. A reconstituted 1 FSS under Lieutenant G O'Neill was responsible for the security of 3 Division headquarters, 152 FSS was earmarked for port security in Port Said with 7 FSS for town security, and two detachments of 902 FSS arrived in Egypt intended for work under the direction of II Corps Headquarters. The work of these sections was, however, limited by the political conditions that followed the ceasefire. Various anti-British organisations distributed inflammatory leaflets in Port Said, but these could not be thoroughly investigated as they originated outside the area to which British troops were restricted. In addition, Corps personnel served in a Joint Services Interrogation Unit, a Special Counter-Intelligence Unit and certain small technical and liaison sections.

A post-script can be added to the work of the Corps in the Suez operation. In 1956 the British Army still maintained a garrison in Libya. Its units, hurriedly reinforced, were put on alert for a move across North Africa into Egypt. A newly arrived despatch-rider inadvertently delivered copies of the operation order for this move to the Tripoli Libyan Army barracks, complete with Egyptian instructors, instead of the nearby British Army barracks. Sergeant P M S Ward of 3 FSS was tasked to retrieve them, which he did by talking his way into the barracks and discovering where the despatch rider had delivered the document—an officers room. Sergeant Ward then entered the room and took the documents from a steel cupboard that the officer, anxious to spend a day of rest in town, had left unlocked.[4] More serious work for 3 FSS in Libya included surveillance of the Egyptian Embassy which was in use as a store house for weaponry and a recruiting office for Libyan volunteers to fight the British, and the security of British Army premises in a local bombing campaign.

Borneo

The next major campaign, that in Borneo from 1963 to 1966, involved a much greater number of Intelligence Corps personnel, serving in roles both interesting and very active—all a reflection of the renewal of the Corps life that had taken place in the late 1950s. Of especial interest is that the lead roles were taken by NCOs.

The campaign arose from the ambitions of President Sukarno of Indonesia to extend Indonesian rule over the three northern areas of the island of Borneo, Sarawak, Brunei and North Borneo (Sabah). All of these had been part of the British Empire and (with the exception of Brunei, which was still a British protectorate) were destined to join the successor Commonwealth nation of Malaysia. A preliminary to the main campaign had been a coup attempt in Brunei in December 1962. The coup plotters were favoured by Indonesia, but acted prematurely, and the coup was suppressed by the rapid arrival of British and Gurkha troops. But this event had served as an alarm signal. A British Military Command for Borneo was established in the same month, well in time before the opening of the main Indonesian campaign in April 1963.

The problem facing Major General W Walker, the Commander, was daunting—mountainous jungle country with no roads or railways, a 965 mile land frontier and a 1,500 mile sea coast to secure against the external threat, with also an internal threat from a 'Clandestine Communist Organisation' of over 20,000, mainly Chinese resident in Western Sarawak. These were interspersed among the towns, villages and scattered settlements which had themselves only a very small police force and no local military organisation. Indonesia initially could attract a following in the border areas, particularly western Sarawak. At the outset, General Walker had but 5 battalions, a few helicopters and a small number of minesweepers; at the height of the campaign, the forces totalled 13 British or Gurkha battalions, 3, later more, Malaysian units, over 70 helicopters, the equivalent of 2 artillery and 2 engineer regiments and a Special Air Service squadron, together with 1,500 locally raised Border Scouts.

The nature of the campaign was a mixture of Intelligence and growing infantry domination of the jungle attained by speed and flexibility, and a 'hearts and minds' campaign based upon small scale military and police development aid, chiefly medical and agricultural. This latter stood in increasing contrast to the severity of the Indonesians. The military domination was achieved by the use of helicopters, both RAF and Royal Navy together with Hovercraft, and of company-sized forward bases from which continuous patrolling was maintained, the patrols being supplied by air drop or helicopters. The Indonesian sponsored insurgents were cut off, ambushed or tracked down before they could approach their objectives. In frustration, Sukarno turned in December 1963 to drawing up his Indonesian regulars, Army, Navy, Marines and Commandos, first to stiffen insurgent groups and then themselves to provide whole units. These, on occasions, landed on the Sarawak coast from submarines or other craft. Some members of these units suffered from malaria and the units' locations were detected from outbreaks of the fever. But these more powerful groups achieved some initial successes. They also attacked Western Malaysia (the Malay Peninsula) with landings on the west coast of Johore and at Pontian in August 1964, and a parachute descent upon Labis in the following month. But the escalation was countered in Borneo by an increase in the number of British battalions and a measure of artillery support to destroy Indonesian encampments and infiltration paths. In March 1966, Sukarno finally fell from power and Indonesia's new government moved to end the confrontation which had proved economically disastrous for the country.[5]

From the outset, the Corps played a distinguished role in Intelligence gathering, on which ultimately all other operations depended. The British force that arrived in Brunei in December 1962 included 21 Intelligence Platoon, Captain J A van Gelder and four NCOs from Singapore; they were reinforced by personnel from 19 and 22 Intelligence Platoons in Malaya and others from Hong Kong. They assisted the Brunei police in the operation of an Interrogation Centre. When the main campaign opened in the following April, an Intelligence Platoon was formed from detachments in Malaya and Singapore and sent to 3 Commando Brigade at Kuching. To meet the expanding insurgent campaign, a system of Field Intelligence Officer (FIO) posts was set up in western Sarawak. The system was later extended to other areas, over 20 FIOs being at work. Each FIO had to cover many hundreds of square miles. The FIOs, mostly Intelligence Corps Warrant Officers and NCOs, might live in a bamboo hut (shared frequently with lizards); they worked through the local community—having first gained acceptance—in a variety of different styles to gather Intelligence.[6] One, for example, entitled himself a 'Field Immigration officer' and as such questioned the numerous traders crossing from Indonesian Borneo. This proved so successful that he issued some traders with cameras—and received in return some useful photographs. FIOs wore plain clothes—sometimes sandals, patched shorts and a local brightly coloured shirt—and might have long hair. Such local necessities however could make convincing briefings of a more orthodox-minded battalion commander difficult (particularly, as happened on occasions, when the unit concerned believed that it had its own sources), until a consistent record of success was established. Gaining the acceptance of the community required tact, sympathy and often a stomach adjusted to anything. Informers, like informers anywhere, varied in reliability, particularly near a pay day. A village or kampong headman was often the most useful contact. Recruitment of agents could be a protracted business.[7] The most reliable were those from across the border in an area occupied by Indonesian troops whose behaviour was ruthless. The FIOs were tasked to work with the local police, and as much as possible learn the local vernacular language. Front organisations of the insurgents, such as, for example, the Sarawak Advanced Youth Organisation and the Sarawak Farmers Association, had to be studied, and known members' hutments raided by surprise. Other sources of Intelligence were the local Special Branch and border scouts, direction signs carved on trees by insurgent groups, boat loadings and movements and reports of the arrival of specialist troops to replace poor quality garrison units, and the local Special Branch. The Intelligence, once collated, provided knowledge of the insurgents' order of battle, strengths, personalities and likely targets.

One FIO, Corporal D R Kitchin, established a firm local ally in western Sarawak who provided a mass of information on a hitherto little known subversive organisation, KONAS, which aimed to subvert the Sarawak Dayaks.[8] This information in turn enabled Corporal Kitching to bring in four leading KONAS figures. During his interrogation of them, he was able both to acquire a full knowledge of KONAS activity in his area and also early intelligence about the more dangerous and specifically Chinese communist PGRS, Sarawak People's Guerilla Movement. This in turn led to successful patrolling and raids on PRGS hideouts.

Friction between the different Indonesian and Chinese groupings was also used to advantage. On another occasion, from conversations with another trader from across the border, Corporal Kitching was able to acquire full details of casualties suffered by the insurgents in a clash with Royal Marines—the total was established from bundles loaded on long boats. One bundle fell open and the trader saw that it contained a corpse. Fortunately, the large distances and foot movement of insurgents made Intelligence long term, giving ample lead time. 'Hot news' could concern an insurgent project three or four weeks away from planned fruition.[9]

FIOs' reports had to be carefully prepared and assessed; they were then sent to both the police and local military command.

Following the late 1963 and early 1964 entry of Indonesian regular units into the fighting and the consequent reorganisation of British forces into four brigades, the system of attaching an Intelligence Platoon to each brigade was extended, 5 Platoon served with 51 Brigade and 15 Platoon with 5 Brigade. There was also an Intelligence Section at General Walker's Headquarters on Labuan Island. Their duties comprised the standard collation, analysis and dissemination of Intelligence material collected by the FIOs and PI staffs, these latter being mainly concerned with mapping and the making of ground models in the absence of adequate local maps. Some platoons specialised, 2 Intelligence Platoon of 19 Airportable Brigade, for example, acquired an extensive knowledge of the Indonesian Police Mobile Brigade. Intelligence Platoons also contributed to the briefings and debriefings of the British and New Zealand penetration patrols. The PI personnel were drawn from the Joint Air Reconnaissance Intelligence Centre (JARIC) Far East and among those who served were Major E Kennington, Lieutenant R Haisley, Staff Sergeants C Edwards, J Kingston, C Bell, J Heredge and G Taylor, together with Sergeant J Schwegmann-Fielding.

Also established in early 1964 was a small interrogation team consisting of Captain N J Flower and Staff Sergeant J Tucker.[10] This team divided its time between Jesselton and working in the field, anywhere where insurgents or Indonesian regulars had been taken. The team, with personnel changed and increased to two officers and six NCOs was moved to Singapore, deploying interrogators forward by helicopters to the points of capture. In 1965 the team was back in Sarawak, commanded by Captain A K Crawford. Some 200 interrogations were carried out; captured documents were also useful. One Corps officer recorded 'Usually the shock of capture, a show of knowledge and a sympathetic European who, to the prisoner's amazement spoke Indonesian was enough to start the prisoner talking!' Information sought and provided covered the size of groups, their equipment, routes and orders; success led to pre-emptive patrolling or strikes and on one occasion to a detailed description of the Indonesian Army coup from an NCO who had served in Army headquarters. Signals intercept Intelligence was also valuable. Counter-Intelligence Security work was less rewarding, the counter-intelligence elements in the Intelligence Platoons often being misused in the absence of an experienced I (B) staff officer.[11] In the operations on the Malay Peninsular, 22 Intelligence Platoon assisted the Headquarters of 28 Commonwealth Brigade in containing the Indonesian incursions.

By the last year of the campaign, Intelligence concerning Indonesian preparations was virtually complete. Indonesian regular units operated very rigidly to set procedures and unit compositions, all identified. None of the final incursions came as a surprise; in most cases, details of the timings and strengths of the forces to be committed were known well in advance. The main source for this Intelligence was the FIOs, almost all Intelligence Corps. Of the FIO organisation the official FARELF report on operations described the FIO organisation as:

> ... a great success and the NCOs themselves displayed great initiative and efficiency. They showed themselves capable of accepting responsibilities far in excess of those normally given to comparatively junior NCOs.

The posting was viewed by most NCOs as a challenge. Although the tour was normally one year only, many volunteered for a second tour, despite long and lonely hours, considerable pressure of work, no garrison amenities and a taxing climate. In so doing they additionally provided valuable continuity when infantry units were rotated. Awards recognised their achievements, Staff Sergeants T Dodridge, L E Stephenson and R H Thompson being awarded the BEM, together with Staff Sergeant P S Brown who had been engaged in air photo-interpretation.

The work of the Intelligence Corps fully justified in the eyes of the whole Army the importance attached to Intelligence by Field Marshal Templer in the 1950s, and his placing of the Corps on a sound basis for the future. Perhaps more than any other, the *Konfrontasi* campaign was a turning point in the Corps' history.

Belize

The Intelligence Corps' contribution to the work of the Army in Belize has been—and still is—in most respects a scaled down version of the Corps work in Borneo. Belize is a small territory the size of Wales on the central American mainland, with a Caribbean coastline. It was a British colony until 1981, for most of the colonial era under the name of British Honduras. The territory has always been claimed by the larger and more powerful Central American republic of Guatemala, a claim strongly opposed by Belizeans.[12] But the claim has necessitated a tri-Service British presence since 1948. This originally comprised one company to 1972, two companies from 1972 to 1975 when the level had to be increased to 1,000 men in response to a Guatemalan concentration of forces on the border, with a further increase to 1,500, an all arms battalion group supported by Harrier aircraft, helicopters and a frigate from 1977. The terrain is difficult. Many border areas in mountainous jungle-covered terrain, have no roads, but there is flatter country in the south where movement is easier.

The Corps is represented by the Force Intelligence staff officer and a Force Intelligence Security Section, together with some personnel serving in a Joint Service Signals Unit. On occasions, when necessary, additional personnel are brought in from Britain. The operational Intelligence work is undertaken by a number of Field Intelligence NCOs, working in plain clothes and living with local communities near the frontier, and by an All Source Assessment Centre (formerly the Intelligence Cell) at Force Headquarters; sources include infantry patrols, observation posts and in theatre and UK-based reconnaissance systems. There is also a Counter Intelligence Detachment component of the Section. Commitments have extended to some internal security work, most notably at the time of independence in 1981 when there was considerable unrest in Belize City, and training the Intelligence Section of the Belize Defence Force.

One example of Operational Intelligence at work can be given. In July 1982 an Intelligent Corps Warrant Officer, acting as Field Intelligence NCO for the Western area, was informed that a car containing four men had been seen crossing the border having first handed in small arms to the Guatemalan border military checkpoint. The sighting had been made by a British Army Observation post on top of a hill in a very isolated area. Accompanied by Police Constable Oscar Wilde of the Belize Police, the Warrant Officer began an investigation and found the car stopped near a customs post, clearly the object of a reconnaissance of the customs post area. While Constable Wilde was questioning the occupants of the car, one of them threw an object out of the window, which was found to be a grenade. The four Guatemalans were then arrested, all proving to be soldiers, with one identified as the commander of the garrison detachment across the border. A second grenade was also found. It was decided to return the four Guatemalans. This gesture headed off a raid about to be mounted by a company of *Kaibuls*, Guatemalan Special Forces, on the Belize border customs post, for which the captured men had been an advanced reconnaissance party.[13]

The South Atlantic 1982

If Borneo and Belize were commitments for which the Intelligence Corps had ample notice, the South Atlantic conflict of 1982 was the reverse. The Argentinian seizures, first of South Georgia and later of the Falkland Islands, were operations that involved very hurried preparation by the Ministry of Defence. The decision to send a recovery Task Force presented special problems for a small Corps already stretched, but some 30 members were despatched to the South Atlantic to serve in a variety of roles, with a further 40, mostly NCOs, deployed on work in connection with the campaign in Britain—at Northwood, the Ministry of Defence and elsewhere.

Shortly after the Argentine invasion, Major D M Burrill took a hurriedly assembled team of two officers, three senior NCOs and a Corporal to Northwood, to provide an Intelligence Section for Major General J Moore's land force headquarters. When Headquarters Land Forces Falkland Islands, LFFI, was formally opened, an additional officer and senior NCO were added, while at Northwood a workable package of basic Intelligence was prepared.[14]

The first Intelligence task, however, was perhaps the most straightforward. A small team of Corps NCOs, headed by Lieutenant Colonel G Redfern, was sent to the theatre for immediate debriefing and tactical questioning, debriefing the Royal Marines repatriated from Port Stanley who were questioned in Uruguay, and also the Marines rescued from South Georgia, debriefed in a ship off Ascension Island. At the same time, the Argentinian prisoners taken in South Georgia were questioned. Valuable material from this work was studied at all levels, from Cabinet to ground force commanders, and the Intelligence gained remained valid to the end of the campaign.

One Intelligence Corps NCO, Staff Sergeant N A C van der Bijl, served as the Operations Intelligence NCO in the 3 Commando Brigade Intelligence Cell, landing amid frequent air attacks at San Carlos with the Brigade Headquarters late on 21 May. Staff Sergeant Van der Bijl remained with the Commando Brigade Headquarters, moving to Bluff Cove Mountain and, following a dangerous Argentinian air attack, to an area east of Mount Kent. This later move had to be carried out at a critical juncture in the preparatory phase of the assault on Wireless Ridge, amid a shortage of fuel and water and while sustaining casualties from a minefield.

Also involved from the start was an Intelligence Corps NCO serving at the time with 22 Special Air Service Regiment, who was later wounded. Following almost immediately were a detachment from Communications and Security Group (UK) who arrived aboard HMS *Intrepid*, an Imagery Analyst at work aboard HMS *Hermes* and the Intelligence Cell of 5 Infantry Brigade who arrived in style aboard *Queen Elizabeth 2*.[15] Then arrived the Corps personnel in the team prepared for the Headquarters LFFI Intelligence Section under Captain D Charters. After the 5 Brigade advance to Goose Green, the Brigade headquarters was flown to Bluff Cove where members of the Intelligence Cell assisted in the rescue of survivors from the stricken *Sir Tristram* and *Sir Galahad* landing ships. The Cell moved next to the Brigade's tactical headquarters on Mount Harriet, from where, under desultory Argentinian artillery fire, the final assault on Tumbledown was directed.

Tasks included interviewing Argentinian prisoners of war, captured document translation, examination of captured equipment, debriefing of civilians and operational intelligence collation, analysis and dissemination. Prisoner interviewing, conducted in a carefully pre-planned humane way, was the responsibility of Joint Forward Interrogation Teams (JFITs): these operated at San Carlos, Ajax Bay and Teal Inlet. Prisoner Intelligence was of particular value in assessing strengths, order of battle, Argentine weapon capabilities and morale. Captured documents were also valuable. One in particular was perhaps the most important piece of ground forces Intelligence acquired after the San Carlos landings. In what was, in some respects, a traditional infantry operation, patrolling was a very important source of Intelligence. In this work, Corps members played a vital part in briefing and debriefing infantry and special forces patrols.

The immensely successful Special Forces 11 May raid on Pebble Island, where a large number of Argentine aircraft were destroyed on the ground and the Argentinian air capacity to harass our landings 10 days later removed, could not have been mounted without the resolution of a particular Intelligence problem, this being principally the work of Major Burrill's team at Northwood, both in the directing, the collection and the analysis of Intelligence. A small-scale counter-intelligence operation was mounted in the aftermath of the re-occupation of Port Stanley, and the screening of some 11,000 captured Argentinian soldiers begun. Of these, some 600 were placed in a Special Category for further questioning by a Joint Services Interrogation Wing team that arrived from Ashford.

The whole campaign, small scale though it was, illustrated vividly the contribution the Corps could make to Service Intelligence—the ability, through experience, to understand and therefore effectively manage, information from all sources and to control, or at least influence, tasking. The almost instantaneous production of so many and varied specialists for an unforeseen operation was yet further proof of the value of a Corps of specialist regular soldiers permanently at work in military Intelligence. Of the Corps' work the commander of 3 Commander Brigade, Brigadier (later Major General) J Thompson wrote later:

> The response by those members of the Corps involved in the operation was positive and professional. As the brigade commander charged with carrying out the initial landings on the Falklands, what impressed me most was the quality of the intelligence assessments that were produced from quite early on and right through the campaign, by the intelligence staffs in my superior headquarters, and in my own headquarters. The 'piece de resistance' was the identification of positions occupied by the Argentine regiments, before we landed, which proved to be amazingly accurate. I also felt that the way the Intelligence Staffs in the theatre of operations coped with the interrogation of prisoners, a mammoth task, when one considers the numbers taken, and the short time available in which to process them, was a model of efficiency, and humanity.

The campaign was also another milestone in the Corps' history in that, for the first time, the principal Intelligence Officer in theatre was an Intelligence Corps officer, Major Burrill.

13

Counter-Insurgency and Military Security Since 1945

The Intelligence Corps has contributed to all the 'withdrawal from Empire' counter-insurgency campaigns, but the contributions made to each have varied. As a continuance of work begun during or at the end of the Second World War, a number of Corps personnel were at work in Palestine and Egypt, and also in Malaya. The Kenya Mau Mau insurrection caught the Corps at its lowest ebb, following the post-war reductions, and with no continuity of experience. With the renewal of the Intelligence Corps in the late 1950s, the contribution made by Corps personnel to the later campaigns could grow both in size and professionalism. Despite this chronological ebb and flow, however, an account of the Corps' contribution is best presented by theatre—the Middle East, Cyprus, the Far East, Africa, and in conclusion a few lesser commitments.

In the campaigns, the Intelligence Corps has contributed to three of Sir Robert Thompson's classic 'five principles' of counter-insurgency campaigning—the need for a co-ordinated plan, the need to establish secure base areas, and the need to concentrate initially on destroying the political infrastructure of the insurgents. In doing so a fourth principle has been carefully respected, the need to adhere to the rule of law.[1]

Of work in the search for and destruction of the insurgents' political infra-structure, one Corps officer wrote later—of Malaya:

> One of Templer's early moves was to reform the intelligence system. Until then the intelligence function was in the hands of the police special branch ... The policemen did the intelligence job as

policemen would do—that is, the whole system was aimed at gathering information which could be used as evidence to secure convictions in court. What was lacking was information about the terrorist organisation and order of battle and their supplies.[2]

This was not the first time, nor the last, that this phenomenon was encountered and the Corps has come to play an increasing part in quests for this information. In the questioning of captives, the wartime approach of civility combined with firmness, the latter conveying unmistakably that the captive was being held until legal trial or the end of a campaign, and that no escape was possible, proved as effective as in the past.

In detail, however, each campaign has generally also provided the Corps with some additional and particular Intelligence requirement.

The Middle East–Palestine

Rising political tensions in the Middle East were contained throughout the Second World War thanks to the arrangements made by Prime Minister Churchill and Generals Wavell and Paget at the statecraft level, and the SIME organisation—down to the humblest Field Security Section NCO—on the ground. The last months of the war however indicated clearly the passions gathering strength, especially in Palestine where Europe's displaced and tortured Jewry sought a home and a renewed Arab nationalism sought both to prevent this and to achieve political independence.

Large scale violence opened with a ferocious Jewish sabotage bombing campaign on the night of 31 October 1945, the Jewish peoples' home guard force *Haganah* with its *Palmach* spearhead groups and the two rival breakaway terrorist groups, *Irgun Zvai Leumi* (IZL) and the *Lochmi Heruth Israel* (the Stern Gang) all being involved. The organisation of *Haganah* was fairly well-known in view of its wartime status. The two break-away groups, however, were small, dedicated and fanatical, and therefore both secure and little known. For the next three years, there followed a succession of violent bombings and bloody killings, targeted increasingly upon the British police and military, especially officers. An initial two divisions of troops in the territory had to be reinforced by a third. But the British Government was not able to devise a political solution and in 1947 announced that Britain proposed to give up the League of Nations Mandate for Palestine and withdraw troops in the following year.

For the Army as a whole, the campaign was a wretched experience, units being committed to riot control, curfew enforcement and the securing of key installations. After major events, such as the blowing up of the British military headquarters in Jerusalem's King David Hotel in July 1946, a 16-battalion cordon and search operation was mounted. The atmosphere was bitter, pent-up Jewish hatred of their Nazi and other oppressors was poured out upon a British Army trying to maintain law and order. The Army itself was in the throes of post-war reorganisation, and had not yet developed its counter-insurgency expertise; particularly at the outset, reliance was placed on the Palestine Police for information. The military-police relationship was not always happy. Overall it must be viewed as an unsuccessful campaign—but one from which lessons for the future were well learnt.

The Intelligence Corps, as a consequence of the Second World War commitments, was well represented in Palestine. Although the number of Field Security Sections was reduced, national service ensured an ongoing supply of capable officers and NCOs. Five FSS were at work; 252 FSS in the south, 272 FSS in the centre and 275 FSS in the north, with 3 FSS under command of 1 Infantry Division in the Tel Aviv area. Lastly 317 (Para) FSS was with 6 Airborne Division, for most of the campaign sited in a kibbutz near Nathanya, though participating in the massive cordon and screening of Tel Aviv; but for the last six months, the Section worked with 252 FSS from a headquarters in Mount Carmel.[3] The Corps also provided personnel for the Canal Zone CSDIC which questioned important insurgent prisoners. In 1946 the CSDIC commander was Major W B Sedgwick, a well-known Intelligence Corps personality.

The special feature of this campaign was the ability of Jewish terrorists, many of whom had served in the wartime British Army, to masquerade as British Army personnel, speaking perfect English and possessing uniforms, equipment and sometimes documents. A large proportion of the time of Corps members had, therefore, to be devoted to a very firm security training of units—many lives were thereby saved. Other tasks included the collation and dissemination of information on insurgent personalities, and forecasting likely insurgent intentions. Intelligence was hard to gain, prisoners refused to talk and the local Jewish population was unco-operative. FSS personnel in plain clothes or disguise entered areas difficult for uniformed military patrols to visit; a system of random searches of people and vehicles also brought some results. Surveillance of individuals, suspect illegal organisations and para-military organisations, the vetting and dismissal of civilian labour, concern with Armenian organisations used by the USSR, and certain pacifist groups were further routine commitments. The FSS were also deployed when ships carrying illegal immigrants arrived—documents checks, investigations into how the immigrants' journeys had been arranged, and into the attitudes of the immigrants themselves.[4] Finally, the Corps had made a contribution to the prevention by the Transjordan Frontier Force, to which Warrant Officer C Barnes was attached, of the entry into the territory of Fawzi Kawukji's 'Arab Liberation Army' in January 1948. Life for Intelligence Corps personnel was fraught. One Corps officer and other personnel kept a small store of hand grenades in the bedrooms of a house they were using to drop from the windows in the event of suspicious noises below during the night; the house was however later blown-up.[5] In the words of one officer 'Any doorway in Jerusalem might hide a gunman of the Stern gang or the IZL, every bend of the road might conceal an ambush'.[6]

The Palestine campaign affected the work of Corps personnel elsewhere, the implications for personnel serving in Austria and Trieste have already been noted. In Cyprus 29 FSS at Famagusta was heavily committed in screening and questioning shiploads of would-be Jewish immigrants intercepted at sea by the Royal Navy.

The campaign also inflicted the heaviest casualties on the Corps of any post-1945 operations. Six out of the 223 British Army casualties were Corps member, Sergeants K C Prince and J R Woozley (the latter killed by Arab terrorists), Local Sergeants C V J Martin and M H Paice, Lance Corporal W B Carrington and Private T W Russell. Sergeants Martin and Paice were kidnapped as hostages against the lives of three convicted terrorists held in Acre gaol. On 30 July 1947, when the terrorists were executed, the two NCOs were strangled and hung from olive trees, their corpses booby-trapped.[7]

Brief residual commitments also remained in Syria and Lebanon, of which the most important was during an uprising against the French at Damascus in May 1945. Intelligence Corps FSS NCOs led units of an Indian Division into the city to restore order. More routine work, until withdrawal in 1946, was the location of illegal hashish crops, and assessing local political sentiment.

The Middle East – Egypt and Libya

Despite the post-war reductions, there still remained a sizeable

Intelligence Corps commitment in the Middle East. In 1947, Headquarters Field Security Wing Middle East under Major H Bickerton-Edwards was responsible for five FSS in Egypt, and one each in Libya, Eritrea, Italian Somaliland, Cyprus and Kenya, in addition to the four in Palestine and one in Greece whose work has already been recorded. There was also a Corps representation in Sudan. By 1950, reductions had scaled the totals down to three Sections in Egypt with one each in Libya, Kenya and Cyprus.

Under a Treaty with Egypt, popular at the time of its signature in 1936, Britain maintained the right to garrison troops in Egypt. By 1946, this presence had become the object of nationalist demonstration and rioting, in the course of which 284 FSS offices were burnt down. In 1947, British troops were withdrawn from the Egyptian cities to the Canal Zone, Britain still wishing to retain a strong presence in the Middle East. Patrolling in the Sinai peninsula by 253 FSS also ceased at this time. The Egyptian Government pressed demands for total withdrawal in an atmosphere of mounting tension, and in October 1951 formally abrogated the 1936 Treaty. A wave of anti-British riots swept through the Canal Zone with attacks on military personnel and families. The Canal Zone garrison was hurriedly reinforced to a total of over 65,000 men.

The military problem centred upon the withdrawal by the Egyptians of the 66,000 strong civilian labour force, and the Egyptian use of Youth groups and armed para-military auxiliary policemen, the *Bulak Nizam*, as terrorists. The Youth groups would include, for example, students tasked to sit on house roofs and sketch British installations. The *Bulak Nizam* and other insurgents would then mount the actual attacks upon Servicemen, families, water supplies, roads, railways and bases. In early 1952, the British Army Commander, General Sir George Erskine, was forced to mount an assault upon the police and *Bulak Nizam* in Ismailia, in this operation over 40 Egyptian policemen were killed. In the ensuing political crisis, King Farouk of Egypt dismissed his militant nationalist government and ordered his army to bring the police to order. This unpopular move led to the King's overthrow in July 1952 and a fresh approach to the political problem in London. Amid continuing rioting and a food blockade, negotiations opened that led to an agreement in 1954 with the new Egyptian leader, Colonel Nasser. Under this agreement, British troops were to withdraw from Egypt, but the bases were to be maintained by civilians and be again available to Britain in the event of a foreign threat. The British troops withdrew in early 1956, but the agreement collapsed when

Colonel Nasser nationalised the Suez Canal Company later in the year.

The work of Intelligence Corps personnel included the provision and collation of Intelligence, where it could be acquired, for GHQ and formation commanders. Such Intelligence was collected from informants, or from persons or documents seized in raids. FS Sections, or detachments were distributed along the Canal towns, an especial problem was the ordnance depot at Tel el Kebir with its 17 mile long perimeter. Egyptian nationalists would use lorries to drag away a section of the perimeter fence, a raid party would then steal arms or stores. FSS personnel undertook screening work during the major cordon and search operations such as those in Ismailia on 21 January 1952 and later again in Ismailia on the 25th. The wider consequences of this latter operation, Erskine's disarming of the Ismailia police and the occupation of the local barracks of the *Bulak Nizam*, have already been noted; on the ground itself more than a thousand regular and auxiliary policemen had to be screened. The work of the FSS was acknowledged in a special message from General Erskine:

> I am extremely pleased with the excellent work done by all ranks of Field Security in the Canal Zone during our recent trouble.

There was also an air photo-interpretation commitment, the Air Photo Interpretation Unit (ME) was tasked to select landing and dropping zones for use in the event of a rescue operation for British civilians still resident in Alexandria and Cairo becoming necessary. One APIU officer of the Corps, Captain C L Kelsey, was killed by terrorists in November 1951 while trying to persuade *Bulak Nizam* auxiliaries to desist. For all, life in Egypt in this period was unpleasant, a pattern of overcrowded tents, poor facilities, no social life, flies and heat, all compounding the tense atmosphere of a terrorist campaign.

The Corps' Security commitment in Libya carried out by 3 FSS, reinforced briefly by 48 FSS from the Cyrenaica area from 1956, lasted until the final withdrawal of British troops in 1969–70.[8] The work was mainly routine frontier airport and seaport Security; there were however occasional crises. The three most serious were in 1949, at the time of the abortive British–Italian agreement on Libya, when large scale rioting broke out and 3 FSS were involved in curfew enforcement, the Suez crisis of 1956 noted earlier, and a final period of acute tension in 1967. Following the Suez episode, British Forces in Libya were substantially reduced leaving only small garrisons in Benghazi and Tobruk/RAF (El Adem); 3 FSS closed down and 48 FSS became the Counter Intelligence Detachment (Libya). Serious rioting broke out in Benghazi against British and American personnel and property during the June 1967 Arab–Israeli War. The CI Detachment's town office was attacked; a Detachment member (unarmed at the time) acted bravely to protect three women trapped in the building, all eventually making their escape. The Benghazi garrison withdrew in February 1968 and the detachment moved to RAF (El Adem) where it came under command of Counter Intelligence Company (NEARELF) and was renamed Army Security Detachment (El Adem). It provided security coverage for, and briefings to, visiting army units exercising in the Libyan desert. After the Libyan Army coup in September 1969, the Detachment provided the first picture of the coup's leader, Captain M Qadhafi. This last Corps unit on the North African coast closed in early 1970 when the Tobruk/El Adem garrison withdrew, ending the British military presence in Libya. One final notable achievement was the discovery, through local contacts, that a large consignment of cheap transistor radios had been unloaded from a Soviet ship and was being widely distributed from the Soviet Embassy.

The Middle East—Jordan, the Arabian Peninsula and Aden

With the withdrawal from Egypt began the Corps' long involvement with the British commitments in the Arabian Peninsula, the Gulf and Aden. These in 1956–57 saw a small detachment of the Corps serving at Aqaba in Jordan, its role being the security of British units in camps there following withdrawal from Egypt. Warrant Officer Barnes took part in both the 1955 and 1956 Buraimi Oasis operations while on secondment to the Trucial Oman Levies. This commitment arose from a dispute between Abu Dhabi, Oman and Saudi-Arabia over water rights at the Buraimi Oasis. A small British-led force was despatched to the oasis while British diplomacy effected conciliation. Warrant Officer Barnes was awarded the MBE for his work. In 1958, following the announcement of an Egyptian-Syrian Union and the Iraq Revolution, 16 (Para) Brigade was sent hurriedly to Amman, in Jordan, to prevent any incursion into this friendly Arab nation. Corps personnel were in the Brigade headquarters. In the Gulf the first Corps presence was that of one or two Warrant Officers and NCOs posted to Bahrain from 1957 onwards on detachment from Aden; this commitment continued until the final British withdrawal from the Gulf. In 1958 one of these, Warrant Officer Barnes, was attached to British and South Arabian forces containing a rising against the then Sultan of Oman in the Jebel Akhdar. In March 1961, at a time when Iraq first appeared to be harbouring designs upon Kuwait, British units were sent to the area from several places; an Intelligence Platoon accompanied the force command, Headquarters 24 Brigade, flown in from Kenya. The Platoon concerned itself with the nature of an invasion threat, and also with security, in particular the investigation of sabotage of an RAF aircraft at Bahrein.

The British Army's two final campaigns in the Middle East were both in the Arabian Peninsula – the operations in Aden and its hinterland from 1964 to 1967, and the Dhofar campaign in Oman of 1970 to 1975. The first of these campaigns arose from the pressures of Arab nationalism, in various local forms and supported by inflammatory propaganda from Cairo and elsewhere, against the precarious British created Federation of South Arabia – Aden and hinterland principalities. An insurgent National Liberation Front, NLF, opened the campaign in late 1963 from bases in Yemen. At the outset the Federation project carried at least a measure of local support as to it had been attached a promise of independence in 1968, together with a remaining British garrison. In 1966, however, following a change of government in London, it was announced that there would be no post-1968 British garrison. Federal Ministers, Federal soldiers and policemen in fear of their own futures, started to waver in support and reliability. The campaign became more difficult and ended in an over-the-beaches withdrawal operation, notably successful in military terms but with no political gains.

Although there was one bomb attack in Aden in 1963, the Radfan border area was the scene of operations in the first half of 1964. Later in that year bombings, killings and intimidation opened in the Aden townships. Civilians and Servicemen's wives and children were especial targets. One bomb planted in a married quarter killed the wife of Major K Wilkes during a supper party. This campaign intensified in 1965 and again in 1966 following the change of policy, and also the appearance of a second rival nationalist movement, the Freedom and Liberation of South Yemen, FLOSY. Sophisticated timed devices and booby traps, rockets, mortars, ambushes and automatic weapons marked the escalation in the streets; the insurgents were now receiving considerable technical and Intelligence support from foreign sources. The Aden Police Special Branch was virtually wiped out, largely as a consequence of this external assistance. The Army's tactics were those of patrolling and pursuit in the Radfan, and in the Aden townships, cordons and searches, house searches, road blocks and patrolling. The conditions—in the Radfan or in Aden—were those of oppressive heat, thirst and discomfort. Danger was summed up by one Corps correspondent:

> We remember the night Ma'alla main road was lit up, literally, by Sergeant Birrell's car colliding with a bazooka rocket. Another rocket narrowly missed Staff Webster's flat and on another occasion two grenades nearly landed in Lance Corporal Crawley's beer whilst he was on a liaison visit ...

The names of members of the Corps were of course on the NLF's assassination list.

The involvement of Corps personnel in operations in the Aden area had begun earlier, with the arrival from 1956 onwards of members of the Corps tasked to provide Intelligence support for British or Aden Protectorate Levies units countering dissidents in the Aden hinterland. Those not serving in staff appointments were grouped together as 4 FSS in 1957. The task, not dissimilar to the former Indian North West Frontier operations, could be adventurous; on one occasion Sergeant Butt acted as 'bait' in a decoy landrover to spring a Yemeni ambush—which then received heavy air and artillery retribution.

In the early 1964 Radfan operations, Corps personnel mostly from 15 Intelligence Platoon under Lieutenant M T J Bourne, were active for over six months in support of 39 Brigade. Their main tasks were studies of insurgent activity based on observation posts, patrol and air reconnaissance reports, the briefing of units and patrols, the assessment of captured weaponry, base security and contacts with local inhabitants.[9] As the campaign developed, tasks and Corps personnel multiplied.

A number of officers were at work in the Joint Staff Intelligence (Middle East), Headquarters, Middle East Land Forces, and the headquarters of 24 Brigade, responsible for the hinterland, and the Aden Brigade, responsible for the townships. The Counter Intelligence Company Aden, which had evolved from 4 FSS, provided Security expertise. With the mounting difficulties within the local police, the Company came to play an increasing role in interrogation at the Fort Morbut Holding Centre, in the collation of Intelligence, and in house raids with the Special Branch. Interrogation and captured documents provided generally full information on the political activities of the NLF, the cell structure and foreign supporters. But this NLF cell system for field terrorism made inroads into the military wing difficult until a very successful surprise raid on an NLF headquarters in September 1965, when commanders and documents were taken. Later, men taken at road checks and found to be carrying weapons or explosives were questioned, their replies leading to buried arms caches and further arrests. One important insurgent leader, under a friendly interrogation by Major Richards, gave himself away by always scratching the inside of his left elbow with his right hand when not telling the truth. He eventually and voluntarily told all he knew. But as a consequence of the efficiency of the questioning, hostile propaganda fell back on the device of alleging abuse.

Other Corps personnel were attached to Royal Marine Commandos, among these was Lieutenant D J Venn, who was involved in a brisk fire fight with insurgents on the Dhala Road in May 1967. It is also right to note that three subalterns of the Corps, C Brittan, E P O Springfield and C D Parr, all served their infantry attachment training period with units in Aden, the latter being mentioned in despatches for leading his platoon during a very fierce fire fight.

The second campaign in the Arabian Peninsula was a notable political and military success. A revolt gathered momentum in the remote harsh and mountainous Dhofar province of the Sultanate of Oman. In part the revolt represented local discontent but it was also supported by the new Marxist régime in the People's Democratic Republic of Yemen (Aden) and the major Communist powers. Small-scale violence began in the late 1960s with the activities of the Dhofar Liberation Front; after the British withdrawal from Aden a new People's Front for the Liberation of the Occupied Arab Gulf (PFLOAG) emerged in 1970, more radical and more violent. PFLOAG received Warsaw Pact rifles, machine-guns, rocket launchers, mortars, 122 mm field artillery and, later surface to air missiles.

At its peak, PFLOAG could field some 2,000 full time and a further 4,000 'part-time' men. It was opposed by the Sultan's Armed Forces (SAF) which were expanded to an eventual 9,500 men, with from 1973 an Iranian battle group, certain Jordani units (mainly specialist up to 1975 when a battalion arrived), and some 500 British Army personnel on loan or contract. The uprising was confined to the Dhofar province. It carried little support elsewhere at the outset, and the July 1970 coup, in which the traditionalist Sultan Said bin Tamiur was deposed by his progressive son Qaboos bin Said, prevented any expansion, as well as returning many Dhofari to law and order.

The campaign was won by a mixture of politico-social reform, essentially the provision of wells, stores, schools and clinics, together with skilful military campaigning. The mix divided PFLOAG; increasing numbers surrendered, many to join the Sultan's forces. The military aim was to disrupt and then cut off PFLOAG's supply routes to the PDRY initially by the holding of the key Sarfait cliff position, then by establishing advance picket lines and finally in 1975 by clearing the areas up to and beyond the picket lines. The British Army assisted in the building up of the Sultan's Armed Forces, especially the *Firqa* or groups of former insurgents, and by the provision of Special Air Service special force units.

The Corps contribution had begun earlier with the early 1967 secondment of Sergeant Chilcott for collation work at the Sultan's Forces headquarters, and the formation in June 1967 of the small Security Unit (Gulf). In 1970, an Intelligence cell was included in the British Army Training Team, its main tasks being the debriefing of insurgents who surrendered and the vitally important collation of all Intelligence.[10] Questioning was undertaken by Warrant Officers Birrell and Capper and the information gained converted to Intelligence by Corps NCOs working round the clock. The Intelligence Support requirement expanded rapidly, and by 1975 the Staff Officers for Operations and for Intelligence, and certain other staff appointments were all filled by Intelligence Corps personnel.[11] In addition, members of the Corps contributed to the specialist work of reviving traditional local and Moslem loyalties to counter revolutionary ideological appeals. This work was one of the decisive factors in the campaign.

There was also a very successful tactical questioning operation in North Oman under Major H M Sloan in early 1971. Roles could be adventurous and hazardous. Captain Abbott was concerned with tactical Intelligence gathering in preparation for the stop-lines. Captain Venn and Warrant Officer Birrell played notable roles in a tense situation following a seaborne landing at a coastal village. Sergeant Duncan on a dhow patrol came under 75 mm artillery and heavy machine-gun fire. Corporal Boden was part of a protection party supplying ammunition to a forward unit across enemy held and mined territory. Sergeant Luttrell raised and ran an Intelligence-gathering Group of Northern Dhofaris. One or two Corps members flew over insurgent-held areas with a former insurgent as a fellow passenger in the helicopter; these latter pointed out insurgent hideous on the ground. This system, named 'the Flying Finger' by its creator,

Warrant Officer Raven, was important in demoralising insurgents in areas they believed safe. A number of Corps officers and NCOs were also serving with the SAS.[12] After the campaign had run down Corps personnel continued to serve on loan with the Oman military intelligence organisation until 1981. The need was emphasised by an event in 1976 of which one Intelligence Corps officer wrote:

> ... on 23 Sept 76 ... 15 members of the PFLO infiltrated into Dhofar carrying well over £100,000 in an attempt to revive the insurgency there. After a very hectic and exciting operation, mounted by the teeth arm units of the brigade, assisted by the entire intelligence community of Dhofar, we managed to force most of the 15 to surrender.[13]

In proportion to the small size of the Corps, its contribution and impact was very great in a classic counter-insurgency campaign.

The Middle East—Lebanon

The Intelligence Corps' last contribution to British Army work in the Middle East was that of the Corps detachment serving in Beirut in 1983–84. The withdrawal of the Israeli Army had led to a resumption of the Civil War; it was hoped, in vain, that a multi-national contingent could act as an interposition force between the city's warring factions. The British component of the multi-national force was located in the eastern suburb of Al Hadath, and the roles of the Corps personnel were surveillance of the city and airfield, and general Intelligence gathering.

The Corps detachment at its maximum totalled seven, and with the exception of one sergeant at work in the British Embassy all were concerned with this provision of operational Intelligence to the Commander British Forces Lebanon.[14] The main sources of Intelligence besides direct observation, were liaison with the US, French and Italian contingents and the Lebanese Army and Police. Both the work and the location brought Corps personnel into the closest contact with the grim realities of Lebanon. Among these realities were assistance, very much appreciated, to the US Marines after the fundamentalist lorry-bomb attacks, the logging of artillery barrages, tank firings and small arms exchanges, the erection of rocket screens, and the close proximity of the Forces headquarters in the Christian sector to the Lebanese Army targets favoured by insurgent artillery and rockets.

Cyprus

The island of Cyprus both as a British colony and from 1960 as an independent state, has provided successive commitments for the Intelligence Corps. The fundamental problem of the island, its four-fifths Greek and one-fifth Turkish population, is well known. In 1954 there emerged a Greek insurgency movement, EOKA, which sought *enosis*, union with Greece. At this time, following withdrawal from Palestine and Egypt, Britain was still anxious to use Cyprus as a major Middle East base and headquarters. There was also strong Turkish opposition both local and mainland to a Cyprus united with Greece, so providing Athens with air base facilities very close to Turkey.

EOKA's campaign took the form of mountain-based guerrillas and town based rioting, terror bombing and assassinations. Students and quite young school children were incited to riot for world propaganda purposes. EOKA was supported by aid and propaganda from Greece itself, again aimed at world opinion, in particular that of the USA. The terror campaign was generally directed at forcing the Greek population to support *enosis*, and was particularly targeted upon police, military and Intelligence personnel, the Cyprus Police being pushed to the verge of collapse. In September 1955, after some nine months of violence, London appointed Field Marshal Sir John Harding as Governor of Cyprus. Harding immediately set up a Cyprus version of the system that had proved successful in Malaya—a Director of Operations, a joint command and control structure for Army, Police and Administration, and a joint Intelligence organisation; the security forces were also increased. By 1956 results were beginning to show. The withdrawal of units for the Suez operation returned some advantage to EOKA but by early 1957 the redeployment of these units and the arrival in Cyprus of helicopters enabled the security forces to reassert control while the political future of the territory was being negotiated. These negotiations resulted in an agreement in 1959 by which Cyprus became an independent state with guarantees for the minority Turkish population and the retention of two 'sovereign base' areas by Britain. As elsewhere, once a proper organisation had been established – in the case of Cyprus not fully effective until 1956–57 – Intelligence played a crucial part in security operations. The early large scale but not always clearly purposeful battalion or brigade sized cordon and searches could be reduced down to small sections of men arriving swiftly in a vehicle and effecting surprise arrests. Particular Intelligence problems were the EOKA

Intelligence gathering and sabotage threats, the initial lack of any proper co-ordination to deal with these threats, the difficulty in convincing some unit commanders of the day-to-day reality of the threats, and the language difficulty.

The Intelligence Corps contribution was threefold, the provision of headquarters Intelligence staff officers and NCOs, of Field Security Sections, and of a Port and Travel Control Security Unit—the first peacetime use of such a unit. The headquarters elements included members of the Security Identification Section (Cyprus), personnel attached to the Police Special Branch, translators, an official (Captain L Savery) who controlled counter-gangs, a headquarters security section and personnel for operational Intelligence support staffs. These latter would work closely with infantry battalion Intelligence Sections, providing continuity as well as expertise. The language difficulty was in part, but only in part, overcome by Corps personnel who had studied classical Greek at school or university.

From 1955 147 FSS was serving in Nicosia responsible for the Western half of the island, it was joined at the end of the next year by 253 FSS responsible for Eastern Cyprus. Some examples of their work show the meticulous attention to detail that was necessary. An FSS NCO insisted, despite outraged protests, that some small clay Madonnas imported as 'religious symbols' into the island be dissected—inside were pencil bombs. Ammunition and grenades wrapped in oil cloth would be found at the bottom of barrels of olive oil or in bales of tobacco. Apparently innocent fishermen's marker flags would indicate a motor tyre inner tube lying on the sea bed with, inside, grenades and ammunition packed in vaseline. FSS personnel worked closely with the Navy's mine-sweepers and patrol craft.[15] Another example was the watch upon the movements of certain professional ladies around cafes favoured by EOKA activists.

The Port and Travel Control Unit arrived in 1956 and operated until 1960 with detachments at Famagusta, Limassol and Larnaca, and a mobile detachment with the RAF at Nicosia.[16] The Group's main concern was the prevention of the smuggling of Greek insurgents, weaponry and political propaganda into Cyprus. All vessels arriving or leaving were searched; the work was monotonous and at times dangerous as EOKA limpets or time bombs were occasionally left on board. The Group had also to provide a Postal Detachment of NCOs for watch on incoming parcels. This watch on occasions provided leads on those despatching parcels containing ammunition or propaganda from abroad, leads that added to knowlege on insurgent organisation and finances, and on the activities of foreign agencies.

Adventures that befell members of the Corps will illustrate the nature of the campaign. Major S Macpherson, within a fortnight of his arrival to command Field Security Middle East, found a time bomb in his garden. Two bombs exploded in the house of Sergeant Stafford of 147 FSS; Sergeant Stafford and Sergeant Crane were both within 10 yards of another bomb exploding in Metaxas Square, Nicosia. The Famagusta interception barge of the Port and Travel Control Unit was sunk by a bomb placed adjacent to its propeller shaft, and a Headquarters Intelligence Corps officer, Captain Wildash, found a large time bomb in the glove pocket of his car.

The ending of the EOKA uprising and formal independence led to reductions in troop levels and a series of reorganisations within Military Intelligence in Cyprus, Corps personnel assuming new roles—the Security of the Sovereign Base areas and later the increased provision of both Intelligence and Security specialist personnel.

The former EOKA leader, Grivas, did not accept the independent state of Cyprus, as although meeting the wishes of the Greek Cypriots, it fell short of the aims of his campaign. In 1963–64 and again in 1967, he attempted to eliminate the government of Archbishop Makarios. In December 1963, violence erupted in Nicosia and two British battalions moved out of the Sovereign Base Area to prevent further killings; Intelligence for the operation was provided by Major K M L Frazer and his Cyprus Counter Intelligence Company, and Major M J D Perrett-Young, the Cyprus Base Intelligence Officer.[17] With the arrival of 16 Parachute Brigade units and headquarters from Britain in January 1964, the Corps work was extended by contributions from the Brigade's Intelligence Officer and 6 Parachute Intelligence Platoon. The Intelligence problem for the next two years was that of the clandestine arrival into the island of large numbers of Greek soldiers with their weapons. The Cyprus Base Intelligence Officer at this time was Major B A H Parritt who was awarded the MBE for his work.

Cyprus was, and remains, a territory of interest to the Intelligence agencies of a number of countries; a high standard of security vigilance is essential. The Corps commitment in Cyprus continues, with officers posted to the Joint Intelligence Staff in Cyprus, a senior NCO at the United Nations Force Headquarters and Corps members of all ranks serving in 11 Security Company. One small but amusing event illustrates the importance of security. An attractive lady collided with an infantry subaltern while skiing, the encounter led to a dinner invitation from the lady. The subaltern was however prudent, and became even more so on being told by Corps officers of the lady's connections with a particular embassy.

The Far East—Malaya

The Malayan Emergency (1948–60) was the largest scale of the decolonisation campaigns and was to provide the pattern for all future British counter-insurgency operations. The insurgents' hard-core was the Chinese Communist members of the World War II Malayan people's Anti-Japanese Army led by Chin Peng, a wartime resistance leader. At the end of 1945, 6,000 of these handed in their weapons, but some 4,000 did not do so and spent 1947 in preparing for an uprising. The conditions seemed propitious. Britain had withdrawn from India, the Communists were winning in the Chinese civil war; the terrain of primaeval jungle or rubber plantation estates was ideal. The 'Malayan People's Anti-British Army' of 10 regiments, all but one Chinese, in practice planned their campaign to lead from terror to the seizure of 'liberated areas', and after expansion to an Indochinese style guerilla army war.[18] Chinese labour on the estates and in the towns was available to help, under threat if not voluntarily.

After mounting industrial unrest, the campaign of violence opened in April 1948 with acts of sabotage, and the first killings of Europeans in June 1948. Worse followed in the next month. The Malayan civil authorities were ill-prepared—the police force was not properly reformed and trained, the Peninsula's garrison was six Gurkha battalions in the throes of reorganisation, together with three British battalions and an artillery regiment. By 1950 the total commitment had risen to 24 British, Malay, Gurkha, Fijian and African infantry battalions, and two armoured car regiments.

The principles conducting the campaign, set out in the Briggs Plan of 1950 and carried out by General Sir Gerald Templer from 1952, are well-known: domination of the populated areas to create a sense of security, and the resettlement of the Chinese estate labour into well-policed villages. These two measures combined to deprive the insurgents of their food and supplies, so forcing them to come out to battle on the Army's terrain. The other principles were the creation of an integrated civil police and military organisation with joint operations committees and operations rooms, at all levels, and the expansion of efficient gathering and pooling of all Intelligence. This latter was effected by a system of Intelligence Committees working to a (civilian) Director of Intelligence, the military being represented by a Military Intelligence Officer working with each district's unit or formation.

At the outset of the violence, the Corps contribution was limited to the four remaining FSS in the theatre, 355 FSS responsible for the centre and south of the Malay peninsula, 358 FSS responsible for the north, 1 FSS in Johore and the Singapore Special FS Section. An early reinforcement was 103 Air Photo Interpretation Section.[19] As the campaign progressed, more personnel became involved. But the campaign was at its height in the worst years of the post-war reductions. Most Intelligence staff appointments were held by other officers, though a practice of using National Service Intelligence Corps officers as district Assistant Military Intelligence Officers grew up.

Close integration with police and infantry formations and units also makes it difficult to discern the particular work of Intelligence Corps members. On the Operational Intelligence side, a good example is that of 1 FSS, which became affiliated to 48 Gurkha Brigade in early 1949, the NCOs of the Section working with battalions as unit Intelligence Sections. This brought them up to the crucial tactical point of the campaign, persuading the villagers and estate labourers compelled by terror to supply food for the insurgents to give information to the Army. Success was achieved either when the villagers became convinced that the Army was winning and could protect them, or by a specific enquiry. These enquiries followed a cordon and search, adult villagers would be given paper and pencil and invited to offer information anonymously, the papers then being placed in a sealed ballot box to be opened later.[20]

103 APIS began its work at Kuala Lumpur, it later provided a detachment to work with the RAF at Butterworth in North Malaya. The work was painstaking, carefully examining photographs of dense forest in search of minute clues to insurgent movements or hides and then setting these clues against other available Intelligence or in use with surrendered insurgents or police informers. A large number of successes enabled air strikes to be mounted or police and military patrols to be briefed.[21]

Routine Security work remained important. A sergeant of 355 FSS was tasked to investigate leaks of information about a particular operation and he visited the local battalion concerned. On the wall of the Commanding Officer's office was a large map with details of the operation. Local personalities came in and out of the office and 25 civilian contractors had been informed the operation was taking place.

In mid 1953 the Field Security Wing Headquarters (Malaya) took over the screening and pass issues for civilian labour in Army employ in the whole mainland Malay Peninsula, to relieve the pressure on Sections. Eleven detachments and a Central Pass Issue Office were at work. These detachments also supported infantry units and were on occasions able to collect insurgent movement Intelligence.[22]

Field Security Sections personnel also worked closely with the local Special Branches. In 1949, for example, the Singapore Special FSS captured five insurgents, weapons and propaganda material in a raid. In 1953, the Special Military Intelligence Unit was formed in Kuala Lumpur, the unit having particular responsibilities with the Special Branch for the acquisition of Intelligence. A number of Corps NCOs were at work in this organisation, in particular on interpretation and document translation duties, briefing, the preparation of Intelligence Summaries for units and the maintenance of insurgent orders of battle for each Malay State.

The developing expertise of the Corps and its varied work is well summarised in a recollection of Second Lieutenant W Ryrie:

> As a Second Lieutenant, I was the assistant to the major who was the Military Intelligence Officer for the state of Pahang at Kuala Lipis. As it happened, the state of Pahang was where the communist terrorist headquarters were, although they were constantly on the move in the jungle. Our main task was to track them down by means of every kind of intelligence—informers from the towns and villages where supplies were obtained, captured documents from camps overrun by our patrols, prisoners and aerial photographs. ... The success we achieved in the year (1953) was that at the start of the year we knew where Chin Peng had been four months before and when I left we knew where he had been six weeks before. Eventually, some time later, they got so close to his tail that he fled over the border into Thailand and Pahang was declared 'White'.[23]

Operations from 1954 onwards were more of a 'mopping-up' nature. A little before it was taken over by the Joint Air Photographic Interpretation Centre (Far East), 103 APIS reduced its number of detachments and turned to civilian work, advising on possible routes for water-pipe laying to remote villages. A few operational commitments remained, personnel being attached to 17 Gurkha Division. With the independence of Malaya in 1957, Security work was reduced to that necessary for British Army military garrisons and depots.

In accordance with the Intelligence Platoon concept, four platoons, numbered 19 to 22 were formed in 1960, covering the Malay Peninsula and Singapore.[24] One of these platoons had an additional South East Asia Treaty Organisation commitment, participating in exercises. Later in the decade, Corps specialists undertook Security duties in respect of small British units, mainly Royal Engineers, in Thailand.

The important roles played by members of the Corps in the Borneo *konfrontasi* operations have already been set out. For the remainder, in the years to final withdrawal in 1970–71, routine duties included preparation of politico-military briefings, essential security training of British, Malaysian and other South East Asian personnel, and participation in exercises.

The Far East—Hong Kong

The Intelligence Corps' second field of duty in the Far East was and still is Hong Kong. The immediate post-war concern of Corps personnel in Hong Kong was the control of refugees, investigations into war crimes, and the issue of passes.[25] Over a million people had fled from Hong Kong to China during the Japanese occupation; they and others sought to return. In the first six months after liberation, some 2,000 persons were processed each day. Routine Security work has continued in Hong Kong continuously since that time, in two particular periods amid tension.

The first of these periods was in 1949, when Chinese revolutionary sentiment was at its height following the Communist victory in the civil war. The garrison had to be reinforced to approximately division strength. The second period was during the Chinese 'Cultural Revolution' of 1966–67 with disturbances involving screaming, hysterical 'Red Guards' both in the urban areas and on the border. There has also been a Corps Air Photo Interpretation representation in the territory following the move of JARIC (Far East) from Malaya.

Africa—Kenya

The Corps' post-1945 commitments in the Horn of and in Black Africa began with the work of 261 FSS, based on Asmara in

246

Eritrea in 1948-50. Members of the Section provided local knowledge and some linguistic expertise to infantry patrols operating against *shifta* dissidents.

In Kenya, 277 FSS continued work in the immediate post-war years, both in Kenya itself and in both the British and former Italian Somaliland; its members included a number of locally recruited African personnel. The Section's disbandment in 1950, however, left no Corps presence in East Africa and no continuity of Intelligence when the Mau Mau uprising began in 1952.

Mau Mau was an uprising of sections of the Kikuyu group of peoples, the sections being surplus resident labour removed off white settlers' farms, the landless in the Kikuyu homelands, and the urban underpaid or unemployed. Military operations were limited to the towns and settled areas adjoining Kikuyuland, and Kikuyuland itself; Intelligence gathering was primarily a Kenya Police concern. The Corps' contribution to this campaign, effectively one of four years, was two of the Divisional Military Intelligence Officers in the affected districts, an FSS (East Africa) for field Security for units and headquarters, and personnel, under Major C A Lowe, for the East Africa Air Photo Interpretation Section.

The DMIOs were concerned with collection and collation of operational Intelligence; as the campaign developed, former Mau Mau members were used in village level Intelligence gathering and pseudo gang work; particularly successful was Major A Parry at Nanyuki. The main task of the FSS was investigation into the very limited number of Mau Mau cells in locally recruited African units and in military installations. The cell members, Kikuyu and a few Kamba, were providing weapons and medical supplies to insurgents, or on occasions were found to be tasked to kill senior officers. Other work included the screening of military labour, some enquiries in the large detention centres where detainees volunteered information affecting the Army, and enquiries into forged movement permits and bus transport services.

The APIS task was exceedingly difficult, Mau Mau using game tracks and well-hidden and camouflaged huts and hides. Mosaics of the Aberdare and Mount Kenya mountain areas were produced for infantry units, advice offered on air supply dropping zones in two major operations, and on the planning of tracks to be built by the Royal Engineers. Some targets were also given to the artillery and bomb strike analyses prepared for the RAF.

After the end of Mau Mau, the Army maintained a brigade in Kenya until 1964, the year after independence. The tasks undertaken by Intelligence Corps personnel serving with the Brigade headquarters are a useful example of the work of the Corps during a 'decolonisation'. Routine work included vetting of civilian labour and the surveillance of hotels used by Army and RAF families, technical surveillance being necessary on occasions. Briefings, including air photographs, would be given to military and police personnel engaged in raids to recover stolen army property, including firearms. All four East African territories were the targets of the Intelligence services of several Communist countries; military Intelligence help was sought by local police in watching arrivals and movements of people in transit, the watch on occasions being from helicopters. A Corps NCO was sent to Stanleyville in the Congo with a platoon of infantry in late 1960 when it appeared that British lives were at risk; another provided Intelligence support to an infantry company in Zanzibar at a time of rioting in 1961. Corps officers and NCOs were also involved in enquiries into the political implications of a mutiny of the Junior Leaders Company of the King's African Rifles at the turn of the decade.

Africa—Cameroons, Mauritius, Zimbabwe

Intelligence Corps personnel have also served in two other areas of or near Africa, Southern Cameroons in 1961 and Mauritius in 1969.

The Southern Cameroons was an area of Nigeria between 1920 and 1961; it had previously been a part of the German colony of Kamerun, most of which passed to the French after the First World War. After Nigeria and Cameroun both became independent in 1960 and amid much political controversy, a plebiscite was arranged for the area to decide which new state it should join. A British battalion under United Nations auspices maintained order, and the plebiscite result favoured Cameroun. A transition period was planned but this proved too slow for a radical nationalist insurrectionary force, the ALNK, *Armée de Libération Nationale Kamerunaise*, which launched an insurgency campaign.[26] An Intelligence Centre was opened to support the British force; its particular concern was interrogation carried out in May–August 1961.[27] Interrogation revealed the training of insurgents by Algerians in Morocco, and by the Chinese. A report on the questioning noted that 'By far and away and best results were achieved by patience, fair treatment and keeping any promises made—this attitude made a great impression on the prisoners'.[28] An example of the success of the questioning was a raid on the camp of the 1st Mobile Battalion of the ALNK in which a number of weapons were found.

Mauritius's transition to independence in 1968 was marred by inter-communal rioting, Creole and Moslem. Two companies of Light Infantry were despatched from Malay to restore order. To assist in the running of an Operations Room 'with daily briefings, riots, arsons, murder and what have you' two NCOs were also loaned by the Commander Intelligence Corps, Far East Land Forces.[29]

The Intelligence Corps's last African commitment was a five man contribution to the Commonwealth Monitoring Force (CMF) in the territory at that time known as Zimbabwe–Rhodesia, now Zimbabwe.[30] The role of the Force, Operation *Agila*, was to supervise the cease-fire and at times fragile peace between the Rhodesian Security Forces (RSF) and the Patriotic Front (PF) insurgents, centring upon 39 rendezvous points and 14 assembly areas, and also to be present during the February 1980 elections. Three of the Corps personnel served at Headquarters, Mobile Force and two on the staff of Major General J Acland at Government House. Of their duties Lieutenant McMahon later wrote:

> Our principal role was to go out to all the outlying stations and bring back unbiased reports of who was there and what was going on. This task in a country the size of France and where the only way of travelling was by means of the few MF helicopters was often long and tedious ... where everyone had some kind of prejudice after fifteen years of war, a mobile unbiased investigation and reporting team proved indispensable, not only for the MF Commanders but, also, on many occasions for our political masters as well.[31]

Three other British territories, two now independent, have required a small Intelligence Corps commitment at times of internal tension or external threat. These were British Guiana at times of communal and labour tension, notably in 1964, Malta prior to independence and Gibraltar.

In conclusion it may justly be claimed that the British Army has won for itself the reputation of being the world's most professional, and the world's most humane, counter-insurgency force. The gathering of Intelligence has been a crucial component of that reputation; the Intelligence Corps has played a vital part in that duty.

14

The Corps Renewed, 1957–90

This last chapter sets out to record the work of the renewed Intelligence Corps and its growth in professionalism and range of duties following the decision in favour of the Corps made in the mid-1950s when Field Marshal Sir Gerald Templer was Chief of the Imperial General Staff. The Corps' work now extends from contributing to strategic Intelligence to the main day-to-day operational commitments, military Intelligence support for the British Army of the Rhine and to Intelligence training for the Corps' Regular and Territorial Army personnel together with a number of Army schools and units.

Expansion

The decisions of the mid-1950s, recognising that the provision of Intelligence requires even in peace time a new dimension of Intelligence expertise, has led to a small but steady numerical expansion of the Corps, and more important, where professionalism is so closely linked with experience and continuity, new structures and career patterns to provide the trained personnel. The three most important decisions were first that the Intelligence Corps should be allowed 100 full Regular commission career officers, eligible for Staff College and promotion to any rank.[1] Secondly, a professional system of trade testing for soldiers and NCOs was introduced.[2] The third major decision was that the Corps should leave the now seriously decrepit Maresfield Camp and have a new home at Ashford, Templer Barracks. The decisions were all linked together with a War Office statement that the Intelligence Corps was now accepted as a permanent component of the Army. The Corps could now be geared to meet the demands of the modern era.

Although the three Second World War components, Strategic Intelligence, Operational Intelligence and Security remain, the spectrum has increased enormously. The continuing military threat of the Warsaw Pact required detailed studies of equipments, orders of battle and tactics, these latter no longer in abstract as in 1939–40 but related to particular terrain and conditions. Increased complexities of technology include computers and computer security, electronic Intelligence, electronic counter and counter-counter measures, air and ground photography and fibro-optical equipments—all now immediate battlefield or Security Intelligence requirements. Terrorism has developed, and continues to develop, even more horrifying dimensions. Also in the nature of the contemporary world, military contingency planning has to cover a number of other possible overseas operational commitments that have, or may require, a British Army presence. Even if no actual operations are in progress, emergencies can arise. Prior Intelligence study can make military intervention, if it becomes necessary, more efficient and save lives. Officers and NCOs of the Intelligence Corps are involved in such contingency planning at major military headquarters. One example may be given, the different possible roles of 84 Intelligence and Security Section of the Allied Commander Europe's Mobile Force (Land), which provides Intelligence support for a variety of NATO flank contingencies.

Despite this expanding range of commitments, it again seemed that in the mid-1960s the Intelligence Corps might be disbanded or mutilated, its specialist personnel distributed around other Corps. Fortunately these ideas, put forward on two occasions, were set aside. The successes of the Corps in the Borneo operations played a significant part in the battle for survival at the time; the lessons of 1939–40 were also recalled. The two Radcliffe Reports, of 1961 and 1962, together with the 1961 Romer Report which recommended the creation of a specialist security staff for each Service, also served to emphasise an important aspect of the Corps' work.

At first it was thought that a structure of all-purpose Intelligence Platoons attached to all formation headquarters, but controlled by a Theatre Intelligence Unit or, later, Intelligence or a Counter-Intelligence Company was appropriate.[3] In the event, maintaining a balance of skills, security, air photo-interpretation and interrogation, proved neither very practical nor, very often, what particular situations needed. Following careful study by Lieutenant Colonel R Dodds, an improved structure was introduced in 1966, that of Intelligence and Security Groups, a

Lieutenant Colonel's command, with functional companies. Three such Groups were initially created, for Germany, the Far East and for the Volunteers (TA). The Far East Group lasted only briefly, but in 1972 an Intelligence and Security Group (UK) was formed. In certain detached areas such as Cyprus and later Hong Kong, Intelligence and Security companies were established.[4]

The movement of the Corps Depot and Headquarters to Ashford provided a great lift to morale. Training could now become very much more professional and thorough; the Corps basic training is as arduous as those of other Corps and most regiments in the Army. Good training, however, must be enjoyable, and members of the Corps have therefore also participated in numerous Army diving, desert navigation or climbing expeditions. In one of these, to the Himalayas, Captain D Brister was killed by a snowfall. Almost every year, an adventurous training expedition, to the Canadian Rockies or the Himalayas, or sailing in the Baltic or around the West European coasts, is mounted by members of the Corps themselves; all are important adjuncts to other forms of training. The Corps has also been able to develop its esprit as a 'family' with its own customs and traditions.[5]

As a consequence of the decision of 1957, the Corps is allowed a small number of newly commissioned officers from the Royal Military Academy Sandhurst; the first Regular subaltern, Second Lieutenant J D Landolt, was commissioned into the Corps on 1 December 1958. Corps officers also returned to the Staff College, Captain D S Hawker's entry in 1961 being the first since the years of the Second World War. In the field of professional training, the Commandant of the Tri-Service Defence Intelligence and Security School, the successor to the old School of Military Intelligence, is an Intelligence Corps Colonel's appointment.

The growing professionalism of the Corps has also been evident in its Territorial Army units. The importance the post-1945 Army attached to TA units of the Corps was evident as early as 1947, but the various component units and sub-units have had to pass through a number of reorganisations before the present very satisfactory structure, the Intelligence and Security Group (Volunteers) was formed in 1967.[6] Initially, the Group comprised three companies. Over the years, the total has been increased to six. With one company as an exception, the entire Group is a BAOR reinforcement.

The companies of the Volunteers Group are functional, each with different antecedents. The predecessors of the 2 Security Companies, 20 and 23, include first the Port and Travel Control

Group, formed in 1947, mainly from various wartime members of the Corps. Numbers for this unit were maintained by inputs from disbanded Artillery regiments, initially anti-aircraft and later coast defence. In 1956, this Group at its height was able to provide sections, on mobilisation, for 13 ports and airports.[7] In 1960 however, a run-down began; 1963 saw the Group's disbandment and surviving personnel transferred to 18 Counter Intelligence Company as 10 Port Security Platoon. Other antecedents included the Territorial Army Field Security Sections formed for each of the TA Divisions. Their training was co-ordinated by Command level Regular Army training teams; some training in Germany was arranged on occasions. There were special problems for the newly forming FSS, all were too small to exist on their own and had to live in a TA Centre in which another unit was the senior partner, and Sections were only allowed to recruit to 70 per cent of establishment.[8] In a reorganisation in 1961, all the Command Intelligence Units and Field Security Sections were subsumed into a United Kingdom Intelligence Unit (TA) commanded by a Regular Lieutenant Colonel, Lieutenant-Colonel C T Carter, and comprising seven Counter-Intelligence Companies, which lasted until the 1967 Volunteers Group.[9]

21 Intelligence Company has its origins in two entirely distinct units. In 1947 the Air Photo Interpretation Centre (TA) was formed. Its first Commanding Officer was Major Murray-Thriepland, and the unit contained a number of World War II strategic interpretation experts. The second unit was 100 Army Photographic Interpretation Unit (APIU) TA. In 1949 the Air Photo Interpretation Unit (TA), later APIS (TA), was tasked with the provision of Sections for service in the field; training in Germany began in 1960, Sections were specifically earmarked for RAF bases in Germany. Despite their different backgrounds, the 1967 amalgamation proved a great success.[10]

22 Intelligence Company was formed from the holding pool of Corps officers who had learnt Russian at different Joint Services Schools of Languages during their National Service, together with NCOs recruited and trained in Operational Intelligence. With the end of National Service and the passing of time, the Company had to turn its attention to the teaching of Russian, often from the beginning; remarkable success was achieved thanks particularly to the work of a team of teachers headed by Major B S Fitzjohn. The Company was later divided, a new 24 Company being formed for Operational Intelligence support for BAOR formation head-quarters.

29 Intelligence and Security Company is tasked to be an

immediate mobilisation reinforcement to Headquarters United Kingdom Land Forces. Standards in all the Companies are maintained by trade testing, and in the case of 22 Company also by Army Language examinations.

Other Intelligence Corps TA officers serve in the BAOR Watchkeepers and Liaison Officers Pool, usually with Intelligence Staffs at Corps and Division Headquarters when on major exercises, and in a small Technical Specialist Officers reserve pool; these latter are mainly scientists.

A postscript to the TA side of Corps work can add that two Intelligence Corps TA officers, both with considerable World War experience, Lieutenant Colonel K Garside and A J L Cahill, commanded the University of London Officers' Training Corps in the 1950s and 1960s, and other Corps TA officers have served with this unit.

The Intelligence Corps in BAOR

This history must however conclude where it began, in emphasising that members of the present day Intelligence Corps are first and foremost practical soldiers and as such are fully committed to the main tasks of the British Army.

The changing organisation of the Intelligence Corps in Germany reflects the on-going post 1957 renewal.[11] The Field Security Section concept lasted until 1958, Cold War problems replacing those of the Second World War. In early 1953, Headquarters Field Security was formed at Hereford. This Headquarters, which moved to Mönchen-Gladbach in 1955, controlled the remaining eight Field Security Sections centred on Dusseldorf, Krefeld, Lüneberg and Berlin. In 1958–59 these were replaced by a 'Counter Intelligence Unit' at Mönchen-Gladbach with four offices, North (Verden), Central (Herford), South (Dusseldorf) and Berlin, each commanded by a Captain and, except Berlin, each with outstations. Two years later the 'CI Unit' became a Theatre Intelligence Unit, a Lieutenant Colonel's command from 1962; in accordance with the Intelligence Platoon concept, the eight detachment offices became Platoons. With the further development of the Group structure, the Intelligence and Security Group (Germany) assumed responsibility for military Security, the various platoons being slotted into two Security Companies and also into 3 Intelligence and Security Company, Berlin.

The Security tasks remain unchanged, protective Security surveys and inspections, provision of specialist advice, investigations, the vetting of locally employed civilians, liaison with the local German police and Security agencies, Security advice for high risk personnel, key point Security, Security Intelligence and casework, and Security coverage of major exercises, where troop movements are often under scrutiny by individuals from a remarkable variety of distant countries with equally varied reasons advanced for their presence. In Berlin, 3 Intelligence and Security Company has rather wider roles in view of the city's special status.

A few other specific examples of Security work can be provided. Residual tracing of Nazi war criminals and surveillance of German political life, especially of extremism in trade unions, was continued until the early 1950s. The 1948–1949 Berlin airlift required reinforcement of FSS staffs in Berlin to vet the large numbers of civilians needed to unload aircraft. In the 1950s, refugees from East Germany were still being questioned by Corps members on their arrival. Today, adverse foreign intelligence agencies and terrorist organisations, notably the IRA, make regular attempts to breach Rhine Army Security or attack British Army personnel and constant vigilance is required.

The Intelligence and Security Group (Germany) also took over responsibility for most Air Photographic Intelligence work in BAOR which, from 1964 onwards, had been the responsibility of the Army Photo Interpretation Unit (BAOR), the successor unit to the Second World War 21 Army Group APIU.[12] Air Photograph capabilities have been greatly increased with the entry into service, in the years 1965–1970, of turbo-jet drones to overfly battlefields. Exercise Imagery analysis work is now carried out under field conditions; evaluated exercise Intelligence being produced from negatives, dispositives or prints by Corps personnel, on occasions in full chemical protective clothing. Equipment now extends to infra red line scan and airborne radar systems; the Imagery Analyst may require multi-strand light tables, computer systems, co-ordinator graphs and stereo-microscopes with a zoom capability. The analyst—himself or herself—will need to be familiar with binary coding, computer software, radar and thermal return patterns as well as the traditional skills of mensuration and trigonometry. For his evaluation he will also have to know the equipments and organisation of foreign armies. A Second World War interpreter would still recognise, however, the continuing need for patience, experience, an enquiring mind and keen eyesight.

Knowledge and experience of Imagery Analysis work is shared with United States Army and Canadian opposite numbers by liaison and exchanges of personnel. Other small Corps detachments of Imagery Analysts work under RAF control elsewhere in Germany. All make notable contributions to NATO aerial reconnaissance competitions, often leading to a team win.

The greatest professional advance of the Corps in Germany, however, lies in the field of Operational Intelligence. In 1955, the two senior officers of the Corps in the Intelligence Branch at Headquarters BAOR were but Majors, the long serving 'Bish' Brzezicki and G Hartman. By the late 1980s, the Assistant Chief of Staff Intelligence (ACOS G2) at Rheindahlen (Headquarters BAOR and Northern Army Group) was an Intelligence Corps Brigadier, the ACOS G2 British Sector Berlin was a Corps Colonel and the Chief G2 at the Headquarters of the 1st (British) Corps at Bielefeld was a Corps Lieutenant Colonel; these posts being General Staff are however not 'tied' permanently to Corps officers. All the Staff Officers Grade 3 G2 at Division Headquarters, together with certain specialist Staff appointments at Rheindahlen are Intelligence Corps officers in 'tied' posts. Trained Operational Intelligence Warrant Officers and NCOs are serving in 7 Intelligence Company of the Intelligence and Security Group (Germany). These specialists in Warsaw Pact Armies are attached to different formation headquarters. Their work in the field has been greatly assisted by the Wavell battlefield computer system which can store, process and recall Intelligence data for all formation headquarters along the whole British front, or any sector of it.[13]

Strategic Intelligence

As in the Second World War, members of the Corps are also still involved in Operational Intelligence and in Electronic Warfare.

Further Strategic Intelligence work is undertaken by officers and NCOs of the Corps at the Joint Air Reconnaissance Intelligence Centre (JARIC) at RAF Brampton; this work has also now moved into very advanced technology. JARIC is the heir to the Second World War ACIU of Medmenham. This ACIU was closed and moved as the Army Photographic Interpretation Centre, APIU (UK), to Nuneham Park in 1946 and then absorbed into JARIC in 1953.[14] Early in 1956, it was decided to train selected senior Corps NCOs in photo-interpretation work, an initial six being successfully trained and then employed at JARIC, which itself moved to Brampton in 1957.[15] By 1958, Corps NCOs were replacing officer photo-interpreters in BAOR and the work became part of the Corps trade test procedures in the next decade. The Executive Officer at JARIC together with all Army air photo-interpretation personnel are now all Intelligence Corps.

The Corps in the 1990s

Readers of this history will have noticed the important role played by women Intelligence personnel serving with Intelligence Corps members from the First World War onwards. Women personnel are now full members of the Corps, women officers being commissioned directly into the Corps from Sandhurst, and women soldiers being trained at Ashford. In almost all postings, women members of the Corps work with male members, and women officers are eligible for the widest variety of appointments.

Two other events epitomise the Corps as it enters the 1990s. On 1 February 1985 the Intelligence Corps was re-defined by the Executive Committee of the Army Boards as an 'Arm' in place of its former status as a supporting Service. And the Corps' commemoration, in 1990, of its 50th Anniversary as a distinct, badged, Arm of the Army can justly be seen as a moment of family pride in achievements increasingly professional and successful. Hardly were the celebrations over than the Corps was faced with its biggest commitment since the Second World War, the Gulf operations. An account of the Corps' role in the Gulf must, however, await the next volume of the Corps' history.

Glossary

AAPIU	Army Air-Photographic Interpretation Unit.
ACIU	Allied Central Interpretation Unit, (air photography).
APIC	Army Photo-Interpretation Centre.
APIS	Army Photographic-Interpretation Section.
APTIUME	Air Photo-Interpretation Unit Middle East.
ATS	Auxiliary Territorial Service, (the Army's Women's Corps in the Second World War).
BAR	British Army of the Rhine, (post First World War).
BAOR	British Army of the Rhine, (post Second World War).
BEF	British Expeditionary Force.
BETFOR	British Element Trieste Force.
BIC	Burma Intelligence Corps.
BOOB	Burma Order of Battle, (the compilation of Japanese Army units in Burma).
CIU	Central Interpretation Unit, (air photography).
CPIS	Central Photographic-Interpretation Section, (South East Asia).
CSDIC	Combined Services Detailed Interrogation Centre.
DF	Direction Finding.
DMI	Director of Military Intelligence.
DMO	Director of Military Operations.
ENIGMA	German enciphering machine for signal communication.
FARELF	Far East Land Forces.
FIAT	Field Intelligence Agency (Technical), (1945).
FIO	Field Intelligence Officer.
FID	Field Intelligence Department, (South African War).
FIU	Forward Interrogation Unit.
FSP	Field Security Police.
FSRD	Field Security Reserve Detachment.
FSS	Field Security Section.

GOC	General Officer in Command.
GOC-in-C	General Officer Commander in Chief.
GSO	General Staff Officer (GSO1, Lieutenant Colonel, GS02 Major-GS03, Captain).
I(A)	The acquisition and use of Intelligence concerning an adversary.
I(B)	The prevention of an adversary's acquiring Intelligence about our own capabilities.
I(C)	Censorship and Propaganda.
I(X)	Administration of Intelligence resources.
IFBU	Indian Field Broadcast Unit.
INA	Indian National Army, (Japanese sponsored).
IO	Intelligence Officer.
ISUM	Intelligence Summary.
JARIC	Joint Air Reconnaissance Intelligence Centre.
JFIT	Joint Forward Interrogation Team.
L o C	Lines of Communication.
LRDG	Long Range Desert Group.
MAIU	Mediterranean Allied Interpretation Unit, (air photography).
MEIC	Middle East Intelligence Centre.
MPAJA	Malayan Peoples Anti-Japanese Army.
NACIU	North African Central Interpretation Unit, (air photography).
NEARELF	Near East Land Forces.
PAIFORCE	Persia and Iraq Forces, (Second World War).
PI	Photographic Interpreter.
PIU	Photographic Interpretation Unit, (Royal Air Force).
PWIS-H	Prisoner of War Interrogation Section—Home, (Second World War organisation).
PWE	Political Warfare Executive, (Second World War).
RFC	Royal Flying Corps, (the Army's Air Corps until the formation of the RAF in 1918).
RSS	Radio Security Service, (established in 1939 by MI5 to intercept signals from German agents in Britain).
SCO	Security Control Officer.
SDEATIC	South East Asia Translation and Interrogation Centre.
SHAEF	Supreme Headquarters Allied Expeditionary Force.
SIME	Security Intelligence Middle East, (Second World War).
SLU	Special Liaison Unit, (theatre and field links for the provision of *Ultra* Intelligence).
SMI	School of Military Intelligence.

SWS	Special Wireless Section.
SOE	Special Operations Executive, (Second World War).
SWG	Special Wireless Group.
ULTRA	The decyphering Service of German Enigma Signals, operating from Bletchley Park.
UNFICYP	United Nations Force Cyprus.
WAAC	Women's Army Auxiliary Corps, (the Army's Women's Corps in the First World War).
WEC	Wireless Experimental Centre, (India Command).
WIS	Wireless Intelligence Section.
WRAC	Women's Royal Army Corps, (post Second World War Women's Corps in the Army).
Y	Tactical level Signals Interception, (Second World War).

Appendix A

The Founder Members of the First Intelligence Corps, August 1914

1. Section 1 comprises Second Lieutenant R Rolleston-West's List of the Intelligence Corps original contingent with the BEF who sailed from Southampton on 12 August 1914. Notes indicating their later postings have been added where these are known. The volunteers from the Metropolitan Police are shown in Section 2 below.

Regular, Territorial, or Reserve Officers, and their Regiments of Origin

Captain (Temporary Major) T G J Torrie	27th Cavalry (IA), later killed, Somme, 1916.
Captain J Montgomery	7th Dragoon Guards.
Captain F W Hunt	19th Cavalry (IA), later killed, Gheluvelt, 1914.
Captain J A Dunnington-Jefferson	Royal Fusiliers.
Captain A E G MacCullan	4th Hussars.
Lieutenant A H Lean	Highland Light Infantry.
Lieutenant D C M Laurie	8th Hussars.
Lieutenant G H Bell	South Lancashire Regiment.
Lieutenant A H Smith Cumming	Seaforth Highlanders, killed in a mortar accident near Meaux, 1914.
Lieutenant J H M Cornwall	Royal Field Artillery.
Lieutenant A C Graeme Harrison	4th Hussars.
Lieutenant B N Nicholson	14th Hussars.
Second Lieutenant (Temp) A E Richardson	Rifle Brigade (Quartermaster).

Scout Officers (Temporary Commission)
Second Lieutenant P Allsopp

Second Lieutenant Lord B Blackwood Later killed, Yser Canal, 1917.
Second Lieutenant G Chapman
Second Lieutenant P Cockerell   Examiner of Documents.
Second Lieutenant E de Trafford
Second Lieutenant A J Evans   Examiner of Documents.
Second Lieutenant F Hughes
Second Lieutenant E H King   Served with 19th Infantry Brigade, later killed Ypres, 1917.

Second Lieutenant Sir N Monson
Second Lieutenant C R Williams
Second Lieutenant J Martin Smith   Died of wounds received while serving with 9th Lancers, Retreat from Mons, 1914.

Second Lieutenant J Addison
Second Lieutenant C Agnew   Examiner of German prisoners.
Second Lieutenant E H Barker   Served with the 18th Hussars.
Second Lieutenant F H Bevan   Served with the 5th Cavalry Brigade. Captured by the enemy.

Second Lieutenant
  W L Blennerhasset   Examiner of German prisoners.
Second Lieutenant L O Bosworth   Staff.
Second Lieutenant R B Bourdillon   Examiner of Documents. Served with the 3rd Army.
Second Lieutenant T Breen   Examiner of Documents. Captured by the enemy.

Second Lieutenant G E Bridges
Second Lieutenant G O M Campbell Photographer.
Second Lieutenant W Chapman
Second Lieutenant W D Drury   Later wounded.
Second Lieutenant C Fairbairn
Second Lieutenant W G Fletcher   Served with 19th Infantry Brigade, later killed, Neuve Chapelle, 1915.
Second Lieutenant W G Gabain   Served with the Cavalry Division, later killed, Flanders 1918.
Second Lieutenant K T Gemmell   Served with the 3rd Army.
Second Lieutenant G A Gladstone   Served with the Royal Flying Corps. Captured by the enemy.
Second Lieutenant J V Hay
Second Lieutenant H W le Grand   Captured by the enemy.
Second Lieutenant C L Lindemann
Second Lieutenant J C Lumsden   Served with 4th Army (Ciphers).
Second Lieutenant W L McEwan   Served with 3rd Army.
Second Lieutenant E W Powell   Served with RFC.
Second Lieutenant M T Rogers   Served at GHQ.
Second Lieutenant A Sang   Served with the 19th Infantry Brigade, died of wounds, Marne, 1914.

Second Lieutenant E G Sawyer		Served with the Cavalry Division.		
Second Lieutenant J T Seabrook		Killed Flanders, 1914.		
Second Lieutenant R F Speir		Served with the Cavalry Division.		
Second Lieutenant M Spicer		Served with RFC.		
Second Lieutenant R R F West		Served with 19th Infantry Brigade.		
Second Lieutenant H Wolf Murray		Examiner of Documents.		

2. The first 24 Metropolitan Policemen who joined the Intelligence Corps:

Police Rank	Army Agent Class	Name	Daily Rate of Pay including Plain Clothes Allowance	Service Pay to men
Inspector	2nd Class	Curry	14/11	8/- per diem
Sergeant	2nd Class	Kirchner	9/2)	
Sergeant	2nd Class	Frost	9/2)	
Sergeant	3rd Class	Hill	8/7)	
Sergeant	3rd Class	Gough	8/1)	
Sergeant	3rd Class	Hansen	8/1)	
Sergeant	3rd Class	Brown	8/1)	7/- per
Sergeant	3rd Class	Bannon	8/1)	
Sergeant	3rd Class	Read	7/10)	diem
Sergeant	3rd Class	Barrett	7/10)	
Sergeant	3rd Class	Clancy	7/6)	service
Sergeant	3rd Class	Palmer	7/6)	
Sergeant	3rd Class	Fitzgerald	7/6)	allowance
Sergeant	3rd Class	Warner	7/6)	
Sergeant	3rd Class	Canning[1]	7/6)	
Sergeant	WO2	Rendall	7/6)	
Sergeant	CQMS	Byart	6/-)	
Constable		Durkin	6/6)	
Constable		Worth[2]	5/9)	
Constable		Kite	5/9)	
Constable		Park	5/7)	
Constable		Lander	5/7)	
Constable		Bradford	4/-)	
Constable		Holmes	4/-)	

(*Source: WO File extant in 1969*)

Notes:

(1) Later Head of Special Branch (Scotland Yard) and Deputy Assistant Commissioner.
(2) Later Chief Constable, 'C' Division Metropolitan Police.

Appendix B

Field Security Sections and Reserve Detachments, Second World War

1 FSS: France (2 Division) 1939-40; UK 1949-41; Burma (2 Division) 1942-45.

2 FSS: France (GHQ) 1939-40; UK (SOE duties) 1941, thereafter Burma 1942-45.

3 FSS: France (1 Division) 1939-40; UK 1941-43; North Africa, Italy (1 Division) 1943-45.

4 FSS: France (3 Division) 1939-40; West Indies 1941-45.

5 FSS: France (5 and 4 Divisions) 1939-40; North Africa, Italy, Greece 1944-45.

6 FSS: France (GHQ) 1939-40; Sierra Leone 1940-43; Burma (81 West Africa Division) 1943-45.

7 FSS: France (I Corps) 1939-40; UK (Lerwick) 1941-42; North West Europe (Lines of Communication) 1944-45.

8 FSS: France (II Corps) 1939-40; UK 1941-42; North West Europe (Lines of Communication Bayeux, Caen) 1944-45.

9 FSS: France (Dieppe) 1939-40; UK 1941-42; North West Europe (52 Division) 1943-45.

10 FSS: France (Cherbourg) 1939-40; UK 1941-45.

11 FSS: France (Brest) 1939-40; Northern Ireland 1941-44; Normandy, North West Europe (53 Division) 1944-45.

12 FSS: France (Nantes) 1939-40; North Africa (1st Army) 1942-43; Italy 1943-45.

13 FSS: France (St Nazaire) 1939-40; North Africa, Sicily 1942-43; Normandy, North West Europe (51 Division) 1944-45.

14 FSS: France (Le Havre) 1939-40; Northern Ireland 1940-42; Burma (14 Indian Division) 1942-43.

15 FSS: France (Le Mans) 1939-40; UK 1940-42; Singapore (18 Division) 1942.

16 FSS: France (Marseilles) 1939-40; London District 1940-44; North Africa, Italy 1942-45.

17 FSS: France (5 Division) 1939-40; Northern Ireland 1940-42; Sicily 1943; Syria and Lebanon 1944-45.

18 FSS: France (Boulogne) 1939-40; Aldershot 1940-45.

19 FSS: France (48 Division) 1939-40; UK 1940-41; Middle East 1941-43; D Day, North West Europe (50 Division) 1944-45.

20 FSS: France (50 Division) 1939-40; Cyprus, Syria, Egypt 1941-44; Greece (Athens) 1944-45.

21 FSS: France (51 Division) 1939-40; Northern Ireland 1941; North Africa 1943; Sicily 1943-45.

22 FSS: France (44 Division) 1939-40; UK 1940-43; North Africa (44 Division, Lines of Communication) 1942-45.

23 FSS: France (42 Division) 1939-40; UK 1940-42; North West Europe (42 Division, Antwerp Port) 1944-45.

24 FSS: France (III Corps) 1939-40; UK 1940-42; Iraq 1942-44; Italy 1944; Greece 1945.

25 FSS: UK 1941; Burma (IV Corps) 1942-45.

26 FSS: Norway 1940; UK 1940-43; North-West Europe (59 Division) 1944.

27 FSS: Norway 1940; UK (47 Division) 1941.

28 FSS: Norway 1940; Egypt 1941; Syria and Lebanon 1941-45.

29 FSS: France (Port Section) 1940; Combined Operations FSS, Argyll 1941-42; Madagascar 1942; Burma 1943-44.

30 FSS: France (GHQ) 1940; 1941; North West Europe (Lines of Communication, Brussels) 1944-45.

31 FSS: France (Le Mans) 1940; UK 1941-42; North Africa (1 Division), Italy, Greece, Austria (46 Division) 1943-45.

32 FSS: France (45 Division) 1940; UK from 1940.

33 FSS: France (30 Division, Marseilles) 1939-40; UK 1941; North-West Europe (3 Division) 1944-45.

34 FSS: France (Paris) 1940; UK 1940-44; North West Europe (I Corps) 1944-45.

35 FSS: Norway 1940; Iraq 1940-42; North Africa; Salerno, Anzio, Italy, 1943-45 (56 Division).

36 FSS: Norway 1940; North Africa (GHQ, later 2 Armoured Division) 1940-41; Egypt (Cairo) 1941-45.

37 FSS: Norway 1940; France 1940; UK; North Africa, (Alamein, 1 Armoured Division) 1941-42; Italy 1944-45.

38 FSS: Iceland 1940; Italy (Bari Port) 1943-45.

39 FSS: Norway 1940; UK 1941; North West Europe (15 Division) 1944-45.

40 FSS: Iceland 1940-42; North West Europe (Lines of Communication, Falaise, later German Dutch border) 1944-45.

41 FSS: UK 1940; North West Europe (Lines of Communication, XII Corps) 1944-45.

42 FSS: UK (55 Division) 1941-45.

43 FSS: Northern Ireland (VI Corps) 1941-44; Kent (pre-invasion security) 1944-45.

44 FSS: London District 1940-45.

45 FSS: UK 1940-44; Tunisia 1943 (S Force); Normandy, North-West Europe (XXX Corps) 1944-45.

46 FSS: UK 1940-44; North West Europe (Lines of Communication, Brussels, R Force) 1944-45.

47 FSS: Northern Ireland 1941-42; North Africa 1943; Italy (Port Section Bari, Ravenna) 1944-45.

48 FSS: Northern Ireland 1942-45.

49 FSS: UK 1941-44; North West Europe (Lines of Communication, Normandy, Brussels) 1944-45.

50 FSS: UK 1940-44; North West Europe (Lines of Communication) 1944-45.

51 FSS: UK 1941-42; North Africa (1st Army) 1942-43; Sicily, Italy (Taranto) 1943-45.

52 FSS: Dakar Expedition 1940; Gibraltar (Port for commercial traffic) 1940-45.

53 FSS: UK to 1944; North West Europe (VIII Corps) 1944-45.

54 FSS: Gibraltar (Town) 1941-45; Section torpedoed en route.

55 FSS: North Africa 1942-43 (6 Armoured Division); Sicily, Italy, Austria.

56 FSS: UK 1940-42; North Africa (23 Armoured Brigade at Alamein, later 43 Division) 1942-44.

57 FSS: UK 1941-43 (XII Corps); North West Europe (43 Division) 1944-45.

58 FSS: UK 1940-45.

59 FSS: Sierra Leone (Freetown Port) 1940-44; North West Europe (Lines of Communication) 1944-45.

60 FSS: Iceland 1941; UK 1942-44; Normandy, North West Europe (49 Division) 1944-45.

61 FSS: Normandy, North West Europe (11 Armoured Division) 1944-45.

62 FSS: North Africa, Sicily, Italy (IX Corps) 1943.

63 FSS: Hertford (SOE duties) 1941-42.

64 FSS: UK, Guildford (SOE duties) 1941-42; Normandy, North West Europe (11 Armoured Division) 1944-45.

65 FSS: UK, Aylesbury, London (SOE duties) 1941-44; Holland 1944.

66 FSS: Nigeria (Lagos) 1941-44; North West Europe (Ostende) 1945.

67 FSS: UK 1942; West Africa 1944-45.

68 FSS: UK 1941-42; North Africa (1st Army); Italy (V Corps); Austria 1942-45.

69 FSS: Egypt 1942; Malta (by submarine) 1942-45.

70 FSS: Gambia 1942-44; North West Europe (Lines of Communication); Germany (US 9th Army) 1945.

71 FSS: Iraq, Palestine 1941-45.

72 FSS: Iraq, Iran (Teheran, Abadan) Palestine 1941-44; North West

Europe (Lines of Communication) 1945.

73 FSS: Iraq, Iran 1941-44.

74 FSS: Iceland 1941-43; UK 1944; North West Europe (XXX Corps) 1944-45.

75 FSS: Jamaica 1941-44.

76 FSS: Bermuda 1941-44.

77 FSS: North West Europe (Guards Armoured Division) 1944-45.

78 FSS: Netherlands East Indies 1941-42; reformed Durham 1944-45.

79 FSS: S. Caribbean 1942-45.

80 FSS: London District 1940-42; North West Europe (Lines of Communication) 1944-45.

81 FSS: Nigeria 1942-44; Burma (82 West African Division) 1944-45.

82 FSS: India (Karachi Port) 1942-43.

83 FSS: India (Bombay Port) 1942-43.

84 FSS: UK (SOE duties); (Dieppe 1943) 1941-44.

85 FSS: North Africa; Italy (Port Section) 1943-45.

86 FSS: North Africa; Italy (Port Section) 1942-45.

87 FSS: Gibraltar 1942-45 (Dockyard).

88 FSS: UK 1940-42; North Africa (78 Division) Italy 1943-45.

89 FSS: UK, Bruneval Raid 1942; North Africa; Sicily, Italy, 1943; (Para) Arnhem 1944.

90 FSS: UK (79 Division) 1942; Normandy (Guards Armoured Division) 1944-45.

91 FSS: North Africa; Italy (US 5th Army, Port Section) 1943-44.

92 FSS: UK 1942; Ethiopia (Diredawa, as 3 East Africa Section) 1942-44; France, Belgium 1944-45.

93 FSS: Nigeria 1943-44; North West Europe, Rhine (VIII Corps) 1944-45.

94 FSS: North Africa 1943; Greece (Piraeus Port) 1944-45.

95 FSS: War Office Control 1944; Colombo 1945.

96 FSS: North Africa 1943; Italy 1945.

97 FSS: Egypt 1943; Italy from 1943.

98 FSS: North Africa 1943; Dodecanese 1943; UK 1944; Normandy (Mulberry Port Section), Belgium 1944.

99 FSS: Bahamas 1942-44.

100 FSS: Italy 1943; SHAEF HQ Section 1943-45.

101 FSS: Glasgow 1939-45.

102 FSS: Gateshead 1939-45.

103 FSS: Stranraer 1940-45.

104 FSS: North Shields 1940-45.

107 FSS: Tilbury, Southend, Dagenham, Gravesend.

108 FSS: Stranraer 1939-45.

109 FSS: Southampton 1939-45.

110 FSS: Plymouth 1939-45.

111 FSS: Weymouth 1949-45.

112 FSS: Falmouth 1939-45.

113 FSS: Avonmouth 1940-45.

114 FSS: Barry 1939-45.

115 FSS: Newport 1939-45.
116 FSS: Swansea 1939-45.
117 FSS: Cardiff 1939-45.
118 FSS: Liverpool 1939-45.
119 FSS: Birkenhead 1939-45.
120 FSS: Fishguard 1940-45.
121 FSS: Holyhead 1940-45.
122 FSS: Heysham 1939-45.
123 FSS: Harwich, Southend to Norfolk 1939-45.
124 FSS: Dover 1940-45.
125 FSS: Chatham 1940-45.
126 FSS: Portsmouth 1940-45.
127 FSS: Devonport 1940-45.
128 FSS: Southampton 1940-45.
129 FSS: Glasgow 1940-45.
130 FSS: Liverpool 1940-45.
131 FSS: London 1940-45.
132 FSS: Fowey 1940-45.
133 FSS: Liverpool 1940-45.
134 FSS: Middlesbrough 1940-45.
135 FSS: Edinburgh 1940-45.
136 FSS: London 1940-45.
137 FSS: Grimsby 1940-45.
138 FSS: Great Yarmouth 1940-45.
139 FSS: Glasgow 1940-45.
140 FSS: Liverpool 1940-45.
141 FSS: Glasgow and Ayrshire 1940-45.
142 FSS: Plymouth 1941-45.
143 FSS: Aberdeen 1941-45.
144 FSS: Whitehaven 1941-45.
145 FSS: Avonmouth 1941-45.
146 FSS: Fleetwood 1941-45.
147 FSS: Glasgow 1941-45.
148 FSS: Glasgow 1941-45.
150 FSS: UK 1942-45.
151 FSS: UK (War Office Reserve) 1942-45.
152 FSS: UK 1942-45.
153 FSS: UK 1942-45.
154 FSS: UK 1942-45.
155 FSS: Newfoundland 1941-44.
156 FSS: UK 1943-45.
157 FSS: UK 1943-45.
158 FSS: UK 1943-45.
159 FSS: UK 1943; (Channel Islands after Liberation) 1945.
160 FSS: UK 1943; (Channel Islands after Liberation) 1945.
161 FSS: UK 1943; (Channel Islands after Liberation) 1945.
200 FSS: Perth, Leuchars airfields 1939-45.
201 FSS: Shoreham, Newhaven airfields 1939-45.

202 FSS: Poole airfield 1939-45.

203 FSS: Poole airfield 1939-45.

204 FSS: Liverpool airfield 1904-45.

205 FSS: Milford Haven airfield 1904-45.

206 FSS: St Eval airfield 1940-45.

207 FSS: Inverness (No.1 Protected Area) 1940-45.

208 FSS: Stromness Orkney (for 'Shetland BW' duties and No.2 Protected Area) 1940-45.

244 FSS: Italy 1944.

251 FSS: Port Said 1940-45.

252 FSS: Greece 1941; Palestine (Sarafand, Tel Aviv, Gaza) 1940-45.

253 FSS: Egypt (Canal Area) 1940-45.

254 FSS: Egypt, Libya (XIII Corps) 1940-41; Egypt 1941-45.

255 FSS: Palestine 1940; East Africa 1941; Syria, Lebanon 1941-45.

256 FSS: Egypt 1940-41 (XIII Corps); Lebanon (Beirut airport), Palestine 1942-45.

257 FSS: Palestine 1940-45.

258 FSS: Alexandria 1940-45.

259 FSS: Cairo 1941-45.

260 FSS: Sudan, Eritrea 1941-42; Tripoli 1943-45.

261 FSS: Sudan, Ethiopia (Massawa) 1941-45.

262 FSS: Palestine (9 Australian Division), Syria, Lebanon 1941-44; Egypt 1945.

263 FSS: Greece, Crete 1941; North Africa (8th Army); Malta 1943; Sicily, Italy 1943-45.

264 FSS: Syria (Damascus) 1941-45.

265 FSS: Syria, (Deraa, Homs), Iraq (Basra), Transjordan 1941-44; North West Europe (Lines of Communication) 1944-45.

266 FSS: Egypt (XIII Corps and GHQ) 1941-42; Iraq (Basra) 1942-45.

267 FSS: Egypt (Lines of Communication, Western Desert, Alexandria) 1941-45.

268 FSS: Lebanon 1941-44; Greece 1944-45.

269 FSS: Sudan, Eritrea 1941; Ethiopia (Addis Ababa, Harar) 1942; Aden (Port) 1943-45.

270 FSS: Crete 1941; North Africa; Italy, (7 Armoured Division Salerno) 1941-43; North West Europe 1944-45.

271 FSS: Alexandria, Egypt (Lines of Communication) and occupied Libya 1940-45.

272 FSS: Cairo Base 1941; Libya, Syria, Egypt 1943-45.

273 FSS: Egypt 1941; Iran (Teheran) 1942; Canal Zone 1943; North West Europe (Lines of Communication) 1944-45.

274 FSS: Egypt 1941; Syria 1941-43; North West Europe (Lines of Communication Ostend) 1944.

275 FSS: Syria (Latakia) to 1944; North West Europe (Lines of Communication Lille) 1944-45.

276 FSS: UK 1942; Egypt 1942; Palestine, Italy 1943-45 (Rome 1944).

277 FSS: UK 1941; Cairo Special Duties 1942-45.

278 FSS: UK; North Africa, Italy (X Corps) 1942-44; Greece 1945.

279 FSS: Greece, Crete 1941; Palestine, Syria, Lebanon 1941-43; Iran 1943-45.

280 FSS: Egypt, Sudan (Port Sudan, Khartoum) 1942-45.

281 FSS: Syria (Aleppo) 1941-45.

282 FSS: Egypt, Cyprus, Palestine 1941-45.

283 FSS: Iran (Abadan and 5 Indian Division) 1942-45.

284 FSS: Canal Zone (Port Suez, Port Tewfiq) 1942-45.

285 FSS: East Africa 1940-41.

286 FSS: East Africa 1940-41.

287 FSS: East Africa 1940-41.

288 FSS: East Africa 1940-41.

289 FSS: Cyprus (5 Indian Division) 1941; Iraq (Baghdad) 1943.

290 FSS: North Africa (with Indian personnel, 4 Indian Division); Italy, Greece 1941-45.

291 FSS: North Africa, Dodecanese 1942-43; Italy, Greece, 1944-45.

292 FSS: Cyprus 1942-45.

293 FSS: Middle East: East Africa 1942-43.

294 FSS: UK 1941-42; East Africa (as 5 EAFSS) 1942-43; Ceylon 1943; Burma (11 EA Division) 1944-45.

295 FSS: Egypt (Airports) 1942-45.

296 FSS: Syria 1942-43; Iran (Teheran) 1943-45.

297 FSS: North Africa (10 Armoured Division) 1942-44; Syria 1942-44; Greece (Rhodes) 1944-45.

298 FSS: India 1942-43; Burma (70 Division, Special Forces) 1944-45.

299 FSS: Egypt 1941-45.

300 FSS: North Africa and Italy (SOE) 1943-45.

301 FSS: UK (Aldershot) 1942; North Africa, Italy (SOE) 1942-45.

302 FSS: UK (Southern Command) 1940-42.

303 FSS: UK (Eastern Command) 1940-42.

304 FSS: UK (Northern Command) 1940-42.

305 FSS: UK (Western Command) 1940-42.

306 FSS: UK Scottish Command and Combined Operations Training Centre) 1941-45.

307 FSS: UK (London District) 1940-42.

308 FSS: UK (London District) 1940-42.

309 FSS: South East England 1940-42; North West Europe (2nd Army) 1944-45.

310 FSS: North Africa, Sicily, Italy (8th Army) 1942-45.

311 FSS: North Africa (Allied Forces Headquarters) 1943-44; Italy 1945.

312 FSS: UK 1941-42; Italy, Salerno (5 US Army) 1943-45.

313 FSS: UK 1943; Egypt (Alexandria); Italy 1943-45.

314 FSS: UK 1942; Sicily, Italy 1943-45.

315 FSS: Italy 1943-45.

316 FSS: London (Port) 1943-44.

317 FSS: North West Europe, Normandy, Rhine Crossing (6 Airborne Division) 1944-45.

318 FSS: London 1943-44; North West Europe (Lines of Communi-

cation, Ardennes) 1944-45.

319 FSS: Faroe Islands 1940-45; North West Europe (Lines of Communication for Denmark) 1945.

320 FSS: North West Europe (Ghent) 1944.

321 FSS: North West Europe (Amiens) 1944.

322 FSS: North West Europe (Antwerp) 1944.

323 FSS: North West Europe (Antwerp, Hamburg) 1944-45.

324 FSS: North West Europe (Antwerp) 1944.

325 FSS: North West Europe (Antwerp) 1944.

326 FSS: North West Europe (Boulogne) 1944.

327 FSS: North West Europe (Rouen, Mass) 1944-45.

328 FSS: North West Europe (Brussels) 1944.

329 FSS: North West Europe (Lines of Communication) 1944-45.

330 FSS: North West Europe (Lines of Communication) 1944-45.

331 FSS: North West Europe (Brussels) 1944-45.

332 FSS: North West Europe (Lines of Communication) 1944-45.

333 FSS: North West Europe (Lines of Communication) 1944-45.

334 FSS: North West Europe (Lines of Communication) 1944-45.

335 FSS: North West Europe (Lines of Communication) Antwerp 1944-45.

336 FSS: North West Europe (Lines of Communication) 1944-45.

337 FSS: North West Europe (Lines of Communication) 1944-45.

338 FSS: North West Europe (Lines of Communication) 1944-45.

339 FSS: North West Europe (Brussels) 1944-45.

340 FSS: North West Europe (The Hague) 1945.

341 FSS: North West Europe (Lines of Communication) 1945.

342 FSS: North West Europe (Lines of Communication) 1945.

343 FSS: North West Europe (Lines of Communication) 1945.

344 FSS: North West Europe (Lines of Communication) 1945.

351 FSS: Singapore 1941-42.

352 FSS: Singapore 1941-42.

353 FSS: Singapore (III Indian Corps) 1941-42.

354 FSS: Ceylon 1942-45 (Raised locally).

355 FSS: Ceylon, 1944-45, Malaya 1945.

356 FSS: Ceylon (HQ South East Asia Command) 1944-45; Burma 1945.

357 FSS: Ceylon, Burma 1944-45.

358 FSS: Ceylon: Malaya 1945.

401 FSS: Reformed UK 1944; Belgium 1945.

406 FSS: Reformed UK 1944; Italy 1944-45.

407 FSS: Reformed UK 1942, Egypt, Cyprus 1942-43; Italy, Greece 1944.

409 FSS: Tunisia 1943; Italy, Greece 1943-45.

410 FSS: Italy (Taranto) 1944-45.

411 FSS: Italy (1 Armoured Division) 1944-45.

412 FSS: North Africa; Sicily, Italy (50 Division, XIII Corps) 1943-45.

413 FSS: Libya (Benghazi, Derna, Tobruk) 1942 (late) to 1945.

414 FSS: Iraq (Baghdad) 1943-44, UK 1944-45.

415 FSS: Iran (Oilfields) 1943-44; North West Europe (Ardennes) 1944-45.
416 FSS: Egypt 1944, Italy 1945.
417 FSS: Italy (Arezzo) 1944-45.
418 FSS: Italy (Arezzo, Siena, Perugia) 1944-45.
419 FSS: Italy (Udine) 1944-45.
420 FSS: Italy 1944; UK 1945.
421 FSS: Italy 1945.
423 FSS: Italy 1945.
426 FSS: Italy 1945.
427 FSS: Italy (Siena, Milan) 1944-45.
428 FSS: Algeria 1943-44; Italy, Austria, 1945.
429 FSS: Italy (Bari) 1945.
547 FSS: India 1944.

II—British Army FSRD

1001 FSRD: UK 1943-44; Belgium, Holland 1944.
1002 FSRD: UK 1943-44; Caen, Helmond 1944.
1003 FSRD: UK 1943-44; Normandy (2 Army HQ) Nijmegen, Goch 1944-45.
1004 FSRD: UK 1943-44; Arras, Ypres, Oudenarde 1944-45.
1005 FSRD: UK 1943-44; Normandy (2 Army HQ) 1944-45.
1006 FSRD: UK 1943-44; Normandy, later Tactical HQ 21 Army Group 1944-45.
1007 FSRD: UK 1943-44; R Force 1944-45.
1008 FSRD: UK 1943-44; Normandy (2 Army HQ) 1944-45.
1009 FSRD: UK 1943-44; Normandy (2 Army HQ) 1944-45.
1010 FSRD: UK 1943-44; Normandy, R Force Antwerp 1944-45.
1011 FSRD: UK 1943-44; Normandy, R Force Rouen, Belgium 1944-45.
1012 FSRD: UK 1943-44; Normandy, R Force Holland 1944-45.
1013 FSRD: UK (London District, SAS training Ayrshire) 1943-44; Normandy 2 Army HQ 1944-45.
1014 FSRD: UK (London District, SAS training Ayrshire) 1943-44; Normandy 2 Army HQ 1944-45.
1015 FSRD: UK 1943-44; North West Europe (1 Canadian Army) 1944-45.
1016 FSRD: UK 1943-44; North West Europe 1944-45.
1017 FSRD: UK 1943-44; North West Europe 1944-45.
1018 FSRD: UK 1944; North West Europe (1 Canadian Army) 1944-45.
1019 FSRD: UK 1944; North West Europe (1 Canadian Army) 1944-45.
1020 FSRD: UK 1944; North West Europe (1 Canadian Army) 1944-45.
1021 FSRD: UK 1944; Normandy (2 Army HQ) 1944-45.
1022 FSRD: UK 1944.

1023 FSRD: UK 1944; Normandy 1944.
1024 FSRD: UK 1944; Normandy 1944.
1025 FSRD: UK 1944; Normandy 1944.

III—East Africa FSS

1 East Africa FSS: Kenya 1939, Ethiopia (11 and 12 EA Divisions 1941), Mombasa 1942-45.
2 East Africa FSS: Kenya 1939, Ethiopia (11 and 12 EA Divisions 1941) Dar es Salaam 1942-45.
3 East Africa FSS: see 92 FSS.
4 East Africa FSS: Kenya (Nairobi) 1942-45.
5 East Africa FSS: see 294 FSS.

IV—1941 British Indian Composite FSS

(1) No 1 L of C Section: Iraq (Basra) 1941.
No 2 L of C Section: Iraq (Basra) 1941.
No 1 Composite FSS: Iraq (Basra) 1941, became 402 FSS in 1942.
No 2 Composite FSS: Iraq (Shaiba) 1941.
No 3 Composite FSS: Iraq (Railways) 1941, became 404 FSS in 1942.
No 4 Composite FSS: Iraq (Baghdad) 1941, became 403 FSS in 1942.
No 5 Composite FSS: Iraq (Mashe), became 407 FSS in 1942.
S Composite FSS: Iraq, became 408 FSS.

(2) 401 Composite FSS: Iraq 1942-44; see also under British FSS.
402 Composite FSS: Iraq, Iran (Doroud) 1942-45.
403 Composite FSS: Iraq (Baghdad) 1942-45.
404 Composite FSS: Iraq 1942-45.
405 Composite FSS: Iraq (Kirkuk) 1942-44.
406 Composite FSS: Iraq, Lebanon, Palestine (8 Indian Division) 1942-44; see also under British FSS.
407 Composite FSS: Iraq (10 Indian Division) 1942; see also under British FSS.
408 Composite FSS: Iraq, Palestine, Syria, Lebanon (31 Indian Armoured Division) 1942-45.

V—Burma FSS 1941-42

(1) Maymyo FSS: Retreat from Burma 1942.
      Rangoon FSS: Retreat from Burma 1942.

(2) Mandalay FSS: Burma 1942.
      Railway FSS: Burma 1942.
      Maymyo FSS: Burma 1942.
      Maymyo FSS: Burma 1942.

(3) No. 2 Burma FSS: Dibrugarh, late 1942.
   No. 4 Burma FSS: Silchar, late 1942.
   26 Division FSS: Manipur Road, late 1942.
   Gauhati FSS: Gauhati, late 1942.

VI—1942-45 British Indian Composite FSS

550 FSS: Ceylon; Burma 1944-45.
551 FSS: India (Karachi Depot Section) 1942-45.
552 FSS: India, Ceylon (Colombo Port) 1942-45.
553 FSS: India (Madras Port) 1942-44, Dibrugarh 1945.
554 FSS: India (GHQ) 1942-45.
555 FSS: Burma (2 Division, Kohima, then XIV Army) 1942-45.
556 FSS: India (Karachi Port) 1942-45.
557 FSS: India (Bombay Town) 1942-45.
558 FSS: India (Calcutta Town) 1942-45.
559 FSS: India (Madras Town) 1942-45.
560 FSS: India (Cochin Port) 1942-45.
561 FSS: India (Chittagong Port) 1942-45.
562 FSS: India (Calcutta, then Kharagphur Town) 1942-45.
563 FSS: India (Calcutta City) 1942-45.
564 FSS: India (Vizegapatam Port) 1942-45.
565 FSS: Burma (5 and 14 Indian Divisions) 1942-45.
566 FSS: India 1943; Burma (XV Corps) 1944-45.
567 FSS: India (Bombay Port) 1943-45.
568 FSS: Burma (7 Indian Division) 1943-45.
569 FSS: India (XIV Army HQ) 1943-45.
570 FSS: India (Poona) 1944-45.
571 FSS: India 1944-45.
572 FSS: India (Ranchi) 1943.
573 FSS: Burma (IV Corps HQ and 17 Indian Division) 1943-44.
574 FSS: India (Chittagong Port) 1943-45.
575 FSS: India, Burma (XXXIII Corps Lines of Communication, later Rangoon) 1944-45.
576 FSS: Burma, (2 Division, Kohima) 1944-45, Ledo 1945.
577 FSS: (Composite British Indian) Burma (Lines of Communication) 1944-45.
578 FSS: India (Lahore) 1944-45.
579 FSS: Burma 1944-45.
580 FSS: India (Calcutta) 1944, Ceylon (Colombo), Burma (Rangoon Town) 1945.
581 FSS: India (Calcutta then Chittagong) 1944, Burma (Rangoon) 1945.
582 FSS: India (Patna) 1944, Burma 1945.
583 FSS: India (Calcutta Airport) 1944-45.
584 FSS: Burma (20 Indian Division) 1944-45.
585 FSS: India (Calcutta City) 1944-45.
586 FSS: India (Dacca City) 1944-45.

587 FSS: India 1944-45.
588 FSS: Burma (Lines of Communication) 1944-45.
589 FSS: Burma (IV Corps) 1944-45.
590 FSS: Burma 1944-45.
591 FSS: India; Burma (Lines of Communication) 1944-45.
592 FSS: Burma (Lines of Communication) 1944-45.
593 FSS: India (Calcutta Port) 1944-45.
594 FSS: India (Jhansi) 1944-45.
595 FSS: (Airborne, Composite British Indian) 1945.
596 FSS: India (Madras) 1944-45.
597 FSS: India (Cocomada) 1944-45.
598 FSS: India (19 Indian Division) 1945.
599 FSS: India; Burma (81 West African Division) 1944-45.
600 FSS: India (United Provinces) 1943-44.
601 FSS: India; Burma (14 Indian Division) 1943-45.
602 FSS: India; Burma 1943-45.
603 FSS: India 1943; Burma (19 Indian Division) 1944-45.
604 FSS: India, Ceylon 1943; Burma (20 Indian Division) 1944-45.
605 FSS: India, 1943-44; Burma (23 Indian Division) 1944-45.
606 FSS: India 1943-44; Burma (25 Indian Division) 1944-45.
607 FSS: India 1942; Burma (14 and 26 Indian Divisions) 1942-45.
608 FSS: India 1943; Burma 1944-45.
609 FSS: India (39 Indian Division) 1943-45.
610 FSS: India 1943; Burma (26 Indian Division) 1944-45.
611 FSS: India (Gauhati) 1944-45.
612 FSS: India (Calcutta) 1943-44.
613 FSS: India (Bombay) 1943-45.
614 FSS: India (Rawalpindi) 1943-45.
615 FSS: Burma (US Army) 1944-45.
616 FSS: India (Bombay Port) 1943-45.
617 FSS: India (Nagpur) 1944-45.
618 FSS: India (Rawalpindi, N.W. Frontier Province) 1944-45.
619 FSS: India (Central Command, Agra) 1944-45.
620 FSS: India (Delhi District) 1944-45.
621 FSS: India (Southern Command Bangalore) 1944-45.
622 FSS: India 1943-45.
623 FSS: India (Madras area) 1944-45.
624 FSS: India (Allahabad) 1944-45.
625 FSS: India 1944-45.
626 FSS: India (Nagpur) 1944-45.
627 FSS: India (Deolali) 1944-45.
628 FSS: India (probably Calcutta) 1944-45.
629 FSS:)
630 FSS:)   India (Dinjan Airfield, security for Assam—China air
)   route) 1944-45.
631 FSS:)
632 FSS: India (Bombay Port) 1944-45.
633 FSS: India (Madras) 1944-45.

634 FSS: India 1944-45.

635 FSS: India 1944-45.

636 FSS: India (Special Forces) 1943-44, Burma 1944-45.

637 FSS: India (Security for Force 136), 1945.

750 FSS: India (Dinjan Airfield) 1944-45.

751 FSS: India 1944-45.

752 FSS: India (Calcutta Port) 1944-45.

753 FSS:)

754 FSS:)

755 FSS:)

756 FSS:) India 1945 (training for projected invasion of Malaya).

757 FSS:)

758 FSS:)

759 FSS:)

760 FSS:)

Appendix B—Notes

1. This list is as near complete as can be established in respect of Sections. There are however gaps that can no longer be filled in respect of all locations in which FSS served. Some sections trained to serve in one area or for one commitment only. Others existed only briefly or were disbanded before 1945.
2. The term FSS is used throughout. In 1939-40 the term FSP, Field Security Police, was in use.
3. Other Sections were formed in 1945 for certain specific post-war commitments. Those formed after the cessation of hostilities are not shown here.
4. Most of the officers of the British FSS were Intelligence Corps but on occasions officers of other regiments were in command. In India, commanders were usually Intelligence Corps (India) officers. Indian soldiers, and some officers, wore the Indian Army Intelligence Corps badge.
5. The collection of material for this list owes much to the extensive research by Colonel F G Robson, Lieutenant-Colonel A Williams, Mr J Hillyer-Funke and Mrs B Tate in respect of the British Army and Lieutenant-Colonel A A Mains in respect of the British Indian Composite Sections.

Appendix C

Wireless Intelligence Sections and Other Wireless Intelligence Units, Second World War

1. British Expeditionary Force, France 1939.

There was no Intelligence Section attached to No. 2 Company, GHQ Signals (No. 1 Special Wireless Group from 6 July 1940), but special Intelligence Staff Officers served there and at GHQ for the Company's work. There were three Sections, 101, 102 and 103 for I, II and a possible III Corps; the Headquarters Section of ISWG was called 100 Section.

2. GHQ Home Forces, 1940–41.

No. 1 Special Wireless Group with No. 1 Company at Egham and No. 7 Company at Radlett. (Sections numbered 200–210 existed briefly)

- 40 Wireless Intelligence Section (attached to 101 Special Wireless Section)
- 41 Wireless Intelligence Section (attached to 102 Special Wireless Section)
  This SWS later moved to Gibraltar, probably without a WIS.
- 42 Wireless Intelligence Section (attached to 103 Special Wireless Section)
- 43 Wireless Intelligence Section (attached to 104 Special Wireless Section)
- 44 Wireless Intelligence Section (attached to 105 Special Wireless Section)
- 45 Wireless Intelligence Section (attached to 106 Special Wireless Section)

46 Wireless Intelligence Section (attached to 107 Special Wireless Section)

47 Wireless Intelligence Section (attached to 108 Special Wireless Section)

48 Wireless Intelligence Section (attached to 109 Special Wireless Section)

49 Wireless Intelligence Section (attached to 110 Special Wireless Section)

With from 1943–44

50 (later 111) Wireless Intelligence Section (attached to 111 Special Wireless Section)

116 Wireless Intelligence Section (attached to 116 Special Wireless Section)

118 Wireless Intelligence Section (attached to 118 Special Wireless Section)

3. Middle East 1941–43.

The parent body was 2 Special Wireless Group which included WIS for training, and 5 and 7 Intelligence Schools, both at Heliopolis. A mobile section of 2 SWG operated at Army Headquarters, this later became 2 Special Wireless Section

(Unnumbered) Wireless Intelligence Section attached to 100-x Special Wireless Section (7 Armoured Division).

40 Wireless Intelligence Section (attached to 101 Special Wireless Section)

42 Wireless Intelligence Section (attached to 103 Special Wireless Section)

44 Wireless Intelligence Section (attached to 105 Special Wireless Section)

45 Wireless Intelligence Section (attached to 106 Special Wireless Section)

49 Wireless Intelligence Section (attached to 110 Special Wireless Section)

4. Tunisia 1942–43 (1st Army)

53 Wireless Intelligence Section (attached to 1 Special Wireless Section)

46 Wireless Intelligence Section (attached to 107 Special Wireless Section)

52 Wireless Intelligence Section (attached to 113 Special Wireless Section)

55 Wireless Intelligence Section (attached to US Army 128 Radio Intercept Company).

8 Special Wireless Company was formed at Bizerta for work on Italian intercept.

5. *Italy 1943–45*.

Several sections from the 1st Army were reformed and some from the 8th Army redesignated. A 3 Special Wireless Group was formed as a parent body, with a 2 Special Wireless Company, and later 5 Special Intelligence Company and 7 Signals Intelligence Company.

1 Wireless Intelligence Section (attached to 1 Canadian Special Wireless Section and, later, the New Zealand Corps and a US Army unit).

22 Wireless Intelligence Section (attached to 2 Special Wireless Section)

23 Wireless Intelligence Section (attached to 3 Special Wireless Section)

29 Wireless Intelligence Section (attached to 9 Special Wireless Section)

(this latter was formerly 40 WIS and was again renumbered 9 WIS when part of 7 Company).

101 Wireless Intelligence Section (attached to 101 Special Wireless Section)

42 Wireless Intelligence Section (attached to 103 Special Wireless Section)

44 Wireless Intelligence Section (attached to 105 Special Wireless Section)

45 Wireless Intelligence Section (attached to 106 Special Wireless Section)

46 Wireless Intelligence Section (attached to 107 Special Wireless Section)

49 Wireless Intelligence Section (attached to 110 Special Wireless Section)

A Mobile Section of 3 SWG served in Greece.

6. *North West Europe 1943-45*.

(i) 6 Intelligence School, initially at Loughborough but expanded to provide for a Special Training and Research Wing and located in Hampstead.

(ii) For 21 Army Group:

1 Special Intelligence Company (attached to 1 Special Wireless Group)

WI Section (unnumbered) (attached to Mobile Section 1 SWG).

8 Wireless Intelligence Section (attached to 8 Special Wireless Section)

43 Wireless Intelligence Section (attached to 104 Special Wireless Section)
108 Wireless Intelligence Section (attached to 108 Special Wireless Section)
109 Wireless Intelligence Section (attached to 109 Special Wireless Section)
110 Wireless Intelligence Section (attached to 110 Special Wireless Section)
111 Wireless Intelligence Section (attached to 111 Special Wireless Section)
116 Wireless Intelligence Section (attached to 116 Special Wireless Section)
118 Wireless Intelligence Section (attached to 118 Special Wireless Section)

7. *India 1942-45.*

The parent body was the Wireless Experimental Centre, New Delhi, with 'A' Special Wireless Group.

1 Wireless Intelligence Section (attached to Mobile Section A (later 3) SWG.
22 Wireless Intelligence Section (attached to 2 Special Wireless Section) Ind
25 Wireless Intelligence Section (attached to 5 Special Wireless Section) Ind
26 Wireless Intelligence Section (attached to 5 Special Wireless Section) Ind
6 Wireless Intelligence Section (attached to 6 Special Wireless Section) Ind
24 Wireless Intelligence Section (attached to 6 Special Wireless Section) Ind
51 Wireless Intelligence Section (attached to 112 Special Wireless Section) Ind
23 Wireless Intelligence Section (attached to 112 Special Wireless Section) Ind
54 Wireless Intelligence Section (attached to 115 Special Wireless Section)

Some of the WIS were later renumbered, the new numbers being the same as that of the parent SWS.

The material for this Appendix was compiled by Major H Skillen who served with several of these Sections in the Second World War.

Appendix D

Awards to Members of the Intelligence Corps 1940-91

1. Honours and Awards conferred upon officers, non-commissioned officers and soldiers of the Intelligence Corps, and officers of the General Staff who were formerly Intelligence Corps officers, for services in the Second World War and its immediate aftermath.

Distinguished Service Order	15
Order of the British Empire, Commander	3
Officer	49
Member	139
Military Cross (and Bars)	21
Distinguished Conduct Medal	4
George Medal	3
Military Medal	11
British Empire Medal	36

2. Honours and Awards conferred upon officers, non-commissioned officers and soldiers of the Intelligence Corps, and officers of the General Staff who were formerly Intelligence Corps officers since the ending of the Second World War.

Companion of the Order of St Michael and St George	1
Order of the British Empire, Commander	7
Officer	39
Member	137
George Medal	1
Military Medal	1
Queen's Gallantry Medal	22
British Empire Medal	134

These totals include nine members of the former WRAC, permanently employed Intelligence Corps at the time of their awards.

3. In addition, over 200 foreign decorations have been awarded to members of the Intelligence Corps since its formation. These have included many of the highest honours, that can be conferred upon non-nationals by Belgium, Denmark, France, the Netherlands, Norway, Oman and the United States.

Appendix E

Training of Intelligence Corps Personnel 1940-45

The training levels and standard of Intelligence Corps personnel in the Second World War varied very considerably. Some officers, particularly in the early stages, had very sketchy training indeed, on occasions no training at all. Others, together with the majority of the Corps's soldiers, received a thorough training on well-instructed courses.

Soldiers were selected by personal interview, a major criterion being the rubric that 'In many ways Intelligence is more dependent than other arms on the quality of its personnel'. The interviews were all conducted by officers of the MI Directorate, its sponsoring branch in the Adjutant-General's Department, or by officers of the Corps Depot.

Soldiers were given an eight weeks basic training course, comprising Organisation and Administration, Map Reading, Motor Cycling, Fieldcraft, Lecture practice, Tactics (in particular night patrols), First Aid, Drill and Physical Training, Unarmed Combat and Weapon Training. Thereafter they received special training, almost invariably either Security or Signals Intelligence. The Security Training was carried out at the School of Military Intelligence from 1942. Signals Intelligence personnel were trained at Harpenden.

In 1942, the 'Other Ranks' Wing of the Corps Depot moved from Winchester to a very large country house in South Yorkshire, called Wentworth Woodhouse, soldiers training beginning there in the autumn. Routine military training cadres were provided by the Irish Guards, a strange and strained relationship recalled only by some with humour. Intelligence Corps practices, such as the overnight promotion of a somewhat unsoldierly but linguistically endowed private to be a Warrant Officer, were apt to leave Irish eyes unsmiling.

In the early years of the war, officers who had been members of pre-war school or university cadet corps were generally commissioned direct. Some but not all, were sent on attachment to an infantry unit.

Most were given a course at the Officers Wing of the Depot at Oxford. The criterion appeared to be how urgently the officer's services were needed as much as his own particular need for training. The five weeks Officers course included Organisation (all arms, British and German), Staff Duties, Map Reading, Tactics and Exercises, Languages, Drill and Physical Training, Unarmed Combat, Weapon Training and Unit Administration. This course was moved to Wentworth Woodhouse in December 1943. On leaving Oxford, the Depot Mess was presented with a silver cup by Oriel College and a silver snuff box by Pembroke College. The Mess gave silver ash trays to both Colleges. Oriel College made the Depot Commander a member of their Senior Common Room for so long as the Intelligence Corps remained in being.

By 1941, the majority of the officers of the Corps were selected either from the ranks of the Corps, or from applicants, or linguistically qualified candidates at wartime Officer Cadet Training Units (OCTUs). Of them all, a post war War Office report somewhat condescendingly remarked:

> As regards officers, the chief criticism, and a fair one, levelled against Intelligence officers in the early days by commanders and staffs was their lack of military knowledge, often coupled with allusions to long haired intellectuals. It must, however, be accepted that men of this type will be present in fairly large numbers in the Intelligence organisation in war, for they are the kind that study languages and other subjects of Intelligence interest and travel extensively. Provided that they are given the opportunity to train as soldiers and are attached to regiments to get some background, they can and do make first class Intelligence officers and Intelligence staff officers.

The first wartime specific Intelligence training took place at the 'Intelligence School', Minley Manor, near Camberley. This opened in September 1939 under the control of the Staff College, three, later four, week-long courses being held. In May 1940, the School was moved to Swanage, living in two hotels under the title of the 'Intelligence Training Centre'. Two long 'War Courses' and shorter interrogation and unit intelligence officer courses were held there until in August when the Centre moved to Smedley's Hydro at Matlock in Derbyshire, where it remained until 1945.

The Centre changed its name to the 'School of Military Intelligence' (SMI) in 1942. Initially, the courses offered were a four (later five) week War Intelligence Course and a course on Interrogation. Security (for NCOs as well as officers) was soon added. A little later, a Photographic Interpretation Wing, offering both short and longer courses, opened. Interrogation was, however, removed to Cambridge for language tuition reasons. There were also other shorter courses at Matlock to meet specific needs; unit intelligence officers courses, senior officers courses and special courses for 21 Army Group officers, and officers proceeding to the Far East. ATS officers and NCOs selected for work with the Intelligence Corps attended some of these, and certain other specialist, courses. Over 3,000 officers attended the 40 War Intelligence Courses, and the Field Security Wing trained 899 officers and 5,350 soldiers.

At Cambridge, the Interrogation Wing's main course was one of five weeks for German speaking interrogators, but there were also courses for Italian and Spanish speaking officers, special Axis armies courses for Signals Intelligence personnel and German Army courses for unit officers. Between 1941 and 1944, 747 officers were trained in German interrogation and order of battle and 38 officers in the Italian equivalent; these two figures are tri-Service. The Axis armies courses lasted five weeks, the majority of students being soldiers rather than officers. The courses included the organisation of the German Armed forces, German map reference systems, signals procedures, and language teaching. In total 75 officers and 470 soldiers were trained in 10 of these courses held in 1942 and 1943. Accommodation was in Trinity and St John's Colleges, instruction took place at the Hawks Club, the instructors messed at the Blue Boar Inn.

At its peak, early in 1944, the SMI staff totalled 28 officers and 179 soldiers.

One rather unusual specialist school, the British Army Control Commission School, operated at the Beach Hotel, Worthing from September 1944 to May 1945. This School was tasked to train control officers in command of sections for each German Army Military District. These sections were to supervise armistice and demilitarisation terms in the event of a surrender by a largely or partly intact German Army. The directing staff numbered 10, all majors and the majority Intelligence Corps. In the event, only one such section was ever formed, for Wehrkreis XI at Hanover; the destruction of the German Army negated its purpose.

In the early months of the war, there was also a two month special secret course at Cambridge designed to train military officers to administer Germany in the event of a Nazi collapse. This course was discontinued in 1940.

The particular problem of Middle and Far Eastern languages was resolved on a tri-service basis, linked also with the India Office's training programmes. Initially bursaries were offered to boys of 17 or 18 (ie below the age of call-up) to study Japanese, Chinese, Turkish or Persian at the School of Oriental Studies, together with a very few for Eastern European and Baltic languages at the School of Slavonic Studies. These courses, 18 months in the case of Japanese and Chinese, a year for other languages, were found to be too long, and new arrangements introduced whereby students learnt either to interrogate in Japanese or to translate Japanese, in a 15 month course. Students held the rank of private soldier (or equivalent in the other services) and attended occasional drill parades. Teaching was at first far from satisfactory due to the absence of good Japanese speakers. Canadian Japanese were used as teaching assistants for conversation but they had no knowledge of grammar. In 1944, teaching improved with the arrival of R P Dore (later Professor), commissioned into the Corps as a subaltern.

The original intention appears to have been that on completing the course they should have served as senior NCOs, but in the event they were commissioned, either on arrival in India or before. Others, mostly recent graduates with promising degrees in languages, were sent on a five month course in Bedford.

Theatres overseas formed their own Intelligence Schools in which courses both for Corps personnel (sometimes recruited locally) and regimental personnel requiring Intelligence training were held.

The most important of these was in India, at Karachi where the first specific Intelligence Training in India began in 1941. This was at an 'Intelligence School', Karachi, which offered Operational Intelligence courses for officers. In October 1942, a 'Field Security Headquarters Training Depot and Centre' was opened also at Karachi. This headquarters was commanded by Lieutenant Colonel J C de Vine, who included five other British Army Intelligence Corps officers on his instructing staff at one time or another. Colonel de Vine had earlier been a police officer in India, leaving the service in 1936. On the outbreak of war, he had joined the FSP as a private, later serving in France. Early in 1943, the Depot and Centre changed its name to the 'Intelligence Corps (India) Depot'; it was responsible for all Security training. In June 1945 it was merged with the Intelligence School to form an 'Intelligence Corps Training Centre'.

The Depot provided a variety of courses in a 'British Wing' and an 'Indian Wing'. The 'British Wing' ran 33 main Security Courses and 20 Cadre Courses together with other specialist courses in Urdu and Burmese, the latter for Chindits. Interestingly, nearly 300 American service personnel were trained. The 'Indian Wing' ran 27 main Security Courses and a similar number of Cadre Courses.

In the Middle East, three week courses in Intelligence were held in Cairo in 1940–41, together with an air photograph interpretation course at Heliopolis. Early in 1942, an 'Intelligence Training Centre' was opened at Helwan, this centre provided operational intelligence and German interrogation courses. In May 1942, the 'Intelligence Corps Depot and Field Security Wing (Middle East)' was moved to Helwan. At its greatest extent, in 1943, the 'Middle East School of Intelligence' was providing short courses for unit Intelligence Officers, GS03 staff officers, Intelligence NCOs at unit and formation headquarters, Field Security Section personnel and technical intelligence staffs. The school's work was developed by some notable instructors in particular Lieutenant Colonels C R Wordsworth and O E Ormsby. Courses on the German Army for British, Indian and Polish officers were held in Baghdad.

A 'North African Intelligence Training Centre' was formed in June 1943 as a joint Anglo–American school. It was sited near Algiers until 1944 when it was moved to Pozzuoli, near Naples. Its British Commandant was Major A Rowan-Robinson. The training provided was limited to one week courses for GS03 staff officers and unit Intelligence officers and NCOs. The students included French and Brazilian military personnel as well as British and American. The courses did much to unify, or at least co-ordinate, Intelligence doctrine and practices.

The war years saw continuous debate about the size and higher organisation for the Corps. From the end of 1947, the Colonel in command of the Intelligence Training Centre (School of Military Intelligence) became a Brigadier and was restyled 'Commandant, Intelligence Training Establishment'; at the same time the posts of Commandant and Assistant Commandant of the Corps were abolished.

Officers were commissioned as Second Lieutenants but on an appointment became acting Lieutenants. From July 1940, 50 per cent of the Corps officers in cipher work were Captains or above, 66 per cent in the cases of Corps officers engaged on other duties. Many rose to be majors or above. After much negotiation, it was agreed in 1942 that all officers holding authorised appointments of the Intelligence Corps could draw staff pay except officers in the Intelligence Pool (awaiting posting) or in an administrative capacity at Matlock or at the Depot.

Soldiers, traditionally from military police days, drew an extra shilling a day as police money; in 1941, Royal Signals tradesmen's rates of pay were substituted for personnel in Signals Intelligence units.

Appendix F

The Intelligence Corps as a Family

In 1946, the Wentworth Woodhouse Depot of the Intelligence Corps was closed, and a new Depot opened at Oudenarde Barracks in Aldershot. At the same time the School of Military Intelligence (SMI) at Matlock was moved to buildings that now form Pierrepont School at Frensham, near Farnham. In 1948 the Depot was again moved to Maresfield Camp, near Uckfield in Sussex, the SMI following a little later. Finally, in 1966, the Depot moved again to form part of the Intelligence Centre at the new purpose-built Templer Barracks, Ashford. The SMI also moved to Ashford becoming the Instructional Wing Intelligence Centre and then the School of Service Intelligence on becoming tri-Service in 1969. It is now known as the Defence Intelligence and Security School. Also at Ashford are the office of the Intelligence Corps Association, the Corps' welfare organisation of present and past members, and the Intelligence Corps Museum.

The design for a Corps badge submitted to King George VI by the Secretary of State for War, Anthony Eden, on 25 July 1940 and finally approved was a rose flanked by laurel leaves, resting on a scroll inscribed 'Intelligence Corps', the whole surmounted by a crown. The specimen badge was in brass, and submitted together with it were the Royal Coat of Arms button and the soldiers' shoulder emblem 'I.C.' The rose was a double rose and although the Royal Submission did not include a description of the colours of the badge when used as a crest, there are two examples of the rose being coloured as a Union Rose in 1940. Later, in the Corps Journal, the rose was coloured only in red, but this was corrected in 1954 when the St Edward's Crown was introduced. The rose is a heraldic emblem of secrecy, and its use as such originates in mythology. Legend has it that Cupid gave a rose to a god to bribe him not to divulge what he had seen or heard of the love affairs of Venus. From this legend grew the practice in ancient times of suspending a rose from the ceiling over the table in a banqueting hall as a symbol of silence and trustworthiness, a reminder to all guests that anything said or done at the banquet was not to be divulged. Hence the term *sub rosa*. The laurels signify victory, and the crown allegiance to the Sovereign.

The Colours of the Corps, to be seen on Mess Kit, the Corps Stable Belt and the Corps Tie, are green, grey and scarlet. The green derives from the green tabs and hatbands of Intelligence Corps officers from 1916 onwards, the colour of Field Security Police cap covers, and the World War II armbands and Intelligence corps shoulder flashes. In the autumn of 1977 the Corps adopted its distinctive green beret, following approval from the Army Dress Committee.

In 1964, the Queen approved the Intelligence corps Motto, *Manui Dat Cognitio Vires*—Knowledge Gives Strength to the Arm. The motto was drafted by Mr B G Whitfield of Eton College from an idea of Major General A C Shortt.

The Corps Quick March 'The Rose and the Laurel' was approved in 1953. The Colonel Commandant had attended three passing-out parades at Eaton Hall which were commanded by Senior Under Officers from the Intelligence Corps. General Davidson noted with regret that the Corps had no Regimental March, and that during the march past the 'British Grenadiers' was played in lieu. He decided to put this right at once, and was fortunate in being able to persuade the Staff of Kneller Hall to arrange a Corps March based on the tunes of 'Let Bucks a-Hunting Go' and 'Sly Renard'.

The Corps' Slow March is to the tune of 'Trumpet Tune (and Ayre)' by Purcell, scored by Lieutenant Colonel R Bashford MBE LRAM ARCM, then Director of Music at the Royal Military School of Music, Kneller Hall. The March was accepted and approved by the Corps Committee in 1971.

On 11 June 1977, HRH Prince Philip, Duke of Edinburgh was appointed the first Colonel-in-Chief of the Intelligence Corps by Her Majesty the Queen.

The Colonels Commandant of the Intelligence Corps have been:

General Sir Bernard Paget, GCB DSO MC	1943–52
Major General F H N Davidson, CB DSO MC	1952–60
Major General A C Shortt, CB OBE	1960–64
Major General R E Lloyd, CB CBE DSO	1964–69
Lieutenant General Sir Richard Fyffe, KBE CB DSO MC	1969–72
General Sir Michael Gow, GCB	1972–86
General Sir Charles Guthrie, KCB LVO OBE	1986–

Until 1974, the Inspector of Intelligence (from 1970 the Inspector Intelligence Corps) was not an Intelligence Corps officer. Among those who held the appointment Brigadier R M Bremner, 1970–73, was held in particular regard and affection by the Corps. From 1974 the Inspector, a title changed to Director Intelligence Corps in 1976, have all been Intelligence Corps officers. Brigadier Mears was the first Corps officer to reach this rank and Brigadier Ford was the first Director whose whole Service was with the Corps. The Inspectors and Directors have been:

Brigadier B E L Burton, CBE	1957–1959
Brigadier (later Major General) J M L Gavin, OBE	1959–1962
Brigadier B T V Cowey, DSO	1962–1963
Brigadier A W Vickers, DSO OBE	1963–1966
Brigadier T F R Bulkeley, MBE	1966–1967
Brigadier J A MacKenzie, CBE DSO MC ADC	1967–1970
Brigadier R M Bremner, OBE ADC	1970–1973
Brigadier (later Major General) P A M Tighe, MBE	1973–1974
Brigadier K J Mears, CBE	1974–1976
Brigadier P E B Madsen, CBE	1976–1979
Brigadier M J D Perrett-Young	1979–1981
Brigadier B A H Parritt, CBE	1981–1986
Brigadier M P Ford	1986–1989
Brigadier A K Crawford, CBE	1989–1991
Brigadier E P O Springfield	1991–

From 1949, on the Saturday nearest to 19 July—the date on which Army Order 112 of 1940 gave approval to the formation of the Corps—'Corps Day' has been held at Maresfield or at Ashford. The day has also been commemorated in all stations where Intelligence Corps personnel serve.

The Corps has formal Alliances with the Australian Intelligence Corps dating from 1950 and the Canadian Forces Intelligence Branch from 1983. There is also an affiliation, dating from 1983, with the Royal Navy patrol vessel HMS *Leeds Castle*. Bonds of friendship have been established with the United States Army Military Intelligence Corps and the Malaysian Intelligence Corps.

The Intelligence and Security Group (Volunteers), like a number of other Territorial Army units, is adopted by a City Livery Company, the Worshipful Company of Painter-Stainers. The link was first simply one of the former Headquarters APIS (TA), adopted in 1964, but it was extended to the Volunteers Group as a whole in 1967. The Company has generously placed Painters Hall, in Trinity Lane, at the Corps' disposal for a number of functions.

The Intelligence Corps Collect, accepted and approved in 1971, was written by the Reverend B W Howarth CF. It is divided into four parts—invocation of God's name, description of an attribute of God, petition and conclusion. The Text is:

O God, who alone givest true wisdom: Grant to thy servants of the Intelligence Corps such gifts of understanding and truth, that by their vigilance thy people may live their lives in freedom and in peace, to thy glory and the welfare of this realm; for thy holy name's sake. Amen.

The 'Angel of Guildford Cathedral', the golden angel weather vane mounted on the tower of Guildford Cathedral, was presented by the parents of Sergeant R D Adgey-Edgar *in memoriam*. Sergeant Adgey-Edgar died from injuries received on duty in 1944.

In June 1949 the Intelligence Corps Roll of Honour for Second World War, containing 214 names, was lodged in Winchester Cathedral by the Colonel Commandant, General Sir Bernard Paget, and housed in an oak lectern. In June 1978 at a simple ceremony in Winchester Cathedral, the Dean handed over the Corps Roll of Honour and its container to a bearer party from the Intelligence Centre Ashford led by Lieutenant Colonel J H S Burgess and WO1 (RSM) W Ward for transfer to the Corps' new home at Ashford. On Sunday 23 July 1978, it was accepted in the Parish Church of St Mary the Virgin by the Vicar, Canon Aubrey Wright, from the Colonel Commandant, Major General J M Gow.

In the South Transept of Ashford Parish Church, the Roll, inscribed in two books, is now housed in a glass cabinet. It consists of:

Book 1, (1939–45), containing the 215 names of those members of the Corps who lost their lives during the Second World War, and
Book 2 (1946 onwards), containing the 36 names of those members of the Corps who have lost their lives on active service since Second World War.

A page of each book is turned every month by a young recruit under training.

In the Corps Museum a register is kept of a further 33 names of Intelligence Corps members who have died whilst serving, though not on active service, from 1945 to the present day.

Notes

Prologue: The Role

1. The term IC, to cover censorship and propaganda, and IX, to cover administration have also been employed at times. They are noted here for interest but are not used in this work.
2. Paper, 'The Use of Ultra', 5 October 1945. Sir Edgar Williams kindly made available a copy of this paper to the author. A copy is also to be found in folio WO 208/3575 in the Public Records Office.

Chapter 1: The Forebears of the Intelligence Corps

1. This chapter is in part based upon a fascinating study of early British military Intelligence, Lieutenant Colonel B A H Parritt, *The Intelligencers*, (Privately Published, 1972). As Brigadier Parritt, the author was Director of the Intelligence Corps from 1981 to 1986.
2. Parritt, *Intelligencers*, p. 21.
3. André asked to be shot, a request refused as he was in disguise, and he met his death on the gallows. Later his body was returned to Britain and a memorial to him placed in Westminster Abbey.
4. The first was Major General Sir Patrick MacDougal.
5. This important office and proud title lasted until 1965; one of the Division's publications at this time was the first edition of *Staff Duties in the Field*. Parritt, *Intelligencers*, p. 156.
6. Other interesting travels are noted in Thomas G Fergusson, *British Military Intelligence, 1870–1914*, (London, Arms and Armour, 1984), pp. 92–93. They included an officer looking for any untoward Russian troop movements on the Russo-German border in 1891, another officer similarly engaged in Bessarabia the next year, and visits to look at new artillery in France and Germany.
7. Fergusson, *British Military Intelligence*, pp. 114–115. Almost all Boer soldiers were 'teeth arm' while the British Army had a large logistic 'tail'. Most Boer soldiers also were mounted and throughout their lives accustomed to shoot accurately, with movement and fire assets superior to those of Britain.
8. Parritt, *Intelligencers*, p. 179.
9. Jock Haswell, *British Military Intelligence*, (London, Weidenfeld, 1973), p. 62 notes in particular that scouts seldom saw the value of negative information, an area being unoccupied or a water resource unused, and they failed to draw a clear distinction between what they thought they were seeing and what they actually did see.
10. The Army instituted language examination in 'Cape Dutch'. One of the earliest officers to pass, with success to the point of passing for a Boer, was Captain Ironside (*later Field Marshal Lord Ironside CIGS*).
11. The courses continued as long as the British garrison remained in South Africa, a little

before the outbreak of World War I. Notes taken by a student on a 1912 course are in the Intelligence Corps Museum, the chief instructor was Ironside. The range of subjects had been extended to include a greater study of Intelligence sources, 'Savage Warfare' (ie black uprisings), agent handling, cryptography, foreign (especially Japanese) Intelligence activities, security in the field, aircraft reconnaissance, tactical questioning, and the detection of spies.

12. Lieutenant Colonel David Henderson, *Field Intelligence, The Principles and Practices*, (London, HMSO, 1904) quoted, Fergusson, *British Military Intelligence*, p. 166.

13. Henderson, *Field Intelligence*, p. 1.

Chapter 2: The First Intelligence Corps, 1914

1. Thomas G Fergusson, *British Military Intelligence, 1870–1914*. (London, Arms and Armour, 1984), pp. 168–169.

2. Notebook kept by Captain F C Rasch, student attending Intelligence Course, Pretoria, 1912, Intelligence Corps Museum. In capital letters Rasch wrote down the teaching in respect of this campaign, 'the Intelligence Officer was the man who counted'. In the absence of maps, distances between settlements were estimated on the basis of travel time.

3. The first head of MO1 was Colonel E A Altham who had been the Intelligence staff officer in South Africa in 1899. The first head of MO2 was Colonel W R (later Field Marshal Sir William) Robertson, also an officer of considerable general and FID Intelligence experience.

4. Its creation had followed reports, probably correct, of a German spy network in Britain. So successful was Kell that on the outbreak of war in 1914 he was able to arrest every member of a very real German spy network, except one.

5. Military attachés, of course, were an important source of intelligence at this time. The British Military Attaché in Berlin from 1903 to 1906, Count Gleichen, an officer with considerable Intelligence staff experience from the 1880s onwards, was notably successful in this work.

6. The manual further envisaged duties divided into an Information Sub-Section 1(a) concerned with general functions, information from prisoners and documents, and the provision and pay of guides and interpreters, and a Secret Service Sub-Section 1(b) concerned with the organisation of Secret Service, codes and ciphers, flags of truce and correspondence with the enemy, and Intelligence Police.

7. Kirke Papers (Intelligence Corps Museum).

8. This course may be seen as the forerunner of the Regimental Intelligence Officers course, still run at the Intelligence Centre, Ashford. Subjects covered included 'Acquisition of Intelligence', 'Organisation of Secret Service', 'Cyphers and Cyphering', 'Intelligence in Peace, work junior officers are likely to be called upon to carry out'. 'Intelligence in Indian Warfare', 'Intelligence in European Warfare, with illustrations from the Russo-Japanese War' and 'On Intelligence duties and the Organization of the Intelligence Department in the South African War'.

9. Influential in the lobbying for a peacetime corps was Colonel David Henderson of the former FID.

10. The names of these, the founder members of the first Intelligence Corps, appear at Appendix A.

11. This role was a development of the duties envisaged in the *Staff Manual—(War) Provisional 1912*, which had listed the duties of an 'Intelligence Police' as the prevention of unauthorised persons gaining access to headquarters camps and offices; the taking charge of all persons brought in for examination; the carrying out of arrests and searches as ordered, and acting as special messengers for the Intelligence Section.

12. One exception was Haig's I Corps, their staff at this stage maintaining that Intelligence Corps officers were unnecessary.

13. Kirke Papers (Intelligence Corps Museum.)

14. James Marshall-Cornwall, *Wars and Rumours of Wars*, (London, Leo Cooper, 1984), p. 16.

15. Brigadier General J E Edmonds, *Military Operations, France and Belgium, 1914*,

(London, Macmillan, 1928), p. 51.

16. Major Baird's diaries from August 1914 to December 1915 were kindly loaned to the Intelligence Corps by his son, the Rt. Hon. The Earl of Kintore, with whose permission these extracts are quoted. Baird later became Minister for Transport (1922–24), Governor-General of Australia (1925–1930), and Chairman of the Conservative Party (1931–36)

17. Second Lieutenant Smith's name appears on the 9th Lancers Memorial and Roll of Honour, in Canterbury Cathedral, as attached to the Regiment.

18. An account of this event, including Rawlinson's immediate recognition of its significance and Sir John French's initial snub appears in L S Amery, *My Political Life*, II, (London, Hutchinson, 1953), pp. 38–40.

19. Readers who find this remarkable should read Carl Zuckmayer's sardonic play about the Kaiser's Germany, *The Captain of Köpenick*, in particular Act III, Scene 15.

20. The French Army had been campaigning in Morocco, on an extensive scale, from 1912. The French commander, Lyautey, had used air reconnaissance effectively and the experience so gained had given France a notable lead in this field. See Anthony Clayton, *France, Soldiers and Africa*, (Brasseys, London, 1988).

21. Field Marshal Viscount French, *1914*, (London, Constable, 1919), pp. 43–44.

22. For further details see WO2 G Downton, INT CORPS, 'Notes and Pictures on the History of Photographic Interpretation', Intelligence Corps Museum, and John W R Taylor and D Mondey, *Spies In The Sky*, (New York, Charles Scribner, 1972), pp. 19–25.

23. Kirke Papers (Intelligence Corps Museum).

24. An asset enjoyed by the Allies was the use of French internal cable communications; these released wireless facilities for Intelligence work.

25. Wing Commander M T Thurbon, 'The Origins of Electronic Warfare', and Major General R F H Nalder, *Royal Corps of Signals* (Royal Signals Institution 1958), 'The Signal Service in France 1914–1919' (Institution of Royal Engineers 1921); both articles quoted in Fergusson, *British Military Intelligence*, p. 196.

26. Edmonds, *Military Operations, France and Belgium*, II, pp. 348–349.

27. Richard Holmes, *The Little Field Marshal, Sir John French*, (London, Jonathan Cape, 1981), p. 246.

28. Edmonds, *Military Operations, France and Belgium*, II, p. 387.

29. 'Military Intelligence and incidents connected therewith during the War', lecture given by Macdonogh at the Royal Artillery Institution, subsequently printed.

Chapter 3: The Western Front, 1915–18

1. This chapter, recording these skills, of necessity covers a number of events and techniques set out in Jock Haswell, *British Military Intelligence*, (London, Weidenfeld, 1973), viii, ix, and Christopher Andrew, *Secret Service, The Making of the British Intelligence Community*, (London, Heinemann, 1985), iv. This work however seeks to add material upon the work of the Corps, rather than upon other agencies and the Intelligence staffs.

2. Colonel J M Cowper, *A Short History of Queen Mary's Army Auxiliary Corps* (privately published). The WAAC were restyled QMAAC in 1918. I am most grateful to Lieutenant Colonel S Wing, WRAC, for the loan for this publication.

3. Not all were satisfied with this. Lieutenant Dunkels, Intelligence Corps, whose civilian occupation had been selling diamonds for De Beers, used one of his family's five Rolls Royce cars specially armour plated. (Woolrych Papers, Intelligence Corps Museum).

4. Hotblack Papers. Woolrych noted that in August 1915 a Pole provided material to form three closely printed pages of information, five appendices, four maps and two diagrams. Hotblack and Woolrych Papers, Intelligence Corps Museum.

5. Note by Captain E L Philip, Intelligence Corps, Intelligence Corps Museum. The note records the stool pigeon's usual ploy was to sit and listen before encouraging prisoners to talk. Excellent German was necessary.

6. Bosworth Papers (Intelligence Corps Museum).

7. A collection of such drawings is included in the Woolrych Papers (Intelligence Corps Museum).

8. James Marshall-Cornwall, *Wars and Rumours of Wars*, (London, Leo Cooper, 1984), pp. 18–19.
9. Philip, Note.
10. Marshall-Cornwall, *Wars*, p. 19.
11. Field telephones at the time used a single wire laid out on the ground, and a ground return. The general assumption had been that conversations could only be intercepted on the line itself, so no security precautions were taken.
12. Material kindly supplied by Corporal Shirley's son, Mr R Shirley. Shirley was transferred to prisoner questioning duties in mid-1917 but returned to ITOC work as it was called, from September 1917 to March 1918, being awarded the Military Medal. In the last months of the war Shirley returned again to prisoner questioning. R A B Young, 'Even Wars Have Ears', *The Territorial*, February 1938, notes the mining example.
13. Haswell, *British Military Intelligence*, p. 125, provides an example of a useful message signed 'Albert Elisabeth', the names of the King and Queen of the Belgians.
14. Sir Ivone Kirkpatrick, *The Inner Circle*, (London, Macmillan, 1959), p. 13 notes that the German Army was so concerned that 14 days leave was given to any soldier who shot down a pigeon.
15. The idea was then taken over by GHQ who used the balloons as a means of disseminating propaganda into German troop areas.
16. Young, 'Even Wars'. This group of Corps personnel were officially designated as 'the pigeons'.
17. Payne-Best transcripts, Kirke Diaries, 12 April 1915, IWM; quoted Andrew, *Secret Service*, p. 214.
18. The Woolrych Papers, Intelligence Corps Museum, contain messages and give further methods for this, the most difficult stage. The methods included the bowl of a pipe, hollow teeth and specially manufactured keys. Women crossing the frontier carried the messages in basket handles, chocolate and tins with false bottoms. In August 1983, 41 Security Section of the Corps' Intelligence and Security Group (Germany) made contact with an 84 year old Belgian, Karel Vernimmen, who had, as a student, gathered intelligence for the British Army. He had bicycled through German encampments and recorded notes in his bicycle handlebars, the notes were later passed to another Belgian for onward transmission. The Corps presented Vernimmen with a Corps plaque at a ceremony in Antwerp. Lieutenant Colonel D J Venn 'An Agent of the British in Occupied Belgium', *The Rose and the Laurel*, December 1983.
19. Kirke Papers, Intelligence Corps Museum. The wrong assessment was particularly unfortunate as the French had warned of a gas attack on the British front and the RFC had spotted cylinders. Later Plumer was warned of a gas attack on his front, took precautions and the attack failed.
20. For an example of the latter see Brigadier General Sir James Edmonds, *Military Operations, France and Belgium 1918*, III, (London, Macmillan, 1939), p. 17. The Americans correctly assessed the direction of the May 1918 German 'Chemin des Dames' offensive one month prior to the attack.
21. In London MO7, Colonel H F Coleridge a former FID officer, was in charge of this work. Before his arrival in France, John Buchan had been Director of Information for the Foreign Office.
22. Kirke Papers (Intelligence Corps Museum).
23. The early months of the war were characterised by numbers of visitors, official, unofficial, wanted and unwanted, to the battlefield areas—press men, voluntary service, political lobbyists, cranks and others.
24. General Sir Horace Smith-Dorrien's personal diary, entry for 21 September 1914. The general noted that the farmer and 15 others had been shot in the previous two days. (PRO. CAB 45/206).
25. Baird Diaries.
26. Baird Diaries.
27. William Allison and John Fairley, *The Monocled Mutineer*, (London, Quarter Books, 1978), pp. 122, 126–128.
28. Kirke Papers (Intelligence Corps Museum). The offender was General Rawlinson.
29. Marshall-Cornwall, *Wars*, iii, 'Charteris, however, with breezy optimism disregarded

the sounder and more cautious forecasts which emanated from the War Office ... I was appalled to find what a mistaken view he [Haig] held about the German troops confronting us'.

Marshall-Cornwall also notes Haig's visit to a German prisoners camp from which fit men had been removed on Charteris's instructions to convince Haig of the poor state of the enemy, and Charteris's refusal to accept Marshall-Cornwall's identification of three fresh German divisions at Cambrai in 1917, established from prisoner questioning, a refusal that led to the costly failure of a British attack. Woolrych felt the same and wrote of Charteris' departure: 'We were all relieved. We knew only too well how dangerous Charteris could be. He had many qualifications for a good intelligence chief but they were offset by the almost insane optimism which informed his judgement and the advice he gave to the C-in-C.'

Chapter 4: Other Theatres of Operations and Training, 1914–18

1. For a general account see Colonel R Meinertzhagen, *Army Diary 1899–1926*, (Edinburgh, Oliver and Boyd, 1960), pp. 81–205.
   An interesting paper by F S Joelson, 'The East African Intelligence Department' in the Intelligence Corps Museum notes three agents, Weinhold, Brown and Lewis as notably successful. Joelson was himself an officer in the Department.
2. Colin Forbes Adam, *Life of Lord Lloyd*, (London, Macmillan, 1948), pp. 69–70.
3. Brigadier General C F Aspinall-Oglander, *Military Operations, Gallipoli 1*, (London, Heinemann, 1929), p. 230. Another example of useful questioning is reported on p. 320.
4. Compton Mackenzie, *Gallipoli Memories*, (London, Cassell, 1929), p. 379.
5. Compton Mackenzie, *My Life and Times Octave 5, 1915–1923*, (London, Chatto and Windus, 1966), p. 25.
6. Adam, *Lord Lloyd*, p. 65.
7. Brigadier General F J Moberly, *The Campaign in Mesopotamia 1914–1918*, (London, HMSO, 1924), Appendix XXX, pp. 537–538.
8. After the withdrawal from Gallipoli, Mackenzie was obliged to report only to an organisation known as the Eastern Mediterranean Special Intelligence Bureau at Alexandria. He was not permitted to contact direct any other Intelligence organisation, which handicapped his work, while his links with Alexandria led to his being distrusted by Army Headquarters Salonica. He himself became Director of an Aegean Intelligence Service based on the island of Syra, in 1917.
9. Compton Mackenzie, *My Life and Times, Octave 5*, pp. 47–48.
10. 'Composition of the Headquarters of the British Forces at Salonika, September 1917; p. 6 'Intelligence Corps'. (Intelligence Corps Museum).
11. Other related staff included a meteorology section of three officers and twenty soldiers, and a Royal Engineers Field Survey Company. A full and interesting account covering the whole period November 1917 to February 1919 appears on War Office file *WO 106 1550*, 'The Service of Intelligence in the British Forces in Italy' prepared by the (Canadian) Chief of Intelligence, Brigadier General C H Mitchell, and dated 30 May 1918, (Public Record Office).
12. Report by Brigadier General R St G Gorton, November 1918 to the DMI, (Intelligence Corps Museum).
13. GHQ Ireland 'Record of the Rebellion in Ireland in 1920–21 and the Part Played by the Army in Dealing with it. II. Intelligence' (Intelligence Corps Museum).
14. One on the War Office Roof and one in Suffolk were War Office controlled, those at Seaham, Peterborough and Westgate were Post Office controlled, and one at Aberdeen was Admiralty controlled. The intercept station was at Devizes. Papers relating to Sir R Nesbitt-Hawes (Intelligence Corps Museum).
15. No record survives as to why green was chosen. Napoleon's *Corps des Guides et Interprétes* had worn green coats and green waistcoats, green being Napoleon's favourite colour; this appears to be the most likely inspiration. During the Indian Mutiny an Intelligence Officer penetrated the mutineers' lines to bring Intelligence to the besieged garrison of Lucknow. He achieved this disguised as an Indian. On his

arrival the wife of the British Resident in Lucknow cut up the green baize of the Residency billiard tables to provide him with a green uniform. This may be the first occasion that a British Intelligence Officer wore a green uniform, but it is almost certainly not the reason for the later selection of green.

16. Professor J H Priestley was also Pro Vice-Chancellor of Leeds University from 1934 to 1939.
17. D Buxton, 'The 10th Bn Royal Fusiliers (Intelligence) (b)', unpublished paper kindly made available by the author. It should be noted that most officers received awards as 'Intelligence Corps' and so are not included in Buxton's totals. In the First World War length of service requirements for the Meritorious Service Medal were dropped; later the British Empire Medal was introduced to replace the MSM in this capacity.
18. Woolrych Papers, Intelligence Corps Museum.
19. American officers were also attached to GHQ BEF for Intelligence training. James Marshall-Cornwall, *Wars and Rumours of Wars*, (London, Leo Cooper, 1984) p. 40.

Chapter 5: The Years of Neglect, 1919–29

1. James Marshall-Cornwall, *Wars and Rumours of Wars*, (London, Leo Cooper, 1984), p. 4.
2. Brigadier General Sir James E Edmonds, *The Occupation of the Rhineland 1918–1929*, (London, HMSO, 1944), pp. 69–70.
3. Marshall-Cornwall, *Wars*. p. 41. Marshall-Cornwall notes that he persuaded the head of the relief organisation to allow an officer to be incorporated into each of the missions.
4. 'Memorandum on the work of the Section of Civil Affairs and Security, General Staff, British Army of the Rhine', written by Lieutenant Colonel R W Oldfield, 12 December 1929. (Intelligence Corps Museum).
5. Oldfield Memorandum.
6. In these plebiscites of areas with very broadly speaking German urban and Polish rural populations, the British were suspected by the Poles of supporting German claims while the French supported the Poles. There was therefore an element of anti-British sentiment in the activities of the Polish partisans. As a rejoinder to this murder, a British infantry battalion mounted a series of raids, capturing a partisan leader and 35 of his followers. Four were sentenced to death by the inter-Allied Plebiscite Commission but the sentence was later commuted.
7. The officer was Lieutenant Colonel R W Oldfield, RA. His rank, a grade above that of a normal GSO 2 (Major), was intended to secure authority among the Germans and to equate with his French opposite number.
8. Active espionage took the form of a careful, politically-motivated, collection of grievances against the occupying armies. More active German espionage was targeted against the French. Oldfield Memorandum.
9. An interesting short catalogue of these appears in Edmonds, *Occupation*, pp. 278–279.
10. Major General Sir Kenneth Strong, *Intelligence at the Top*, (London, Cassell, 1968), p. 8. Goebbels had referred to the French as *dreckige Waschlappen* (dirty dischcloths) for which he was arrested. The Oldfield Memorandum notes a prohibition on the wearing of party uniforms in the Occupied zones, a measure which temporarily reduced membership.
11. The Oldfield Memorandum gives some examples of the agents, including a Cologne police official, an employee of the German Communist Party, a Communist and a National Socialist militant both in need of money, and an English petty trader. Some were paid in cash, others in goods. The German police helped to recruit agents who were in touch with, or members, of left-wing parties.
12. Oldfield Memorandum. The language difficulty largely precluded this despite German Communist endeavours to learn Esperanto.
13. Marshall-Cornwall, *Wars*, pp. 59–60.
14. A remarkable account of a unit Intelligence officer's duties appear in Darrell Bates biography of Lord Twining, *A Gust of Plumes*, (London, Hodder and Stoughton, 1972), pp. 41–53. The account reveals all the confusion in the minds of people at the time

both in respect of policy when Twining arrested de Valera in a surprise raid and was then ordered to release him for political reasons, and at personal level where Twining found himself physically unable to shoot a man on the run out of what was clearly an IRA meeting.

15. It is purposeless to enter into the detail of recriminatory arguments over this. The IRA claimed the personnel were tasked to kill militant Republicans, a number of these were however implicated in previous IRA attacks and killings. The British also suspected, with good reason that the IRA was planning a germ warfare campaign against troops and horses.

16. Some idea of the complex, cumbersome nature of the dual system can be formed from the requirement that captured IRA documents—one of the few useful Intelligence sources—were analysed by the military if concerned with operations, arms, training and organisation, but by the police if they concerned individuals, addresses, Sinn Fein police, courts, or organisation and propaganda. Each was in theory to supply copies to the other; the reader may need to be reminded that copying machines had not been invented.

17. General the Rt. Hon. Sir Nevil Macready, *Annals of an Active Life*, (London, Hutchinson, n.d.), II, p. 463.

18. John Ferris, 'Whitehall's Black Chamber, British Cryptology and the Government Code and Cypher School, 1914–1929' *Intelligence and National Security, II* (1), 1987, p. 70. The station at Aden was in fact much more concerned with the Italian Air Force than the Italian Army.

19. The Branch Intelligence Officers Course at Ismailia in 1927, for example specifically included aerial reconnaissance and liaison with the RAF. John Cloake, *Templer, Tiger of Malaya*, (London, Harrap, 1985), p. 44. F H Hinsley and others, *British Intelligence in the Second World War, I*, (London, HMSO, 1979), p. 29 notes also '... although the RAF School of Interpretation had been set up in 1922, the Army provided all its instructors and pupils until 1938'. The course, at Farnborough, included titling strips, the making of mosaics, and a measure of stereoscopy. Some 500 students had attended the course by 1939.

Chapter 6: The Rebirth of the Corps, 1939–40

1. F H Hinsley, and others, *British Intelligence in the Second World War, I.*, (London, HMSO, 1973), p. 76. The key word is 'circulated', much was known in the War Office of German equipments and probable tactics. The expertise, however, was not made available for proper analysis and training at field formation level. The clearest indicator of this failure was the surprise German breakthrough on the Meuse.

2. Hinsley, *British Intelligence*, p. 77 notes the Army's surprise, after the outbreak of war, at the power and speed of German offensives; the use of tanks and aircraft; and, despite reports, the existence of certain weapons and the capacities of others for example, the anti-tank capability of the 88 mm anti-aircraft gun. And p. 113 adds 'From the COS papers it appears that no systematic study was made before May 1940 of the relevance of MI reports on the Polish campaign to earlier reports of Germany's interest in *blitzkrieg* methods or of the possibility that she would use them in Western Europe'.

3. 'Notes on MI Directorate' by Brigadier L A New, Intelligence Corps Museum. The personnel consisted of 6 GSO1s, 18 GSO2s, 21 GSO3s, 4 attached officers, 2 quartermasters, 5 Warrant officers, 17 NCOs, 3 retired officers, 7 civilian assistants, 1 chief constable, 2 assistant chief constables, 1 inspector, 3 map-curators, 30 ex-soldier clerks, 18 draughtsmen, 2 photographers and 7 printers.

4. 'Intelligence Corps War Establishment', *Army Council Instructions for the week ending 16th December 1936.*

5. Davis undertook this work as a civilian, receiving £30 per month in addition to his pension. He was initially appointed for two months only, this apparently being considered sufficient time.

6. The CMP is of course now the Royal Corps of Military Police (RMP).

Notes

7. The courses, for which Davis and two or three CMP NCOs were the instructors, covered general field security work, interrogation technique, orders of battle of an enemy army, propaganda and morale and motor cycle riding. The number of courses increased in 1939, some students being recruits to MI5.
8. The actual staff were Captains Woolrych, Wallerstein and F E P Suthrell, Sergeants W B Smith, T F Shelton, McIntyre, Corporals P Pawson and R F Carter, and ATS Kay Murray, Clair Hupton, May Lunn, Emma Skinner and D Heddington.
9. Sullivan Papers (Intelligence Corps Museum).
10. M Muggeridge, quoted Jock Haswell, *British Military Intelligence*, (London, Weidenfeld, 1973), p. 171.
11. As a consequence of this misunderstanding, FSP became changed from Police to Personnel.
12. Ewan Butler, *Mason-Mac, The Life of Lieutenant General Sir Noel Mason-Macfarlane*, (London, Macmillan, 1972), p. 106.
13. Sullivan Papers, Intelligence Corps Museum. A full list of all the World War II FSS is shown in Appendix B. Sullivan also notes other small groups of people who had attached themselves to the Intelligence Corps—RAF Liaison Sections, King's Messengers, and the 'Twelve Apostles', officers mostly recalled from retirement for a mixture of liaison with French formations and VIP visitor escort duties.
14. Ronald Lewin, *Ultra Goes to War*, (London, Hutchinson, 1978), p. 63.
15. These difficulties in sum were that the Blenheim aircraft used were too vulnerable; the Spitfire adaptations were few in number and constrained by weather; and the photographs too small scale. Much effort had also been spent on updating out-of-date maps of Belgium, or photography of the Ruhr.
16. Major General Sir Kenneth Strong, *Intelligence at the Top*, (London, Cassell, 1968), p. 63. Pre-war calculations of the order of battle strength of the German Army had been very accurate; deductions from this in respect of strategy and tactics were, however, almost non-existent. For a useful summary of the position in 1938, see Ernest R May (Ed), *Knowing One's Enemies*, (Princeton, Princeton University Press, 1986), ix, 'British Intelligence and the Coming of the Second World War in Europe' by Donald Cameron Watt, in particular pp. 253–54.
17. Arthur Marshall, *Life's Rich Pageant*, (London, Hamish Hamilton, 1984), pp. 144–147.
18. Captain Sir Basil Bartlett, *My First War*, (London, Chatto and Windus, 1940), *passim*.
19. K Vignoles to the author, 24 October 1987. Vignoles was also with 3 Division. The documents were soon on their way to Corps Headquarters as the Corps Commander was visiting the 3rd Division at the time. Captain Osman later died of wounds sustained at Dunkirk.
20. Major L F Ellis *The War in France and Flanders, 1939–40*, (London, HMSO, 1953) pp. 148–149. Ellis comments, in this Official History of the campaign, 'by doing so, he [Gort] saved the British Expeditionary Force'.
21. R C Symonds to the author, 11 August 1987.
22. Bosworth Papers, (Intelligence Corps Museum). Bosworth was one of the Officers' Emergency Reserve Officers serving with the Corps.
23. Interview, Sir Tom Normanton, 9 November 1987. Normanton's SLU duties had provided him with these VIP numbers. Ironside, out of touch with Gort, directed Normanton to pass Intelligence to a formation that it was proposed to land at Calais on that night. Normanton made contact with a Royal Army Medical Corps column and arranged for the Intelligence to be passed on before accepting medical treatment.
24. Hinsley, *British Intelligence, I*, pp. 146–147. The Luftwaffe used either low grade codes or signalled en clair.
25. Examples appear in *The Diary of a Staff Officer*, (London, Methuen, 1941), written by an Air Liaison Officer who remained anonymous, pp. 3, 25.
26. Bartlett, *My First War*, pp. 88–89, 96. Bartlett notes receiving a report that said '... all German Jews with a red J (instead of the usual black J) on their passport must be detained. The Germans have apparently issued a number of red J passports to their own agents'.
27. Lieutenant Colonel B G H McNabb to the author, 3 November 1987.
28. Hinsley, *British Intelligence, I*, p. 148.
29. The Earl of Perth to the author, 16 July 1987. Lord Perth added 'With hindsight I

doubt this did much'.

30. Various earlier plans had been fashioned for British landings in Norway, ostensibly to support the Finns in their fight against the Soviet Union, but in practice to cut German iron-ore supplies. In support of one of these, in February 1940, at least one FS Section was actually embarked before the operation was cancelled.

31. Two officers and five NCOs, all Scandinavian language specialists, had had to be withdrawn from the Corps in France.

32. Michael Pertwee to the author, 31 July 1987.

33. The personnel were told little of their wartime duties. Some on mobilisation expressed surprise that they might have to be posted elsewhere, or even wear uniform. As with the BEF Sections, officers either wore the insignia of units in which they had served previously or General Service insignia; soldiers wore CMP uniform.

34. At the time of the moves Lieutenant Colonel Davis was Commandant with Major Woolrych as his Chief Instructor—other early instructors included Captains V L Armitage, the Earl of Northesk, L Wallerstein, P H Bickerton-Edwards, R M Brooker, A S Wilkinson, Lieutenant T M Muggeridge and WO1 W B Smith, the first Regimental Sergeant Major. With the appointment of Colonel Jeffries as Commandant in December 1940, Davis became Assistant Commandant.

35. One such was Eric Birley, a classics scholar who applied his pre-war card-indexing system in respect of Roman Army units to the Wehrmacht, building up a remarkably accurate store-house of information. But in the course of his work Birley came across highly classified information from an Axis source predicting an offensive in a particular theatre, one reason for the prediction being the presence of a large number of Intelligence Corps personnel. Professor E Birley to the author, 21 September 1987.

Residual anti-Intelligence Corps prejudice also sometimes made it easier for Intelligence work and briefings to be undertaken by officers badged to other arms, a point made to me, from personal experience, by Sir Edgar Williams, 30 November 1987. Some Intelligence Corps Officers, for this reason and for their own safety in the event of capture, wore the badges of their previous units in operational theatres. One of the most notable of these was Colonel J O Ewart.

Chapter 7: Strategic Intelligence: The Corps Contribution

1. J C Masterman, *On The Chariot Wheel*, (Oxford, OUP, 1975), p. 222.

2. Some measures of the MI5 requirement can be gauged from the numbers, over 20,000 Germans (including Austrians) and 4,000 Italians.

3. Lord Rothschild, *Memoirs of A Broomstick*, (London, Collins, 1977), pp. 25, 29–32.

4. Among the minor changes was an expansion of MI11 to provide Security training for the US Army in Europe.

5. A very complete compilation of the evolution of the Directorate of Military Intelligence throughout World War II, noting all the sections, sub-sections and establishments is to be found in 'War Diary, DMI, Organisation and Establishments' of which a copy (Number 1185) is in the Intelligence Corps Museum.

6. Lieutenant Sherman, a pre-war journalist, had joined the ATS as a private and had been commissioned in 1942. She recalls with pride her being awarded an Intelligence Corps badge to wear above her tunic breast pocket. Mrs M Bean (Captain Sherman) to the author, 28 September 1987.

7. Sir Brinsley Ford to the author 19 October 1987; article in *The Times* 10 April 1985, M R D Foot and J M Langley, *MI9, Escape and Evasion 1939–1945*, (Boston, Little and Brown, 1979).

8. Major P M Lee, Imperial War Museum Tape Interview.

9. Lord Annan to the author, 22 September and 2 October 1987.

10. W D Combs to the author, 31 July 1987; C R Tangye to the author, 12 January 1988.

11. Professor N Gash to the author, 17 August 1987.

12. One very useful document was one that portrayed the heraldic signs favoured as divisional emblems by the German Army.

13. Mrs Bean to the author, 28 September 1987. Mrs Bean noted that Geopolitics was regarded with particular suspicion.

14. Captain Malcolm was awarded the US Legion of Merit for her work, a very unusual honour.

Notes

15. Anthony Powell, *Faces In My Time*, (London, Heinemann, 1980), vii, notes in particular the arrangements for the release of Polish units interned in Central Asia, vendettas amongst Polish officers (Pilsudski versus Sikorski factions) and the request of the Belgian government in late 1944 that 30,000 restless and often communist members of the Resistance be brought out of Belgium to Britain for military training and a 'cool off' period.

16. The technology of this in very simple terms was a typewriter-like machine to which were fixed a series of rotor wheels that made alterations in the lettering according to their setting; the settings could provide for the same original letter actually to appear in two or more different letters in the enciphered version. The addition of extra wheels and other devices added to the complexities. A German Enigma machine captured by Polish forces in 1944 is on display at the General Sikorski Museum in London, and one is being acquired for the Intelligence Corps Museum.

17. Ralph Bennett, *Ultra In the West*, (London, Hutchinson, 1979) pp. 29–30. Other research departments at Bletchley amassed expertise on the German terms for the working parts of artillery and armour, logistic returns, German State Railways consignment numbers, navigational beams and the German Y Service. The other notably useful book specifically upon Bletchley is Ronald Lewin, *Ultra Goes to War*, (London, Hutchinson, 1978). This work has, of course, drawn upon all the volumes of F H Hinsley others, *British Intelligence in the Second World War* for further illustration of the importance of *Ultra* in the conduct of grand strategy and of particular campaigns.

18. Early in the war, signalled Intelligence was kept secure by hand ciphers, but later, to cope with the heavy loads, machines were used. But certain commanders were apt to stuff an *Ultra* message into their trouser pocket and become irritated when asked to return it to secure filing.

19. Professor Lindars began his work at Bletchley as a civilian. He was later enlisted into the Intelligence Corps in which he was eventually commissioned in mid-1945. The late Rev. Professor B Lindars to the author, 9 July 1987. Fletcher served only in 1941–42 before discharge and re-engagement as a civilian.

20. Neither this listing of officers nor that of NCOs is complete, as no complete list from the time survives.

21. 'The work in the Park required people of the calibre of Gordon Spinney (Cpl) who had worked in the State Paper Room of the British Museum, Dr Herbert Murrill (Sgt), Head of Music at the British Broadcasting Company, Asa Briggs (CSM) now Lord Briggs, and many similarly qualified people, yet they were all liable to sudden attacks from "Authority" and incarceration in the guardroom for failing to get a "short back and sides", or failing to wear a cap or failing to salute an officer. From being privileged people selected for our "special qualifications" we became literally part time prisoners of war.' Mrs E Baly (Staff Sergeant E V Deacon), 'Enigma Indeed ...' *The Rose and the Laurel*, 1978, p. 37.

22. Another useful if unspectacular role of the Y service was the monitoring of British army signals while on exercises.

23. A D Peck to the author, September 1987.

24. Miss E Roberts (ATS) to the author, 31 December 1987.

25. I am most grateful to the late T X H Pantcheff for much of the material that follows.

26. Colonel Scotland's Intelligence experience began in South West Africa in 1904–07 when, as a supplier to the German Army engaged in suppressing indigenous uprisings, he had been given a commission in the German Army to facilitate his work. In World War I he had worked in prisoner of war camps and, on occasions, crossed into German occupied Belgium masquerading as a Welfare officer to gather useful intelligence. He describes his service in *The London Cage*, (London, Evans, 1947).

27. Ranks given in the lists that follow are those reached by the end of the war; many officers started as Lieutenants. Terry appears in the Army List as General List but he transferred later into the Intelligence Corps.

28. Letter Mrs D I Taylor (who as Private Stainier served at Beaconsfield) to the author 29 March 1988; Letter to Intelligence Corps Museum from Mrs Taylor, 30 January 1988.

29. One precise case was that of the ship *Rostock* sailing from L'Orient to Santander in Spain in September 1944 with a naval crew and certain key technologist personnel on board.

30. Pantcheff recalled the delight of the Pole on being questioned and his remark 'I knew one day someone would need to know and I packed my mind systematically. Now I will unpack it for you'.
31. This had a sequel. The leaders of the project were sent to a camp in Perthshire. Included among them was one unfortunate who had not been involved. The others blamed him for the failure, and he was found hanged. Major Pantcheff carried out an investigation into the murder, as a result of which five Germans were hanged for the crime and others received prison sentences.
32. Major R C Goldsmith to the author, 30 April 1987. Major Goldsmith, an RAMC officer, was on board the ship at the time.
33. T X H Pantcheff to the author, 19 February 1988.
34. RAF Medmenham, to last to 1975, centred on Danesfield House, on the banks of the Thames. The site was selected for its proximity to Stanmore, High Wycombe and Heston.
35. Of these officers Lieutenant Falcon later became a Lieutenant Colonel, Lieutenants Simon and Espenhahn become Majors and the others all Captains.
36. The full range of CIU's work, the largest part of which was RAF, is set out in Ursula Powys Lybbe, *The Eye of Intelligence*, (London, William Kimber, 1983).
37. The initial V stands for *Vergeltung*, revenge.
38. A painting by Terence Cuneo of the *Bodyline* team at work at Medmenham hangs in the Officers Mess, Intelligence Centre, Ashford.
39. The process would have been completed had the RAF not been required to attack targets directly concerned with the Normandy landings.
40. 'The pictures when they arrived confirmed my worst fears. There were German tanks and armoured vehicles parked under the trees within easy range of the 1st Airborne Division's main dropping zone.' Brian Urquhart, 'The Last Disaster of the War', *The New York Review of Books*, 24 September 1987. Urquhart, (not an Intelligence Corps officer), was the Chief Intelligence Officer (GSO2 (Intelligence)) of the Airborne Corps.
41. As it happened an air photograph of a rocket at Peenemunde had been taken in mid-1943, but it had been confused with a water tower, and its significance only realised a year later.
42. Captain H B Eaton, *APIS, Soldiers with Stereo*, (Ashford, Intelligence Corps, 1978), pp. 48–49.
43. Names of a number of personnel who served in the Executive and its attached FS Sections are held at the Intelligence Corps Museum, but the lists are incomplete.
44. Blizard worked under the cover name of Major Blunt (a choice of name in no way connected with the art historian). It should be recorded that the failures of the Dutch Section of SOE occurred in late 1943 and 1944, and were not the responsibility of Blizard.
45. Churchill's *Times* obituary summarises his remarkable career and personality, *The Times*, 2 May 1972.
46. M R D Foot, *SOE in France*, (London, HMSO, 1966), p. 286. Michelins refused a similar proposal and their factory was badly damaged by the RAF.
47. The Italians supplied two important figures, as 'hostages', evidence of intent, while the armistice negotiations were in progress. These were looked after by Major Lee and his FS staff.
48. Patrick Howarth, *Undercover*, (London, Routledge, 1980), pp. 191–193.
49. By the end of the war, Lee's records totalled 40,000 names. Agents authorised to report to No 1 Special Force came down the Western side of Italy, through passes in the Appenines. IWM Tape, Major P M Lee.
50. C I Isolani to the author, 8 November 1987.
51. Woodhouse transferred into the Corps from the Royal Artillery. After the war he became a Member of Parliament, a junior Minister and Director of the Royal Institute of International Affairs.
52. A Panzer Division was sent to Greece which might otherwise have been available for use against the Allied invasion of Sicily.
53. Woodhouse very early on advised that unless the British government stated that it would suppress any ELAS coup, eventual civil war was certain. This advice was

unfortunately proved correct in the immediate post-war months.

54. Howarth, *Undercover*, p 110.
55. In his *Apple of Discord* (London, Hutchinson, n.d.), pp. 77–81 Woodhouse conclusively rebuts charges that General Zervas's non-Communist EDES collaborated with the Germans.
56. See Nicholas Hammond, *Venture Into Greece*, (London, Kimber, 1983).
57. A copy of a report on his work by Major A W E Winlaw, well portraying the hazards and difficulties of work in occupied Greece, is in the Intelligence Corps Museum.
58. This history has as a rule taken the *Army Lists* as the authority establishing whether or not a particular officer was a member of the Corps at any one particular time. An exception has been made for Major Leigh-Fermor. He is technically recorded General List in the Army Lists, but he himself believed he was Intelligence Corps and his DSO citation notes him as Intelligence Corps. The General List record may well have been a security cover.
59. Bishop Stephen Verney to the author, 30 July 1987. Bishop Verney added 'We worked for several months in Khania, the capital of Western Crete, and were able to make contact with a number of German officers and non-commissioned officers. The people who were willing to speak to us, mostly Germans opposed to Hitler, or Poles and Austrians, or Germans who had fallen in love with Cretan girls'.
60. Kemp's arrest was a diplomatic manoeuvre—to ensure these officers, with first hand knowledge of the non-Communist Polish Home army were *incommunicado* while negotiations over the future of Poland with Britain and the USA were in progress. They were later released. Although the project to assassinate Sikorski was being inspired by a Polish officer believed to be in Soviet intelligence service (NVKD), the main motivation was not ideological but differences in views between the officers of General Anders' army, mainly from eastern Poland, and the London Poles, mainly from west Poland. Interview, Patrick Howarth, 7 September 1988.
61. J A F Ennals to the author, 14 September 1987. Ennals added that at the end of the war he rode side by side with the Yugoslav X Corps Commander entering Zagreb.
62. D E N Peploe, writing to the author, 7 August 1987, of this work comments 'It was intended that I should report on their morale and motives for volunteering for dangerous clandestine work; these motives could be various and were not always creditable. A general assessment had to be made of the readiness of potential agents for undercover work. There was also routine work such as the vetting of individual histories and assistance in devising cover identities, etc'.
63. Lee, IWM Tape.
64. Many (Lee states 36 out of the original 39 and including H. Rée and his brother later killed in North Africa, and A Baird, E G Bisset and J Macalister) were commissioned. Several moved to operational work in the field, in which the two latter were killed. Languages included French, German, Italian, Spanish, Dutch and Norwegian. One of the Corps's NCOs, Mallison, subsequently became a professor.
65. B Blount to the author, July 1987. Blount subsequently became Director of Scientific Intelligence at the Ministry of Defence.
66. R Dahl to the author, October 1987.

Chapter 8: Operational Intelligence: The Corps Contribution

1. Sir Edgar Williams 'The Use of Ultra', 5 October 1945, WO 208/3575. This chapter has drawn freely on the four volumes of F H Hinsley and other *British Intelligence in the Second World War*, (London, HMSO), for examples of the contributions made by Ultra material in the major campaigns.
2. Among the non-linguists were a number of Royal Army Service Corps clerks that had been recruited for the clerical side of traffic analysis in 1939 and were transferred to the Intelligence Corps in 1940. A few of these proved so valuable that they were commissioned into the Corps. A list of Wireless Intelligence sections and units appear in Appendix C.
3. Teams consisted of British officers, South African Military Police and East African drivers, orderlies and interpreters. Memoir by G K Young, Oxford Development

Records Project Collection, 'The British Military Presence in East and Central Africa', Rhodes House, Oxford.

4. An FSS had earlier been attached to the Western Desert Force from April 1940.

5. A post-script to this incident, indicating the improvised nature of training at the time was that Sergeant Jacobs was armed only with a pistol, a weapon that he had never actually fired.

6. Clayton had served in World War I and was commissioned into the Intelligence Corps in 1940.

7. Colonel Haselden was listed as missing. An unconfirmed Arab source reported that he led a party of survivors southwards, was caught but jumped out of a lorry and escaped. He was later betrayed by a Libyan and recaptured, after which nothing further was ever heard of him.

8. Heliopolis's No. 5 Intelligence School was reinforced by personnel from No. 4 School in Britain. The School had in fact earlier broken Italian codes and ciphers.

9. Mr J Agius of Valletta kindly supplied me with a list of 70 names of Malta citizens who served in the Intelligence Corps. Of these 30 can be identified as officers in the *Army Lists*.

10. These were 252 FSS (Lieutenant F Whitty), 279 FSS (Captain H M Trethowan), 263 FSS (Captain Fox), and 'B' FSS. There was also an Australian FSS.

11. This Section was in technical terms a Type B Section. These comprised 2 officers and 78 soldiers of the Royal Signals and 2 officers and 5 NCOs of the Intelligence Corps. In 1943 these latter were increased to 3 and 13 respectively.

12. A sixth FSS, 270 FSS, was also despatched to Crete but seems never to have arrived.

13. N Hammond, *Venture Into Greece*, (London, William Kimber, 1983), p. 16.

14. M E Allen to the author, 6 April 1988. Mr Allen later finished a distinguished career as an Ambassador.

15. The list is incomplete but the following are examples. 37 FSS was with 1 Armoured Division, 254 FSS was with 4 Indian Division until early 1942, 256 FSS was with XIII Corps, 263 FSS was with 8th Army Headquarters and 270 FSS was with 7 Armoured Division. 366 FSS was at GHQ and as such was responsible for the security of the Prime Minister's August 1942 Cairo Conference.

16. A Terence Cuneo painting of Captain Makower and Sergeant Swain at work by their vehicle in the desert is in the Intelligence Corps Officers' Mess at Templer Barracks, Ashford. (*See Plate 9*)

17. Letter, Captain E M St G Moss to his parents, 14 September 1942. Mr Moss kindly gave the Corps a xerox of this fascinating description of events.

18. *The Daily Telegraph*, (obituary), 12 January 1988.

19. The deployment of the operational Intelligence FSS at this time was as follows: Army Headquarters and Lines of Communication, 263, 267 and 271 FSS—the latter having escaped from Tobruk; XIII Corps, 254, 255, 256 FSS; XXX Corps and 7 Armoured Division, 270 FSS; 4 Indian Division 284, 290 FSS; 1 Armoured Division, 37 FSS; 2 Armoured Division 36 FSS; 8 Armoured Division 56 FSS; 10 Armoured Division 297 FSS; 44 Infantry Division 22 FSS; 50 Infantry Division 412 FSS. The Australian, New Zealand and South African Divisions possessed their own FSS.

20. The major was held against the establishment of 7 Intelligence School, which had joined 5 Intelligence School of Heliopolis. Later in 1943, the Schools were retitled Special Intelligence Companies.

21. These included 106 Special Wireless Section (SWS) with 45 Wireless Intelligence Section (WIS), 105 SWS with 44 WIS and 110 SWS with 49 WIS followed later by 101 SWS with 40 WIS and 103 SWS with 42 WIS. An ad hoc 100-X (Armoured Division) SWS (Experimental) was formed for 7 Armoured Division; All were joint Royal Signals and Intelligence Corps and except for that of 7 Armoured Division structured on the Type B establishment, (see note 11).

22. The WIS was in Party B of the Corps headquarters for the night withdrawal. They managed to evade a German encirclement that captured Party A, the first party to move. The Intelligence Corps element included Captain A D Peck, one sergeant and four corporals of 44 WIS, together with a few additional personnel from the ad hoc 7 Armoured Division SWS. Earlier in the day they had intercepted a message giving Rommel's plan for the capture of Matruh, but had unwisely not drawn the deduction

that they should have done from the clarity of the message, intercepted by 12 foot rod aerials rather than the 30 foot mast. The close proximity of the enemy was first revealed by an artillery bombardment during which intercept work continued. War Diary of 105 SWS, PRO file WO 169/5492.

23. Williams 'The Use of Ultra'.

24. Dr H Beckhough to the author, 7 March and 15 March 1988. He adds 'We were nicknamed "The Madhouse" because of the loud noises emanating from our secret quarters when any group or member "cracked" a code, breaking a whole sequence of messages'.

    F H Hinsley, *British Intelligence in the Second World War*, (London, HMSO, 1981), II, p. 377 notes that the Army's Y Service strength in the Middle East increased from 1300 in May 1942 to 2,400 to July.

25. Bletchley Park had earlier broken both the ciphers used between the German Air Force and the Afrika Korps (Scorpion) despite the long distance and faint signals and between Field Marshal Kesselring's headquarters in Rome and the Afrika Korps.

26. The sections were 101 SWS at Cairo and 102 at Gibraltar. Both included Intelligence Corps personnel. Material was sent to Bletchley daily by air. F T Prince to the author, 21 July 1987.

27. H T Shergold to the author, 16 September 1987.

28. The 1st Army's Sections conformed generally to the pattern of those of the 8th Army. At 1st Army HQ was 1 SWS with 53 WIS; at V Corps 10 7 SWS and 46 WIS; at IX Corps 113 SWS and with 52 WIS; at II (US) Corps an American Radio Intelligence Company was supplemented by 55 WIS.

29. The Divisional Commander opted to land from the sea in the event.

30. Letter, C A P Cockell to Intelligence Corps Headquarters, 1987.

31. In the case of the Sicily landings, the following arrangements were made. At 8th Army, 2 Special Wireless Section, Royal Signals with 22 Wireless Intelligence Section Intelligence Corps (10 officers and 28 soldiers); at XIII Corps 106 SWS with 45 WIS (3 officers and 17 soldiers); at XXX Corps 110 SWS with 49 WIS (3 officers and 17 soldiers), with a further element, 5 Wireless Intelligence Company, at 15 Army Group Headquarters—in all totalling approximately 20 officers and 87 soldiers.

    For the Italian Mainland landings, the two Corps WIS, 45 and 49, were both increased to 10 officers and 28 soldiers, and additional support provided as follows: For the Salerno landings, 44 WIS was attached to the American 5th Army and 21 WIS was working with 113 SWS at X Corps headquarters; for the Taranto area 46 WIS was working with 107 SWS at V Corps Headquarters. These three section, 44, 21 and 46 each comprised 10 officers and 28 soldiers; 21 WIS was later renumbered and redeployed.

32. Major Fugelsang was not at this precise time Intelligence Corps, but was transferred into the Corps very shortly afterwards.

33. Among the valuable material gleaned was that certain coast defences thought at first to be artillery were identified as being only machine gun emplacements.

34. Captain H B Eaton, *APIS: Soldiers With Stereo*, (Ashford, Intelligence Corps, 1978), p. 34.

35. It was not uncommon for a sortie to take 700 prints; some 6000 or more might have to be collated and distributed each day. A division might receive a 100.

36. M E Allen to the author, 6 April 1988.

37. The US unit also worked briefly in Naples, but was then moved to prepare for the Allied landings in the south of France.

38. H T Shergold to the author, 16 September 1987. The SS General Wolff proved particularly helpful, ordering all inmates to talk freely and asserting that the Nazi régime's fall released them from any former oath of loyalty.

39. Captain Isolani, of part Italian family origin, had only acquired British nationality in 1938 and fought in this campaign under the name of Captain Arnold. Letter to the author, 8 November 1987.

40. D Macfarlane to the author, 27 July 1987; *The Times*, 11 October 1988, (obituary), Duke of St Albans.

41. Initially the British forces were a brigade plus additional units in the Athens area, a brigade less certain units at Salonika, and an Indian Army brigade at Patra.

42. No 89 (Para) FSS was formed early in 1942. Corporal (later Warrant Officer) Loker was the first Intelligence Corps member to parachute. Captain Dunbar, Warrant Officer and Sergeants van Laer and Grazebrook were the four Corps members at Bruneval.
43. W D Stallybrass to the author, 3 January 1988.
44. A useful summary of *Ultra*'s contributions up to 6 June 1944 and afterwards appears in Ralph Bennett, *Ultra In The West*, (London, Hutchinson, 1979), ii. Bennett was himself an Intelligence Corps officer serving at Bletchley Park.
45. A recent scholarly evaluation appears in Michael I. Handel (Ed), *Strategic and Operational Deception in the Second World War*, (London, Frank Cass, 1987) chapter by T L Cubbage, 'The Success of Operation Fortitude: Hesketh's History of Strategic Deception'.
46. The June 1944 distribution was as follows: 21 Army Group, 1 Wireless Intelligence Company and 1 Special Wireless group, both semi-mobile; 2nd Army, 1 Special Intelligence Company, 8 SWS and 53 (Cipher) SWS; I Corps 108 SWS; VIII Corps, 109 SWS; XII Corps 104 SWS; XXX Corps 110 SWS. In addition reinforcements for the 21 Army Group that followed included 111 SWS, 118 SWS, 54 (Cipher) SWS and 7 SWS. The two cipher SWS only occasionally included Intelligence personnel. The Winter 1944–45 distribution is set out in Appendix C.
47. S Edwards to the author, 27 July 1987.
48. Eaton, *APIS*, p. 33. There was also formed a Canadian APIS to support the 1st Canadian Army. British instructors played an important role in their training.
49. 'The analysis of air photography not only served to build up accurate and often very full maps of enemy defences and static installations such as supply dumps but also, by the analysis of traffic densities and the types and directions of the freight carried—troops, arms, supplies—enabled us to establish a comprehensive pattern of enemy movement and keep abreast of changes in it.' Major General Sir Kenneth Strong, *Intelligence at the Top*, (London, Cassell, 1968), p. 132. Strong added that equally useful could be pilots' own observations.
50. Captain J W Barber, 'Service with No 4 Special Force Unit (SOE)', *The Rose and Laurel*, 1978.
51. A full study appears in Bennett, *Ultra in the West*.
52. Eaton, *APIS*, pp. 50–51.
53. T Peters to the author, 20 and 31 July 1987. Mr Peters subsequently enjoyed a successful career as a diplomat.
54. Among the Corps officers working with this unit were Captains F Hogwood, W D Stallybrass and J B da Silva.
55. A Terence Cuneo painting of Captain Galloway in action is in the Intelligence Corps Officers' Mess at Ashford.
56. An excerpt from one report may be quoted '... Captain Royce went down again with a member of Operational Research Staff 2nd TAF and stayed for a week in several of what had been the big communication centres of the salient. By extensive interrogation of local civilians they accumulated much information on the extent of the dislocation and delay imposed by the Air Forces', *Operational Research in North West Europe, The Work of No. 2 Operational Research Section June 1944–July 1945*.
57. A W E Winlaw to the author, 8 July 1987.
58. D Macfarlane to the author, 27 July 1987.

Chapter 9: Security: The Corps Contribution

1. A list of these appears in Appendix C. The list does of course also include FSS attached to combat formations.
2. Tape prepared by T Allbeury, April 1988.
3. A composite British Indian FSS generally comprised a British Army officer, warrant officer, two sergeants and four corporals together with an Indian Army Viceroy's Commissioned officer and eight soldiers, these latter could on occasions be Gurkha, Burmese or Karen.
4. Location of individual sections are noted in Appendix C.

Notes

5. Geoffrey Household, *Against The Wind*, (London, Michael Joseph, 1968), p. 128. Household added that the inquisitiveness was usually but not always innocent.
6. The first four had been numbered 1 to 4. The new Composite sections were numbered 401–408, see Appendix C.
7. The command lay initially with GSI(b) British Troops Iraq later re-designated 10th Army, or less formally PAIFORCE.
8. DDMI PAIFORCE was also Head of the Combined Intelligence Centre IRAQ (CICI) and as such linked political with military intelligence. Commanders of the FS Wing in 1943 included Majors G Household, L Inrig and V C Martin.
9. C Crisp, 'At The Teheran Conference', *The Rose and Laurel*, 1978.
10. Access to the ships had also to be controlled lest agents ashore attempted to communicate with agent handlers on board. Exceptions had to be made for French crews wishing to join the Free French.
11. 'Couldn't you have stayed with the girl just a bit longer, until breakfast time, say? I'm sure she could have told you a lot more', asked Lieutenant Oldfield during one such investigation. Richard Deacon, *'C', A Biography of Sir Maurice Oldfield*, (London, Macdonald, 1983), p. 51.
12. H T Shergold to the author, 16 September 1987.
13. R D Wise to the author, 25 August 1987; D Hamblen to the author, 12 September 1987; T Allbeury, tape, April 1988.
14. December 1944 may be taken as a typical month with 48 arrests, 33 line—crossers, 11 stay-behinds, 4 parachutists. Agents masqueraded as doctors and refugees, others sought employment with the British Army. Detection followed a watch on the numbering of lira notes, departure from cover stories, repetition by two or more agents of cover stories, and return passes found sewn into clothing, among other give-aways. Women agents had identity particulars sewn into underwear, their style of operation was traditional.
15. W D Gibson to the author, 8 January 1988. Leaflets were printed with photographs of those shot and were dropped by the RAF over the Axis spy-training establishment.
16. Full and rewarding accounts of FSS work appears in Norman Lewis, *Naples '44*, (London, Collins, 1978), and in H O Dovey, 'The Unknown War: Security in Italy 1943–45' *Intelligence and National Security*, III, No. 2, April 1988, pp. 285–309.
17. The Headquarters staff included Lieutenant L C Buss. In early 1944 it was located at 18 Bishopwood Road, Highgate.
18. The Field Security Reserve Detachments were numbered 1001–1025; the Counter Intelligence Units were 101-103; the Censorship Sections included 25 Field Censorship, 4 Prisoner of War Censorship, 4 Special Censorship, 1 Telegraph and 2 Special Mail Censorship Sections.
19. W D Gibson to the author, 8 January 1988.
20. 'Notes concerning 19 FS Section in NW Europe', paper prepared after the war for the Rhine Army School of Intelligence by Lieutenant Colonel M F R Hockcliffe, who had commanded the Section in Normandy.
21. Michael Pertwee wrote in his autobiography 'They were reportedly well-trained and hard to spot. We were supplied with a list of questions, which had to be fired at anyone suspected of being one of these agents ... an immediate correct answer was expected ... "What's Bing's surname?." There were about 20 questions, simple to a genuine American, difficult for a phoney'.
22. Michael Pertwee later wrote in his autobiography. 'In the main they were a miserable and inefficient bunch, with little chance of getting away with anything; ill-trained, of low intelligence and even lower morals. They were mostly traitors, dropped into their country of origin, having been more or less press-ganged into service'.
23. Sir John Killick to the Inspector of the Intelligence Corps, 10 August 1971. The one survivor was Sergeant Zuker who spoke fluent Dutch and was able to escape. Those killed included Corporals Maybury and, later, Corporal Scarr.
24. Hockcliffe, 'Note'.
25. Norman Kirby, *1100 Miles with Monty, Security and Intelligence at TAC HQ* (Alan Sutton, Gloucester, 1989) *passim*.
26. K B Pepper to the author, 20 July 1987.
27. 'If we decided that an arrival from abroad, whether passenger or crew, gave rise to

suspicion, we would serve a detention order under Regulation 18B'. B H Kemball-Cook to the author, 7 October 1987. Those so detained were taken for further specialist interrogation.

28. Michael Pertwee to the author, 31 July 1987.
29. From an autobiographical manuscript awaiting publication, ix. V Bonham-Carter to the author, July 1987.
30. Sir A Rouse to the author, 7 July 1987.
31. Commitments arising from the Pacific War are dealt with in the next chapter.
32. The first two were 52 and 54 FSS, the third was 87 FSS. Two NCOs of 54 FSS, A J Sydney and W Y Brown lost their lives en route to Gibraltar when their ship was sunk. In 1943 most of 87 FSS were posted to Italy and the remainder absorbed into 54 FSS.

    For further details of the Gibraltar Security problem see F H Hinsley and C A G Simkins, *British Intelligence in the Second World War, IV*, (London, HMSO, 1990), pp. 159–162, 205. One Gibraltarian was arrested.
33. Paper by B Ardill.
34. Later Major Ardill became the Defence Security Officer and one of his NCOs who has been commissioned, Lieutenant Littlefair, took over Port Security.
35. The Portuguese was detained in Britain until 1945. Somewhat pathetically, all he had asked from the Germans was the cost of his daughter's education at convent school.
36. B H Kemball-Cook to the author, 7 October 1987.
37. H Montgomery Hyde, *Secret Intelligence Agent*, (London, Constable, 1982), ii. The Americans accepted examination of mails if actually passing through Britain, but initially objected if mails were intercepted at sea. In late 1940, they conceded in respect of Pan American Clippers and ships calling at Bermuda.
38. Readers may need to be reminded of the very large German colonies in Latin America, 4,000 in Colombia alone for example. These were, very unwisely, allowed to move about the Caribbean for some time after the outbreak of war.
39. Household, *Against the Wind*, p. 134.
40. Household, *Against the Wind*, p. 124.

Chapter 10: The War Against Japan: The Corps Contribution

1. The author would wish, at the outset of this chapter, to record his profound gratitude to four Burma campaign officers of the Intelligence Corps, J G Charles White, Alan Stripp, the late Louis Allen and Stanley Charles for their most generous advice and guidance in preparing the text.
2. In respect of language, the reader may find it useful to be reminded that Japanese characters 'reveal neither meaning nor pronunciation at sight. Each has to be learnt and moreover one has to learn the 214 radicals under which they are normally classified in dictionaries as well as the order in which the strokes are written, since this alone enables them still to be recognised when they are written cursively or abbreviated. Finally in Japanese most of them have at least two different pronunciations and sometimes a surprisingly wide range of meanings'. Alan Stripp, 'Breaking Japanese Codes', *Intelligence and National Security*, II, 4 (October 1987), p. 135.
3. 15 FSS was attached to 18 Division. The escapees from Singapore were Captain S J Lemin, Sergeants A K H Boyd, H G Gibberd, D O'Shea, J Taylor; the five who died in captivity were WO2 J W Wright, Sergeants J B Nunn, W Shaw, Corporals S Livesley, J E Harris; the five who survived captivity were Corporal L Dorfman, Lance Corporals J D Smith, J Ullman, E P Wrigley and Rifleman S Burney.
4. The mission included Malayan officials commissioned in the RNVR or other units. It was later reinforced by an Australian Army party that was in Java and, briefly only, by Dutch personnel.
5. Sir Robert Black to the author, 29 August 1987.
6. Lieutenant Colonel A A Mains, 'The Indian FSS' (unpublished paper), Intelligence Corps Museum. Colonel Mains, a 9th Gurkha Rifles officer, was the GSO2 (IB) in Burma. He notes these four sections as having but 10 days training and only half of the members being equipped with any form of firearm. The Burmese members of the

sections deserted at the end of the retreat, on the day immediately preceding an Army Order granting honourable discharge.

7. Dr J J Grant to the author, 11 July 1987.

8. 'War time Experiences—Captain G R Lock', Intelligence Corps Museum. Lock wrote 'I found it embarrassing that I was the only person in the section who really knew anything about Sumatra or could read Dutch or Malay, so that all material that came into, or went out of, the section had to be shown to me'.

9. Stripp, 'Japanese Codes', p. 138 describes this section as 'a small exotic plant grafted on to the large and flourishing European parent'.

10. W C Smith, (Sergeant), 'Wireless Experimental Centre Hill of Happiness, Anand Parbat Delhi, 1943–46' *The Rose and the Laurel*, 1986.

11. Some remarkable photographs of WEC at work, left to the Corps following the death of Mr W M Allen who served as an officer of the Corps at the WEC, are held in the Corps Museum at Ashford. They show the wide variety of personnel.

12. Stripp, 'Japanese Codes'.

13. The best estimates available suggest December 1941–May 1942, 6; First Arakan, October 1942–Spring 1943, 30; Assam Front 1943, none; Second Arakan, September 1943 to May 1944, 70; Kohima, March–June 1944, 200 at the most; Imphal, March–June 1944, 130, including 12 officers; Kabaw Valley and Chindwin, July–December 1944, 200 at the most; 1945 campaign up to Sittang battles, 1000. One major was captured and interrogated by Captain (later Major) R Gibson. The rest included a few junior officers but the large majority were ordinary soldiers.

14. In a letter to the author, 6 July 1988, S T Charles notes that among the many difficulties were the Japanese prisoner's total lack of any anticipation that he might be questioned in Japanese—a lack that had to be made up by the making of preliminary 'Japanese-like noises' before any questioning, and also dialect—British interrogators using a Japanese that might be described loosely as 'BBC', unsuited to a peasant farmer from a remote island. Kyoto, Osaka and Kobe Japanese was relatively easy, Tokyo was 'a sort of Japanese cockney' and Shikoku very heavily accented. The difficulties of guttural pronunciation were worsened by the speed at which a prisoner might speak. Also interesting is Dorothie Storry, *Second Country*, (Ashford, Paul Norbury, 1986), Appendix A.

15. The quality of early interrogators, very often businessmen from China (some were even White Russians) commissioned in India into Indian regiments, logistic units or general list was uneven. This situation reflected the lack of pre-war preparation; the 1943 *Army list* records but 10 First Class and 3 Second Class Interpreters among Regular Officers.

16. On 8 June 1945 the Intelligence Corps officers were distributed as follows: Lieutenant-Colonel F R Fugelsang at HQ APIU; Captain R H Burroughs at APIS, 347 Wing RAF; Lieutenant T P Cliffe at HQ 14th Army; Major P W Murray-Thriepland at APIS CPIC; Major N C A Simon and Lieutenant R J Boulton at HQ 12th Army; Lieutenant T G Jarvis at APIS 23 Division.

17. Captain H B Eaton, *APIS, Soldiers with Stereo*, (Ashford, Intelligence Corps, 1978), pp. 23, 29, 30, 38, 48, 52–53.

18. For more detailed accounts of Force 136 operations in Malaya see Ian Trenowden, *Operations Most Secret, SOE; The Malayan Theatre*, (London, William Kimber, 1978).

19. S T Charles to the author, 6 July 1988.

20. S T Charles to the author, 6 July 1988.

21. Professor D L Snellgrove to the author, 21 September 1987.

22. Professor H Lloyd Jones to the author, 3 August 1987.

23. Louis Allen (Lieutenant Louis Levy), *Burma The Longest War*, (London, Dent, 1984) pp. 506–510, Louis Allen to the author, 5 July 1988. The document was mixed up in a bundle of maps and personal effects, rain and blood soaked, its identification reflected the value of earlier 'scanning' experience. The order set out precise routes to be used after feint attacks by three columns, projected attacks on the lines of the routes, and arrangements for reconnaissance of river banks and the collection of crafts for crossing the Sittang River.

24. Note by Captain F W Barks, Intelligence Corps Museum.

25. 'Log of Events of a Field Security Section, October 1942 to December 1944', paper

prepared by FS C(CI) Wing, Advanced HQ, Allied Land Forces, South East Asia, 15 May 1945, Intelligence Corps Museum.

26. 'Extracts from the Akyab Diary of an FS NCO' attached to 'Counter Intelligence Activities on Akyab Island', paper prepared by FS (CI) Wing Advanced HQ, Allied Land Forces, South East Asia 25 February 1945, Intelligence Corps Museum.

27. W Lough to the author, February 1988.

28. The Force had originally served in Iran under the title of 303 Brigade. It had been using Bren gun carriers, with a mocked up superstructure simulating tanks, as part of a deception to deter any German incursion into Iran.

29. Colonel Turnbull who had been a Regular infantry officer for a while before the war served during World War II in the Corps. After the war he became a writer of history, biography and fiction. I am grateful to his widow, Mrs E Turnbull, for the loan of a copy of a synopsis of a book on D Force that, prior to his death, he had been planning to write.

30. A protective screen of booby traps reinforced by a standing patrol was put around a chosen area. Effects—firecrackers, slabs of gelignite, dried gun cotton, verey lights fired from hollowed bamboos—would be laid on a frontage of 600 yards to a depth of 100 yards; they were designed to last 30 minutes when available—real artillery support would be provided. In good conditions a company could simulate a brigade.

31. Major General C E Lomax, commanding 26 Indian Division, in which the brigade was serving, described the success of the Ramree Island operations as a 'classical example of tactical deception'. It had involved three companies, one British, one Pathan and one Punjabi Moslem, and a supporting artillery battery.

32. Rupert Croft-Cooke, *The Blood Red Island*, (London, Staples, 1953), is an account of the author's experiences in Madagascar in 1942. A postscript describing his own work is written by Richard Colby.

33. Mains, '*Indian FSS*'.

34. Examples, including caricature drawings depicting Indian soldiers being driven blindfolded into battle by British officers with lashes amid sinking British ships and wrecked aircraft, are to be seen in the papers of R Mayne, Intelligence Corps Museum.

35. Note book, 7688 722 Sergeant W L Brown, Intelligence Corps Museum.

36. Laurens van der Post, *The Night of the New Moon*, (London, Hogarth, 1970). Van der Post's linguistic abilities enabled him to carry out this work; in the last days before the Japanese surrender he also learnt much from very careful observation of the Japanese officers and guards behaviour in face of disaster.

Later, as Military Attaché in Batavia, van der Post's wartime knowledge of the Indonesian nationalist movement was especially valuable.

Chapter 11: Aftermath

1. *The Stars and Stripes*, (US Army Newspaper), 1 April 1946, notes that 10 months of surveillance had preceded the arrests, which were almost all achieved without trouble.

2. In Cologne for example one of the FSS, under the command of the Area Security Officer, Major M Pertwee, unearthed a German General living under an assumed name; he was an important capture being one of the last men to see Hitler alive.

3. B K Blount to the author, 21 July 1987. Colonel Blount was instrumental in saving the large number of research institutes grouped in the Kaiser Wilhelm Gesellschaft. The other three powers wished to break up the KWG but a semantic name change, from KWG to Max Planck Gesellschaft, preserved the structure.

4. T X H Pantcheff to the author, 6 November 1987. See also T X H Pantcheff (trans. Lisolotte Julius) *Der Henker vom Emsland, Willi Harold 19 Jahre Alt*, (Koln, Bund-Verlag, 1987).

5. P J Prior to the author, 25 March 1988. Captain Prior commanded 45 FSS in Hanover at this time. On one occasion he successfully observed a rendezvous at Hannover station of a Soviet courier with a Soviet agent who had been 'turned'; he himself was disguised as a Scottish infantry medical orderly dispensing contraceptives near the station. The courier was then tailed and caught.

6. The paragraphs that follow and the quotation included within them, are based on and

taken from an address 'Dr Adenauer A Reminiscence' given by Lord Annan to the *Deutsch Englische Gesellschaft*. Lord Annan very kindly supplied the author with a copy of the text.

7. Professor N Gash to the author, 17 August 1987.
8. Klagenfurt controlled 16 and 55 FSS at Wolfsberg, 62 FSS at Villach, 88 FSS at Millstatt, and 91 FSS together with a CSDIC (to 1947) at Klagenfurt. Graz controlled 31 and 96 FSS at Leibnitz, 97 FSS at Brüch. 263 and 422 FSS at Graz, 409 FSS at Weiz and 418 FSS at Leoben. The Frontier Sections were 62, 91, 410 and 313 FSS.
9. W D Gibson to the author, 8 January 1988.
10. 'It was surprising how many people maintained that they were simple peasants with no interest in politics and yet had hands which had clearly never handled anything heavier than a fountain pen', 'The Intelligence Corps in Trieste', paper written by Sir Robert Andrew, Intelligence Corps Museum. Sir Robert served with the Corps as an NCO in the years 1948–50; his paper gives some interesting examples of line-crossers whom he had to question, a defecting Romanian rear-admiral, a disillusioned Yugoslav trade union leader, a Russian naval petty officer who may have been a plant, and an Italian who admitted to working for the Yugoslav security agency.
11. 89 FSS returned to Britain for demobilisation in September 1945 ending a span of service that had included action in Algeria, Tunisia, Sicily, Italy, Greece, France, Holland, Germany, Denmark and Norway.
12. T X H Pantcheff to the author, 6 November 1987. See also T X H Pantcheff, *Alderney, Fortress Island*, (Chichester, Phillimore, 1981). In the case of one SS officer, the report was later found to be inaccurate.
13. J G C White to the author, 24 April 1988. The Mobile Sections may not have been briefed, for security reasons, on all the information available at SEAC, information which of course would have been given to the *Zipper* commanders if the operation had been mounted.
14. These were 565 and 566 FSS who in the event went to Singapore direct, 571, 481, 606, 355, 757, 759, 753, and 755 FSS who landed at Port Dickson at various times, 489 and 358 FSS who were disembarked at Penang from a cruiser, 756 FSS who landed at Port Swettenham and 758 and 760 FSS who landed a little later.
15. These Sections were initially 625, 556 and 596 FSS in Sumatra, and 605, 624, 622, 681, 597, 601, 356, 611 and 900 FSS with later 358 FSS relieving 356, 762 FSS relieving 611, and 481 Port Security Section relieving 900 FSS. These reliefs were occasioned by the withdrawal of the sections for enquiry into the disappearance of a quantity of treasure looted by the Japanese. An officer of another branch of the Army not connected with Field Security was later convicted at a Court-Martial.
   Corps Officers also served in SEATIC detachments that were sent to Java and Sumatra.
16. L Coe to the author 21 December 1987. Mr Coe served with 601 FSS at the time.
17. The account of this commitment that follows is based on a letter from A F Young, who served with 354 FSS, to the author, 15 January 1988.
18. Louis Allen (Lieutenant Levy) to the author, 1988, n.d.
19. Professor R Greenwood to the author 16 July 1987. Professor Greenwood, at the time a captain, was one of the officers.
20. These figures unfortunately do not include ATS personnel. In respect of officers, they also represent a slight reduction from the May 1945 peak of 3,040 Intelligence Corps officers, with 1,554 attached regular officers.
21. General Paget's other proposals included the permanent separation of the Directorate of Military Intelligence from Operations. Intelligence courses for regimental officers, proper attention to Intelligence at the Staff College, and that a reserve of Army Intelligence Officers be created.
22. Paper 'Note on Military Intelligence After the War', by the Assistant Chief of Staff, G-2, Allied Forces Headquarters, Major General T S Airey, 8 January 1945. The author is indebted to Mr D A Prater for a copy (No 12) of this paper.
23. The first Intelligence Corps Territorial Army units were formed in 1947. They were specialist units for air photograph interpretation and travel control security, based in London. The further development of Territorial Army Intelligence Corps units is examined later.

24. The 1951 *Army List* for example noted 7 majors, 110 captains, 4 Quartermasters and 42 lieutenants or second lieutenants on short regulars or short service commissions, plus a further 44 national service subalterns, a total of 207, serving in the Intelligence Corps. The same list recorded total officer figures for an average line infantry regiment of some 150–60, the Army Catering Corps 245, the Royal Army Dental Corps 377, and the Royal Army Pay Corps 839, this total including a major-general and 3 brigadiers.

Chapter 12: Conventional and Sub-Conventional Wars, 1945–90

1. Captain H B Eaton, *APIS, Soldiers With Stereo*, (Ashford, Intelligence Corps, 1978), p. 61.
2. The initial command team of 904 FSS on its departure was Captain D W Sanders MBE in command, Lieutenant E Rhodes as second-in-command and WO2 L Praill as CSM. Captain Sanders was later relieved by Captain W R Wells, in turn relieved by Lieutenant C A Vearncombe. WO2 Moorcroft relieved WO Praill.

   A very interesting account of the work of 904 FSS, 'History of 904 FSS, Feb 1953 to Feb 1954', written by Colonel Devitt is in the Intelligence Corps Museum. The paragraphs that follow have drawn upon this account.
3. Eaton, *APIS*, p. 64 APIU(ME) officers studied with some nostalgia damage inflicted on airfield premises that they had themselves used a few years previously.
4. P M S Ward, interview, 1 June 1988.
5. In September 1965 the Indonesian Communist Party had attempted to seize power, possibly with President Sukarno's connivance. The attempt was bloodily suppressed by the Indonesian military and Sukarno's days became numbered.
6. The NCOs concerned had no special training for this role and in an attempt to co-ordinate their work a 2 Intelligence Company was set up in Labuan. Terrain and distance made this largely impractical; it was agreed later with hindsight the FIOs should have been attached to the Intelligence Platoons of the Brigade operations in the area.
7. Captain Althorp and WO2 Brown in 'Hot But Worthwhile', *The Rose and Laurel*, 1968, wrote: '... To distract a man from his normal day to day routine, carried on without change from his forefathers, in order to aid a government for which he cared little and an Army of which he knew little, could prove extremely difficult indeed. Common topics of conversation tended to be drink, food, love and somewhat surprisingly, the Queen. Many kampong headmen proudly displayed a tattered photograph of the Queen on their bamboo walls, which had been torn from old magazines during one of the rare visits down-river. One had a photograph of King George VI and saluted it regularly in homage. The Federation of Malaysia was relatively unknown, but the former white ruler from across the seas was revered, honoured and respected. For this reason, on matters of trust and confidence, there is no doubt that the Queen's (or King's) representatives, the British soldiers or FIOs possessed a definite advantage over others.'

   The article is a valuable account of the work of FIOs in the Borneo operations.
8. KONAS stood for *Kommando Nasional Rajkat Sarawak*. The full story of this event is set out in Jock Haswell, *British Military Intelligence*, (London, Weidenfield, 1973), pp. 38–240.
9. Corporal Kitchin later rose to become a Staff Sergeant in the Intelligence Corps, from which he was commissioned into another arm.
10. Captain Flower was at this time serving in the infantry, he subsequently transferred to the Intelligence Corps for the rest of his career.
11. It had been planned to provide a trained Intelligence Corps 1(B) officer and two CI Sections for Borneo, but the personnel were not available—a lingering result of the lean years.

    At one stage the Indonesians had recourse to propaganda leaflets of World War II Japanese design depicting a lady scantily dressed encouraging British soldiers to return home.
12. The political issues are complex. A useful summary appears in Major General Edward

Fursdon, 'Belize' *Army Quarterly and Defence Journal*, January 1988, Vol 118, 1.

At the time of writing the British presence is viewed by Guatemalans with feelings not unmixed, as the presence, from the Guatemalan point of view contains Honduras and Mexico, who also have territorial claims, prevents left wing Guerrilla penetration from Belize into Guatemala and insulates Belize from other ideological and Superpower rivalries in the region.

13. The *Belize Tribune*, 8 August 1982, provides an outline report of this incident, naming the Guatemalan officer, Lieutenant Jose de Leon Flores, commanding at Melchor de Mencos.
14. The full team consisted of Major D M Burrill, Captains A Thomas and D Charters, WO2 Vygrass, Staff Sergeants Horman, Cowdrey and Neville and Corporal McDonald, with a little later Major M Dawkins as Special Intelligence Adviser.
15. This cell was in fact 81 Intelligence Section and included Lieutenant Whipple, Staff Sergeant Peck, Sergeant Massey, Corporals Ramsey and Waine and Lance Corporals Lovell and Stoker. Of their journey one wrote 'Eating QE 2 gourmet meals on the way to war, practising small arms drill among the staterooms and practising Intelligence work among the purple padded armchairs of the ladies hairdressing salon: these were so bizarre that the whole experience had an element of make-believe'.

Chapter 13: Counter Insurgency and Military Security, 1945–90

1. Sir Robert Thompson, *Defeating Communist Insurgency*. (London, Chatto and Windus, 1966). The fifth principle, a clear political aim on the part of the government, is a political and not an Army matter.
2. Sir William Ryrie to the author, 22 July 1967.
3. The FSS commanders were Captains R M Richards and E E Bartholomew, 252 FSS; Captain T Keen, 257 FSS; Major F G M Wheeler, 272 FSS; and Captains R Fraser and J P T Linklater, 317 FSS. This latter section was notably successful in Haifa.
4. David R Johnston-Jones, 'Palestine Memories', *The Rose and the Laurel*, 1987. '317 FSS used to cover these operations and it was a matter of pride to produce a report by dawn for delivery to Divisional HQ immediately after breakfast.'
5. Jock Haswell, *British Military Intelligence*, (London, Weidenfeld, 1973), notes this incident. The officer concerned was Captain (later Lieutenant Colonel) R M Richards.
6. David R Johnston-Jones. 'There and Back Again'; paper in Intelligence Corps Museum, Ashford.
7. Both NCOs had been wearing plain clothes when they were kidnapped. Insurgent propaganda alleged 'spying' in attempting to justify the killings. A seventh Corps casualty was Corporal J H Dunsby, killed in a traffic accident.
8. In the last months of the British presence in Libya, 3 FSS was retitled FS Section Tripolitania.
    The reader may need to be reminded that in 1948 there was still a divisional headquarters, three infantry battalions and two armoured regiments in Libya. Most of these units were moved to Egypt in 1951–52 or later to Cyprus, but Libya was used for training purposes until 1969, a Field Security detachment remained at the RAF Station at El Adem until 1970.
9. Some of the leading figures were Warrant Officer Hobson for photo interpretation work; Staff Sergeant Gardener and later the Arabic speaking Sergeant Birrell for prisoner questioning and local contacts, Sergeant Varley and Lance Corporal Cartwright for Security and Staff Sergeant Roussel, Corporal Jenkins and Private Holden for Operational Intelligence. Also at work in the Radfan was Major J H S Burgess, at the time an infantry officer; immediately after the campaign Major Burgess transferred to the Intelligence Corps, finishing his service as a Lieutenant Colonel.
10. The members of this Cell, known as the 'Spooks', were Warrant Officers Birrell and Capper; Sergeant Duncan; Corporals Mutch and Mackrell, and Lance Corporal Davis.
11. These included Major P Boxhall and Captains D Venn, A Abbott and J Antcliffe. Captain Abbott was awarded the MBE and Sergeants Duncan and Ryles the BEM for their work in the campaign.

12. In the various Arabic Peninsula operations for which the General Service Medal was awarded, the total issues to Intelligence Corps personnel amounted to 'Arabian Peninsular' 12 medals, 15 clasps; 'Dhofar' 31 medals, 21 clasps; 'Radfan' 29 medals, 1 clasp; 'South Arabia' 89 medals, 28 clasps.

13. Unpublished source. PFLOAG had by this time changed its title to PFLO, the People's Front for the Liberation of Oman.

14. Those who served in the Lebanon included Major J Goodall, Warrant Officers Hill and Nutt, Sergeant O'Connor, Massey and Powell and Corporals Gebbie, Simm, Cockles and Diamond. Brief accounts appear in Warrant Officer Hill, 'Op Hyperion—Beirut 1983' and also 'Op Hyperion—Beirut 1983–84' in *The Rose and the Laurel* of 1983 and 1984 respectively.

15. Gregory Blaxland, *The Regiments Depart*, (London, William Kimber, 1971), p. 314; G A M Howes to the author, 6 October 1989.

16. A number of Intelligence Corps Territorial Army travel control specialists were called forward to serve with this unit for periods of several weeks.

17. Major Frazer passed a warning message to Major General P Young, the Commander, in the midst of a morning Church Service.

18. The insurgents later changed the name of their force to the Malayan Races Liberation Army.

19. The officers commanding these sub-units included: 355 FSS, Captains R Innes, J McPhail, L G Masterton, G F O'Neill; 358 FSS, Captain G W Turrell (killed in a vehicle accident), Lieutenant P W Hunt (killed by insurgents); Singapore Special FSS, Captains Graham-Martin, Pearson, C F Vinn; 103 APIS, Majors A L Cary, D C Morgan.

20. Sometimes a regimental band would play while the paper and pencils were distributed. The tactic was tried again later in Kenya, but without success.

21. An observation from Captain H B Eaton, *APIS, Soldiers with Stereo*, (Ashford, Intelligence Corps, 1978), p. 62, is also illustrative. 'During 1954 we laid and issued over 1,000 annotated mosaics ... in 1948 the figure for the year was 10'.

22. Detachments generally consisted of two NCOs. One such detachment, in the Cameron Highlands, found that it appeared on an insurgent death list, and hurriedly exchanged its Landrover for a light armoured car.

23. Sir William Ryrie to the author, 22 July 1987.

24. The institutional arrangements are complex. In 1957 FSW Malaya was closed down and its personnel transferred to a reformed 355 FSS. This FSS was broken down in 1960 to 19 Platoon, (Seremban), 20 Platoon, (Kluang), 21 Platoon, (Singapore and Johore), and 22 Platoon, (Taiping and Penang), controlled by a Headquarters Intelligence Corps (Far East).

    In 1967 the brief-lived Intelligence and Security Group (Far East) was formed to last only to 1970.

    The Intelligence Platoon concept is described in Chapter 14, *infra*.

25. Again the institutional arrangements are complex. From 1945–59 a FSS (Hong Kong) was in existence; in 1959 the Corps provided a Counter-Intelligence Unit (Hong Kong) and 23 Intelligence Platoon. In 1961 the C1 Unit became a C1 Company, but was reduced to C1 Platoon in 1965. In 1967 10 Intelligence and Security Company was formed as part of the Intelligence and Security Group (FARELF).

26. The ALNK had its roots in an anti-French political movement, the UPC (*Union des Populations de Cameroun*), which had led to French military intervention in the 1950s.

    The aims of the ALNK were complete unification, the withdrawal of all British and French forces from both parts of Cameroon, and the ending of all agreements with Britain and France. The movement was described as 'a mixture of patriots and bandits'.

    Paper 'Cameroons 1961' by Captain R Seager, Intelligence Corps Museum.

27. Personnel involved included Major T A Cave and Lieutenant A I Kennedy, Warrant Officer E A Ceulemans and Sergeants R Finlayson and P French. Questioning was carried out in French.

28. Unpublished source. This report also noted that there were effects of magical practice to be noted on some men taken in for questioning.

29. Staff Sergeant Conway, 'Mauritius', *The Rose and the Laurel*, 1969. The second NCO was Corporal Dowling.

30. The 1,400 strong Force comprised Australian, New Zealand, Kenyan and Fijian

military personnel; the 1,100 British troops formed by far the largest contingent. Over 50,000 former insurgents were handled by the Force.

31. Lieutenant I I McMahon, 'Operation Agila', *The Rose and the Laurel*, 1980. The members of the Corps concerned were Lieutenant McMahon, Warrant Officer Greenwood, Staff Sergeant McCabe, Sergeant Buckley and Lance Corporal Grant.

Chapter 14: The Corps Renewed, 1957–90

1. The paper recommending this permanent cadre was submitting to the Executive Committee of the Army Council at the height of the post-Suez reappraisals, on 22 January 1957 (ECAC/P (57)7). At the time, of the Corps Officers 79 were on Extended Service Commissions, 73 on Short Service Commissions and 47 on National Service Commission. The number of career Regular Officers has since been increased, but a high percentage of the Corps officers are, however, former NCOs.

2. At the outset five trades were tested, these were then combined into one 'A' trade of Operator Intelligence and Security. Since that combination, however, certain other specialists trade-testing developments have taken place to meet particular needs.

3. The first 4 Intelligence Platoons, Nos 2 to 5, were formed in 1959 for the 3 brigades and divisional headquarters of 3 Division, a fifth platoon was formed a little later for the Parachute Brigade. All were under the administrative command of Major F G Robson, Commander, Intelligence Corps Strategic Reserve. Later 20 more Intelligence Platoons, numbered 1, 7–23, 39 and 40 were formed.

4. These included 10 Company Hong Kong and 11 Company Cyprus.

5. This aspect of the life of the Intelligence Corps is set out in Appendix F.

6. When the Territorial Army was re-formed in 1947, National Service conscripts were technically required to serve in it for a period of time (the precise length was several times changed) after their national service. The requirement remained a largely paper exercise and the TA returned to what it always had been, a Volunteer force of enthusiastic spare-time soldiers. Most of course had national service experience until the 1960s, when basic training had to be resumed.

7. This Group was re-named Travel Control Security Group in 1957. Its centres were firstly at 18 Cadogan Gardens, Sloane Square and later la Iverna Gardens, Kensington and 1 Fitzjohn's Avenue Hampstead; outstations were scattered all over Britain. Its maximum establishment was one of 159 officers and 523 soldiers Intelligence Corps, 12 officers and 154 soldiers WRAC, and 98 attached Royal Army Service Corps personnel.

8. An exception to this constraint was the section attached to 16 Airborne Division, allowed to recruit above War Establishment.

9. The Companies were numbered 11 to 19; 11 Company as a BAOR reinforcement, the remainder were allotted to the home military Command Headquarters.

10. One of 21 Company's most notable officers was Major (later Lieutenant-Colonel) P W Moth who began his TA Service as a private in APIU (TA).

11. Readers may find it useful to be reminded of the changes in the size of BAOR. In 1948 the BAOR was reduced to two divisions, a parachute brigade and the Berlin brigade. With the Cold War at its height, Headquarters 1st (British) Corps was re-formed in 1951 and two more divisions sent to Germany in 1952. Various changes both in the numbers and size of divisions have taken place since then. In the late 1980s the 1st (British) Corps comprised three divisions in Germany and a fourth, as an immediate reinforcement, in Britain.

12. There was a brief interim stage during which the Theatre Intelligence Unit, BAOR commanded an air photo-interpretation company. Individual officers and Warrant Officers were attached to formation headquarters Intelligence Platoons, as noted earlier.

13. Readers who have served on field Intelligence staffs and have kept careful records of tanks and vehicles destroyed on their front to pass upwards or downwards in complex messages, will appreciate the immense saving of time and energy Wavell affords.

14. APIU (UK)'s first Intelligence Corps Commander since 1945 was Major F S Austin, who assumed command in 1953. The post was combined with that of Deputy

Commander of a Joint Air Photo Interpretation Centre, JAPIC from 1952 onwards, and is now one always filled by an Intelligence Corps Lieutenant Colonel.

15. The training of photo interpreters suffered many vicissitudes. Courses were run at Nuneham from 1947 but in 1956 an Air Photo Reading Branch of the School of Military Intelligence was formed at Maresfield and courses were begun at JARIC for members of all three Services in the same year. Training was later moved to RAF Wyton.

Index

Aden in 1939–45   168
 post-war   234, 235–237
Agent handling before 1900   1, 2, 3, 5,
 7–8
 in 1914–18   34–37
 in 1919–39   58
 in 1939–45   81, 139, 187
 in Korea   217
 in Borneo campaign   220–221
Air photography in 1914–18   23–24,
 31–33, 38, 50, 51
 in 1919–39   61
 in 1939–45   70, 73, 95–99, 117, 118,
 119–120, 131–132, 135–137,
 144–146, 148–149
 in war against Japan   179–181
 post-war   212, 215, 244, 247, 255–27
Algeria   158
Austria *also* Austria-Hungary
 1914–18   49–51
 post-1945   201–202

Balloon Observation   11, 12, 31
Belize   169, 170, 223–225
Borneo, campaign in   219–223
Burma, in 1939–45   175, 183–190
 post-war   3209–210

Cameroons, Southern   170, 248–249
Censorship   51, 74, 77, 83, 85, 152, 167,
 168, 169, 192
Corps of Guides, pre-1900   3–4, 5, 7
Counter-Insurgency, major post-1945 cam-
 paigns Palestine   229–231
 Egypt   231–233
 Jordan, Arabian Peninsula,
 Aden   234–239
 Lebanon   239
 Cyprus   240–242
 Malaya   243–246
 Kenya   246–248 *See also Security*
 Cyprus   231–240–242

Dardanelles   44–46
Deception plans and disinformation   10,
 25, 38, 143–144
 in war against Japan   189–190
Denazification   161–162
 in post-war Germany   194–201
 in Austria   201–202
Dhofar   237–239
Directorate of Military Intelligence   5, 6, 8, 15, 52, 56, 63,
 65–66
 structure in 1939–45   81–88

Documents, Intelligence from in Boer
 War   11
 in 1914–18   28, 29, 44
 in 1939–45   72, 87, 115, 119
 in war against Japan   179–180,
 183–184, 185–186
 in Falklands War   226

East Africa in 1914–18   43–44
 in 1939–45   114–115, 115–129,
 170–171
 Zanzibar in 1961   248 *See also* Kenya
Egypt (and Sudan) 1882–83   7–8
 in 1914–18   44–47
 in 1939–45   157–158
 post-war   231–233
 in 1956 Suez operation   217–218

Falklands War   225–227
Field Intelligence Department (Boer
 War)   8–13
Field Security Sections, list of 1939–45
 Sections   262–273 *See also Security*

Gibraltar   168, 249
Greece (and Macedonia) in 1914–18   44,
 48–49
 in 1939–45   104–106, 117–118,
 140–141
 post-war   206
Group System, Intelligence and Security
 Groups   251–252

Hong Kong   173, 209, 246

Indian Army Intelligence   4, 14, 155,
 172–173, 176, 191
Indonesia (to 1949 Netherlands East
 Indies) in war against
 Japan   173–175
 post-war   207–209, 210
 Borneo campaign   219–223
Intelligence Corps major events, etc,
 role   xv–xvii
 formal formation in 1940   77–79
 strengths in 1943–45   211
 post-1945 run-down   211–213
 post-1957 renewal   250
 in Territorial Army   252–254
 designated as an Arm   257
 women personnel admitted   257
 honours and awards   279–280
 homes, customs, uniform, Colonels Commandant, Directors   78, 211,
 287–289
Inter-Services Topographical Depart-

ment   76, 83, 87, 176
Iran in 1939–45   155
Ireland in 1914–18   51
   in 1919–21   60–61
   in 1939–45   167
Iraq in 1914–18 (Mesopotamia)   46–47
   in 1939–45   154–155
Italy campaigns in, in 1914–18   49–50
   in 1939–45   102–104, 133–140,
      159–160

Jordan (pre-1946 Transjordan)   231, 234

Kenya in 1952–63   246–248
Korean War   214–217
Kuwait   235

Lebanon   *See Syria and Lebanon*
Libya in 1940   1942   115–129, 154
   post-war   218, 233–234
Long-Range Desert Groups   116–117

Madagascar   110, 190–191
Malaya in 1941–45   173–175
   post-war   206–208
   emergency in   243–246
Malta   167, 249
Maltese members of the Corps   117
Manuals for Boer War   9
   for 1914–18   13, 15, 37
   for 1939–45   61, 86–87
   for war against Japan   179
Mauritius   249
Norway in 1940   75–65
   post-war   205–206

Oman   234 *See also* Dhofar

Palestine in 1914–18   47–48
   in 1939–45   157
   in 1945–48   229–231
Prisoner Questioning before 1900   2, 3
   in Boer War   11
   in 1914–18   23, 29–30, 38, 49–50, 51
   in 1939–45   72, 91–95, 114, 117, 119,
      130–131, 138–139, 150
   in war against Japan   178–179, 183–185
   in Borneo campaign   222
   in Falklands War   226–227
   in Aden   236–237 *See also* Documents
Propaganda and Political Warfare in
      1914–1   38
   in 1939–45   74, 109–110, 140
   in war against Japan   182
Psychological Warfare   115, 132–133, 150,
      151, 238–239
Recruitment in 1914–18   16–17,
      52–53
   in 1939–45   63–68, 77–79
   post-war   212–213, 281–285, 250–252

Russia operations in   51, 59–61

Scouragers   1
Security in Boer War   10
   in 1914–18   39–41, 50–51
   in Germany 1919–28   55–58
   in 1939–45   68, 71–74, 75–77, 115, 128,
      141, 146, 152–171
   in war against Japan   186–188, 190–
      9192
   in post-war Austria   201
   in Korea   215–217
   within BAOR   254–255 *See also*
      Counter-Insurgency for major post-
      1945 campaigns
Signals Intelligence in Boer War   11
   in 1914–18   24–25, 28, 33–34, 48,   in
      1919–39   61
   in 1939–45   69, 72–73
   as Y Service   74,, 85, 88–91, 107–108,
      112–113, 114, 117, 118, 119,
      120–127, 132, 134–135, 144,
      147–148, 168
   in war against Japan   176–178, 183, 185
   List of Wireless Intelligence
      Sections   275–278 *See also Ultra*
Somalia   14–15, 114–115
Special Operations Executive   99–109
   in war against Japan   181–182
Syria (and Lebanon)   118–119, 155–157,
      231
   Lebanon 1983–84   239

Territorial Army, Intelligence
      Corps   252–254
Topographical and Statistical Depart-
      ment   5–6
Training, Intelligence training gen-
      erally   16, 55, 211–213
   of Boer War FID   11
   for and in 1914–18   16, 54
   of Intelligence Corps personnel
      1939–45, 65–68, 77–79, 281–285
   post-war   211–213, 250–252
Trieste   203–205
Tunisia   132–133, 158
Turkey in 1919–22   59

Ultra   69–70, 72, 85, 88–90, 112–113, 118,
      121, 124, 132, 135, 143–144,
      147–148, 176

Women Personnel in 1914–18   28
   in 1939–45   84, 86, 90, 93
   accepted into Intelligence Corps   27

Y Service *See also* Signals Intelligence

Zimbabwe   249